LEGAL METHOD, SKILLS AND REASONING

...rcester, WR1 2JF.

...ate below.

Third Edition

Language skills, study skills, argument skills and legal knowledge are vital to every law student, professional lawyer and academic. *Legal Method, Skills and Reasoning* suggests a range of 'how-to' techniques for perfecting these academic and practical skills. It explains how to work with legal texts; how to read and write about the law; how to acquire effective disciplined study techniques; and how to construct legal arguments.

Packed full of practical examples and diagrams across the range of legal skills from language and research skills to mooting and negotiation, this new edition will be invaluable to law students seeking to acquire a deeper understanding of how to apply each discrete legal skill effectively.

This restructured third edition is now additionally supported by a companion website offering a wealth of additional resources for individual and group work for both students and lecturers.

For students, the companion website offers:

- workbooks for each Part, containing guided practical and reflective tasks;

- checklists to help monitor progress in specific skills;

- self-test quizzes to consolidate learning for each individual legal skill.

For lecturers, the companion website hosts:

- a set of PowerPoint slides of the diagrams in the text;

- specimen seminar plans, with supplementary notes to provide support and inspiration for teaching legal skills;

- sample legal skills assessment, and accompanying answers.

www.routledge.com/textbooks/9780415458511

Sharon Hanson is Senior Lecturer in Law at Canterbury Christ Church University where she is course co-ordinator for the undergraduate legal studies programme.

LEGAL METHOD, SKILLS AND REASONING

Third Edition

Sharon Hanson

Routledge·Cavendish
Taylor & Francis Group
LONDON AND NEW YORK

Third edition published 2010
by Routledge-Cavendish
2 Park Square, Milton Park, Abingdon, Oxon OX14 4RN

Simultaneously published in the USA and Canada
by Routledge-Cavendish
270 Madison Ave, New York, NY 10016

*Routledge-Cavendish is an imprint of the Taylor & Francis Group,
an informa business*

© 1999, 2003, 2010 Sharon Hanson

Previous editions published by Cavendish Publishing Limited
First edition 1999
Second edition 2003

Typeset in Helvetica Neue by RefineCatch Limited, Bungay, Suffolk
Printed and bound in Great Britain by
MPG Books Group, UK

British Library Cataloguing in Publication Data
A catalogue record for this book is available from the British Library

Library of Congress Cataloging in Publication Data
Hanson, Sharon, LLB.
    Legal method, skills, and reasoning / Sharon Hanson. – 3rd ed.
        p. cm.
    Rev. ed. of: Legal method & reasoning. 2nd ed. 2003.
    1. Law—Great Britain—Methodology.   2. Law—Great Britain—Interpretation
and construction.   3. Law—Great Britain—Language.   4. Law—Methodology.
I. Hanson, Sharon, LLB. Legal method & reasoning.   II. Title.
KD640.H36 2009
340′.1—dc22
                                                                2009006587

ISBN10: 0–415–45850–1 (hbk)
ISBN13: 978–0–415–45850–4 (hbk)

ISBN10: 0–415–45851–X (pbk)
ISBN13: 978–0–415–45851–1 (pbk)

ISBN10: 0–203–87674–1 (eBook)
ISBN13: 978–0–203–87674–9 (eBook)

CONTENTS

FIGURES

TABLES

PREFACE TO THE THIRD EDITION

This extensively revised and expanded third edition retains the user friendly and practical approach of the first and second editions while adding new chapters exploring study skills and self management, IT skills, use of the law library, the contexts of law, oral skills and examination strategies. For the first time, the book is also supported by an extensive companion website.

The title of the book, as well as its content, continues to grow. Now legal method and reasoning have been joined by skills, to give the title *Legal Method, Skills and Reasoning*. The changes made reflect the need for new law undergraduates to grasp a broad range of skills. As a consequence there are five new chapters at the start and end of the book (Chapters 1, 2, 3, 10 and 11) covering these areas.

As with previous editions, the book enters into a direct dialogue with the reader, explaining how to break into legal texts and showing how to understand and construct arguments. It covers basic issues of concern for many students as well as more sophisticated skills relating to arguing and reading the law.

Practical manuals do not aim to be encyclopaedic, and this one is no exception. It aims to engage the reader in a highly personalised conversation, at times presuming to voice their worst fears, 'What if I am not good enough?', 'What if I cannot understand?', 'What if I fail something?' At every point the book gives a context, so, instead of plunging into pages of detailed diagrams and narrative concerning access conventions for law reports and statutes, the student is more casually talked around the law library and its print and electronic collections. Libraries are daunting places to the new undergraduate, but they become the core of intellectual and creative work when properly understood and used.

I retain my belief in the importance of diagrams to demonstrate interconnections that are not apparent from just reading or hearing narrative. They remain one of the particular characteristics of this text.

I am also particularly delighted that it has now been possible to add a companion website containing student and teacher areas, intended to provide 'food for thought' for the further development of basic legal method, legal reasoning and legal skills. For the student there are a range of exercises with suggested answers to test development of reading and arguing skills. There are also glossaries of troublesome terms. For the teacher there are suggestions for practical class-based exercises, PowerPoint slides and specimen assessments with guidance answers. This material has been carefully considered as I thought long and hard about how a companion website could be of use to students and teachers.

INTRODUCTION
TO THE BOOK

Careful thought has gone into the structure of this book. If it is approached in order, you will gain skills vital to the academic stage of legal education. If you already possess some knowledge and wish to look only at specific skills, then many discrete chapters stand alone, such as Chapter 4 on domestic and European legislation or Chapter 5 on reading law reports.

This is a method and skills book and it is therefore no substitute for texts in your substantive areas of study such as criminal law, the law of contract, or the English legal system. The book draws on a range of areas of law to demonstrate skills development and to alert you to some of the confusions and mistakes easily made. It is a book that bridges the gap between substantive legal subjects and the skills that need to be acquired in relation to:

■   commencing study;

■   finding the law;

■   reading the law;

■   writing legal answers;

■   argument construction;

■   speaking the law (in presentations, moots or negotiations).

The nature of legal study, and the range of skills required to engage in that study, can be described, like many things in life, as a journey. We will use this journey theme throughout the book, to assist you in making interconnections. The climbers on the front of this book have just reached the end of their journey to the summit of a mountain. They reached the end successfully because they were well prepared, appropriately dressed, had the necessary ropes in place and knew how to build stamina for the task. They achieved their goal by working together, with each individual also using their own independent skills.

If you were climbing a mountain you would not knowingly set out in bad weather. You would not set out without a reliable map giving clear guidance on distances, tracks and paths. But a map is not much use without a compass to indicate the right direction of travel. The map has an indication of north printed on it, but only a compass can show you where north is. You of course would need to make sure you had a reliable and finely calibrated compass. It would not be wise to climb a mountain with a novelty compass designed to be a toy.

With a reliable map and a reliable compass you will know where you are and how you got there and be able to plan where you are going. If you know something about the movement of the sun, or the positioning of the stars, you may well be able to navigate roughly without a compass. In life, as in study, knowledge determines what you are able to do.

You would no doubt wish to take climbing ropes, a torch in case you found yourself in the dark, and emergency food supplies to keep your energy levels high. You would prepare yourself by finding out what is available and which is the best approach for you to take.

Many students embark on the journey of studying without the equivalent of a map that indicates the area incorporated in study, or a compass indicating the appropriate direction. A study map is essential because you need to see both the fine detail and also the larger context within which the detail is situated. Zooming in and zooming out of your map of the terrain of law reveals the complex, sophisticated understanding required. This ability to see the micro and macro contexts is one that will be referred to several times in this book. The competent study of law ideally involves you, the student, in the micro tasks of discussions concerning the meaning of words and phrases used in legal rules, and the macro tasks of reviewing the entire legal system, or a discrete area of law, considering appropriate reforms.

There will be many journeys throughout your study of law. As you constantly end one and start the next you always begin from a stronger position, as preparation is built in to all of the tasks you perform. Each part and chapter of this book begins with a quotation. Look at the quotation for Part One and consider how it might relate to your studies at the start of your journey.

HOW TO USE THIS BOOK

Successful legal study depends upon the simultaneous development of the different, but complementary, skills set out in Figure I.1. Developing competency in any one skill can be relatively easy. However, addressing the full range of skills can be more of a challenge. At the beginning of law study it can be all too easy to feel overwhelmed by too much information, too soon. It is particularly important to remember that you are not expected

Study skills	how to develop independent and highly efficient learning strategies
IT skills	email, word-processing, virtual learning environments, internet searches, e-library use, database manipulation
Language skills	how to competently understand and use ordinary English and legal English terminology
Critical thinking skills	how to develop the ability to constantly question, seeking the underlying assumptions behind arguments, taking nothing for granted, seeking evidences for your assertions, questioning your own positions
Legal research skills	how to find law and texts about law through highly effective library skills
Legal method skills	how to approach legal documentation
Argumentative skills	identification, construction and evaluation skills
Reading skills	how to read legal rules, judges' opinions, academic critiques of law reports and more
Writing skills	how to write notes, summaries, essays, legal problem solutions, exams, reports and more
Speaking (oral) skills	debating, mock trials (mooting), mediation, negotiation, presentation
Substantive law	legal knowledge, for example of criminal law, contract law and so on

Figure I.1 The skills required for the successful study of law

to be highly competent in every area immediately. You should also remember that you will already have some competencies in place, which can be developed further.

For many of you this will be your first sustained time away from home, without the guidance of school patterns or teacher-discipline. You may need to work hard to develop your skills of self-management and independent learning. At university the academics who teach you are most likely also to be researchers and writers. They, like you, are engaged in study. They will expect you to develop your own timetable and to work independently to prepare for group work. You will be expected to read, and if you choose not to you will lack understanding and fall behind. You must monitor your own progress. Your university lecturer is not there to cajole, entreat or bully you.

Some of you will be beginning your legal studies as part-time students, with a number of other family or employment responsibilities. It is worth understanding from the start that, unlike individual topics which may be spread across terms or years, you will need to develop the full range of skills simultaneously. Remember that you can develop competency in English by reading good novels, and you can increase your IT competency by experimenting with the internet.

Or, on the other hand, you may have studied English as a second language, and be moving away from your home country to study in England. It may take a few months to become accustomed to being surrounded by English and to understand the range of accents that you will hear. You may find that you encounter difficulties relating to the meaning of words as law brings its own technical vocabulary. You will also encounter some issues with grammar, spelling and structure. Do not panic; these matters just take time. As the weeks pass you will not feel so pressured.

All areas of skills development will be tackled during the course of the first year, and in most cases over the course of the first term[1]. Being aware of the range of skills in which you need to develop competency is a good beginning. Many students are unprepared for the broad range of competencies required to engage in effective legal study. They find the need for excellent IT, language, oral and library skills particularly unexpected.

Structure of the book

The chapters in this book are grouped into four parts:

- **Part One: Preparing for the Journey** contains three chapters dealing with the development of good study skills and library skills, e-learning strategies and basic IT skills. Finally it introduces you to the contexts of law.

- **Part Two: Mapping the Territory** contains three chapters dealing with essentials: reading texts of law (legislation, treaties and law cases) and reading texts about the law (philosophical or historical texts, social scientific texts, or textbooks explaining areas of law)[2].

- **Part Three: Arguing the Law – The Construction of Argument** contains two chapters dealing with the anatomy and design of argument construction and legal reasoning.

- **Part Four: Putting it All Together – Last Things as You Arrive** contains three chapters dealing with writing skills, oral skills and examination techniques.

The function of this 'how to' text

This book will consider all of the above skills, study skills, and effective methods for presenting work in writing or in speech alongside reference to the contexts of English law and the basic structure of the English legal system. Throughout, however, you will note that the primary focus of this book is inevitably text based. Texts of the law (statutes, law reports) and texts about the law (textbooks, journals, reports, proceedings in Parliament, articles) will be the main objects of analysis. Studying these will help you to:

---

1 To assist you to have a view of where you are in each of these areas you can make use of the skills checklists on the companion website.

2 This distinction between texts *of* law and texts *about* law is important to grasp. Texts *of* law contain the actual legal rules. These are called primary texts. Texts *about* law look at law from a range of perspectives, questioning, critiquing or summarising the state of law. These are called secondary sources because they are commentaries about the legal rules in the primary texts.

■   understand the ways in which legal rules are put together;

■   acquire skills of argument construction, analysis and critique;

■   appreciate links between and within the texts;

■   understand the importance of language and appreciate contexts such as culture or politics;

■   use your knowledge and understanding of legal rules to solve legal problems and answer posed essay questions for both coursework and exams.

As you gain increasing competencies in these areas you will increase your critical ability to analyse law. This will sharpen your thinking. You will learn to ask questions, never taking anything for granted and always looking for evidence to support arguments.

The majority of books on the market that deal with legal skills and legal method (that is, the way in which legal rules are used to resolve certain types of disputes) do so in the context of legal process or legal theory. Inevitably, many of these books tend to be weighted in favour of explaining the English legal system, its processes, personnel and doctrines. They do not give time to an appreciation of how to break into texts, how to read and understand them. But if you cannot get inside legal rules, and fully appreciate their various dimensions, you will not be able to be successful in your legal studies.

Although this text acknowledges the complexities of legal rules, the importance of critique and the construction of arguments, it also attempts, in a user-friendly manner, to make interrelationships within and between texts. It presents language clearly, and uses these interrelationships to allow the commencement of the task of understanding and reading the law, of seeing and evaluating arguments and of constructing your own arguments.

Essentially, this is a book about practical matters. The practical skills of studying, using IT, practical thinking and legal research, intellectual and presentational skills, all rely on reader reflection and activity. If you actively engage with the book, you will develop your critical thinking[3] skills and your ability to engage in highly competent analysis. The text draws a map of your studies, setting out the territory at the macro level. But it also provides smaller maps to enable you to locate and understand legal texts. Ultimately you will be able to recall relevant memorised knowledge concerning general or specific contexts and apply or interpret it confidently with a clear understanding of the interrelationships between rules, arguments and language, in the search for plausible solutions to real or imaginary problems.

This text is not a philosophical enquiry that asks why English law prefers the methods of reasoning it has adopted. Although such texts are of the utmost importance, they will mean more to the student who has first acquired a thorough competency in a narrow field of practical legal method and practical reason. Then a philosophical argument will be

---

3   This is discussed in detail in Chapter 2, and referred to in Chapters 6, 9 and 10.

appreciated, considered, evaluated and either accepted or rejected. This is not a theoretical text designed to discuss in detail the importance of a range of legal doctrines such as precedent, although you must also carefully study these. Further, this is not a book that critiques itself or engages in a post-modern reminder that what we know and see is only a chosen, constructed fragment of what may be the truth. Although self-critique is a valid enterprise, a fragmentary understanding of 'the whole' is all that can ever be grasped. We can only ever see part of the whole collection of stories that is the law. This means we should approach the study of law carefully, checking that our arguments and our criticisms are plausible, and checking that the arguments and criticisms of others are also plausible.

The book will draw attention to the fact that there is often more than one solution to a legal problem. Judges make choices when attempting to apply the law. The study of law is about critiquing the choices not made as well as the choices made.

The diagrams used in this text are integral to the successful understanding of legal skills, legal method and legal reasoning as presented in this text. They have been specifically designed to:

- provide a way of taking students to deeper levels of understanding;

- give a basic description or blueprint for an area;

- demonstrate interconnections between seemingly disconnected areas, texts and skills.

An ability to comprehend diagrammatic explanations will be encouraged throughout the text. Diagrams present another way of seeing, and the sheer novelty value of seeing the interconnections in a diagram can sometimes be enough to transform confusion into comprehension. It is hoped that you will also begin to construct diagrams for yourself.

This is above all a 'how to' text, a practical manual. Bearing in mind the list of skills set out, it concerns itself primarily with the issues identified in Figure I.2. Carefully read the list as it constitutes your marching orders for the rest of the book and for your legal study.

The parts and chapters in this book are intended to be read, initially, in order, as material in earlier chapters will be used to reinforce points made later. Parts One to Three lead you through various skills to Part Four, which concentrates on piecing together a range of skills to engage in the finished products of written coursework, oral skills presentations and written examinations. Colloquially the header for this final part remains as in earlier editions 'putting it all together'.

Patient study will be rewarded by clear progress in the ability to research and understand the substantive law, and to move towards interpretation and argument construction using legal rules and academic texts. If you work through this text methodically, you *will* reach a place of understanding where you know how to present arguments competently. You can then develop these skills during the course of your studies.

How to . . .

1. Effectively engage in general study skills and become an independent and interdependent learner.
2. Engage in efficient legal research using your institution's print and electronic library collections as well as non-academic open access internet resources.
3. Develop an awareness of the importance of understanding the influence and power of language, including how to effectively use legal dictionaries and glossaries
4. Understand the European influence on English law.
5. Identify the relationship of the text being read to those texts produced before or after it.
6. Effectively use and deploy IT resources
7. Read and understand texts *of* law: law cases, legislation (in the form of primary legislation or secondary, statutory instruments, bye-laws, etc.) and European Community legislation (in the form of regulations and directives).
8. Use texts *about* the law and texts *of* the law to construct arguments to produce plausible solutions to problems (real or hypothetical, in the form of essays, case studies, questions and practical problems).
9. Make comprehensible the interrelationships between cases and statutes, disputes and legal rules, primary and secondary texts.
10. Read and understand a range of different texts *about* the law: secondary textual sources from the discipline or from other disciplines such as philosophy, psychology, sociology, anthropology, history and politics.
11. Identify, construct and evaluate legal arguments.
12. Search for intertextual pathways to lay bare the first steps in argument identification.
13. Write legal essays, answer problem questions, perform oral skills and prepare for exams.

Figure I.2 The function of this 'how to' text

COMPANION WEBSITE

This third edition of the text also introduces a new dimension: the companion website, where you can find extra material, templates for the range of self-management charts referred to in the text, extra exercises to hone your skills, along with skills checklists to check your progress. There are also three workbooks to enable you to compile sets of tasks that demonstrate you have understood a particular area. Each comes with a self-marking scheme.

The companion website does not give you copious links to other sites, primarily because you need to discover these for yourself. However, specific links are referred to as appropriate.

PART ONE:
PREPARING FOR
THE JOURNEY

"The journey of a thousand miles starts with a single step."

Lao Tzu

The chapters in Part One of this book deal with the essential basics of studying. They prepare you for the specifics of law study by showing you how to develop competent general study skills and how to use the library effectively. They also offer a brief initial understanding of some of the basic contexts that affect your study of law.

Part One is about first things coming first and contains three essential chapters. Chapters 1 and 2 are particularly designed to give you a firm basis for developing your skills in two important areas, general study skills and using the library. It is a good idea to keep the quote from this chapter ahead of you as you approach the first term of your study of law. Take just the one step, then the next, and do not be daunted by the steps you have not yet taken. When you reach your journey's end, even if you stumbled a little along the way, it is not the individual steps that are in your mind, but the sheer joy of the destination being reached.

The first step of your legal study is for you to tackle the first things, the preparatory skills that always need to be practised.

Chapter 1: This chapter focuses on study skills. Many students consider that study skills are either unimportant or they are something they have already learnt. Some study skills may well be in place from school or access studies, but the sheer range of basic study skills is usually not well established and therefore these skills need to be ascertained and practised until they are second nature. Many students, for example, are not prepared for the enormous emphasis on IT skills at university. There are few universities where it is not necessary to have access to your own computer, printer and the internet. This allows you to study at a convenient time rather than having to fit your schedule in with the opening times of your institution's study spaces. Nor are students prepared for the freedom given to them to manage their independent study programme for seminars and assessments. The relationship with lecturers and tutors needs to be understood if you are to get the most out of your experience of university. These and other matters are therefore discussed in Chapter 1.

Chapter 2: Landmarks and signposts looks at the law library. You may think it strange to include this but your ability to use the law library competently is essential for your success in the study of law. The university library will contain a vast academic print collection as well as subscriptions to many electronic collections which link to resources far in excess of those you can see on the library shelves. The law library also contains large numbers of highly specialised legal resources, both print and electronic, to enable you to access and search legal rules. You need to find your way efficiently and competently around these resources.

Both print and internet sources can sometimes lack authority and the opportunity will be taken in Chapter 2 to discuss how you can test the authority and reliability of retrieved material.

Chapter 3: The contexts of law considers the bigger picture. Law is viewed on a larger map, where it is easier to talk about the factors that influence the development and the interpretation of English law. It considers sketches of law at the level of the power of language, aspects of its history and discusses briefly how the language of law and the history of law have shaped legal doctrine and legal methods. English law will also be briefly viewed in its European context as one of a number of world legal systems. Law is used by many and we will question its ideology of neutrality through the lens of legal philosophy.

At the conclusion of Part One you will then be well-equipped to turn to Part Two and begin the task of breaking into legal texts to understand their language and meaning and to comprehend the relationship between judges and legislators in terms of law making and the interpretation of law.

FIRST THINGS FIRST

" What lies in our power to do lies in our power not to do."

Aristotle

After reading this chapter you should be able to:

- appreciate the range of skills competencies required to engage in good study;

- understand the concept of learning and teaching styles, recognising which you prefer and appreciating how you can be a flexible learner;

- identify inefficient study habits and take action to avoid them;

- understand the cycles of academic life throughout the year and the term;

- appreciate how courses and modules make up parts of the degree programme;

- construct a personal independent study timetable;

- appreciate the need for excellent IT skills and develop a plan to acquire them;

- understand the structure of your particular course and the preferred methods of communication, including virtual learning environments (VLEs).

CHAPTER SUMMARY

Study is a disciplined enterprise. You are responsible for the choices you make, and you always have choices even if you do not like any of them. It is you who is reading for a degree, and no one else can do it but you. You do not, however, study in a vacuum. Balancing your social, work, family and university lives demands interdependency and teamwork.

This chapter asks you to consider your goals and how you will achieve them and challenges you to develop your own interpersonal skills. It starts off by posing several basic questions:

- What is studying?

- What existing knowledge and skills can I bring to the enterprise of studying at university?

- Where am I in my understanding of learning?

- How can I begin to develop reliable independent learning skills?

It then introduces you to the general cycles of the academic year and the term, and helps you manage your lecture, seminar and independent study timetable as well as your assessment or examination timetable[1]. For too many students university simply happens to them. They do not make proper use of the opportunity to become independent learners, and do not succeed in acquiring a useful intellectual education which can open up the future in terms of life-changing career opportunities. Too many students see university as a necessary evil and then enter the world after university ill-prepared with a worrying lack of self-awareness. Do not let this be a description of you.

The chapter also highlights the importance of understanding your university department's communication protocols. It discusses the importance of developing competency in the use of IT systems such as email, VLEs, internet searching and word processing. The importance of competent library and IT research skills is referred to, but these are dealt with in more detail in Chapter 2.

Overall, this chapter deals with all the small things that can easily be overlooked. Yet it is these small things that will point you in the right direction for success in your main goal, that is legal study and obtaining a good degree.

---

1   Exams and revision warrant special discussion and are covered in more detail in Chapter 11.

IDENTIFYING YOUR GOALS

At the outset of your study of law it is vital to take an opportunity to consider carefully what you want and how you are going to achieve it. This book assumes that one of your goals is to be a successful law student. Every student will come to law with different past experiences of study. You may be apprehensive and wondering if you are good enough. You may be extremely confident that you know what is needed. Or you may be returning to study after a gap of a few years, or even longer, worried that you may not be able to keep up with the demands of university level study. All of these concerns are absolutely legitimate and apply equally to full-time and part-time students. Whatever your age or experience and hopes and concerns, you will probably find some aspects of studying law a challenge. This chapter will assist you to start your studies in a focused manner, allowing you to create sustainable study and organisational habits.

This is the time to consider the year ahead. Reflect for a moment on the following three questions:

■   **Why** are you at University?

■   **What** do you want to achieve?

■   **How** will you achieve it?

Write down your answers to these questions and keep them safe. You may need to remind yourself of your answers if you hit times of demotivation or lose self-confidence. Studying law can be difficult and highly pressurised at times. More students than you might guess seriously consider that they are not good enough to study law, or not good enough to stay at university. Often they are not being fair on themselves and all that is needed is a good chat with their personal tutor[2]. He or she will probably suggest that the student talk to his or her subject tutors or will do so on their behalf. Or a student may be referred to student support for further assistance. Tutors may also suggest that matters be discussed with friends and family.

One way to begin to achieve your goals is to make yourself aware of the range of issues involved in studying and the skills and strengths that you will need to succeed. It is also good to take the time to consider the skills and strengths that you already have.

You also need to familiarise yourself with your timetable, lectures, seminars, and begin the task of becoming an independent learner. To do this you need to understand something about the mechanics of study and how to learn. While you will be guided in broad outline by your lecturers and seminar leaders it is left to you to learn.

---

2   An allocated lecturer who is not a subject-based tutor and who can be contacted if there are matters that intrude on your ability to study.

STUDYING AND SKILLS

Studying is about learning: learning about yourself, learning about academic subject areas and learning *how* to learn. It is not just the law itself (substantive law) that has to be learnt and understood. A good student should be able to understand, evaluate and use information about studying itself and consider a range of ways of seeing, arguing and thinking. It is good to begin with a basic appreciation of what learning by itself actually is, and what learning involves.

The *Shorter Oxford English Dictionary* defines 'learning' as the obtaining of knowledge about a skill or an art through personal study, reference to personal experience and teaching. In fact, study is defined in several ways, although perhaps the definition that sums up the view of many students is as follows:

. . . a state of mental perplexity or anxious thought.

Studying is an action. It is not passive; it is dynamic, and interactive. Yet too many students see studying as a passive process of soaking up and memorising what is, hopefully, just handed out by the teacher. It is, however, an engaged, proactive process of searching for other ideas, weighing up possibilities and alternatives, criticising and evaluating.

Skills required for successful legal study
You will spend much more of your time studying alone than you will spend learning from your teachers. You are your own best teacher and the quality of your learning habits will determine the quality of your work, your final degree result and your future career (whether in the law or not). The following pages will highlight the range of skills needed for successful study and as you progress through this text many of these skills will be developed. Before going any further, consider Figure 1.1 which sets out the wide range of skills required for legal study. These skills can be hierarchically grouped into the generic skills listed below. To be successful, all these skills need to work effectively together:

■   study skills;

■   IT skills;

■   language skills;

■   critical thinking skills;

■   legal research skills;

■   legal method skills;

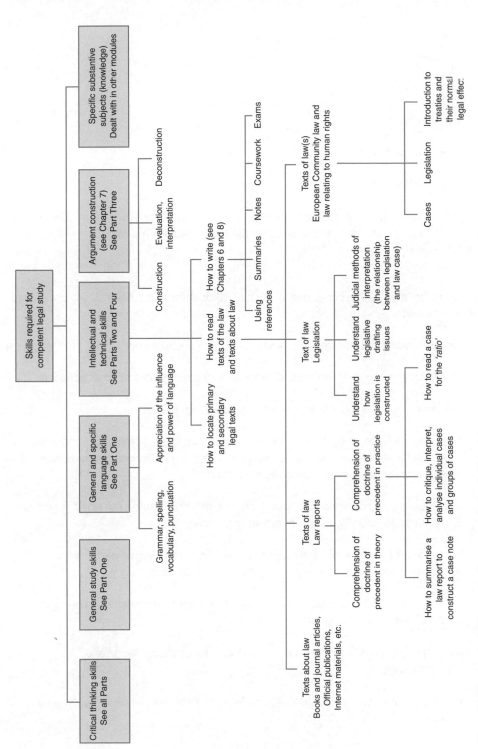

Figure 1.1 The range of skills required for successful legal study

- argumentative skills;

- reading skills;

- writing skills;

- speaking (oral) skills;

- substantive skills.

These skillsets each encompass a range of sub-skills as set out below. Do not be tempted to ignore these lists as they are essential for informing you about the skills which you should be developing.

Study skills

It is vital to be alert to the core need for highly competent study skills. Skills under this heading include:

- understanding and appreciating how your course is structured;

- understanding the different roles of lectures and small groups such as seminars;

- managing your personal study time by pre-planning the week;

- organising a *place* to study. This includes setting up filing systems for handouts, notes made from books, articles or lectures, subject specific problem questions, essay questions and past examination papers;

- developing your powers of concentration so that you are able to sit down for up to two hours and read in a useful, meaningful manner;

- learning to be a highly competent user of the library facilities, using physical resources such as books and journals as well as electronic resources;

- developing writing and reading skills (this also comes under language and legal method skills);

- developing the ability to execute tasks using your legal knowledge and understanding;

- competently using distance learning guides if you are taking a distance learning course or a self-study scheme.

IT skills

This includes becoming competent in the use of:

■   word-processing and email programs;

■   internet searching;

■   databases;

■   your university's electronic library (e-library);

■   the VLE, if used by your university.

   You will find online teaching materials for most of the above in several places on your university's website as well as attached to the learning tutorials for the VLE your institution uses. The teaching and learning unit in your institution will also have student specific learning material on its webpages. We will return to some of these skills later in this chapter. Competent use of your university's e-library is dealt with in Chapter 2.

Language skills

Students need to be competent users of language as the quality of your language skills determines the effectiveness of your communication. This involves demonstrating competency in the areas of:

■   grammar;

■   punctuation;

■   spelling;

■   vocabulary (in terms of both standard English and the development of technical legal language);

■   reading (primary texts *of* law and secondary texts *about* law);

■   writing (notes, summaries and extended academic writing);

■   speaking;

■   interpretation of arguments by analysing the language in which the arguments are presented.

Some time is taken in Chapter 3 to consider these, and there are also relevant exercises on the companion website.

Critical thinking skills

The overarching skill of critical thinking is introduced later in this chapter and integrated throughout this text. It is essential for you to utilise a critical approach to studies, taking nothing for granted and questioning everything. This involves developing your skills of:

■ searching for hidden assumptions;

■ justifying your own assumptions;

■ judging the rationality of those assumptions;

■ testing the accuracy of those assumptions.

Legal research skills

Legal research involves the finding of primary and secondary sources, and is covered in detail in Chapter 2. To be successful you need to become competent in:

■ searching for and finding library resources, both in hardcopy and the electronic formats;

■ retrieving law reports and legislation in hardcopy and e-formats;

■ retrieving academic journal articles in hardcopy and e-formats;

■ bibliographic searching.

Legal method skills

These skills concern formal ways of understanding and analysing issues relating to the law and to legal method, including:

■ handling, applying and interpreting law reports, UK legislation and delegated legislation, case law of the European Court of Human Rights, treaties generally and human rights law;

■ argument construction and deconstruction;

■ answering legal problem questions and constructing essays;

■   legal reading and writing skills;

■   oral argument skills.

Legal method skills are particularly addressed in Chapters 4, 5, 9, 10 and 11. Exercises on the companion website also encourage the practice and development of these skills.

Argumentative skills

The importance of these skills cannot be underestimated because your level of competency in these areas will determine your grades. They include:

■   locating arguments;

■   critiquing and creating arguments;

■   understanding a range of different argument strategies.

These skills are referred to in Chapters 6, 9 and 10, but are the subject of in-depth consideration in Chapters 7 and 8.

Reading skills

These essential skills include:

■   engaging in active reading for sense;

■   looking for markers in the text to aid reading;

■   scanning for information;

■   appreciating when to read carefully and when to skim read.

Reading skills are considered in relation to reading legislation in Chapter 4, in relation to law reports in Chapter 5 and in relation to secondary literature in Chapter 6.

Writing skills

Good writing skills are an essential component of successful study. Your level of competency in this area will also be an important factor in the grades you achieve for assessed written work. Students should become competent in:

■   taking notes;

■   writing summaries;

■   referencing.

Writing skills are covered in detail in Chapter 9.

Oral skills

Oral skills can be as important as written skills. They include:

■   preparing an argument in an oral format;

■   mooting, negotiation, mediation and debate;

■   developing and delivering a competent presentation.

Oral skills are dealt with in detail in Chapter 10.

Substantive skills

This refers to knowledge of particular areas of law, such as criminal law, and is outside the remit of this text. However, it is important to be aware that memorising chunks of your substantive law subjects is not enough to guarantee success. Never underestimate the importance of the general range of study skills, English language skills, legal method skills, critical thinking skills and argument construction skills that you will need to achieve your potential.

It is essential to realise that deficiency in one group of skills can affect performance in all areas, and therefore affect your grades. It is possible to divide these sub-skills into even smaller constituent parts. The complexity of interconnections shown in Figure 1.1 is not specific to the law. If you were studying life sciences or history, you would need a similar set of generic and specific skills.

Before moving on, take a moment to consider which of the skills described above you may already have a basic competency in, which skills you are deficient in and which skills you are good at. This will help you focus on developing the entire range of skills to your highest possible competency.

Studying law

On your law degree programme you will constantly engage with ideas, theories and concepts. You will be taught to find the assumptions on which these ideas or theories are based, and to critically question these assumptions. You need to develop an inquiring mind, one that is flexible and can take on new ideas and critically evaluate them. You will be required to locate and find a range of materials to develop your understanding and application of ideas, legal rules, and theories. You must develop the ability to be able to recognise arguments, the weaknesses in arguments, and to construct your own arguments. You will also need to be able to handle materials sourced in the library, e-library or elsewhere thoroughly and competently.

In order that you can reach a place of complex and sophisticated deeper understanding of the topic you are studying, you should be constantly seeking to understand, and plausibly interpret what you are reading and then consider competing interpretations. In the context of our theme you should *not* stay safely on the lower slopes of the mountain too long; you should train, prepare and begin to climb higher with the aim of achieving greater clarity of vision. A law degree is often seen as a dry and boring programme of study to those who do not know much about it. But the study of law will touch your imagination and provoke your emotions. You will learn how to exercise judgments and make judgments. As you learn you will develop the range of required skills.

You are on a course of study leading to a degree. Each year you take a range of courses and obtain credits at certain grades which determine your degree result. Each course has a teacher who has preset the assessments and the weekly topics in lectures and smaller seminar groups. He or she presents the course in the order that they consider most conducive to delivering a thorough understanding of the topic. From the first week of your study on a particular module or course you are on a journey. Each step from preparation to the final destination is connected to the one before. You should aim to make links between the various topics on your course, rather than moving from one to another without any regard for what has gone before. Each topic you learn and each unit within that topic should be constantly related back to your existing knowledge.

If you do not take this approach to your courses you are not obtaining the level of understanding that your teacher intends. Past information and learning is not being used to inform you with regard to new topics and therefore you may be stuck in a reactive narrow state. Students who just try to do, or avoid doing, the work for this week, or those who try to understand this week's work without a context of knowing what went before, will not attain a sufficient level of understanding.

University is not about getting by; it is certainly not an institution run on the same lines as school. At school you will have been directed by your teachers. At university there are lectures to guide you, seminars to discuss the detail of topics and vast libraries of information at your disposal. However, you must set your own learning agenda. You chose to be at university. And you can choose to make the best use of the learning and feedback opportunities available to you. If you do not, you may obtain a degree that is not a reflection of your true potential, or even fail. The choice is in your hands.

> At university your learning will primarily take place at your own direction. You are your own teacher, and you need to be as disciplined as you can be.

It is worth remembering that you have studied before, so you are not beginning an entirely new enterprise. You may have studied at a school or college, completed private training for a work placement or employment, or engaged in the more experimental learning of new experiences such as parenthood. The big issue to consider is whether your previous study habits are a positive influence on you, or whether you have developed bad habits which should be dropped.

Many students commencing study at university find the new-found freedom strange, difficult to cope with, and easy to get lost in. In school classes with relatively small numbers you may have had a teacher alongside you encouraging you personally. At university you will often be in large groups – there could be up to 300 students in one lecture – where the lecturer does not know you personally, and probably never will. You may be on a course where many seminars are student led, and you will see the tutor only to assess how you present the thoughts derived from previous seminars. You may feel that you are being asked to do things you have not done before but everyone has some past experience of writing an argument, or evaluating the writing of someone else.

Life at university allows you the freedom to explore books and the electronic learning resources – to prepare when you wish, and to talk to your peer group about ideas. Many students make the mistake of allowing old school habits to tip over into their behaviour at university instead of cultivating an independent, adult approach to learning. Indeed we live in an age of 'life-long learning' where more and more people of all ages become students either full time or part time, formally or informally, and they all share in common the need independently to manage and control their own route or path through learning.

It is a standard required skill of the university student that they should develop independence. Not only does the UK Quality Assurance Agency for Higher Education (the body that checks to ensure universities maintain their own academic standards and quality) require it to be instilled in students, but it is also an essential academic and vocational requirement for the study of law. Lawyers generally are professionals who deal with the practical side of their client's everyday issues, including divorce, buying a house, making a will, financial arrangements, commercial contracts and employment issues. They set their own timescale for reaching answers to the questions that client issues bring up. Law students begin the training to be able to do this as they start the academic aspect of their education and take responsibility for planning their own learning.

LEARNING THEORY AND STYLES

You may not realise it but your personality has a major impact on how you learn. Recognising some things about yourself and your learning early on in your studies will be of tremendous benefit. Stop reading for a moment and think why you study using the processes that you use. *How* do you approach the task of studying?

Some students just want to be given all necessary information and memorise it. This of course will not necessarily be enough to obtain even a low grade pass for assessments and exams. Other students just like to be left alone to find out information for themselves, preferably without the need to engage in teamwork. But this will not necessarily be enough to get a very good grade, as interaction, and exchange of ideas, are part of the learning process. Being open to the ideas of others and using them to inform your own ideas is important for your development. Some students are only interested in grades from day one, and will choose only to understand the skillsets that need to be engaged with to get the high grades. Other students have a range of things they want to get out of university and are more interested in an instrumental approach, focusing on the least they can do to get a pass, or how to achieve both a good degree and a good social life.

From reading this you may already know where you fit in the above stereotypical groups. Are you an instrumentalist? Do you want to focus only on the skills associated with achieving high grades? Are you interested in minimal rote learning? It is useful at this stage to consider learning preferences, in order to understand that there are theoretically quite a few different preferences, and that many people use several of them when engaging in learning. Some students really enjoy learning through problem solution, engaging in role play, going off and researching an area alone or just soaking up information delivered in a lecture. Which method you prefer will give you your 'preferred learning style'. Finding your preferred method will help you make the most of your independent learning time. You may be tempted to skip this section but please try not to. You should take the time to get to know your strengths and weaknesses in learning.

Below you will find three sets of learning styles which have been described by different educationalists. Set one has been advanced by Stella Cotterell[3], set two by David Kolb[4] and set three by Peter Honey and Alan Mumford[5]. You will note that many of the features of each overlap.

Cotterell's learning styles
Cotterell outlined four key learning styles, as described below:

■   visual;

■   auditory;

■   kinaesthetic;

■   interactive.

Visual learners are most happy learning from written information, diagrams and pictures. If they are in a situation where they cannot take notes they will be stressed or de-motivated. Some visual learners will take their own notes even when they have been given pre-prepared ones. Think about whether you do this, and if so why? Written assessment works extremely well for visual learners. Some theorists split this group into those who relate best to print, and those who relate best to pictures, graphs and diagrams. Over half the population would fall into this grouping.

Auditory learners work best with oral skills. They like to listen to lectures, and may not take notes or write anything at all until after the lecture. If they see written information it will not make much sense until it is heard. One way in which this group find it easier to learn is

---

3   Set out in Stella Cotterell, *The Study Skills Handbook* (3rd edn Palgrave, 2008).
4   David Kolb, *Experiential Learning* (Englewood Cliff, Prentice Hall, 1984).
5   Peter Honey and Alan Mumford, *The Manual of Learning Styles* (Peter Honey, Maidenhead 1992) 5.

to read aloud from their notes and books. Auditory learners can be particularly good speakers. You may be surprised to hear that about one-third of the population fall into this category.

Kinaesthetic learners have a style which involves efficient learning through movement and/or touching. It relates to practical approaches, such as watching others do something and then repeating it. Kinaesthetic learners are often thought particularly slow in grasping information but this only because popular teaching styles favour visual learners and, to a lesser extent, auditory learners. They may go to different spaces to memorise different information and classify it in their head according to place. Or they may pace or jog whilst learning. Very few people rely on kinaesthetic learning as their only preferred learning style.

Interactive learners like to learn through discussion with peers and teachers. This style is particularly well suited to small group learning. Many students will say that they enjoy learning this way, but if it is not backed up by notes of the session made by the student the learning can be lost.

It is interesting that we tend to use the above preferences together when engaging in simple tasks such as rote learning. Verbal memory can be enhanced by uniting it with visual memory. Making notes and using differing colours to highlight, or using different patterns in your note taking, increases your ability to remember the text. You can also utilise kinaesthetic memory, for example, moving around and talking over the text to yourself[6].

Kolb's learning styles

A different way of clustering learning styles was developed by David Kolb. He classifies four main learning styles characterised by the terms:

■   accommodator;

■   converger;

■   diverger;

■   assimilator.

Accommodators are characterised by their ability to plan and to execute the plan. They are prepared to take risks, and get involved in new experiences, and are extremely able to adapt to new situations. They are not afraid to throw away theories that clearly do not fit the situations they see, and they have an instinctively intuitive ability to jump straight to the solution to a problem without following a step-by-step problem-solving methodology.

---

6   Some students may be concerned that they have a bad memory, or believe that as you get older your ability to remember diminishes, and lose confidence. Mid-life memory loss is not substantiated by very much hard evidence. Mental processes do *change* with age and speed is lost, but we develop efficient strategies for the manipulation of data. Our application and understanding is enhanced. This more than makes up for the loss of speed which is hardly noticeable! The issue is how much the brain is *used* rather than the *age of the user*. To remember is to involve oneself in an active process.

They also rely extensively on gathering information from others. Whilst accommodators are socially relaxed they can be perceived as bossy or lacking in patience.

Divergers utilise their imagination to view situations from a range of different perspectives. They are good at any activity that requires the creation of sets of ideas, such as brainstorming. They are social, and tend to pursue their academic interests in the areas of the arts.

Convergers have a much stronger skill in the area of practical application of ideas. They are particularly good at locating answers when only one solution is correct. They tend to enjoy technical tasks, and excel at problem solving.

Assimilators have a major strength in the area of theoretical models. They can look at a range of seemingly disconnected facts and give an integrated explanation, if there is one to be found. They enjoy logical thought and, if a theory does not fit, they will carefully review the facts, and seek another theory.

Honey and Mumford's learning styles
Honey and Mumford, whose work was much influenced by Kolb, also identified four main types of learning styles:

- activist;

- reflector;

- theorist;

- pragmatist.

Activists prefer to learn 'by doing', so that their learning is based on experience. This is similar to Kolb's converger, and Cotterell's kinaesthetic learner. They are extremely open to new ways of doing things, but this can foster a tendency to be always moving on to new experiences. Activists can be easily seduced into thinking that the actual experience is the learning (which it is not).

Reflectors are most happy learning by observation, researching materials, reading them, reflecting on them and reaching conclusions. What can be a problem for these students is the tendency to collect too much information, making it difficult to reach a conclusion. The reality of academic life is that of course there is always more information to find but there are also reasonable places to stop.

Theorists work best when constructing theories. They like to think things through logically, organising their views into theories like Kolb's assimilators. They can, on the negative side, jump to conclusions too quickly without taking care to reflect critically on their material and findings.

Pragmatists learn by translating what they know, whatever that may be, into practical experience which they experiment with in a range of situations. This is again similar to

Kolb's assimilator. This preference for practical experience can again mean a tendency to jump to conclusions prior to the outcome of analysis.

Honey and Mumford also discussed the fact that many learners only use and feel comfortable with one way of learning. What do you think? Would you be happy to try a few? You could think about this now. When you were reading the learning styles above did any mirror how you approach learning? Had you even thought of some of them? Honey and Mumford consider that there is a benefit in trying all learning styles despite your natural, preferred approach, because different learning styles can be more or less suitable for different learning situations. For example, the activist style is particularly useful when searching for data, such as the primary sources of law, law cases, legal rules and texts. Once you have retrieved the data you may find it more useful to adopt the reflector style, which is extremely productive for considering the tasks to be done (such as sorting, classifying and time-management). The pragmatist learning style is good when repeating learnt techniques and is therefore suitable for practising worked examples to learn methods of problem solving. The theorist learning style is excellent for working towards understanding objectives and information, leading to summarising. Use Table 1.1 to tick the learning styles that you think you currently use and also the styles that you would like to use. You can then make an effort to incorporate your chosen styles into your developing study strategies.

You can use different learning styles to develop study strategies for the full range of teaching methods with which you will be presented. Lecturers will use words, PowerPoint slides, handouts, videos and snippets of recordings to share information with you. Your seminar or tutorial leaders will use small groups to engage in discussions and role plays and you will be asked to engage in investigative research. You need to take as much as you can from all of these learning opportunities, regardless of your preferred style. If you need to learn from auditory information and this is not your preferred learning style, then you need to consider what skills you must develop. If you need to learn from purely visual information and you naturally prefer auditory, again you need to consider how you can adapt to learn from this situation. Awareness of learning styles suited to differing learning opportunities enables you to get the most out of your university education, and acquire the habits of flexible learning.

Learning theories

With his co-researchers, Kolb also developed the concept of the learning cycle. His main interest was in experiential learning (learning by doing) and he was of the opinion that this approach reflected the natural learning process of the individual.

Kolb's learning cycle[7] has four stages, as shown in Figure 1.2. It begins with an actual experience (stage 1), which becomes the object of careful reflection and observation (stage 2) with a view to learning from it. Patterns are then sought and the experience is conceptualised (stage 3). Finally, the learner experiments (stage 4), seeking to learn from the experience to be able to make best use of it in another situation.

---

7   One of the best discussions can be found in D. Schon, *The Reflective Practitioner* (Basic Books, NY 1983).

TABLE 1.1 WHAT IS YOUR STYLE OF LEARNING AND WHAT ARE YOU WILLING TO TRY?

Learning style	Description	Yes, this is me	No, this is not me	Don't know	I might try this
COTTERELL'S LEARNING STYLES					
VISUAL	Deals well with visual information, writing, diagrams				
AUDITORY	Deals well with heard information and engages in oral skills				
KINAESTHETIC	Learns through touching and moving, watching others and doing				
INTERACTIVE	Learns through discussion groups with students and teachers				
KOLB'S LEARNING STYLES					
THE ACCOMMODATOR	Organises plans and sticks to them, good at taking information from others but can be a bit bossy and/or impatient				
THE DIVERGER	Looks at situations from a range of perspectives using imagination				
THE CONVERGER	Practically applies ideas, excelling and enjoying solving problems with only one right answer				
THE ASSIMILATOR	Good at logical thought, devising theories and producing overarching explanations of a range of seemingly unconnected facts				
HONEY AND MUMFORD'S LEARNING STYLES					
THE ACTIVIST	Learns by doing and very open to new ways of doing things				
THE REFLECTOR	Learns by watching (observation) and by researching and reflecting on materials				
THE THEORIST	Constructs theories but has a habit of jumping to conclusions in the absence of supportive evidence if they are not careful				
THE PRAGMATIST	Translates knowledge into practical experience				

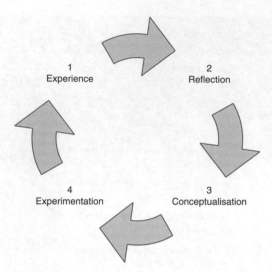

Figure 1.2 Kolb's learning cycle

Once you have completed one cycle of learning as set out above in Figure 1.2, you start the next, this time with greater proficiency and knowledge. Therefore your next learning experience will start at a higher level of competency. Steadily, your understanding increases with each loop, like a knowledge spiral, shown in Figure 1.3.

Figure 1.3 The knowledge spiral

These models of learning show how we can move away from the slavery of information reproduction to obtaining deeper understanding of information. They both demonstrate how knowledge is developed out of understanding and vice versa. Are you beginning to see how the acquisition of knowledge without understanding hampers knowledge use?

Kolb's work on learning styles, and the establishment of what is now known as the experiential learning theory was preceded by two other important schools of thought, the **behaviourist** view of learning and the **social cognition** school. It is useful to summarise these to give you as broad an introduction as possible to learning.

The behaviourists consider that what is important with regard to learning is encouraging students to change their behaviour. Change their behaviour and you change habits so that students automatically improve their study techniques. As a psychological theory it depends on rewarding 'good behaviour' so that it is positively reinforced. Learning then is said to be characterised as response/reward reinforcement, which changes behaviour. Behaviourists prefer an incremental approach to learning, taking small steps to build on what has gone before and allowing time for the skills to develop, all the time rewarding good behaviour. As you might by now suspect, this approach to learning can be rather mechanical. But it has its place, perhaps in those areas of study where there is only one right way of doing things. However, in the study of law it is often not the simple case that there is just one right way of doing something. You could try a reward approach to your own studying, however, as it may help you build disciplined habits.

The social cognition school factors into its theory the complexity of human ways of seeing and thinking, and the vast range of rationales adopted for behaviour. It notes how people overwhelmingly tend to fit new information into existing frames of reference or, if we cannot do that, we then change our existing understanding. They note, however, that whatever information is involved we only understand the solution to a problem by internalising our information and considering it within an entire frame of reference. This view of learning underlines the importance of understanding the meaning of things, and suggests studying is dynamic, constantly evolving through questioning and returning to texts. It suggests that we use problem solving as a main vehicle to understanding, and employ a large amount of material to assist with that process. Much of your learning of law will depend upon your understanding of the meaning of rules, theories and ideas and you will no doubt fit each new piece of learning into that framework.

MANAGING YOUR LEARNING

Consider if you have a good track record of working to a deadline and 'getting things done'. In the past your teacher, your employer or your family may have given you a structure for planning your work. At university you have to do this for yourself. There will be many tasks coming your way, so you will need to develop quickly the skill of efficiently setting your priorities.

For each course you are studying ensure you know where to locate the subject hand-book, the reading list, the calendar of lectures and seminars and above all the course or module outline (the syllabus for the course). You then need to prioritise your time in terms of lecture attendance, seminar preparation, seminar attendance and participation, production of course work, revision and taking exams. Always be aware of your own independent study priorities on a daily and weekly basis. Look ahead and plan out the term, and also ascertain when your assessments are set and due for submission, and pencil them in for the year.

You will no doubt bring with you to your new studies some skills for handling stress. As you will probably know stress is a required and normal part of everyday life, but sometimes it can get out of hand. Being well organised in your management of class attendance, independent study and coursework submission will help ensure that you do not experience high stress levels. Being a perfectionist can be almost as great a stress as being a procrastinator. Mark Twain once remarked that he had had many worries in his life – but luckily none of them actually occurred.

You will also have some level of language skills and experience of problem-solving, working as part of a team and using IT. Take some time to reflect on how good each of these skills are and whether you need to develop any of them. Your existing skills will not be of use to you if you do not take the time to reflect on them and how they can be improved.

The cycles and schedules of academic life

Part of preparing for the journey of being a successful law student and ultimately a successful law graduate is to understand the shape of the year, its divisions into terms and vacations, and the weeks in the term. You cannot successfully manage your learning if you do not know the patterns of university life and what is expected when.

The academic year is split into terms of lectures, seminars and assessments, and vaca-tions. This structure determines the flow of your work, setting out your free time and your study time. You need to understand the structure well because you have to fit into it. You may need to slot paid work commitments or family commitments into it as well as your study and leisure activities. Consideration of the shape of the year will allow you to see where you have spaces to do certain things and when you should be busy with your studies. Of course you *know* about terms and vacations but have you really understood how little time you have in a year?

It is equally important to understand the rhythm of your term/semester cycle and the timetable of weekly lectures, seminars and assessments. You will need to organise your study outside the classroom for seminars and assessments as well as increasing your general understanding of the subject.

The cycle of the academic year

Most universities structure the academic year into three terms with short (three- or four-week) vacations at the end of terms 1 and 2 and a longer break in the summer, from the end of June until at least mid-September. Some universities are semesterised, which means the

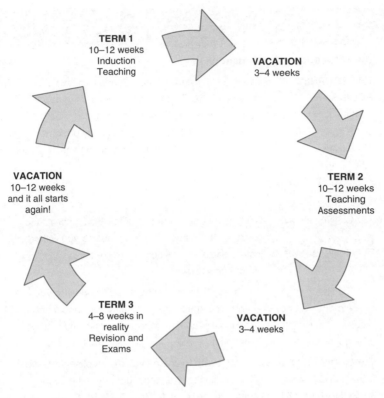

Figure 1.4 The cycle of the academic year

year is broken into two large chunks, split into smaller modules. The discussion that follows discusses the termly pattern, as shown in Figure 1.4, but it can be adapted very easily to slot into the semester pattern if your institution uses it.

Zooming into this cycle in more detail, Table 1.2 sets out the months of the year and maps them against the standard academic activity taking place, so you can begin to see perhaps for the first time the rhythm of the academic year for the typical student. You will realise that you do not actually have a year to study; at best you have nine months. Of this time, only around six months will be spent with teachers or in classes and seminars.

Once you appreciate the structure of the entire academic year, you also need to know and understand how your time is divided at the level of the term, and then at the level of each week. The next section looks at this micro-context and also engages in a discussion of personal management within the termly and weekly cycle. It is at the detailed level that you are most likely to 'lose the plot'.

TABLE 1.2 TYPICAL ACADEMIC CYCLE FOR A YEAR-ONE STUDENT (SPLIT INTO TERMS)

Month	Official activity	Student tasks	Week
SEP	**THE JOURNEY BEGINS** INDUCTION START OF TERM 1 TEACHING (choosing options if applicable for Terms 1 and 2)	This is a whirlwind, a time of highs and lows for most students. Ensure you know your timetable subjects, times and room numbers, and whether weekly or fortnightly, etc. Choose any options. Begin to get to grips with communications, IT and the library.	**TERM 1 TEACHING TERM** 10–12 weeks
OCT	TEACHING BEGINS	Continue your induction. Ask for assistance if you need it. Do not suffer in silence as you will be lost. These are key weeks so make sure you get off to a good start.	
NOV	TEACHING There *may* be a one-week reading week with no lectures	Your study timetable should now be clear to you. Attendance at seminars and lectures should not be an issue, you should *be* there. Use any reading week to catch up.	
DEC	TEACHING DRAWS TO AN END FROM AROUND 12th–17th VACATION	As term draws to an end you may feel settled, and/or aware of what you need to do over the upcoming vacation to be ready for Term 2. You may need to do some catching up if you have lost your focus. You may feel low and demoralised, but it's not too late to make some positive plans to change bad habits, develop good self-management skills and get on top of your work. A chat with your tutor before leaving for vacation can work miracles for your motivation. **(SEMESTERISED PROGRAMMES MAY HAVE EXAMS NOW)**	**VACATION** 3–4 weeks
JAN	VACATION/START OF TERM 2 Teaching begins and moves swiftly. This is the busiest & most tiring term	Enjoy yourself in the vacation, and do take some time out for a rest but ensure you continue planning and studying. Use the vacation to reflect on how you did in Term 1. What worked and what did not? Make specific plans about how to change bad study habits. **THIS IS THE MAKE OR BREAK TERM.**	**TERM 2 TEACHING TERM** 10–12 weeks

Month	Official activity	Student tasks	Week
FEB	TEACHING There may be a one-week reading week with no lectures	You can still make up for lost time and do well, but if you do not work consistently this term you may find that you do not get the grades you want. You should have your study plan not only in place but be working to it. Be careful, it is easy to lose motivation.	**VACATION** 3–4 weeks
MAR	TEACHING VACATION MAY START	It is important to keep going as the term approaches its end as you will be tired. You can make up for lack of good study habits in Term 1, but be careful: it is easy to lose momentum and then fall behind.	
APR	VACATION It can sometimes start in March TERM 3 BEGINS	This is a make or break vacation in terms of exam success. You need to have a proper break and then ensure you do any necessary assessments, and plan your revision timetable in rough. If you have missed important work make sure you catch up.	**TERM 3 REVISION CLASSES** 1–2 weeks
MAY	REVISION & EXAM SEASON You have nearly reached the summit of your journey up the mountain that is your first year of study.	This is again not the time to lose momentum. Look after your emotional and physical health in revision and exam season. If it is better for you to go home for a few weeks to revise when revision classes have ended then you should consider it. Others will want to stay in the hub of things. Everyone is different and you must do what is best for you. **(SEMESTERISED PROGRAMMES MAY HAVE EXAMS NOW)**	**PERSONAL REVISION AND EXAMS RESULTS**
JUN	EXAM SEASON **THE JOURNEY ENDS**	You just need to stay focused, and move on if one exam seemed difficult. Put fears you have failed something behind you and keep your strength up for the next exam.	
JUL	RESULTS If you failed any exam ensure you know what went wrong so that you can succeed in the resits.	If you have failed any exams it is essential to see your tutor before they leave for the long vacation. Put failure in a context. Is it your fault for not studying properly, is this the best course for you? Did you just make a mistake reading the exam question? Work hard for the resits and resolve to develop better revision strategies and if applicable better independent management skills next year.	

TABLE 1.2—continued			
Month	Official activity	Student tasks	Week
AUG	VACATION	RESITS POSSIBLE	
SEPT	**THE NEW ACADEMIC YEAR : IT ALL STARTS AGAIN!**		

The termly academic cycle and your personal timetable

An entire degree programme is made up of 360 credits. Each year of your degree will be worth 120 credits and each course or module will contribute a specific number of credits to that total. You will be required to complete a set number of compulsory courses or modules each year, and you can then make up the rest of your credits for the year by choosing options from pre-set lists. Part-time students usually take six years to complete their degrees, completing one level over two years. Of these two years one year may inevitably be heavier than the other due to timetabling constraints or the subjects on offer.

Options usually have to be chosen in the induction week, if not before. Your choices here are important as you want to get the best results that you can. Consider your options carefully before making your choice.

Let us suppose that you are studying the subjects shown in Table 1.3 in your first year, and you are a full-time student. Taken together these seven subjects equal 120 credits. It would seem from this list that you have five modules or courses in Term 1 and four in Term 2 (note that courses 3 and 5 run across both terms).

TABLE 1.3 HYPOTHETICAL COURSES OF STUDY OVER A YEAR				
	Course or module	Length	Term	Credits
1	Contract law	One term	Term 1	20 credits
2	Critical law	One term	Term 1	20 credits
3	English legal system and methods	One year	Terms 1 & 2	20 credits
4	Philosophy	One term	Term 1	10 credits
5	Criminal law	One year	Terms 1 & 2	20 credits
6	Legal theory	One term	Term 2	10 credits
7	The law of tort	One term	Term 2	20 credits

When you have registered your department will know what courses or modules you are doing. This will determine your lecture timetable and you will find that at most lectures you will be in a group of more than 100 students. You will most likely be allocated to a particular seminar or tutorial group as well. This is a smaller group of students (15–30) which may meet weekly, fortnightly, or at more irregular intervals with a lecturer or tutor to discuss student answers to problems posed by the lecturer. There is sometimes the opportunity to change your small group for another day or time if you have family commitments or other documented reasons for not being able to attend the original class allocated.

You will need to compile your own personal timetable of classes (only a few law departments or schools will issue you with a personal timetable) like the hypothetical one shown in Table 1.4 and you can find template forms for this purpose on the companion website. Here we have put the five hypothetical Term 1 courses or modules introduced above onto a weekly timetable. Table 1.4 does not factor in rooms but it is a good idea to put the room number for each activity on to your timetable. Bear in mind that these can change not only from term to term but from week to week.

Our hypothetical timetable so far includes only the fixed times in the week when you must be in classes, at least in Term 1. However, as we have already seen, you will also be expected to engage in a relatively large amount of independent learning. The amount of study expected of you each week will vary according to whether your course or module is taught over one term or one year, and whether it is a whole unit course or a half-unit course. Just because an option is covered in one term, this does not mean it is a half-unit course. Your courses may state the number of independent study hours they require. If you look at the course or module outline you may find that at the top of the first page it gives you a number of taught hours and student study hours. This could, for example, be 50 teacher hours and 200 independent student hours. Make sure you read the small print. Overall, most individual courses or modules will require you to engage in independent study for 4–6 hours a week. More study may be needed if you are preparing for an assessment. Your personal timetable will affect how much work you need to do. If your friends seem to have less study commitments, do not worry, this is just the way things have worked out.

If you look at the specimen personal weekly timetable in Table 1.4 below you will see that our hypothetical student's timetable of **5** subjects amounts to **12** hours' class attendance. Now we need to factor in independent study time. Five subjects, at 4–6 hours a week independent study will require 20–30 hours a week additional study time. Add to this the 12 hours of class attendance and you get a university week of 32–42 hours, as shown in Table 1.5. More hours may well be required in a week with assessments due.

Even a 42-hour-week, however, leaves you plenty of time for a social life. In our hypothetical timetable we have put all of the independent study hours into the 9–6 Monday to Friday slots. Using the available spaces and allowing breaks, this allows for 24 study hours and still leaves every evening and the whole weekend free. This is enough for five

TABLE 1.4 A PERSONAL WEEKLY TIMETABLE, WITH FIXED POINTS FOR CLASSES

Time	Mon	Tues	Weds	Thurs	Fri
9–10		**Critical law LECTURE** One term module only, Term 1		**ELS & methods LECTURE** Runs all year	**Philosophy LECTURE** One term module only
10–11		**Critical law LECTURE** One term module only, Term 1			**Philosophy LECTURE** One term module only
11–12			**Criminal law LECTURE** Runs all year	**ELS & methods SEMINAR** Runs all year every week	**Criminal law SEMINAR** Runs all year Every two weeks
12–13		**Critical law SEMINAR** One term module only, Term 1 Runs every week	**Contract law LECTURE** Term 1 only		
13–14		**Contract law LECTURE** Term 1 only			
14–16					
16–17					**Contract law SEMINAR** Term 1 only Runs every week
17–18					
18–19					
EVENING					

TABLE 1.5 A PERSONAL WEEKLY TIMETABLE, WITH FIXED POINTS FOR CLASSES AND INDEPENDENT STUDY HOURS ALLOCATED

TERM 1: INDEPENDENT MANAGEMENT OF STUDY

Time	Mon	Tues	Weds	Thurs	Fri
9–10	STUDY	Critical law LECTURE One term module only Term 1	STUDY	ELS & methods LECTURE Runs all year	Philosophy LECTURE One term module only
10–11	STUDY	Critical law LECTURE One term module only Term 1	STUDY	STUDY	Philosophy LECTURE One term module only
11–12	STUDY	BREAK	Criminal law LECTURE Runs all year	ELS & methods SEMINAR Runs all year Every week	Criminal law SEMINAR Runs all year Every two weeks
12–13	BREAK	Critical law SEMINAR One term module only Term 1 Runs every week	Contract law LECTURE Term 1 only	BREAK	BREAK
13–14	STUDY	Contract law LECTURE Term 1 only	STUDY	STUDY	STUDY
14–16	STUDY	STUDY	STUDY	STUDY	STUDY
16–17	STUDY	STUDY	STUDY	STUDY	Contract law SEMINAR Term 1 only Runs every week
17–18	STUDY	STUDY	STUDY	STUDY	STUDY
18–19					
EVENING					

subjects requiring 4–5 hours' independent study each. It is not enough if each module requires six hours' study, in which case you may need to do some additional work at the weekend.

In addition to the study timetable many students need to work in paid employment, sometimes during the day. There is time available in our hypothetical timetable for that, but then study time will need to be moved to the weekend. Some students play sport and are in teams for the university. In this case training and playing time needs to be taken into account. Study hours will again need to be rearranged by you.

> You do not have as much free time as you think if you want to succeed and get a good degree. But you will have enough free time to have fun.

However, be careful to make sure your social life does not impact on your study by leaving you exhausted during the hours you need to study. Whilst you may have paid employment which you are able to do when you are very tired, it is extremely difficult to do good work when you are tired, or indeed to study at all. Try not to fall into the trap of saying you are 'free' or have 'nothing on' if you do not have a formal class with a lecturer. You usually do have something you ought to be studying. But if you organise and manage your study time well, you can be flexible with yourself, and occasionally take a break before working in the evening to compensate.

Many management consultants advise that you also build in crisis time to your planning. This comprises hours that are 'free' but 'in-waiting', in case you cannot study at the time allotted. In our hypothetical timetable, evenings and weekends would be hours 'in-waiting', when you could work if you were not able to study at the times you originally planned.

Whilst the termly timetable may seem daunting, there is of course relief in the form of reading and independent study weeks allowing you to catch up. The vacations also allow you some space to have a break as well as study. Looking back at the short version of the yearly academic cycle in Figure 1.4 puts the termly cycle into context. You are only asked to work to such a packed timetable for around 22 weeks of the year in two terms of 11–12 week blocks. The third term is taken up with catch up, some assessments, revision and exams. However, this does mean that if you fall behind you need to take proper advice from your lecturers and tutors as to the best way of making up time.

Even if you are not formally examined until later in your degree, do not underestimate the importance of doing well in your first year. Law is a highly competitive profession to get into in terms of finding placements (which look good on your CV), obtaining places at law school and securing training contracts or pupillage. This type of competition demands focus and requires you to put in hours of studying. You need to spend time in your first year developing your stamina for the hours of study involved. Often prospective employers look at first year results even though they do not count towards the degree, and of course some of the first year courses of law students count as foundation courses for the purposes of going on to the vocational stage of legal training. The prospective law school for the vocational stage may also wish to see your first year marks in these foundation subjects.

Prospective law firms and vocational law schools will also be interested in your broader activity. What have you done to engage with the life of the university law school? Are you involved in the student law society? Are you involved in client counselling or mooting competitions? Have you got placements? By planning your time effectively, you can ensure you have time available to participate in appropriate activities which will enhance your job prospects.

CRITICAL THINKING

All day, every day, your brain receives information from your different senses. It processes that information in microseconds, often without you even being consciously aware, evaluates it and then decides what to do (whether to ignore or act upon it). Often the action we take in everyday life is in part based on guesswork, which is itself based on a certain level of knowledge and experience. Given that everyday life is a cyclical process of receipt of information, evaluation, guesswork and action, as shown in Figure 1.5, it is obvious that learning is not an exception to the normal rhythms of life. On the contrary it is merely a highly sophisticated and stylised part of it.

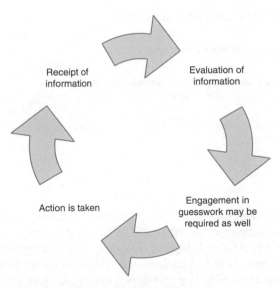

Figure 1.5 The cycle of information receipt, evaluation and action

One important characteristic of highly competent people is that in many areas of their lives they have developed *a critical approach* to what they do, see and think. Not critical in the sense of 'fault finding' but critical in the sense of:

exercising judgments based upon careful:

- ## observation;

- ## investigation;

- ## consideration

of the issues relevant to the matter about which a judgment is to be made.

Most educators and senior managers would state that critical thinking, critical analysis and critical reflection are essential skills sought after in students and employees. Usually, these phrases are not defined but are left as vague attributes. However, the skills involved are not vague, for they are identified by others looking for them. Some people define critical thinking as a skill, or cluster of skills, which includes:

- reasoning logically;

- the ability to locate underlying assumptions;

- analytic and argumentative skills.

In terms of approaches to study, it can mean the ability to be:

- curious;

- flexible;

- sceptical.

Critical thinking is usually thought of as an academic or intellectual skill but it also has crucial practical applications in life. What should be clear is that it is not just a cerebral rational attribute and act. Critical thinking is equally informed by passion, emotion and imagination. Imagination can in fact be essential to leaps of creativity that are later identified as 'critical'. Being a critical thinker therefore is bigger than just cognitive acts of logical reasoning, and the careful consideration of argument. It also involves an ability to find assumptions behind beliefs, actions and behaviour, and bring creativity to the activity of thinking. Critical thinking involves the whole person and can be seen as a life-enhancing necessity:

> I argue that the ability to think critically is crucial to understanding our personal relationships, envisioning alternative and more productive ways of organising the workplace, and becoming politically literate[8].

Critical thinkers will be able to put forward justification for their ideas and actions and those of others. They can compare and contrast, work through processes, subject justifications to a number of interpretations, and they can predict and test the accuracy of those predictions. They can work artificially by constructing models of the 'real' and recognise that is what has been constructed. Critical thinking also involves 'reflection', subjecting your learning to analysis by comparing it with practice.

Critical thinkers are always searching for the hidden assumptions behind what others just call 'common sense', or 'everyday' accepted ways of acting or thinking. They are aware of diversity in values and behaviour. When critical thinkers locate underlying assumptions they know they have to ask if they fit in with current notions of social reality. These assumptions are carefully dissected and their accuracy, as well as their validity, questioned. At this point these competent individuals consider alternative ways of acting and alternative assumptions to back them.

For critical thinkers nothing is closed, fixed, or certain. Everything is potentially flexible, open and possible. They are always questioning what lies behind the ideas, beliefs or actions that people hold or take. This is not to say that critical thinkers hold no strong views or cannot believe in anything. It is possible to hold the strongest convictions that something is right while accepting that all values, views and beliefs are open to question and that there may be alternative views. Critical thinkers can always imagine another plausible story, explanation, or value. They are not going to believe in universal truths without thorough investigation and indeed will probably always remain healthily sceptical of universal views, truths and explanations.

If a critical thinker holds a clear view, it is held lightly with scepticism. If strong evidence to the contrary occurs the view will be reconsidered. As Cotterell notes:

> Scepticism in critical thinking means bringing an element of polite doubt. In this context, scepticism does not mean you must go through life never believing anything you hear and see. This would not be helpful. It does mean holding open the possibility that what you know at the given time may be only part of the picture[9].

Critical thinkers are flexible thinkers, but not fickle thinkers and they are not afraid of alternatives. Constant questioning heightens the awareness of critical thinkers, as they always approach givens as if the view could be otherwise.

---

8 Stephen Brookfield, *Developing Critical Thinkers: Challenging Adults to Explore Alternative Ways of Thinking and Acting* (Jossey Bass, 1987) 14.

9 Sheila Cotterell, *Critical Thinking Skills: Developing Effective Analysis and Argument* (Palgrave Macmillan, 2005) 3.

This takes us a long way beyond the discipline of law, legal method and studying law but the intellectual process involved in critical thinking is the basis of studying. Each discipline may require slightly differing approaches that accord to its accepted practices and procedures, but the foundational importance of critical thinking remains intact within every part of the academic community. Each discipline will have developed its own beliefs, practices and procedures, its own theory and methods and its own underlying assumptions. The study of law is no exception.

Competency in critical thinking develops over time and no doubt all readers of this book will have developed some critical thinking skills outside the study of law, although they may not have put a name to the process. This development can be transferred to your legal studies even if you have never really considered the issue of critical thinking before. In academic studies, critical thinking and a healthy scepticism of universality, are demonstrated by approaches to reasoning. Critical thinkers, for example, are aware that often arguments contain contradictions and these contradictions have to be looked for. They are also able to distinguish between differing types of statement. For example, they can understand the difference between a statement of fact and a statement of opinion. This naturally affects the expertise of their reasoning processes as it makes a great deal of difference whether an argument is based on opinions or facts!

The core of critical thinking is the constant and considered identification and challenging of the accepted truth. It requires the evaluation of values and beliefs as well as competing truth explanations and, of course, texts. It involves both rationality/objectivity and emotions/subjectivity and the questioning of the very categories of thought that are accepted as proper ways of proceeding. If you think critically, you will:

■   *search* for hidden assumptions;

■   *justify* assumptions;

■   *judge* the rationality of those assumptions;

■   *test* the accuracy of those assumptions.

Texts will form the 'bare bones' of much of your studies. They are delivered in language that has to be read, interpreted, questioned and seen in its fragmented contexts, so it is vital to develop a critical approach. The critical thinker has to engage not only with micro-questions within a text, from both superficial and deep readings, but also with macro issues surrounding topics, courses and ultimately the legal system. Much of your degree study will involve working with legal primary or secondary texts, reconciling, distinguishing and/or following the arguments of others, as well as the tentative construction of your own arguments. You must be able to identify arguments set out in texts, offer your views on their weaknesses and strengths, and understand why an argument can be considered good or bad. Much of your time may be spent explaining alternative interpretations that may be very close to one another. When deciding what words mean in texts we make far-reaching decisions and often engage with morals, religion, justice and ethics. Critical thinkers look for hidden assumptions underlying the face value explanations of texts. They are not deceived by theorists, particularly those who make claims of neutrality, and are aware of the power of language and the value of argument. They know that all texts are not logical and do not necessarily feel that they have to be so.

Many students think it strange that in their first term of study they can be asked to critically evaluate an article written by a leading scholar. The rationale for this is that by reading the work of leading scholars students can see the ways in which a strong argument is deployed. Sometimes a theorist who has constructed a very elegant theory from quite normal information known to students is used to teach about theory construction. Students are also asked to read the work of scholars critiquing other scholars, and in this way students begin to understand how to critique themselves.

If you identify and carefully take apart the arguments of leading academics you will learn how they put together an excellent argument. You will begin to extract from an article, or a chapter in a book, the main and secondary arguments. You will identify the evidence that they have used to support their arguments. You will also see many ways of structuring arguments. You will of course come across some academics who argue most elegantly, interlinking the parts of their argument to create a highly persuasive conclusion.

When you read these academics or when you read any material you should be in the process of having a dialogue with that writer 'in your head' as you read, make notes and question. Academics, professionals and especially students cannot find out everything for themselves through firsthand experience of doing research and evaluating it. They have to rely on the work of other people in place of doing the initial research. But that work should only be relied on after you have subjected it to careful consideration and critique. You should never accept the arguments of another without careful reflection and if possible double-checking the evidence supporting the arguments. In other words not just the argument but the evidence it is based on should be subjected to critical reflection and analysis.

It is also important for students to learn quickly that in actual fact theories, interpretation or arguments may only be partially correct. They may, in part, be wrong. As you ask, and answer, some of your critical questions you will develop a better understanding of areas, and this will allow you to engage in discussions of increasingly complex topics. As a result you will come to know a topic, or the main subject-matter of a course, well. In academic life new questions constantly arise and cannot be resolved by an internet search. It is then the task of the astute student to apply known understandings to the new circumstances and questions. You are only expected to identify and understand the relevance of new questions in your area of study to and engage with them. You are certainly not expected to resolve any new intellectual and academic dilemmas.

Critical thinking is a dynamic process involving a range of different mental processes, including attention to detail, focus, organisation and classification, and ultimately evaluative judgment of the arguments you are reading. For the first months of study, and even the first year, critical thinking will be somewhat of an artificial process that you need to keep remembering. Ultimately it will become a way of looking at the world so that you automatically question everything and evaluate it, and where necessary adjust your understanding. If you subject your own arguments to critical evaluation, in time the habit of employing critical thinking as you read and write will become ingrained.

In the academic life of the university it is normal to query the correctness of the reasoning of other academics and to state your doubts. However, just as in real life, there is a level at which we must operate on trust despite all our questions as critical thinkers. We need to trust at times that the argument we read is based on information that is plausibly correct, but we need to make informed decisions about what we choose to take on trust. In academic study it is expected that our belief in certain academic points of view or positions are fully explored so that we more fully understand the basis of that belief. As you acquire better habits of critical thinking as a process you will more naturally become aware that your emotional standpoints, and your attitudes to the author, have to be placed to one side. You will realise that you need to take a neutral objective view as you approach a text and identify and evaluate the arguments to ascertain whether they are plausible or not. At that point you are ready to express your own view, your own argument and forward your own evidence to support it.

Always remember that an author must give you clear reasons for each of his or her arguments before you take a position agreeing or disagreeing with the argument. As you move through the levels of study over the years of your degree you should find that the quality of your reasoning improves substantially. Ultimately you will be able to evaluate quickly and efficiently the reasoning of others, spot internal contradictions in their work and 'read between the lines' and identify or hazard a guess at the underlying or hidden assumptions that the argument is based upon. You will far more easily engage in comparing and contrasting the opinions of the academic authors you read, and you too will be able to form categories and engage in the prediction of outcomes. Above all you become competent in the skill of attention to detail.

Not only are critical thinking skills vital to your study but they will be of enormous value to you in the workplace. They are transferable skills which you can use in all settings to evaluate properly your courses of action. Not only will critical thinking help you save time, you may also be saved from making bad decisions!

IT AND COMMUNICATIONS

This section is not last because it is least important. All the areas considered in detail in this chapter are of comparable importance because they all work together to make you a successful and competent learner.

However, *everything* that you do at university depends on excellent communication skills. Your final degree grade is the total product of the marks you receive for your course assessments (both oral and written) and your examinations. The final grade for each piece of work is affected by your communication skills in the following areas:

■ **Presentation:** grammar, spelling, paragraph use, general layout of your word-processing/ handwriting *or* speed of oral delivery, audibility of voice, body language, etc and referencing of sources whether in oral or written formats.

■ **Content:** the range of academic sources used, the range of legal sources used, the competency of your argument construction.

■ **Structure:** the use of standard academic protocols relating to the structure of written and oral work which usually requires a clear introduction, a main body of discussion relating to sources, and a clear conclusion. Your argument should be signalled in the introduction, worked out in the main body and finalised in the conclusion.

The normal expectation for all written course work and evidence of oral skills is that it is handed in having been word-processed. Many departments require electronic submission of work. In addition many of your sources of required academic reading may only be accessible in electronic format through your institution's library (this is dealt with at length in Chapter 2). Therefore excellent IT skills become essential for the appropriate completion, presentation and submission of assessed coursework.

You can only know exactly what it is that you are required to do, and by when, by locating the information that reports this. That information will be communicated to you by your department, most probably via electronic communication methods such as email. Probably the most important thing for you to do is to familiarise yourself with your department's communication systems and set up a university email account. Most universities require students to register for the university, then register for the library, at which point they may use their library-user ID to register for a university email account.

Your department may also make extensive use of a web-based VLE. All students registered in departments using this will receive all of their announcements via the VLE. In addition each course will have a separate area of the VLE (Virtual Learning Environment) to post course documents for access by students. This may include access to teaching support materials such as handouts, PowerPoint lecture slides and materials for seminar tasks. You need to know how to make best use of this and how to file material electronically by placing a copy onto your computer.

The types of electronic information you may be given from your department and your lecturers then includes weekly, termly and yearly information, all of which is important. For example, you may be informed electronically of:

■ your timetable of classes in a given subject, of tutorials and/or seminars;

■ your timetable of examinations;

- your assessment timetable and protocols for the submission of work;

- the university's attendance policy and forms to use if you are sick or need leave of absence for reasons other than sickness;

- important regulations for your degree course.

If you are staying in university accommodation you should have a broadband facility to enable you to access the internet from your room on your PC. You may need to pay a modest one-off fee for this. If you are staying in private accommodation you may have to organise and pay for landline rental and monthly broadband access yourself. There are a range of options for accessing the internet including using your mobile phone. You may wonder why you need even to think about internet and a PC in your accommodation. As more and more material is delivered by VLEs or the electronic databases in the library, having your own PC will save you from queuing for computing access in the university. This in turn will save you time and stress. Both the VLE and the electronic resources in your university library will be available to you via the internet and your university webpage.

You need to make sure that in the first days of your attendance at university you note down all instructions you are given, even if you think you will remember them. These instructions will cover how your classes, seminars, lectures or tutorials will take place, including what you must sign up to and what training you may need. Every department will have some form of induction for new students and you will be told who you can ask about any issues you may have. With such an overwhelming amount of information at the start of your course, you may think that everyone else seems to know what they are doing and you do not. One of the first things to realise is that whether others do or do not is immaterial. It is *you* who has to know.

CONCLUSION

- As a university student you need to take responsibility for your own learning, identifying your goals, employing appropriate learning styles, planning your time and developing your skills.

- Success in law relies on knowledge of substantive law and the application of competent study, IT, language, research, reading, writing, speaking and critical thinking skills.

- Understanding the structure of the academic year and the termly and weekly timetables is essential for organising your study outside the classroom and balancing your academic, work and leisure activities.

FURTHER READING

There are some excellent books on the market to support study skills and critical thinking and the following are some of the best.

WR McKay and HE Charlton, *Legal English: How to Understand and Master the Language of Law* (Pearson Longman, 2005).

This is excellent for getting to grips with language issues from the technical legal vocabulary through to issues of the appropriate use of grammar. It is presented clearly and in an interesting format, allowing students to improve their skills. The majority of the exercises have answers and are well suited to self-study.

G Price and P Maier, *Effective Study Skills* (Pearson Education, 2007).

This is an excellent guide to study skills dealing in depth with issues as diverse as independent management to getting the best out of group work and writing essays. It is a general book not specific to law.

S Cotterell, *Critical Thinking Skills: Developing Effective Analysis and Argument* (Palgrave Macmillan, 2005).

This is an indispensable book if you wish to take these skills seriously. It is clearly set out with a range of interesting exercises and feedback to assist you to assess yourself.

S Cotterell, *The Study Skills Handbook* (3rd edn Palgrave Macmillan, 2008).

C Gatrell, *Managing Part-time Study: A Guide for Undergraduates and Postgraduates* (Open University Press, 2006).

S Hargreaves, *Study Skills for Dyslexic Students* (Sage, 2007).

E Hoult, *Learning Support for Mature Students* (Sage, 2006).

A Northledge, *The Good Study Guide* (2nd edn Open University Press, 2005).

Specific references to legal writing and issues of reading are given in the further reading sections of Chapters 4, 5, 6 and 9.

SIGNPOSTS AND LANDMARKS – USING THE LIBRARY

2

" A university is just a group of buildings gathered around a library"

Shelby Foote

LEARNING OUTCOMES

After reading this chapter you should be able to:

■ understand the structure and layout of the standard university library and the context of the law library within it;

■ understand the difference between primary and secondary sources of legal information;

■ develop a competent approach to locating, accessing and searching print and electronic resources;

■ use citations to locate primary source material and correctly reference sources;

■ understand the hierarchy of law reports;

■ develop strategies to ascertain the authority and validity of retrieved materials.

CHAPTER SUMMARY

The key tools of the trade of the law student are found in the library, in the millions of words that constitute the body *of* the law and the millions of words that have been used to talk *about* the law. Library skills are crucial to your study of law, indeed without them you will not achieve good end results for your degree. The acquisition of excellent library research skills is an essential task undertaken in the first term, which will then be developed thereafter all the way into the professions or study at post-graduate level.

Today not only are library catalogues computerised but vast reservoirs of electronic resources create a virtual library at the disposal of students and staff[1]. This chapter concentrates on mapping the overall structure of the library, and the law library in particular, along with the range of available resources and their format (whether print or electronic). It covers the location of print and electronic law resources in the university library, search strategies for print and electronic collections and the issue of determining authority and reliability in the texts that you find. It also discusses the vital importance of quickly developing competent IT library skills, such as understanding the nature of databases and gateways to resources.

There are several excellent detailed texts on the market that talk students through the library and it is not the intention of this chapter to repeat that information[2]. These texts are necessary reference texts in their own right and are referred to in the further reading section.

INTRODUCING YOUR UNIVERSITY LIBRARY

Walking into the university library can be a daunting experience. New students of all ages often report a feeling of inadequacy when first confronted with the scenes of a typical library lobby. There are lots of people (all of whom seem to know what they are doing); there are issue desks, banks of computers, banks of photocopiers, unfamiliar signage, student study support staff and private study rooms. There may be coffee bars, and some may have imposing atriums built to a scale which dwarfs individual users; there are cloakrooms and rules about bags. Entrance to the library is often through security checks and the scanning of your library card. Some libraries have not taken on the dimensions of huge factory buildings or implemented security measures, but even these can feel extremely alien to the new student.

Librarians and lecturers do realise, however, that there are several barriers to overcome to enable students to understand how to make best use of the library's print and electronic collections. All libraries arrange a general induction to the layout and range of resources for new students. Additionally the law department, usually in liaison with the law librarian, will arrange for a series of specialist training sessions to introduce new law students to the

---

1   The invention of printing was revolutionary in the spread of knowledge; a revolutionary innovation of similar dimensions has occurred through the electronic communication of knowledge.
2   In addition each university library will have its own information for students.

print and electronic collections. Often there are opportunities for updates and more advanced training throughout the first year and one-to-one assistance may be offered to students who lack confidence. It is important to be aware of what support and training is on offer in your library so that you can make best use of it. Many libraries and departments also provide links to in-house and external online tutorials concerned with using the library. You should check for these on your departmental, library, study support and induction webpages as well as on your department's preferred virtual learning environment (VLE).

In the past, university libraries, with their large print collections, were referred to as storehouses of knowledge. Today the volume of these printed resources becomes insignificant in relation to the huge amount of academic and official, non-subscription and subscription, electronic resources on offer through the library. This huge electronic resource is in turn dwarfed by the number of non-academic and non-official electronic resources generally available, the constant supply of which seems inexhaustible. Figure 2.1 illustrates this. When considering the use of the library it is therefore important to bear in mind the full range of available sources.

In year 1 of a law degree you need to acquire the basic skills of searching, and you will then work hard to build on these to construct sophisticated search strategies that you can rely on. If you are researching a particular law you do not want to overlook reliable and valid information because your library research skills are patchy. Nor do you wish to base

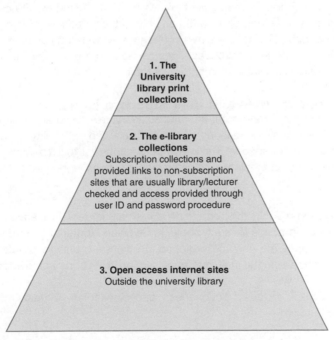

Figure 2.1 How the volumes of different types of legal resources compare

an essay for an important assessment on non-authoritative, non-reliable, non-academic open internet site sources. Many students do, and achieve extremely low marks bordering fail for doing so.

The structure and layout of the law print library

Your university may house the law library in a separate building, or in a separate area of the main library. A few libraries fully integrate law resources into the main classification system of the library without creating a separate space. Whichever system is used the same signpost is required to allow you to begin to locate the actual rooms and shelves where the resources you need are: the computerised main library catalogue. This is the system of classification of the print resources. Each print resource is allocated a *classification number* or a *class mark* and these numbers or marks are grouped in subject clusters and subgroups of subjects. Libraries tend to have signs and leaflets that map the area of the law print collection, indicating which part of the building you go to for particular subjects. So, once you have a classification number or class mark, and a diagram of the library showing the location of the law resources, you will be able to go to the correct area and locate your specific resource.

The classification number is located by searching the main online library catalogue. Many libraries, but not all, have banks of computers around the library and in the reception area, which you can use to look up your book[3]. You can search the main catalogue by author name, title of book, or the subject area you are interested in. You can also search this catalogue from any computer with an internet connection, signing on with the user ID and password given to you when you registered with the library. You can use the main catalogue for a range of purposes, such as locating a particular book or journal, or searching all resources available on a particular topic.

Types of print materials and their standard locations

Print material comes in a range of types and sizes. All law material is not laid out in one integrated sequence but, for reasons of ease of use and rationality of layout, there is segregation into different spaces. The following sections list the types of materials to be found in the law library and their likely clusters and locations.

Reference

There are always some books that tend to be abnormally large. These are usually reference books. It is standard practice for such books to be placed together in a reference section, as it is recognised they are only to be dipped into for small chunks of information. They may be in the law area or in the main reference section in the library or divided between the two areas.

Reference books include dictionaries, encyclopaedias, digests, indexes, and bibliographies.

---

3   If you sign in at the login prompt screen with your user ID and password you will find you are in your own section where you can check what books if any you have borrowed, when they are due back, and reserve books.

Thin resources (pamphlets)

There are also some print resources that are very thin (pamphlets) and again they will tend to be stored together in a separate area of the law library.

Parliamentary papers

There is a vast array of materials generated by Parliament, including verbatim reports of proceedings of the two Houses of Parliament, details of committee meetings, reports and material produced by government departments (reports, statistics, recommendations, and policy reviews). Not all libraries will keep a print collection of Parliamentary papers[4].

Journals

Academic journals (also called periodicals) are an important resource for seminars and assessed work. There are a range of periodicals that are published two, three or four times a year, containing articles by academics or professionals. They exist in most disciplines and constitute the most up-to-date information and analysis of law. The law journals are most likely to be grouped together in the law library. However, some libraries do like to keep all their periodicals together in one place regardless of discipline and here science rubs shoulders with art. It is important to be aware that many disciplines research the law and you are therefore likely to find relevant publications in other disciplines such as psychology, sociology, or history.

Law reports

These are reports of important cases in the courts. They are published in several series, which we will consider in detail when we look at citation later in this chapter. You can find out more about reading law reports in Chapter 5.

Statutes

These are collections of Acts of Parliament, which we will consider in detail later in this chapter, and also in Chapter 4. The statutes are technically referred to as the statute books and each statute, or Act of Parliament, is assigned a chapter number in the statute book of the year.

Books about the law

These tend to be divided into topics and sub-topics, for example criminal law or the law of contract. It is worth remembering that the date of publication of a book is likely to be 6–24 months after the completion of the manuscript of the book, due to the time needed for the publication process. This means that the law described in books may not be totally up to date and you should double check the status of the law to be careful. Also, as with journals, it is important to be aware that many other disciplines interact with the law and you are therefore likely to find relevant books in other subject areas.

---

4   The most extensive collection is housed in the London School of Economics and Political Science Library.

Short loan collection

Many lecturers find it useful to put important books on the short loan system. This means that the book is loaned for only a few hours at a time. Short loan books are often placed behind the issue desks and need to be requested if you wish to view them. Most short loan books are only for use in the library and cannot be removed, although some short loan books can be taken out overnight just prior to the library closing, or for the weekend. Lecturers may also put in short loan a photocopy of an article from a journal not in the print collection or the electronic subscription collection of the library[5]. Fines for such books can be by the hour.

Figure 2.2 sets out each of these resources and the storage types used for them. You will find that many materials, particularly law reports, statutes, and journal articles are stored in both electronic and print formats. There is a lot of cross-referencing between print and electronic versions, for although the strategies for access differ between them, the nature of the two main types of storage, and the functions for their ultimate use, remain the same. They both offer collections of information, explanation, description, innovation and argument as well as records of legal rules from the courts and Parliament.

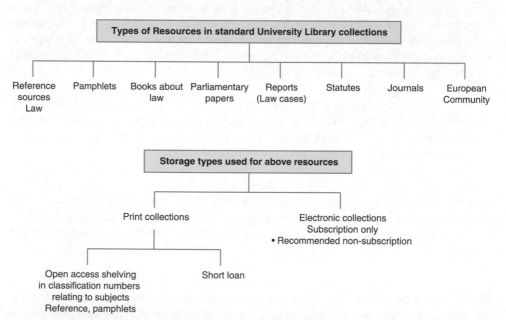

Figure 2.2 Types of resources in standard university library collections

The structure and layout of the electronic collection

The competent location and search of the range of electronic materials is an essential skill for the law student. Initially you may find the array of internet sources overwhelming. But in fact they can be reduced to a few overarching categories within which you can research.

---

5   Some lecturers may also post a digital version of material from a popular library book on their VLE.

These will be set out below. Electronic resources mirror in many ways the materials contained in print collections. The best electronic materials are developed by commercial organisations, with annual subscription fees. However, there is a wide range of additional databases and internet gateways which open a huge array of electronic resources.

An internet gateway, which can be referred to as a portal, is a single website that collects together a range of internet links on related topics. Search engines are powerful tools that have indexed a large number of webpages, and allow you to retrieve data through simple keyword searches. Some gateways and databases are free, whilst others are commercial and require user name and password information. Many will be accessible through the electronic library (e-library) of your institution.

The standard university law library will have subscriptions to many electronic resources that retrieve materials from the UK, the EU and a range of world collections of legal rules. They will also keep lists of free electronic materials available on the internet. There is a great difference between subscription sites, with proper review of accuracy of representation of legal rules and academic commentaries, and non-subscription, open access, sites. That said, you should explore the full range of available data. Some free sites are of great importance. For example, the only official site for revised statutes (that is the most up to date online version of a statute) is the new government UK Statutes Database, which is free to access.

When you sign into the main library catalogue, click on the icon for the e-library and you will be taken into the sources. Your library will often group access by subject. You can therefore click on law and be sent to another listing of sources. Some of these will be subscription sites and some free sites. There will be different access conventions for each of the electronic materials. The majority require an internationally recognised login and password, referred to as an Athens password. Today most university library students' login and password details are also automatically accredited as Athens logins and passwords. At induction you will be told your own library's conventions. Whilst the majority of the electronic collection can be accessed from anywhere, including your home if you have internet access, a few resources can only be accessed from the library itself. The majority of your electronic resources will come to you via the internet. However your library may also have a range of CD-ROMs and microfiche (texts on film viewed through specialised machines, an older form of technology but often libraries have valuable data still stored on it).

When you have your library access sorted out, take time to explore the e-library at your leisure. It will not be time wasted as you need to acquire the skills to access a range of databases quickly and easily, in order to locate materials for seminar and assessment purposes. You would not just walk into a large university library and wander around until you accidentally found the law section and then luckily stumbled across a relevant law book. You would locate the catalogue and engage in methodical search. Many students approaching a database, however, do the equivalent of just aimlessly wandering around. If they do not haphazardly locate any sources and they then erroneously conclude no such sources exist. Map the terrain of the electronic sources as well as you would the library print collection. Your lecturers will be only too pleased to guide you generally as will your law librarian.

Types of electronic materials and their standard locations

The same types of material available in the print collection are available through electronic sources in the e-library, but, with the exception of books, there are also many more materials available in electronic form. Figure 2.3 shows the type of resources generally available. We will now look at each in turn. Some will be familiar from our earlier discussion of print collections.

Reference

Dictionaries, encyclopaedias, digests, indexes, bibliographies.

Parliamentary papers

Reports of proceedings in Parliament, for example Hansard online, which has virtually verbatim debates from both Houses of Parliament, Parliamentary committee verbatim debates, decisions and much other useful data.

Journals

Your library will offer electronic access to the majority of journals kept in its print collection, to online-only subscription journals and to free open access online journals.

Law reports

Specialist subscription and free access sites make differing ranges of cases available in database collections. When a case has also been reported you *must* refer to the most authoritative print version, as the courts do not recognise internet sources. Leading law databases such as Westlaw will retain the original printed page number of the report in their electronic version. This is why you will see numbers in bold throughout the electronic text.

Statutes

Specialist subscription and free access sites make differing ranges of statutes available in database collections. The UK Statutes Database is the only official online facility for accessing statutes.

Books about the law

The one area where the electronic collection differs enormously (at present) from the print collection is in the area of academic e-books. There are not many academic law books available as yet in electronic formats. Many law textbooks come with companion websites and the small collection of e-books is growing but these, as yet, are nowhere near approaching the capacity of the books in the print collection. There is a particularly poor

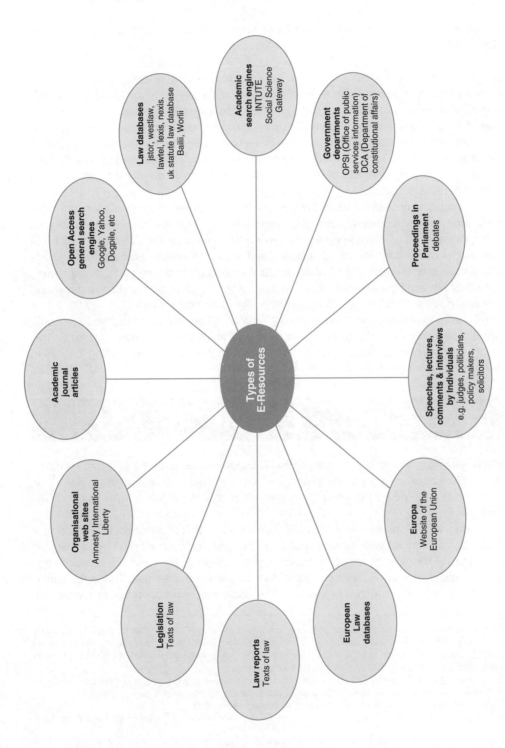

Figure 2.3 Legal electronic resources

selection of law books currently available online in comparison with the thousands of fiction e-books[6].

Open access internet electronic sources located outside the e-library

Here we properly enter the third level of the triangle shown in Figure 2.1 above. In this category the electronic resources are unlimited and extremely varied. They are often updated daily[7]. They may include student sites, propaganda sites, news sites, organisational sites, individual sites, university sites, government department sites, and thousands of other types of sites. Some of these may be of use to you, but you need to be very clear what you are dealing with and have a good strategy for ascertaining the authority and reliability of retrieved data.

A large number of organisations, such as charities and pressure groups, have extensive literature on their sites. Many universities around the world make some aspects of their electronic materials available free on the internet. Some individual academics in university departments make their speeches, lectures and articles available. Some university professors have their own websites, often accessible through their university departments' websites. All these types of sites open another world of electronic source material and many will have links enabling you to go to other sites with similar material.

There is an excellent overall online training tutorial devised by a law librarian, Sue Pettit, to introduce students to the range of material on the internet, and how to use it[8]. This training tutorial also contains invaluable information concerning navigating sites and assessing the reliability of the information you retrieve.

DEVELOPING APPROPRIATE SEARCH STRATEGIES FOR PRINT AND ELECTRONIC COLLECTIONS

William Twining, a well known Professor of Philosophy, once issued a text that he called the *Law Cookbook*, a series of 'recipes' for success in legal method and reasoning[9]. This developed into a popular text, co–authored with Professor David Miers, *How To Do Things With Rules*[10].

The 'cookbook' is an excellent metaphor[11], especially related to electronic and complex print texts. You may not wish to cook, but if you did, you would not start off by cooking the most complex recipe or by simply reading recipes. You would learn the basics of cooking and then add on more complex variants to your simple starting recipes. This is the underlying approach of this section, to lay out some basic research strategies, or recipes, for

---

6 Many lecturers may put e-versions of chapters from books and journal articles that they use for a specific course onto the VLE. There are strict copyright rules about what can be posted and you may find that there are not any on your VLE, or of course your department or particular lecturers may not use the VLE. Lecturers may also put links to websites on their VLE for you to explore.

7 This is why the OSCOLA referencing system states proper practice requires you to put the date of access when using an internet address in circumstances where there is no other print reference to use.

8 http://www.vts.intute.ac.uk/he/tutorial/lawyers accessed 14 April 2009.

9 W Twining and D Miers, *How to Do Things With Rules: A Primer of Interpretation* (4th edn CUP, 1999) Appendix 111, 421–433.

10 W Twining and D Miers, *How to Do Things With Rules: A Primer of Interpretation* (4th edn CUP, 1999).

11 A metaphor can be defined as the act of describing something unknown by reference to something known.

searching print and electronic collections, allowing you to experiment and providing the tools you need to gain a sophisticated appreciation of law library research. Exercises will be suggested but, as with cooking, there is no substitute for trying things yourself. You will learn best by going into the print collections, or logging into the electronic collections, and locating the sources.

Academic study involves the application of proper and rigorous research for materials, followed by your selection of the most appropriate resources, which are then subjected to competent and rigorous interpretation[12]. The effort taken to locate material is only the beginning of academic work, but it is an essential task because you need to locate the most authoritative and correct texts.

How to search the various resources efficiently will be discussed concurrently for both print and electronic formats. As you practise you will find that your skills increase and improve. In addition to the face-to-face training that your department and/or library will provide, there are excellent training guides produced by most university libraries to assist in locating and searching particular print and electronic resources. In addition many databases such as Westlaw contain detailed instructions both in print format, and online. All databases will contain either help tutorials or 'hints' in a dropdown menu. While these can be useful if you have a problem, you should remember:

There is no shortcut to competency in the law library. You have to put the time in.

It is important not to view your institution's electronic resources as an optional extra, but to treat them as an essential and integrated aspect of your university's provision for the study of law.

Search strategies for print and electronic materials will both start in the same place, with a range of questions:

■   What is your search question?

■   What is its most succinct and relevant formulation?

■   Where will you look?

■   How will you ensure that the primary law you have located is current as opposed to out of date? (How do you know that what you have is the latest version of the relevant law?)

■   How will you assess the quality of retrieved secondary material?

■   How do you know that you have located the most current, scholarly material?

---

12 Analysis and interpretation of retrieved material will be dealt with later in the book.

To locate the best, and most relevant, materials you need a carefully thought out strategy based on:

■   **what** you are looking for;

■   **why** you are looking for it;

■   **where** you are looking for it.

The following brief guide to using the law library collection is divided into primary legal sources and secondary sources[13]. This book is concerned with the English legal system, and this section will concentrate on searching for details of the laws relevant to that system, including European Community law as it affects the English legal system.

Primary legal materials – texts *of* the law

Texts of law, or primary legal materials, are documents containing the law itself, such as law reports, statutes, regulations, bye laws, international treaties, European treaties and law from other jurisdictions. They are located in both the print and electronic collections provided by the library. These documents can be official versions, sanctioned in some way by Parliament, the EU or the courts, or they may be unofficial versions reproduced from official versions by other publishers and organisations. You need to know the authority of the version you are reading and whether it can be trusted for reliability, an issue which will be considered later in this chapter.

The text of statutory legal rules can be obtained in full-text form, summary form, or revised form (where amendments to statutes have been put into the text of the original statute)[14]. Law cases can also be retrieved in full text or summary versions. You need to know whether you have the verbatim text or a summary and legal analysis should only be carried out on the full text versions. For statutory legal rules you also need to have confidence that you are using the most up-to-date and correct wording.

INTELLECTUAL HEALTH WARNING!

Primary texts of legal rules located
in law reports and legislation are
not academic materials – they
are **legal** materials

Primary sources can be divided into print or electronic materials, and into subscription and non-subscription or open access internet sites. We will now consider some of these different primary sources.

---

13 In Chapters 4, 5 and 6 this material is explained and its interpretation discussed in detail. This chapter is simply concerned with its location and search strategies to find it.
14 See Chapter 4 for detail about UK and EU legislation.

Subscription only sources of primary law

■ *Halsbury's* **encyclopaedias** cover the laws of England in print and electronic form, dealing with statutes, statutory instruments and commentary on the primary sources.

■ The printed **Law Reports** series commenced in 1865. They are published by a private charitable organisation but are considered official by the courts, as trustworthy records of verbatim reports.

■ Other printed law reports series include the All England Reports and Criminal Appeal Reports.

■ The **Westlaw** electronic database includes legislation, cases and journals and EU law. It is a good site to search for legislation and law reports and contains electronic copies of the law report series. The only official source of electronic statutory material is the UK Statute Law Database, discussed below.

■ The **LexisNexis**® **Butterworths** database can also be searched for legislation and law reports.

Free sources of primary law

By far the largest set of free resources can be found on the internet. These range in reliability depending upon the site.

■ The **UK Statute Law Database** (SLD)[15] is the official government record of all statutes and statutory instruments. Statutory instruments are law made by ministers, local authorities, or other groups, by permission contained within an Act of Parliament. It was launched as free public service in December 2006 and is extremely search friendly. All statutes are shown in their revised form with any changes incorporated into the text of the statute.

■ The **Office of Public Sector Information** (OPSI)[16] contains a collection of Public General Acts going back to 1988, and reproduces the statute in the form in which it was originally enacted. It contains statutory instruments going back to 1987. What is particularly useful about this site is its efforts to get a copy of a statute online within a day of its publication.

■ The **British and Irish Legal Information Institute** (BAILII)[17] contains reports of cases and statutes. It takes its statutory data from OPSI and is a free searchable site.

■ **LawTel** has a large range of searchable legislation and law reports.

---

15 http://www.statutelaw.gov.uk accessed on 14 April 2009.
16 http://www.opsi.gov.uk/acts.htm accessed on 14 April 2009.
17 http://www.bailii.org/uk/legis/num_act accessed on 14 April 2009.

■   The **Official Journal** (OJ) of the EC. It is the official site of EC texts and is updated several times a week.

Check out the free electronic sources as soon as you have become familiar with the print sources, as it is good to know what the original texts look like before becoming immersed in electronic copies, which can be presented very differently. The extra flexibility that you obtain with electronic copies is excellent for research purposes. For example, when a case is retrieved, Westlaw also provides links to all cases cited, and to articles of relevance about that case. In the print collection you would need to laboriously work your way through a range of digests and encyclopaedias in order to achieve the coverage that is instantaneously available on the electronic sites.

Citing primary law

There are particular conventions for citing primary law in the form of domestic and European legislation and law reports of cases in court, which can be most confusing to the new law student. Because law expands exponentially, it can only be contained in sequential volumes of print publications that have the capacity for such expansion. The conventions for properly referencing the location of legal rules can at first sight seem rather problematic and cumbersome but once you have realised the rationale behind the conventions and begun to look at the reports and statutes you will quickly be at ease. If necessary, you will find detailed instructions available from your institution's law librarian and your law department.

A citation is a generally recognised method for referring to the precise location of primary law in a publication. Each publication varies, and the official citations refer to the print versions except in rare cases when the only official version is online. The future may bring many instances of material which is only available online but at present the only example is a series of the Official Journal of the EC.

Although different publications use different conventions, there is an underlying logic that determines any citation. As you can imagine, law changes, new laws are enacted and old laws are abolished in total or in part (technically referred to as repealed) or added to in some way (technically referred to as amended). Citations of primary law must therefore be able to change with the law and all print collections are organised according to a few standard rules. These will now be considered in relation to the law reports, statutes and European law.

Citing law reports

There are a number of publishers of collections of law reports and the editors of each of these will apply different criteria for determining the relative importance of cases and choosing which reports to publish so that they are widely available to practitioners. Such reports are also the staple diet of law students. Like the relationship between the print collections and the open access internet there are, in the scheme of things, a small group of cases reported in print and a vast number that are not reported.

The size and numbers of important cases cannot be predicted each year and therefore publications of law reports must have room to expand. They are therefore published in series. The standard format is to issue smaller looseleaf publications of cases a few times a year, or even every month. Whilst small these pamphlet-sized publications have the publisher, date run and prospective volume number and page numbers, usually running along the spine. These are then bound yearly into a book or books, called a volume for the year. The citation consists of the year, the series and the volume number for the year, which is printed on the spine of the book, along with an abbreviated form of the publication's name. When there is a particularly busy year there will be more than one volume for the year and each will be numbered consecutively, 1, 2, 3 and so on. Each volume will run chronologically from January to December, with volume 1 containing cases from January onwards.

There is no one official publisher of law reports. There are instead many private publishers. However, the courts have determined that one series is deemed the most authoritative and the hierarchy of law reports is discussed later in this chapter.

Some publishers will separate out cases heard in the Court of Appeal and the House of Lords, while some series of reports only deal with specialist areas of law, such as company law, or employment law, other series are generalists dealing with all areas. As you are asked to locate series of law reports in your library you will become familiar with locating them by citation and you will start to internalise the different abbreviations without effort. In your early days of study it may be useful to keep a modest list of abbreviations in your bag as a quick translation. To that end some lists of abbreviations are provided on the companion website for you to download for ready reference.

When a particular law case is cited, the name of the law report series, the year, the volume number if applicable and the page numbers of the report must be given. With this information you can efficiently locate that report in print, and usually electronic, form. The citation also provides the proper reference to include in your written work. However, there are a few issues to be careful about, as explained in the following sections.

Dates and years of publication

For a range of reasons, if a case appears in a volume of reports from a specific year, it may actually have been heard in a previous year. For example, cases may be heard in court late in December and reported in January. Sometimes the editor is slow to realise the importance of the case, or its importance is not realised until another case has referred to it. Then the case can only be published in the next year or even some years later. So whilst it may be published in 2009 it may have been decided in 2000. The year given in the volume is therefore not always the year of the hearing of the case and it is important to check the date in the actual report itself. If you are discussing, for example, the development of the law through cases you must be sure that the year of the volume of the law report in which the case is reported actually coincides with the date of the case itself.

Prior to 1890 no dates needed to be put on volumes of law reporting at all and other conventions were used to locate the case, most usually an abbreviated version of the author's name. Today, the dates of pre-1890 cases are placed in round brackets ( ) in the citation. This indicates the fact that you do not need the date in order to find the case, though it may be helpful. Cases post-1890 include the date in square brackets [ ] to symbolise that information concerning year of the case is necessary to locate it. You will find some exceptions of course as you continue to read citations and locate law reports.

Hierarchy of series of law reports

There are no official government or court published law reports; all law reports are published by private organisations. However, some series of law reports are considered more reliable than others. As the editors of each series of law reports can choose which cases to publish it is likely that some cases appear in more than one series. When this is the case it is essential to be aware of the hierarchy of the various series and their standing in court.

It is good to get into the habit of automatically adopting the rule that you will only use the most authoritative version of the report in your written work. Similarly, should you decide to engage in mooting, a competitive form of formal legal argument between two teams of students role playing counsel, you will lose vital marks if you do not cite the most authoritative law report of the case you are using. The reasons for decisions concerning this reliability have grown over time and it is enough at this point that you be aware of the following hierarchy among modern law reports.

The most reliable reporting is considered to be found in a series of reports called the Law Reports which were commenced in 1865 by the Council of Law Reporting[18] to report all cases:

- where new rules or principles are introduced into the legal system;

- which modify existing rules of principles of the legal system;

- which resolve doubt in relation to a question of law;

- which the Council considers important in terms of instructiveness.

The Law Reports series contains the argument of counsel for the parties and each report is checked before publication by the judges' bench hearing the case. They are therefore considered the most authoritative reports and <u>must</u> be cited in court over and above any other series of reports that may have published a report of the same case[19]. It is good to get into the habit of using these in preference to other reports.

Her Majesty's Courts Service records all the practice directions issued and from these the following hierarchy of other law reports emerges:

---

18 In 1870 it was renamed the Incorporated Council of Law Reporting (ICLR). It became a registered charity in 1970.

19 Woolf CJ *Practice Direction (Judgments: Form Citation (Supreme Court)* [2001] 1 WLR 194 3.1: 'where a case has been reported in the official Law Reports published by the Incorporated Council of Law Reporting for England and Wales it must be cited from that source'.

1.   the official Law Reports published by the Incorporated Council of Law Reporting for England and Wales;

2.   the series of Weekly Law Reports or the series of All England Law Reports may be used if the case is not reported in the series of the official law reports;

3.   if the case is not reported in the series of reports referred to in 1 or 2 then a report from an authoritative specialist series of reports may be cited.

Case names

As a general rule if a case is a criminal case the convention is to note the state by the letter R (which stands for either Rex (King) or Regina (Queen)). The notation signifying dispute is the letter v, which stands for the Latin 'versus', meaning against. However, it is always spoken as 'and' not 'versus'. The defendant's name in criminal proceedings comes second as the notion is that the Queen is bringing a case against the defendant for breach of criminal law. So the criminal case against one Camplin in 1978 together with the case's citation in the law reports would be:

R v Camplin [1978] AC 705.

Having consulted your list of abbreviations and ascertained that AC stands for the official Law Reports series for the **A**ppeal **C**ases, and that the date in square brackets will be the actual date of the volume, you can locate it as shown in Figure 2.4.

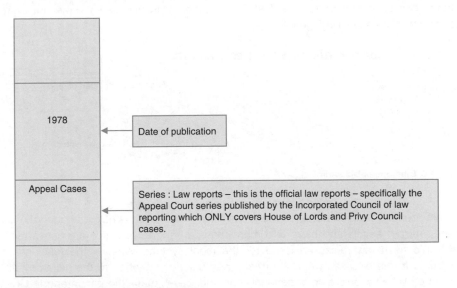

Figure 2.4 Locating *R v Camplin* [1978] AC 705

The case of *R v Briggs* [1977] 1 WLR 605 can be located by date of volume, volume number and series (WLR is the abbreviated version of Weekly Law Reports), as shown in Figure 2.5.

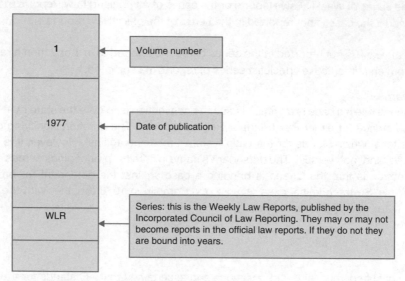

Figure 2.5 Locating *R v Briggs* [1977] 1 WLR 605

The names of cases in areas outside the criminal law note the names of both parties with the complainant's name given first. The notation 'v' is still used and the citation rules are the same, as shown in Figure 2.6.

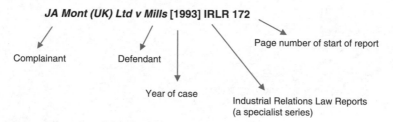

Figure 2.6 Citations outside criminal law

Citing electronic versions of law reports

The electronic collections of law reports are huge, far in excess of those printed. As use of the internet spirals and more and more material reports of cases are converted into electronic form this raises an issue for the legal system. What is the relationship of electronic forms of cases to print formats, particularly in relation to the hierarchy of law reporting? When should a court seriously consider cases that although unreported in print version, are reported electronically?

A first step towards ordering the large mass of electronic reports of cases was to assign cases in the courts a unique neutral citation mark that had nothing to do with a private publisher but is generated by the Courts Service for all cases. Every case in the English legal system is verbatim recorded in writing by court shorthand writers. Since 2001 every approved judgment in the House of Lords, Privy Council, Court of Appeal, the administrative court, and latterly the divisions of the High Court (Chancery, Queen's Bench, Commercial, Admiralty, Family, etc.) has been given a neutral citation by the shorthand writers, as shown in Figure 2.7. It is a very simple citation stating the year, the jurisdiction (for example, UK or EW meaning England and Wales)[20], the court, whether civil or criminal jurisdiction and the sequence number of the case.

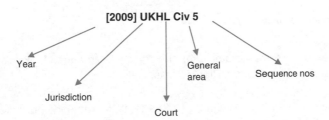

Figure 2.7 Neutral citation

When you locate a case in its electronic format you must be most careful to note where it may be reported in print and ensure you check the most authoritative version. The electronic source does not displace the hierarchy of print series, and it must precede the list of print sources that may be listed after it.

Databases such as Westlaw give you electronic access to the official series of the Law Reports, the Weekly Law Reports, and a large number of specialist reports such as Common Market Law Reports, Criminal Appeal Reports, European commercial cases, human rights law reports and industrial cases reports.

Citing of statutes

Every statute has a long title and a short title. The wording of the short title is given to it within the statute itself. So, for example, the Human Rights Act section 22(1) states 'This Act may be cited as the Human Rights Act'. It is the short title that is used to cite it and since 1963 it is cited together with the year. Every statute has its own number in the year identifying it, as shown in Figure 2.8 for the Human Rights Act 1998. This is its Chapter number in the statute book for the relevant year. The order of citation is:

- short title;

- Chapter number;

- year.

---

20 The House of Lords has UK jurisdiction whilst the High Court has jurisdiction within the English and Welsh legal systems.

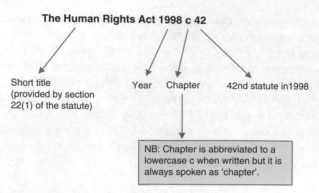

Figure 2.8 Citation for the Human Rights Act 1998

The long title appears immediately after the short title and often looks like a paragraph of text. The long title of the Human Rights Act is:

An Act to give further effect to rights and freedoms guaranteed under the European Convention on Human Rights; to make provision with respect to holders of certain judicial offices who become judges of the European Court of Human Rights, and for connected purposes.

Prior to 1963 the statute was not cited by the chronological year, but by the number of years into the reign of the monarch (called the regnal year). The Chapter number was still used with regnal years. A regnal year starts from the date of accession to the throne but there is a little complication. Parliamentary years run from the autumn to the summer, so it may be possible for there to have been two parliaments in one regnal year depending on when in the year the monarch succeeded. Then both years are referred to and the running order is:

■   short title;

■   regnal year;

■   monarch abbreviated;

■   Chapter number.

For purely demonstration purposes we can convert our citation of the Human Rights Act to a regnal year citation, as shown in Figure 2.9.

There are other conventions that can be quite complicated at first, but you will pick them up as you steadily use the statutes over your years of study.

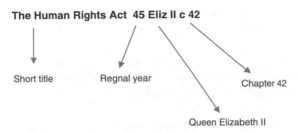

Figure 2.9 The Human Rights Act 1998 in regnal year citation

Locating primary legal sources by topic

Law students are often presented with legal problem scenarios which require them to search for appropriate law reports without being given the details of specific cases or statutes. This is more of a 'fishing' expedition, of course, and far more related to research skills than to your understanding of citations. As we have already seen, a large number of print and electronic sources are at your disposal. We will consider only the best print and electronic sources.

The print collection

There are a range of books arranged as indexes called digests which allow you to search through subjects and sub-topics to locate lists of cases and statutes that deal with a specific subject. Each case or statute is fully and correctly referenced, allowing you to then move on and locate the source. There are also books which tell you how to use the indexes.

The most authoritative source is *Halsbury's Laws of England*. It has a cumulative digest of legal rules and an index. There is no substitute for exploring these yourself and you will be given ample opportunity to do so in the first weeks of your study. You can search by topic, parties' names, or just citations.

You can find specimen library exercises on the companion website in Workbook One.

Electronic databases

The electronic collection provides an excellent source for searching. This is because not only can you search by topic, but you can also refine your search to locate topics occurring together in the text. You can also search for cases by names of parties, year, topic, citation or the use of keywords. So you can find cases you know exist even if you do not know the full citation.

Westlaw is an excellent source of full text data on law cases and legislation. Another exceptionally useful database for historical information is JUSTIS[21] which contains UK, Irish and EU case reports dating back to the earliest year books in 1163 and legislation from 1235.

Again there are many online learning materials that tell you how to use these databases, and you will need to take time to learn how each of these operates. The INTUTE online tutorial mentioned earlier in this chapter can guide you through the main types of electronic

---

21 http://www.justis.org accessed on 14 April 2009.

material available for lawyers (both practitioners and students) and should be your first point of call on your journey round the law e-library.

Secondary legal materials – texts *about* the law

Secondary legal materials are academic materials which describe, discuss and critique the primary legal materials outlined above. They include:

■ journals and journal articles (both academic and professional);

■ reference material;

■ books;

■ debates and proceedings of Parliament;

■ policies, briefings, information and committee reports produced by various government departments.

As students of law studying for a law degree you are engaged in the academic stage of a legal education. Among other things in your learning you are required to keep up to date with some of the latest academic thought in your area. Academic journals contain articles by academics which can critique an area of law, explain the emergence of a new idea or area of law, or offer an academic commentary on an area of law. Books can bring exceptional scholarship to an audience but where they are concerned with actual legal rules you will need to check that the commentary and the rule is up to date.

Your library will subscribe to journals and reference material and in many cases these will be available in both print and electronic formats. Many journals will provide electronic access to current and back issues if your library has a print subscription. Journal articles are never more than two to four months out of date at the date of publication.

Just as you can search texts of law by topic, print indexes and digests, electronic databases allow you to search for secondary texts. When you are engaging in research for seminars and assessment it is particularly useful to be able to search databases of journals. For example JSTOR or INTUTE allow you to search by title, author, or keywords. JSTOR is a large archive collection of out-of-date journal articles, whilst Blackwell Synergy allows search of all of its publications including current journals. But to avoid disappointment get a list from the library catalogue of the range of journals to which your library subscribes. Make yourself familiar with your library's print collection of law journals and also familiar with their electronic collection of law journals. Print collections of journals are reference only and must be read in the library; if an electronic version is available you can read it anywhere with internet access using your library ID and password.

As you move through the first year of your studies you will gain an appreciation of the importance of secondary law texts both from textbooks that explain the general area of law, through to scholarly books which carefully explore one area of law from a complex set of perspectives. As with primary sources, you should also assess whether the author of a secondary text has appropriate credentials.

Books written as student text books, such as this one for example, are not books of any legal authority. Some by longevity and respect for their views do get mentioned in court but it is not common practice. As already discussed books can be out of date before they are published so you do need to consult academic journals for up-to-date legal commentary.

RELIABILITY AND VALIDITY OF INFORMATION SOURCES

Lawyers construct argument based on sound evidence. Whilst legal rules are often the object of consideration, at times our sources are non-legal, secondary commentaries about law. Each of the books in your institution's law library will have been placed there by the recommendation of the academics responsible for that particular area of law. Detailed discussions are entered into between academics with regard to which books should be allowed into the law collection.

Similarly detailed discussions will occur relating to which journals the institution should subscribe to. The vast majority of journals are academic. This means all articles placed in a particular edition of the journal will have been read before publication by two other academics working in the same area, who must agree that the article is academically sound and adds to the current debates. This process is called peer review, or peer refereeing, and the journals which undertake this checking prior to publication are called refereed journals. The peer review process ensures that the article and the journal are reliable. This does not mean that what is said should be believed or should not be questioned, but it does mean that you can read it and trust it to be of an authoritative nature.

As noted above the internet is a vast storehouse of materials and you can retrieve material from a range of sources. When dealing with the internet, how can you work within good academic criteria to ensure the authority and reliability of your retrieved sources? You will be severely penalised for drawing on non-academic sources and you could end up learning wrong law. It is even possible to retrieve erroneously repeated legal rules, or school essays.

If you draw on your institution's electronic collection of subscribed materials, these will again have gone through the same type of academic quality control discussed above. They will have been filtered by your lecturers and your law librarian. However, your e-library may well be linked to databases and search engines that can retrieve less reliable material. It is possible to jump from one link to another and reach a site that is not academically sound. This section provides some guidance on being able to assess the reliability of retrieved electronic material, with the aim of locating relevant good quality academic information.

Obviously staying close to your e-library resources is one way of keeping to good quality material but there will be times when you wish to use material on the Internet and it is wise to have some quality control strategies in place, particularly as anyone can put anything on the internet. The Intute Internet for Lawyers resource provides an excellent tutorial on ascertaining the reliability of retrieved internet sources. It suggests you ask yourself three important questions:

- **Who** has posted this?

- **Why** have they posted it?

- **When** was this information posted?

We will now consider each of these questions in more detail.

Who has posted this?

Initially look for the name of the author, or the organisation issuing the information. Many websites will have a 'contact us' or 'about us' page. Check it to see how forthcoming the individual or organisation is about their aims and qualifications. You can also gain a lot of information from the website's address or URL (the uniform resource locator). Consider the web address for Canterbury Christ Church University's student induction pages[22]. Figure 2.10 shows how you can deconstruct this to learn about the organisation, the type of institution and its location.

If you have a good habit of searching for electronic academic information within your e-library you should be able to rely on your sources. But you should not take anything for granted.

Why have they posted it?

Consider what you can find out about the standpoint of the author. The information that you have accessed could be prejudiced towards one point of view. The importance of academic work is that it is able to sum up evidence on both sides of an argument and move to conclusions based on the weight of evidence. You may have retrieved highly emotive or persuasive material that is not academic. You need to look at any information given to the author, and the business they may be involved in. Is it a government site, a pressure group site, a lone writer with no credentials tied into an organisation? Is it a media or a news site? Is the source a journalist?

When was this information posted?

Information on the internet may have been correct when it was posted but, especially in law, it can easily become out of date. Always try to find the date when the webpage was last updated.

As you become more familiar with internet search techniques you will gain more knowledge of the types of sites that are reliable and those that should not be trusted. Open access internet sites rarely have academic content, so they may be of limited use for your

---

22 http://www.canterbury.ac.uk/induction accessed 24 April 2009.

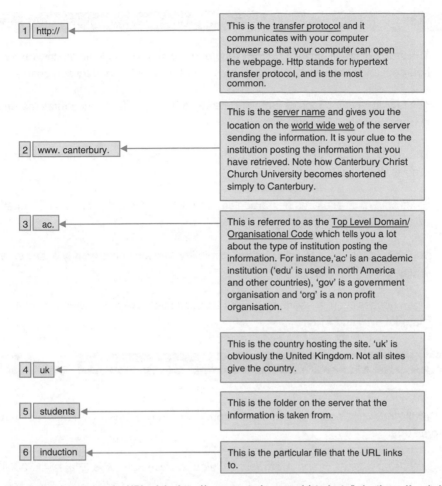

Figure 2.10 Deconstructing the URL of the http://www.canterbury.ac.uk/students/induction.pdf website

work. However, material from news media and sites belonging to non-governmental organisations or important pressure groups can sometimes be valuable. If you know the source of the information, and understand what type it is (for example, non-academic or academic, propagandist, and so on) you will be able to use it properly. For example, you may wish to subject standard news reporting to academic scrutiny and access a site to retrieve suitable data to interrogate.

Do not use open access sites for obtaining an overview of an area of study or research.

CONCLUSION

■ The study of law is exclusively the study of documents containing the law (primary sources) and books and other resources about the law (secondary sources).

■ The law library functions as a major gateway to help you find your source materials, in both print and electronic form.

■ There are particular conventions for citing primary law, and for the hierarchy of law reports, that should be observed.

■ Electronic databases can be particularly useful tools if you do not know the citation of a specific case.

■ You should take care to consider the credibility, version and currency of any source you use.

■ Open access internet sources should be questioned in terms of who posted the material, why and when.

FURTHER READING

The Cardiff Index to Legal Abbreviations http://www.legalabbrevs.cardiff.ac.uk accessed 14 April 2009.

P Clinch, *Using a Law Library: A Student's Guide to Research Skills* (Blackwell, 2001).

P Lawrence, *Law on the Internet: A Practical Guide* (Sweet and Maxwell, 2000).

PA Thomas and J Knowles, *Effective Legal Research* (Sweet and Maxwell, 2006).

PA Thomas and J Knowles, *How to Use a Law Library* (4th edn Sweet and Maxwell, 2001).

THE CONTEXTS OF LAW: SKETCHES OF THE STORIES OF LAW

" [l]egal language, like a song, can be hummed by someone who did not write it and changed by those for whom it was not intended."

M Minow[1]

LEARNING OUTCOMES

After reading this chapter you should be able to:

- appreciate the various historical, political, social, economic, religious, and linguistic contexts that have shaped the law;

- appreciate that legal systems worldwide have traditions and cultures, and that legal systems operate within overarching explanatory paradigms of globalisation, international 'law' and human rights;

- understand the contexts that have shaped the development of the English legal tradition (the common law tradition) and English legal culture;

- understand and explain why attention to the power of language is an important skill for competent legal study;

- list some of the characteristics of legal language.

---

1   M Minow, 'Tolerance in an Age of Terror' (1987) Harvard Law School Public Law Research paper No 07 1987: 1860.

CHAPTER SUMMARY

The extent to which historical, political and socio-cultural circumstances shape law, and the extent to which law through its institutions, personnel, and doctrines is in charge of its own destiny are issues that will be considered at length in many of the courses you will study, such as legal philosophy, legal history, discrimination law, law and religion, human rights law, and law and politics courses. However, it is good to be made aware of the contexts of law at the beginning of your studies. And when we move away from the micro level of the meaning and interpretation of words in statutes and law reports, the fluidity of law across time and in the face of external change becomes very apparent.

This chapter considers law at the macro-level, looking at ways in which linguistic, historical, political and cultural forces have shaped, and go on shaping, English law. This journey into contexts is not irrelevant, because a grasp of some of these background issues, and knowledge of some of the assumptions upon which the law is founded, will give you a greater understanding of it. Once you have gained an appreciation of these contexts, we will go back to the micro-issues of reading and interpreting law, constructing argument, answering legal assessment questions, engaging in oral presentations, and keeping your nerve in exams.

INTRODUCING THE CONTEXTS OF LAW

Claims are often made that the law is objective and neutral. Given the fluidity of law and its vulnerability to a range of external and internal factors its claims to neutrality and objectivity seem compromised. How plausible is it to maintain its neutrality, and what do we mean by this term? Academics take different positions in relation to this question, depending upon their overall philosophical or theoretical positions concerning the development and function of law. Certainly it cannot be denied that modern English law is primarily politically created, with legislation contained in the body of rules. This politically constructed law is then interpreted by judges in the court, who continue to mould it as they have done for centuries. If we consider law to be like a field, politicians determine the broad landscape while judges determine where the gateways in and out of that field might be. They do this by their chosen definitions of rules or words as they narrow and broaden the shape of the law.

Although historical, political, economic and social forces all shape the nature of law, as shown in Figure 3.1, in many ways it can be said that it is language which shapes the law. Language is certainly a powerfully persuasive instrument, as can be seen from the case studies and exercises offered on the companion website. In practice, eloquent poetry-filled speeches and artworks from human rights activists, poets, and politicians sit alongside

English law cases. In some cases you will find the judges deliberately making great use of poetic language, despite the stated objectivity of law and the consistent enforcement of neutrality and literalism for witnesses and defendants[2]. The judges not only demonstrate the way language can affect how the law is interpreted, they demonstrate their ability to change the law by interpretation.

For some, law can be seen in highly politicised, purely instrumental, terms. It might be said to be playing the 'tune' of those who have control of it. But it can also be made to play another tune. It can even be made to play tunes that were never intended. And it can be used for both good and bad. This idea of law as music is forcefully brought home by the quotation at the beginning of this chapter. It is a haunting picture of the flexibility of law.

Whilst the main focus of this chapter remains the English legal system, it is important to bear in mind that English law sits within a broader world context, and has a place within the legal traditions of the world. Legal traditions worldwide encompass the indigenous law of tribes, religious traditions such as Talmudic and Islamic law, or the European civil law tradition, and the English common law tradition. Each tradition gives pride of place to differing conceptions of law. Glenn[3] describes English common law as a legal tradition giving centrality to the ethics of adjudication. By this he means that our legal processes have been honed in order to provide an ethical approach to the role of the court. This gives centrality to the judges, to the adversarial trial and to the inbuilt duality of right and wrong

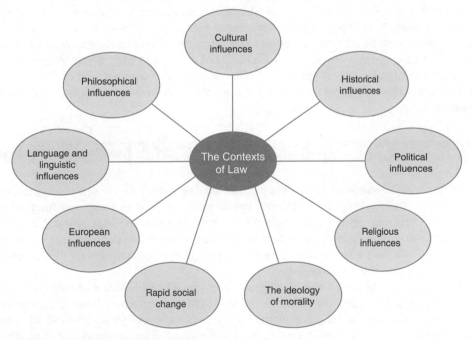

Figure 3.1 The contexts of law

---

2   We will see this in our case studies in Chapter 4.
3   PH Glenn, *Legal Traditions of the World: Sustainable Diversity in Law* (3rd edn OUP, 2007).

and a preference for the judge as umpire rather than the judge as inquisitor. Indeed many mistakenly see our legal system as fixated on the idea of the trial, yet only a tiny percentage of legal disputes go to trial. Most disputes are settled before this stage, and there is increasing resort to negotiation, mediation and other alternative dispute resolution strategies adopted by people who do not wish to go to trial. For Glenn the Talmudic and Islamic law traditions are 'rooted' in the notions of divine revelation and divine later revelation, while the civil law tradition in Europe has been constructed and secularised from early Romano-Christian roots.

The next sections of this chapter will set out these broader contexts of the law, looking at the influences of language and history on law. Along the way we will also discuss some cultural and political influences. The last section of the chapter considers how legal philosophy (a sub-branch of philosophy, and, for that matter, law) steps back to consider the motivations of law. Many other disciplines also interrogate the law, for example the social sciences through the discrete sub-disciplines of psychology, sociology and anthropology.

Before we start, have you noticed that consistently in this introduction reference has been made to the law doing, changing, being shaped and reacting? As sociologists, Peter Berger and Thomas Luckman[4] were keen to point out that institutions themselves do not act. Rather, people acting in a role take social action. The law is a collection of doctrines, legal rules and institutions created, maintained and changed by *people* acting in official social roles as the personnel of the law: adjudicators, lawyers, policy-makers and politicians exercising formal law-making roles with the Houses of Parliament. The law is, therefore, what we make it, what we imagine it to be. Although some of us have more power than others to make it what we imagine it to be. Some of us only see what we are indoctrinated to see, some of us take the script and run with it and do not question it. Part of the lawyer's vocation is to question constantly, and to argue objectively, in order to clarify grey areas in understanding.

LANGUAGE AND LAW

It is important to realise at the outset of your studies that language is a mediating and shaping influence on law, which is in turn mediated and shaped by users and interpreters of the law. You may not have considered this shaping role of language before. You have perhaps taken language for granted as a means of communication. But language is not just packaging, like the paper around a present; language can actually change the nature of what is being presented or described.

Language, like the air we breathe, surrounds us and we barely notice its existence. But we all use language to process internally much of our life. If you have a 'feeling' do you not explain it to yourself and others in words? Do you not look at other people and describe and categorise them in words? Words such as professional, unprofessional, ugly, beautiful,

---

4   P Berger and T Luckman, *The Social Construction of Reality. A Treatise in the Sociology of Knowledge* (Allen Lane, London 1971).

clever, ignorant, helpful, mean, logical, irrational or deceitful, once applied, can be difficult to shift, even if no evidence led to their application. Through language someone can succinctly put into words the feelings of another. That other person relates to that description and takes it for his or her own, usually increasing regard for the speaker. People, feelings and events can all be explained through language.

Language as a social construct

The academic disciplines of sociology, psychology and philosophy present us with several theories about the role of language in the construction of our understanding. Have you ever thought about language as the *creator* of the social world and your understanding of it and your place in it? You were born into a language community. You may well have been confronted with a situation where you needed to change languages due to moving, or because you were born into a dual-language community. Language is a key vehicle through which a person internalises life experiences, thinks about them, tries out alternatives, conceptualises a future and strives towards future goals.

It is true in many respects, in accordance with the views of theorists[5], that our understanding can be reduced to the ability to comprehend the expansiveness and limits of our language and the cultural bounded-ness of our language. As we grow up, 'ways of seeing' are developed that are socially constructed by the limits of a particular language. Yet, as language is all around, there is a temptation to see it as a neutral tool, a mirror that tells it 'like it is'. All language can do is to give someone's interpretation of *their* belief, or *their* experience. What is seen as, or believed to be, the real world may be no more than the language habits of the group. It is, therefore, possible that language can give a biased view of 'correct', 'normal' or 'good' behaviour.

Languages also have their limits. A well-known sociologist of language, Edward Sapir, argued that the limits of our language are the limits of our world[6]. He too argued that in so far as language functions as a shaping and a mediating structure, it is a guide to social reality.

> Language does not exist apart from culture, that is, from the socially inherited assemblage of practices and beliefs that determines the texture of our lives. . . . We see and hear and otherwise experience very largely as we do because the language habits of our community predispose certain choices of interpretation.

If language does not have a word for something or some concept then that 'something' will not be seen nor that 'concept' thought. All language is, however, responsive to what linguists call the 'felt needs' of its speakers. Indeed, it is more likely that not only are thoughts expressed *in* words but that thoughts themselves are *shaped* by language. A good example of felt needs is the vocabulary used to describe weather. Although the English are often said to enjoy talking about the weather, for many decades our essentially mild climate has provided us with the need for only one word for snow. We also have several different words to express cold and a separate word for ice. By contrast, the Aztecs

---

5   See for example the classic work of E Sapir, *Language: An introduction to the Study of Speech* (OUP, Oxford 1921) and BL Whorf, *Language, Thought, Reality* (MIT Press, Massachusetts 1956).

6   E Sapir, *Language: An Introduction to the Study of Speech* (Oxford University Press, Oxford 1921).

living in the tropics have only one word to cover the concepts of 'snow', 'ice' and 'cold'. Separate words are unlikely to be needed in such a warm climate. As English speakers, it is impossible to understand, or make sense of, a language that conflates into one word the vastly differing meanings we attach to 'cold', 'ice' and 'snow'. Coldness is a characteristic of snow, but there can be 'cold' without 'snow'. Ice can occur with or without snow and we would not be able to understand how snow and ice could be interchangeable. In English it is impossible for these two words to become synonyms. Equally, the Inuit people would find it incomprehensible that the English language only has one word for snow. They have many different words describing snow when it is falling, lying, drifting or packing.

This is one small illustration of the way in which our situation gives rise to our language. It can therefore be said that words we use daily, and may not even think about, can actually reflect our cultural understandings and at the same time transmit them to others, even to the next generation. Sensitivity to language usage can reveal a lot about the background and views of the speaker. It is an essential aspect of law.

Language and gender

Language also has the power to shape social rules and reinforce stereotypes. Despite attempts over past decades to strive for gender equality parents and teachers may still tell a boy 'not to cry' because it is not 'manly', or praise a girl for her 'feminine' way of dressing. Here they are using the words for manly and feminine to reinforce attitudes and categories that English culture has assigned to males and females. Innocent repetition of such 'every-day' language reinforces sexism in language and in society. In this way language determines social behaviour. Language, as a means of communication, becomes not only the expression of culture but a part of it. The feminine/masculine vocabulary is rarely questioned, yet its usage creates expectations that determine male as the norm and female as the secondary. Verbal descriptions of sex and gender therefore actually *construct* a social situation, rather than merely describing it.

Such construction of belief can also be found in dictionaries. When defining 'manly' *Webster's Dictionary* lists:

- having qualities appropriate to a man;

- open in conduct;

- bold;

- resolute;

- not effeminate or timorous;

- gallant;

- brave;

■   undaunted;

■   drinks beer.

For 'womanly' one finds:

■   marked by qualities characteristic of a woman, belonging to attitudes of a woman not
     a man.

The female here is defined as the negative of the male. If the male does not have it, and his attributes are worthy of listing, then it is female. In this way, sexism pervades the 'objective' nature of the dictionary, subordinating the female to the male.

The law itself maintains that the male term encompasses the female and many religions maintain that man is made in the image of God; woman in the image of man. The female is once removed in religions and in law. Is this acceptable? If exclusion is necessary on pragmatic terms, why not exclude the male term instead? More interestingly does the law exclude the female because language excludes the female?

Even in the nineteenth century, English law maintained that the Christian 'cleaving of male and female' in the marriage service and contract, meant the subjugation of the female, with the loss of her property and identity to the male. English family law was based upon Christian attitudes to family at a time when the church and the law were intertwined. This intimate relationship between church and state accounted for the rather late introduction of flexible divorce laws in the 1950s. Here religious tradition determined legal regulation. This short consideration of the shaping role of language also shows the way in which language carries cultural ideas into the law.

Modes of language

So far, the discussion has centred on the construction of the world by, and through, language as written word. But we all have different ways of speaking and writing. People use the modes of speaking and writing that their experience and education notes as the most appropriate. However, language exerts power here, too, through the social hierarchy given to 'ways of speaking'. This hierarchy is often based on accent as well as choice of, or access to, vocabulary.

People often change the way they speak, their accent and/or vocabulary according to who is listening. They may mirror the accent of the hierarchical authority figure they wish to be. Or they may change from the informality of family communication to the formality of work. Speakers address the other in the way it is thought that the other wishes or expects to be addressed. People also change the way they speak to 'fit in'.

It has been said that Britain in the 1940s and 1950s was the only place in the world where a person's social status could be noted within seconds, by accent alone. Oral communication and vocabulary was status laden. Accent revealed education, economic position and class. Today, particularly in certain professions (including law), regional accents can often generate discrimination. Such discrimination is not spoken of to those whose speech habits are different; only to those whose speech habits are acceptable, thereby creating an elite.

Given the variety of oral communication, accent, tone and vocabulary, it is clear that it is not just language itself that is important but how it is communicated and the attitude of the speaker. Does it include or exclude?

Written expressions of language are also important. They are used to judge the ultimate worth of academic work and job applicants, and the observation of protocols concerning appropriate answer and letter writing can affect the success or otherwise of that communication. In a legal context, letters of complaint that are well presented are far more likely to be dealt with positively.

So, language is extremely powerful both in terms of its structure and vocabulary and in terms of the way it is used in both writing and speaking. Rightly or wrongly, it is used to label one as acceptable or unacceptable, educated or uneducated, rich or poor, rational or irrational. Remember that language can be used to give character attributes that are completely wrong. For example, a highly articulate, well spoken, English accent with a rich vocabulary leads many to make the assumption that the speaker is well educated, of 'noble' birth and character and is rich. This assumption could of course be baseless.

Language and the role of the lawyer
Lawyers work with language all the time. They have been described as wordsmiths, people whose craft, or trade, is the highly competent use of both oral and written language.

Lawyers work with legal rules that come in two major forms: UK domestic legislation and EC law (where it is said that the legal rule is in a 'fixed verbal form'), and case law or common law. In common law, the judgments of the judges contain the rules of law, but these rules have to be extracted from the text of the judge's decision. Although the judgment is always taken down verbatim by the court stenographer, the rules are *not* in a 'fixed verbal form'. In fact, just the reverse is true. These judgments contain rules in an unfixed verbal format. Both fixed and unfixed verbal forms give a certain latitude to interpreters.

When dealing with legal rules, lawyers determine their likely application to the facts of a case, predict the outcome of the application of the rules and interpret the language constructing those rules. Lawyers need to be acutely aware of the power of language and the particular characteristics of legal language.

The characteristics of legal language
It is often said that law has its own language. It does not, but the language of law does have distinctive characteristics. For example, those social actors engaged in creating law tend to use linguistic terms dealing with generalisations and categories that have to be applied to individual specific circumstances. This is because law as drafted has to be able to apply to a whole range of circumstances, some of which are unknown at the time the law is drafted.

Particular characteristics of legal language are formality, precision and the existence of a technical vocabulary. Often everyday words are used, but given a different, specialised meaning. Many characteristics of legal language have their roots in the historical origins of legal procedure and it is now difficult to provide rational justification for them. They have become fossils or indicators of historical development. Other characteristics remain as justifiable attempts to reach precision in language usage. Figure 3.2 gives a fuller indication of the characteristics of legal language.

Lawyers want to be able to use a distinctive language that is precise, brief, intelligible and durable. But, of course, they fail. Lawyers are particularly reliant on being able to persuade by argument. Argumentation will be considered in Chapter 7, and exercises on the companion website demonstrate the power of figurative and poetic language to persuade. The ability to persuade in the absence of strong evidence on the basis of the use of emotive poetic language gives language its power, and its influence over law. Rules are carried in language, and their meaning is assigned through language.

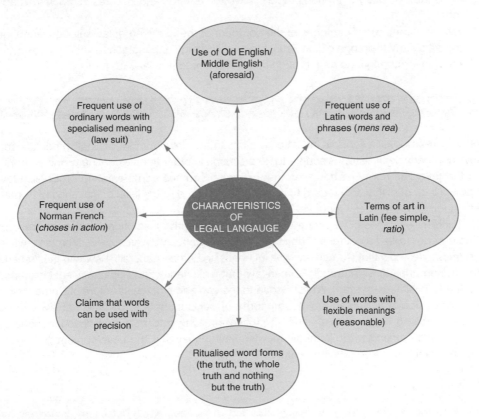

Figure 3.2 Characteristics of legal language

Language and history

As we shall see in the next section, history has played a major role in shaping the content of law. But history has also shaped the language of law[7]. If the words of the law are carefully considered it is possible to see the traces left behind from conquering political and legal systems. Before the Roman invasion in 55BCE the inhabitants of the area that is now England spoke Celtic dialects. Latin did not take a hold until 597CE with the arrival of Augustine's mission from the then Pope Gregory in Rome. Subsequent, post-Augustine, invasions by Angles, Saxons and Jutes brought Scandinavian and Germanic languages into the arena of English, and into the lexicon of English law. It is well known that the Vikings invaded parts of North East England and Scotland, which from 800CE brought further aspects of Scandinavian dialects to English. These linguistic influences seeped into the lexicon of the law. In the mid eleventh century, the Normans stamped a duality of linguistic forms on developing English law that was to dominate it for 300 years. At that time, bringing an action to law in England was linguistically highly complex. Legal proceedings were conducted orally in French but formal written records and statutes of law were made in Latin[8].

Even this briefest of sketches of the contours of the mapping of law through language indicates clearly the range of linguistic, historical, foreign and indigenous influences on the shaping of legal language and through this on the content of law.

HISTORY AND LAW

History textbooks in schools indicate certainty in the development of English politics and law, and early legal histories sought to do the same in order to give continuity and authority to the law. The reality is, however, that historical sources commentating on English law show a lack of clarity with regard to its development and to the level of influence of Roman law prior to the Norman Conquest in 1066.

There is evidence of separate collections of law with jurisdiction in different areas of England controlled by different tribes (for example Danelaw, Wessex law, Mercian law). In addition, we know that Roman law was influential in Europe generally between the first and fourth centuries. It was through Roman law that Christianity first became a legal influence on the English legal system. Whilst Scotland took on some of the structure of Roman law it was not popular in England (although some of our concepts in commercial law can be traced back to Roman law origins). It is also interesting to note that historical sources also provide examples of Talmudic (Jewish) law influencing the development of English commercial law in the eleventh century[9].

---

7   This section is drawn from an excellent practical text on legal language, R Haigh, *Legal English* (2nd edn Routledge-Cavendish, 2009).

8   Latin, slightly adapted, was the acquired sacred language of Christian text and ritual, reminding us of the political connection between Imperial Rome and Christianity from 400CE.

9   Space does not permit extended discussion but see: J Rabinowitz, 'The Influence of Jewish Law on the Development of the Common Law', in L Finkelstein, *The Jews: Their History, Culture and Religion* (3rd edn Harper and Row, New York 1960); EH Burn, *Cheshire's Modern Law of Real Property* (12th edn Butterworths, London 1976).

The development of common law

English law is now characterised by being a common law tradition. This tradition was a by-product of the Norman invasion in 1066, as the conquerors sought over successive centuries to centralise their power in the fragmented land of England. The Normans knew that they could not stamp control on the land working alone. So they developed a flexible system of political control that factored in the entire nation. This system gave power to the aristocracy in return for loyalty to the monarch, who had ultimate control. The Normans were content to combine legal rules of the particular areas with a mix of their own rules. In this way no one group felt that the new legal rules were completely alien. However, because these rules were nationalised, the monarch had the jurisdiction to hear all legal disputes. This meant political control became centralised through the use of flexible, nationalised legal rules. So while indigenous rules operated in selected areas, it was the king who offered the *common* law, the new royal justice to all.

As conquerors, the Normans were unsurprisingly on the receiving end of a hostile response from the people. They needed a judiciary capable of dispensing and developing their unified laws, in a situation where they were not only restricted by language ability but by local hostility. Since the judiciary needed to be highly literate, the aristocracy might have been the obvious choice, were it not for their own hostility. The Normans instead turned to the other main literate group, the church, training the literate Christian clerics to be judges in the royal courts. Christian influences therefore became instilled in the law at many levels, as the legal customs and rules of the tribal areas merged and were then added to by Norman law-making.

The newly appointed judge-clerics travelled the country on the monarch's authority hearing disputes, reading evidences, hearing witnesses and then delivering judgment. These journeys and records formed a travelling, localised justice that was administratively centralised. It was this innovation that was to develop ultimately into nationalised law and a unified legal system in terms of administration, jurisdiction, adjudication and law creation. This construction of a law common to all came in time to be referred to as the common law of England primarily built up of judges' decisions and the commands of the sovereign.

As law professionalised during the eleventh and twelfth century, the teaching of English law took place via apprenticeship. Judges needed clerks, and litigants needed those who understood law to advise them of the procedures and arguments to be given at law. Legal education took place in specialist Inns of Court, the only places which taught the common law necessary for the education of legal professionals who worked in the royal courts of the monarch. They were known as 'inns' because living and working space was merged into one area. The Universities of Oxford and Cambridge at this time limited their offered legal instruction to Roman law. This was deemed to be more academically demanding with its links to classical education. In England, however, Roman law was only used in the church courts of the Roman Catholic Church, still at that time under the political and religious power of Rome. In the sixteenth century the monarch effectively nationalised religion when he removed England from Rome and took over the church's administration. Within three centuries this move was to mould the Anglican Church. The courts of the monarch never used Roman law. However, it was not until the seventeenth century that the first law schools at Oxford and Cambridge began to turn their attention to common law.

The development of the role of barrister was made possible through the creation of the Inns of Court. The earliest Inns of Court were attached to churches because of the close connection between the clerics and the judges. As the common law system evolved and judicial reasoning became more expansive, many justifications for law were grounded in Christian morality and illustrated with references to the Christian sacred text, the Holy Bible. Increasingly in the courts, judges maintained that Christian law was indeed part of the law of England.

Whilst this brief sketch of the origins of common law and the unification of legal codes in England has noted Jewish and primarily Christian influences on the development of English law, some scholars have noted that the structure of Inns of Court attached to churches indicates that Islamic law also exerted a major influence on the structure of English law and the development of its argumentative techniques during the eleventh and twelfth centuries[10]. Glenn[11] notes that the attachment of the Inns of Court to churches mirrored the process whereby the madhahib (schools of Islamic law) were attached to mosques with living accommodation integral to working and teaching space. Glenn concludes that as the Normans were active in Jerusalem in the same period as they were in England it is inconceivable that there was no cross-fertilisation[12]. This was therefore more than mere coincidence (for example due to the role of the law in the hands of political power and the close relationship between political power and religious authority in the eleventh century).

Because of its beginnings in an act of political necessity (to unite hostile forces and allow localised justice to have a centralised control) the characteristics of the common law became its communality, its inclusivity, and its preference for providing supplementary legal rules rather than fixed absolutes. It could be said that this flexibility was the supreme act of political diplomacy of the Normans. Initially, the monarch decided that it was not necessary for the English common law to claim **exclusive** jurisdiction. This allowed space for a range of localised legal systems (Scandinavian, Germanic, Roman, Scottish, Talmudic, Islamic, and indigenous) to exert influence on the shape of English common law. Here you could think of law and justice as privatised at the level of the local and national power. As long as political loyalty locally was intact then local laws were tolerated as part of the nationalised system, with common law, the royal justice, offering dispute resolution in the courts.

In the early centuries after the Norman invasion a number of methods of dispute resolution existed alongside the court-based common law. Most had their origins in dispute resolution within tribal settings, such as the blood feud[13], trial by battle[14] and trial by ordeal. Trial by ordeal came particularly to utilise Christian ritual, whereby the person

---

10 See: R van Caenegem, *Birth of English Common law* (2nd edn CUP, Cambridge 1988); C Burnett, *The Introduction of Arabic Learning into England* (London, British Library 1997).
11 HP Glenn, *The Legal Traditions of the World* (OUP, Oxford 2000) 189–193.
12 See J Bush and A Wijffels, *Learning the Law: Teaching and Transmission of Law in England 1150–1900* (Grande Ohio, Hambledon Press, London/Rio 1999).
13 When the family of a victim sought to extract revenge by killing members of the aggressor's family.
14 When two sides to a dispute resolved it by engaging each other in battle, or by sponsoring a champion to fight on their behalf.

accused was subject to ordeals (such as placing a hand in boiling water). If there was a miraculous recovery it was deemed to be the hand of God showing the defendant to be innocent. The use of the support of the church to trial by ordeal was forbidden in 1215. Inevitably whilst there was some choice between royal justice and concurrent forms of justice, political pressures accompanied by threats of physical torture were placed on defendants and litigants to choose the proffered royal justice. The drawback associated with royal justice was its cost, and the fact that if a person was found guilty of breaking the king's peace, that is acting against the Crown, his lands and monies would be forfeited to the Crown leaving his family destitute. Many people elected to die under torture so that local justice would take effect and land and possessions would pass to the family, not the Crown.

In its pursuit of communality social actors who became part of the common law allowed it to work itself out in different places in different ways. Common law remained flexible, making it capable of intricate adaptations to situations. These adaptations eventually produced the law we work with today, as well as the developed state legislation that we are familiar with and the methods of argument that allow permutations and interpretations of existing rules.

You will note as you begin to read the law that often the justification for a rule is held to be history alone. The implication is that longevity is synonymous with validity. However, tradition develops over centuries and, when we look back, becomes an embellished retelling of doctrine. The tradition can end up attaining an almost mythical or mystical state. Edward Coke, a lawyer of much influence in the seventeenth century, gave the following explanation for the importance of history in relation to law:

> We are but of yesterday . . . our days upon the earth are but as a shadow in respect of the old ancient days and times past, wherein the laws have been the wisdom of the most excellent men, in many successions of age, by long and continued experience, (the trial of light and truth) fined and refined[15].

Often in court it has been repeated that the English judge made, or common law is said to be, the collective wisdom of the ages. This is a powerful *myth*, not necessarily a powerful *truth*.

The eleventh century to the present day

The history of English law from the eleventh to the eighteenth century and beyond is a story of increasing centralisation and ultimately the removal of any choice in legal dispute resolution. It resulted in the development of an all encompassing system of common law applicable to all. Over the centuries strands of tradition have been retold and the story of law has become objectivised, with the role of the law described as a neutral observer.

Law also became a political weapon as it outlawed and made illegal certain Christian religious denominations whilst others aligned with the Crown. Wars of succession to the throne became mediated by religious views and the force and might of the law.

---

15 *Calvin's Case*, 7 Co Rep 1a (Coke's Reports).

The main story of English law from the eighteenth to the twentieth century was the exportation of common law to British colonies. This includes former British colonies such as Australia, Canada, New Zealand, the West Indies and the Caribbean, which have kept these common law roots after obtaining independence. This is why the Privy Council remains the last appeal court for so many nation states. It dates from the time when the relevant state was a colony with a final appeal to the homeland.

If you choose to study legal history other stories will be drawn out, including the long struggle for equality between people and Parliament before the law, and the twentieth and twenty-first century use of law for social engineering. Law has been described as the power discourse of the state. At whatever point we might choose to zoom into the history of the law from the eleventh century on (and we do have authenticated documents of law pre-dating then) we find only conflict and bargaining.

Law cannot be disconnected from history; it is the product of circumstance. Today English law is infused with new types of legal rules from EC law. This has a number of differences from English common law. Much of it is steeped in variants of Roman law, where judges have a different relationship to adjudication. EC law is more open-textured and judges look far more to the end purpose of rules, as we shall see in Chapter 4.

Since 1998 when the Human Rights Act embedded in English law many of the articles from the European Convention on Human Rights and Fundamental Freedoms, English courts have also had to grapple with, and take note of, the judicial decisions of the European Court of Human Rights. This, too, takes a broader approach to interpretation than the linguistic twists and turns of word-by-word interpretation used by English judges.

Legal philosophy

We can obtain another series of snapshots of law by considering it from the pathway of legal philosophy. Although there are many legal schools of philosophic debate, it can be crudely suggested that there are two ways of considering law from a philosophic perspective. One main view is to imagine law as *reason*. From this perspective it is argued that either man, or the cosmos, contains principles of rational and reasonable order. And this order can be seen to be replicated in rational beings. This is the perspective of the **natural law** schools of legal thought. The other view imagines law as a matter of *power*, often sheer will power, whether divine or human. This is the view of the **positivist** schools of legal thought. Law is in this sense a power discourse. Both perspectives are influenced by religious ideas and have room for notions of the divine. They therefore contain reasoning of interest to those people who have religious faith as well as those people who have none.

In natural law schemas, the ideology is of reason ascertainable by each person through their own rational enquiry. Many religions where there is a view that men and women are fallen from God's blessing can find this a problem, as the law thus located by way of human reasoning is flawed. If you are interested in exploring these areas you will find interesting arguments presented by religious professionals constructing differing frameworks to accommodate natural law, alongside the secular forms. Even secular arguments for natural law reject it on the logical grounds of the impossibility of human infallibility.

Positivism argues to the contrary. It states that there is no higher order of things dis-cernible by reason (secular or divine) and that law is created and maintained purely by power and will. Over time this creates habits of obedience to sovereign power. The only matter of importance is that law is properly created. In English law this would mean by the authority of judges or Parliament. In other words, law is law if it is validly enacted. The leading English legal positivist HLA Hart puts forward this view[16]. For him, all rules have both an external and an internal dimension. By this he means that not only do they come from somewhere (the external dimension), but that those to whom the rules apply observe them or react to them (the internal dimension).

Both the value and the problem of this position, lie in its potential for de-politicising legal analysis and unifying moral positions. Under a 'law-is-law' perspective, if a regime is stable and predictable it is a legal system irrespective of the laws enacted and enforced, and irrespective of whether it is lacking in democracy or morality[17]. One of the major criticisms of Hart is by Dworkin[18] who argues that law is *more* than merely rules, that it also includes principles. Dworkin identifies the existence of discretion as a core problem of law. As all interpretation is constructive, he argues, it imposes purpose on the object of interpretation. While interpreters can differ on the 'purpose and value' of assumed common inter-pretations the important decision occurs in the moment of choice, for choice remains at the point one decides what constitutes the 'best' interpretation. Dworkin argues that the law has an investment in the constancy of its power to ensure that all of the law's decisions and interpretations are the *best* decisions and interpretations. Dworkin's problem is that he dislikes the idea of discretion, but where there is choice of interpretation there is always discretion.

Ultimately the Western legal tradition consistently claims that law is a specialist, scientific pursuit separated from other social phenomena. Whilst it can be said that English legal tradition, due to its common law tradition, is different in its structure from the majority of Western legal systems (that are based on variants of Roman law), it is no different in its claims about the unitary and specialist nature of law. It is after all the product of the Normans' rationalisation of a range of localised law in its creation of common law.

It is important at the beginning of your studies to appreciate that the law can change in terms of its content and its form. This in turn allows it be used to play different social, economic and political roles. But whilst law's flexibility allows law's content to change legal institutions it can also promote its unity and thus its unchanging nature. Within this framework if one looks back centuries, considering English law as royal law, judge law, parliamentary law, or a mix of all three, it is argued that the law still retains the unity of an external and internal view of law. Its *external dimension* can always be pointed to in terms of its ideational source (whether that be the wizard, the kings, the judge, the cleric, God(s) or the secular). The ideational core of law is held to be unchanging, and it is with reference

---

16 HLA Hart, *The Concept of Law* (2nd edn OUP, 1994),

17 Therefore a corrupt and immoral regime imposing appalling sanctions on some or all of its people would have the right to do so – because law is not answering to a rational order but to the mere process of lawfully enacted law. If a law states this then a law is a law and is to be followed.

18 R Dworkin, *Taking Rights Seriously* (Duckworth, London 1978); R Dworkin, *Law's Empire* (Fontana, London 1986).

to this core that law claims its unique role to maintain social order by setting up notions of the desirability of communal order. The ideational core constitutes the 'presence' of law but this is not considered at the level of the everyday, where practitioners point to interim institutional sources, the legislature, the courts, the EU and international treaties. This law of the everyday is its *internal dimension*, the law as applied to people.

The positivistic 'law-as-law' philosophy has been firmly in the ascendancy in English legal theory. In the US, however, a movement known as **realism** maintains that law is what really happens-in-practice, at the level of the everyday[19]. To give a flavour of this movement there is no better example than Oliver Wendell Holmes' famous description of law as the experience of life, referring to law as a magic mirror:

> . . . wherein, . . . we see reflected, not only our own lives, but the lives of all men that have been. . . .[20]

On another occasion he specifically alludes to the law using the genre of fairy tales, describing the law as likened to:

> . . . a princess . . . eternally weaving into her web dim figures of the ever lengthening past. . . .[21]

Here the illusion is of a seamless trail of history. In both these quotations, Holmes is referencing both the everyday level of law and its ideational core through his metaphoric references to magic, myth, story and royalty. Indeed the reference to stories is most appropriate in relation to law, and particularly English law. Each legal case revolves around the telling of stories. It can be overlooked that when these stories go to court it is the judge's final legitimation story – the authorised story of the court, patched together from the perceptions and evidence of the stories of the parties – that becomes the written record of the law. From this perspective law can be viewed as dynamic stories: stories whose texts yield information concerning the many contexts of law in action: political, social, institutional, and religious.

As the discussion returns to stories and language so we return to the view of law as a power-filled system of communication. The **critical legal theory** movement argues that legal scholarship fails if it does not look at the power dimensions of the law, through a careful interrogation of its hidden assumptions and figurative language[22]. Goodrich's analysis of law-talk shows that legal language is no more and no less than a social practice patterned by its background, contexts and officials, and that its texts therefore reflect and express:

---

19 The theorists most associated with this stream are Karl Llewellyn, Jerome Frank and Oliver Wendell Holmes.
20 OW Holmes, *The Common Law* (Belknap Press, Cambridge, Mass 1963) 20–21.
21 Holmes (1963: 22). This is an interesting allusion to Tennyson's poem the Lady of Shallot: 'There she weaves by night and day, a magic web with colours gay, cursed to watch the world through a mirror on pain of death to look directly'.
22 Here mention could be made of critical legal scholars such as Peter Goodrich, Costas Douzinas, Peter Fitzpatrick and latterly Adam Geary.

. . . the roles, purposes and ideologies of its participants or subjects, these implicit or unconsciously regulated operative meanings are accessible to study through their expression in the lexicon, syntax and semantics of the text[23].

We could say here that its texts are again a mirror. It has been cleverly argued by White that:

the greatest power of law lies not in particular rules or decisions but in its language . . . in the way it structures sensibility and vision . . . law offers opportunities to tell one's story and be heard. Thus law is a method of translation as well as integration[24].

He continues with:

. . . the text is meant to operate not simply on one occasion but across a range of imperfectly foreseeable occasions, and thus to have the peculiar kind of meaning such a text can have. It creates as it were a new dimension of reality, running across time and space, in which it aims at, even claims, a consistency of result and significance that in the nature of things cannot wholly be allowed. The legal text thus stimulates and works by a desire not for the discovery of actual human intention but for a different sort of meaning: for the creation of a general language of justice that will govern a wide range of particular cases over time in a consistent and fair way[25].

RELIGION AND ENGLISH LAW

The close connections between law and religion have already been signalled in this chapter. This relationship is often mediated by politics and recent legislation has steadily worked towards the secularisation of public space, so that if a speaker wishes space he or she must not have a partisan religious view.

English law has always been very good at protecting individual interests. If you have a dispute with an employer, for example, the law has been shown to appreciate the power differences between you as a sole individual and the resources at your disposal and the organisation you may be in dispute with. Whilst at one time the idea of trade unions and the power to withdraw labour was seen as striking a balance between employees and employer, today the trade unions have very little leeway to strike. Similarly the law recognises certain rights to religious freedom for the individual but it does not recognise the issues of identity (personal, communal and social) involved in religious affiliation. Whilst the law through its institutions declares its equality and neutrality it does so from the somewhat pre-judged assumption that balance between competing worldviews can best be obtained by imposing the position of the secular.

---

23 P Goodrich, *The Languages of Law from the Logics of Memory to Nomadic Masks* (Weidenfeld & Nicolson, 1990) 76.

24 JB White, *The Legal Imagination* (abridged edn, Chicago University Press, Chicago 1985) 114.

25 Ibid. 133–4.

Religion raises particular concerns in the UK precisely because English law neglects the importance of conferring communal rights on religious organisations. This in turn has had a major impact in religio-social communities that elevate the communal dimensions, in some instances causing misunderstanding and hostility towards English law. It is therefore important that matters of religion and their influence in the area of law are properly understood.

After a period of academic disinterest, the relationship between religion and law has re-emerged as an issue of academic study over the past 15 years. Once an area of purely historical interest, scholars are now focusing on the tense relationship between politics, law and religion. The late twentieth century saw religious influences increasingly shaping English society, with repercussions around the world. More and more religious issues of a legal nature are aired both in and outside court.

A worrying trend particularly manifesting itself in the twentieth century is the enactment of law that is draconian in so far as it is taking away rights. Swathes of new anti-terrorism laws have been enacted which, for instance, curtail the freedom of movement of extremists. Whilst assurances have been given that such new powers will not be used out of context, there have already been examples where this is not the case. The government froze the assets of the Icelandic bank at the beginning of the credit crisis in 2008 using terrorism powers to combat a completely unconnected financial crisis. The Icelandic government was naturally incensed to have been on the receiving end of the application of the British government's terrorism legislation. Prior to that in 2007 a pensioner, who had been a labour party supporter all his life, was ejected from the labour party conference for heckling (asking loud questions from the back of the arena during government speeches) by security using terrorism law. Formal apologies were issued in both cases after the action had been carried out by authority of law. It was not suggested the action could not legally occur, but that it was not envisaged that such powers would be used in these circumstances.

What is often ignored in analyses is the highly relevant religious template of English law. The Judeo-Christian tradition has been historically and culturally woven into the fabric of English law. This religious profile or dimension could possibly cause one to query whether there is a rupture in law's story of neutrality. Professional lawyers and judges, as well as politicians, certainly still view the idea of religion in simplistic terms – as a personal preference of individuals of no concern to the state – unless that religious view comes into direct conflict with government policy and law and order. Then it is religion that is seen as the problem to be neutralised. But events in the past ten years have caused a rapid re-evaluation of the power of religion to influence law and the power of law to change the nature of religious freedom.

ENGLISH LAW AND THE IDEA OF HUMAN RIGHTS

International and European human rights have had a powerful influence on the development of English law and the way in which judges interpret the law relating to human rights. Moving forward with a view of human rights as a set of texts, it can be found that conflicts repeatedly occur with the linguistic and textual aspects of legislation. What did the politicians, lawyers and judges intend when they first set out powerful documents such as the Universal Declaration of Human Rights in 1947 or the European Convention on Human Rights 1951 (ECHR)? What do ECHR rights mean when they are considered in English courts by virtue of the Human Rights Act 1998 (HRA 1998)?

What is seen in disputes in the area of human rights and religion, is that behind neutral terms such as 'the law', 'religion' and 'politics', human agency plays the key role in the formation of interpretations that create or break relationships, and ultimately determine what the law is.

The HRA 1998 places important restraints on the English judges and legislature. Legislation ideally should not be enacted in opposition to the Act and the government must declare this for all new legislation (or declare the opposite by issuing a declaration that the legislation is not in keeping with the HRA). English judges, by virtue of the HRA, must take notice of cases in the European Court of Human Rights and apply reasoning from the court to English cases. In time, this Act will have a profound effect on English law as it changes subtly our standard methods of interpretation. We will discuss the influence of the European Union (EU) and European treaties further in Chapter 4.

CONCLUSION

- As you learn the rules of law, and the methods of making law, it is essential to be aware of the contexts within which the law is constructed and applied.

- Language is a powerful influence on law, not only in terms of analysing the rules themselves, but in ascertaining in what way, if any, language influences the constructors, applicators and interpreters of the law.

- Law is carried by words and excellent English language skills are the beginning of basic competency in handling legal rules derived from common law, statutory activity or EC law.

- There are also important historical and political influences on the law, and other disciplines such as philosophy can assist in the understanding of what law might be. As you continue your studies of law you will find many other lenses through which to view the law.

FURTHER READING

For those of you who have found the links between language and law, and the basic introduction to the power of language interesting, you may enjoy reading the following book which takes yet another perspective on the issue of language and law:

P Goodrich, *The Languages of Law from the Logics of Memory to Nomadic Masks* (Weidenfeld & Nicolson, 1990).

The links between law and religion as briefly discussed in this chapter can be explored further in the following:

C Burnett, *The Introduction of Arabic Learning into England* (British Library, 1997).

J Bush and A Wijffels, *Learning the Law Teaching and Transmission of Law in England 1150–1900* (London/Rio 1999).

HP Glenn, *The Legal Traditions of the World* (2nd edn Oxford University Press, 2000). An overview of different legal traditions can be obtained from this book.

J Rabinowitz, 'The Influence of Jewish Law on the Development of the Common Law', in L Finkelstein, *The Jews: Their History, Culture and Religion* Vol 1 (4th edn Harper and Row, 1970).

R Van Caenegem, *The Birth of English Common Law* (2nd edn CUP, Cambridge 1988).

If you are interested in philosophical discussion you could begin by considering some of the following texts:

R Dworkin, *Taking Rights Seriously* (Duckworth, 1978).

R Dworkin, *Law's Empire* (Fontana, 1986).

HLA Hart, *The Concept of Law* (2nd edn OUP, 1994).

OW Holmes, *The Common Law* (Belknap Press, Cambridge 1963).

JB White, *The Legal Imagination* (abridged edn Chicago University Press, 1985).

COMPANION WEBSITE

Now visit the companion website to:

- work through the series of Part One-related exercises in Workbook One;

- tackle quiz questions on library skills.

PART TWO: MAPPING THE TERRITORY

"The world can doubtless never be well known by theory: practice is absolutely necessary; but surely it is of great use . . . before set[ting] out for that country, full of mazes, windings, and turnings, to have at least a general map of it, made by some experienced traveller."

Philip Dormer Stanhope

As students of law it is important to have confidence that you fully understand the origin, format and jurisdiction of the range of legal rules making up the English legal system. It is even more important that you can read these legal rules and make sense of them as well as utilising secondary materials that comment and critique the law. The three chapters in this part are designed to map the territory of law, to show its extent and its limits and to help you understand the primary texts of law and the secondary texts about law.

From Chapter 2 you will already have a basic idea of the types of legal rule in the English legal system. There are four main sources of law that make up the laws of England, as set out in Figure II.1 and described below. Two of these originate within the UK.

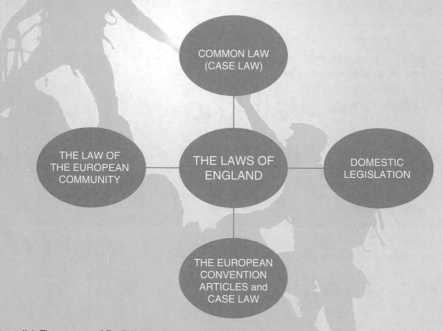

Figure II.1 The sources of English law

Common law

When using the term common law in the sense of a source, it describes the law-making capacity of the senior judges encompassing the case law of the English legal system[1]. The cases will mostly be concerned with issues of the meaning of words and phrases used in legislation or earlier cases. Some cases will produce new legal rules, as the appellate courts do have power to develop the law in this way. This is also referred to as judge-made law.

Domestic legislation

This is the law created by Parliament. This is a superior form of law to the common law and it can change or abolish common law judge-made law.

---

1   You will recall from Chapter 2 that it also bears the meaning of all of the law common to the whole of the English legal system.

European Community law (the law of the European Union)

This source originates outside the English legal system but has legal effect *inside* the English legal system (this has been authorised by Parliament through their enactment of the European Communities Act 1972 as amended). This is a superior form of law to the common law insofar as it has been given legal force by Parliament and where this is the case it can change or abolish judge-made case law in its areas of competency. This law includes:

- legislation of the EU;
- decisions of the European Court of Justice (the Court of the EU).

The European Convention on Human Rights and Fundamental Freedoms (the European Convention)

This source originates outside the English legal system and has limited effect inside the English legal system (where it has been authorised by Parliament through the Human Rights Act 1998). It includes:

- selected articles from the ECHR;
- decisions of the European Court of Human Rights.

The chapters in this part deal with the sources of law as briefly sketched above. However, it is useful to note that English law can additionally be divided into different groupings of literary and historical sources as shown in Figure II.2. English legal sources include both *lex scripta* (written law) sources or legislation, characterised by being in a fixed verbal form, and *lex non scripta* (unwritten law) sources in non-fixed verbal form.

None of these areas are static; all are constantly evolving. You need to know how each area of law can be created and by whom, and how it can be changed. The constant changing of the law makes it extremely important that you can effectively use your library skills to consult the print and electronic collections for the most up-to-date versions of the law in any of these areas.

Chapter 4: Reading and understanding legislation focuses exclusively on legislation. It considers the law made by Parliament, European legislation which has effect in the English legal system by virtue of the European Communities Act 1972 and the articles of the ECHR which have been brought into English law by the Human Rights Act 1998. This chapter not only discusses the creation of legislation but takes time to discuss how to make sense of the format and language of statutory provisions.

Chapter 5: Reading and understanding law cases deals with cases. It looks at the law generated and/or discussed in the English courts, the case law of the European Court of Justice, the Court of the EU and the case law of the European Court of Human Rights, which hears cases under the jurisdiction of the ECHR. In keeping with the approach adopted in Chapter 4, Chapter 5 takes time to discuss how to understand the language of

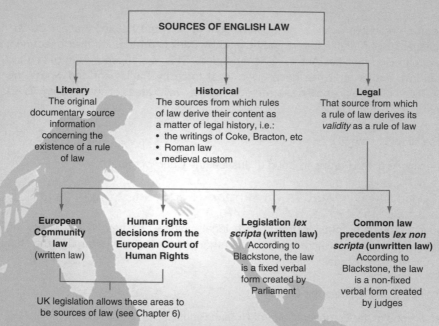

Figure II.2 Groupings of the sources of English law

the judgments. It also indicates how to write a good case note of a case in court and discusses the hierarchy of the law reports.

Chapter 5 discusses the doctrine of precedent, which is key to understanding the particular system judges adopt for reaching decisions in English cases. The doctrine maintains that if a similar case has already been decided by a senior appeal court (the Court of Appeal or the House of Lords) then the case must be decided the same way by all courts, except the House of Lords which allows itself limited practical ability to ignore an earlier similar decision of its own. In tandem with this discussion more detail will be given of the hierarchy of the courts and the development of the system of law reporting which is of key importance for a system based on keeping to the decisions of past cases.

Chapter 6: Reading texts about law turns away from primary sources of law to consider academic commentaries and critiques *about* the state of the law. The chapter introduces a reading strategy to allow you to work through texts and make useful notes.

If you complete the exercises in all three chapters and complement them with those on the companion website you will have a very firm grasp of the range of sources of English law and how to read the law, as well as how to read the secondary texts.

READING AND UNDERSTANDING LEGISLATION

4

" It is one of the finest problems in legislation, what the state ought to take upon itself to direct and what it ought to leave, with as little interference as possible, to individual discretion."

Edmund Burke

After reading this chapter you should be able to:

- competently read, use and understand domestic and European legislation;

- understand the layout of a statute, a statutory instrument and a treaty;

- understand the internal language of sections in a statute;

- distinguish between primary and secondary legislation;

- appreciate the history of the EC and its place within the EU;

- distinguish between primary and secondary EC law;

- understand the relationship between the English legal system, the EC and the EU;

- place the English Human Rights Act 1998 (HRA) in its appropriate context and explain how it relates to the European Convention on Fundamental Freedoms and Human Rights (here referred to throughout as ECHR);

- understand the function and strategies of statutory interpretation.

CHAPTER SUMMARY

This chapter introduces legislation: the first of two important generic sources of English legal rules discussed in detail in this book[1]. This broad heading includes UK statutes, EC legislation (the law of the EU impacting the UK because of our membership of the EU) and the articles of the ECHR (impacting particularly UK law since the HRA 1998). Because of the vast amount of law that is of European origin, most texts, and this one will be no exception, refer to legislation of UK origin as 'domestic' to differentiate it from its European dimension

The standard layout of legislation is explained, along with the need to concentrate on English language skills in order to understand the fundamental importance of prepositional words in legislation. The macro-level of a whole statute and its organisation, and the micro-level of the individual elements of legislation (sections, subsections) and their organisation is discussed. The chapter also considers the difficult but fundamental issue of interpreting legislation.

The second half of the chapter deals extensively with understanding the European influence on English law to provide a stable foundation for understanding the European dimension of English law, that part of English law very much affected by the UK government's international agreements with other European nation states contracted via treaties. A step-by-step approach is taken, introducing treaties generally and describing their standard format. If the concept of treaties is not basically understood you will be at a disadvantage trying to understand the European dimension of English law. This is followed by a consideration of the ECHR 1951 and the way in which it became part of UK domestic law through the HRA 1998. Attention then turns to the treaties setting up the EU, considering the way in which European legislation is given legal force in the English legal system through the European Communities Act 1972.

The chapter ends with a consideration of statutory interpretation and the role of the judges when they are called upon to determine the meaning of domestic or European legislative provisions.

The overall aim of this chapter is to provide a commentary concerning the relationships and differences between the legislative areas of the UK, the ECHR and the EU to assist in the management of the study of these complex areas[2].

INTRODUCING LEGISLATION

There are three major sources of law that can be included under the broad heading of legislation:

---

1   The other is common law discussed in detail in Chapter 5.
2   Case law from the courts will be considered in Chapter 5.

■   domestic legislation;

■   EC (often popularly called EU) legislation;

■   the ECHR.

Getting to grips with these different legal rules can seem difficult. To handle competently primary texts of law, you need to be able to:

■   locate and understand the various sources of the rules;

■   learn how they can be used to provide a resolution to disputes of a legal nature;

■   learn how to engage in applying and interpreting the rules;

■   understand the interconnections between the main sources of English law and in particular the relationship between cases and legislation.

In order to give a context for the reading and analysing techniques that enable legislation to be properly understood, it is necessary to describe the nature of legislation and how it is implemented. As an important source of law it is of course studied in more detail in courses on constitutional and administrative law (or public law), the English legal system, European law and human rights.

Domestic legislation

Domestic legislation is the law made by the authority of Parliament. When directly created by Parliament the legislation is an example of a primary source of law. The technically correct term for such a piece of legislation is a 'legislative Act'. This is the dominant form of law making within the modern English legal system.

In addition to creating legislation, Parliament can delegate, to another person or group, by an Act of Parliament, the power to create a limited range of laws for others. For example, powers can be delegated to a:

■   local authority;

■   government minister;

■   professional body.

When the relevant institutional representative follows the procedure laid down to create law aimed at specific groups or areas, the legislation that is created is referred to as secondary legislation[3], but it also has a range of other synonyms as shown in Figure 4.1.

---

3   The word secondary as used here should not be confused with secondary texts of law, or secondary sources of law. Note the whole phrase 'secondary legislation'. It is a primary source of law, as it contains the legal rule(s).

a statutory instrument (SI)

OR

delegated legislation

OR

secondary legislation (for it is once removed from parliamentary power)

Figure 4.1 Synonyms referring to secondary legislation

The legislation giving the power to make such secondary or delegated legislation is referred to as the *primary legislation*, or the *parent Act*. The metaphor implied by the phrase *parent Act* describes very well the relationship between the primary legislation and the secondary legislation. The secondary legislative Act is the *child*. It looks to the *parent* (in an ideal world) for its authority and the parent has the power to take that authority away. Again the range of synonyms used can be confusing and these are noted in Figure 4.2.

Primary legislation

OR

Public General Act

OR

Act of Parliament

OR

Legislative Act

OR

Statute

In addition there is a cluster of primary legislation that is NOT applicable to all, which is referred to as Private Acts of Parliament. This is when the act goes through the full procedure and is primary legislation, but it only refers to a small area, a few people or even just to one person (a name change by Act of Parliament, for example).

Figure 4.2 Synonyms referring to primary legislation

The law of the European Community

The second source of law caught within the broad heading of legislation created and/or authorised by Parliament is the legislative law of the EC. In 1973, the UK joined the EC. At the time Parliament enacted the European Communities Act 1972 which made provision in section 2 for EC law, created in the areas covered by the treaties signed by the UK government, to have superiority over any conflicting UK legislation. So, in areas within the competence of the EC, if there is a clash between national law and EC law, the latter must prevail. This scenario is in fact provided for in the Treaty setting up the EC in 1957. If the UK wished to join the EC in 1972 it had to make legislative provisions that would ensure the appropriate superiority of EC law. Furthermore, the UK government promised to legislate where necessary to ensure that Community law was observed in the UK.

The EC has now come to be a larger creation called the European Union (EU), with 29 nation states in membership at the time of writing this text. The EC still exists within the larger EU. Newspapers, news media and the public generally now all speak of the European Union or EU. But to be technically precise from the point of view of law, all of the law-making powers are still contained within the smaller unit of the EC. The EU label allows states to come together to engage in informal co-operation in various areas, areas that may in time be the subject of more formal legal regulation with the agreement of all the states, or those involved. We will discuss the EC and EU in more detail later in this chapter.

There are several different types of law in the EC with differing effects. Each effect is laid down in the treaties of the EC, and now the EU, and each type of law is specifically referred to in English legislation. Some EC law is immediately incorporated in the body of English law, by virtue of existing powers in the European Communities Act 1972 as amended. Some types of EC law have to be specially enacted by Act of Parliament.

Since the enactment of the HRA 1998, English courts have to decide human rights cases by considering cases in the European Court of Human Rights.

UNDERSTANDING DOMESTIC LEGISLATION

Having spent time discussing the power of language, considering issues of meaning and becoming alerted to the influence of figurative language, the importance of excellent language skills for the study of law should be clear. In its legislative format, the language of the law can:

- be in an unusual grammatical form;

- be potentially confusing;

- be tediously literal, dense text;

- exhibit scant punctuation;

- Be liberally peppered with alphabetical and numerical dividers.

To read and understand legislation involves the act of interpretation. Legislation is read for a range of different purposes but they all involve interpretation. A prosecutor or defence lawyer may wish to make legislation suit their view of a legal situation. Judges need to determine the meaning of legislation and apply it to one of the parties in the legal dispute being heard. Others may interpret from a more open position, merely asking: What does this legislation provide for? How might these legal rules apply to this factual situation?

What is the general social impact of this legislation? Does this legislation effectively address the issue?

It can be argued that an interpreter creates something new when they engage in interpretation. It could be the case that an interpretation which is triggered by the text bears no resemblance to the writer's intention. This can be an important issue when related back to the interpretation of a statute as drafted.

Whether an interpreter of a legal text is interpreting from the point of view of a student, a lawyer, a law professor, or an organisation, that interpreter has to be able to adapt their methods according to the type of document they are dealing with. Whether it is ever possible to find the real meaning of words is questionable, but many interpreters do find plausible meanings that others can agree with. When judges speak, the power of their authority ensures that this is the given meaning, until another judge or the legislature changes that meaning. Much of the authority of the English courts lies in their ability to know what the law means and to apply it.

This chapter will demonstrate the importance of developing expertise in various techniques for breaking into legislative texts and using a range of skills and methods to evaluate, analyse and critique them. These skills require constant practice and reflection to learn, but then the techniques can be applied easily. Each type of legal text requires different methods of analysis. Practice steadily increases intellectual awareness, language appreciation, skills of prediction concerning interpretation difficulties and the ability to evaluate. Immediately the interconnections between a range of skills becomes apparent. Overall, there is a need to engage in the following:

1. Language analysis:

- sophisticated comprehension skills;

- vocabulary skills;

- grammar skills;

- excellent reading and writing skills.

2. Diagrammatic methods for organising texts:

- tree diagrams;

- flow charts;

- algorithms;

- Venn diagrams.

3. Textual methods for organising texts:

■   Tables;

■   paragraph analysis;

■   linking and summarising.

4. Identification of interrelationships between different types of legal rules

5. Knowledge of substantive law, for example, the law of contract

Many people do not know how to listen to, or read for, an argument. They hear or see words and do not know how to capture the potential meanings and arguments, truths and errors that they carry. They do not know how to split the text into its small chunks, its building blocks. Think of statute as its own form of map, with pointers to various parts of it and the whole working together. Then you will see how to use the statute and how to under-stand it as a whole. Reading legislation requires many skills. But the reality is that every skill that is necessary for the competent study of law is interconnected and most inter-pretational problems, whether purely theoretical (what is this law?) or practical (what does this law mean for the defendant?) require the competent handling of interconnected skills of language use, legal rules and facts as shown in Figure 4.3.

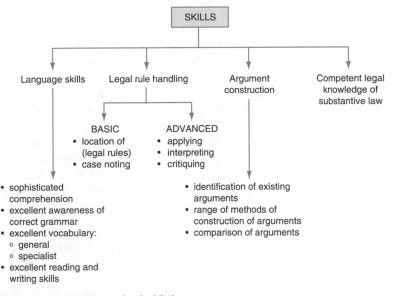

Figure 4.3 Skills required for interpreting legislation

Types of domestic legislation: primary and secondary

Parliament authorises the creation of a range of different types of legal rule that are collectively referred to as legislation (Acts of Parliament). These are set out in Figure 4.4. They are all united by the fact that they are created in a fixed verbal form. The phrase 'fixed verbal form' means that only *those* words in that order, those exact words, were agreed by Parliament as containing the legal rule[4].

A characteristic of legislative rules is that they rarely come as a single rule, they are usually enacted as part of a collection of rules linked by the fact that they deal with similar issues as indicated by the long title, rather than the short title, of legislation. They also come with attached definitions, defences, modes of interpretation and guidelines for operation.

Legislation is enacted in various timescales. Sometimes legislation is a reasonably well considered response to a particular issue such as consumer protection. Sometimes, legislation is quickly created as a reaction by Parliament to a crisis or public outcry or a one-off situation, for example, in response to an act of terrorism. Of course, in reality, it is the government of the day that determines what issues are put into the parliamentary law-making machinery. But this text does not discuss the reasons for the enactment of legislation in detail, it concentrates on the techniques for *understanding* such rules and the processes of *interpretation* that the courts, officials, ordinary people and law students follow in order to apply these rules. Although each piece of legislation responds to particular issues, the finer details of the situations to which the rules will have to be applied will vary enormously. Therefore, another characteristic of legislation is that it is drafted in a general way, in order, it is hoped, to be applicable to the widest possible range of situations. This often presents a major challenge to those drafting the legislation and to those who are subsequently called upon to interpret it.

Another factor that must be borne in mind when considering the meaning and application of legislation is that it may have changed in some way since enactment. For example, it may have been changed by:

■ parliamentary authority, through legislation amending it (adding to or subtracting from it) or by repeal (abolishing it);

■ the House of Lords or the Court of Appeal determining the meaning of words and phrases used to make up the legal rule; UK courts have no power to amend or abolish legislation but their power to interpret legislation can have a major impact on the application of the legislation;

■ EC legal obligations directly entering English law and conflicting with the legal rule.

---

4   Although, as you will see in Chapter 5, judges interpreting words and phrases in court will often deal in the substitution of words.

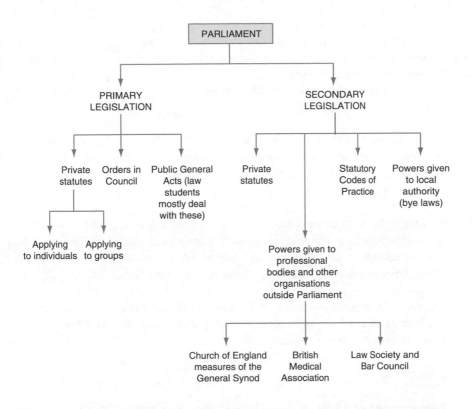

Figure 4.4 Types of primary and secondary legislation

Procedure for the enactment of primary legislation

There is a strict procedure determining the journey of draft legislation to the status of law. This will be considered in detail in English legal system courses, constitutional law or public law courses or institutions courses.

There are three main types of legislative act that can become a primary Act of Parliament:

■ **Public General Acts** mostly originate through the daily work of government departments and affect the general public. Some may be the result of implementing electoral promises. On occasion they can be created in response to public concern over a controversial problem.

■ **Private Acts** affect only specific private individuals or specific companies, or geographic areas and are actually advanced by groups outside of Parliament who are requesting powers that they cannot enjoy without an Act of Parliament granting them. They are used, for example, in relation to nationalised industries.

■ **Hybrid Acts** occur when only a small locality or group are particularly affected by the legislation in ways that may be onerous, but the legislation then permits work of national benefit and importance.

In addition there are:

■ **Private members' bills** which are non-government sponsored pieces of legislation which the government may or may not take over. If it is clear it has support it could finally reach the statute book as a Public General Act, a Private Act or a Hybrid Act.

In this chapter we will only be concerned with the detail of one of these types: Public General Acts.

Whilst prospective legislation is going through the processes required to become an Act it is called a bill, for example a public bill, a private bill or a hybrid bill (or a private member's bill).

It is worth noting that statutes can be enacted to consolidate existing law in a particular area, bringing together common law judge-made rules, customary legal rules, and/or existing legislation together into one statute. There are two types of statutes that work in this way:

■ **consolidating statutes** bring together disparate statutory provisions throughout the statute book and re-present them in a logical order. There is no change made to that existing law;

■   **codifying statutes** restate legal rules previously contained in a range of places: common law, custom and statutes. Not all codifying Acts get it right. A good example is the Theft Act 1968. It codified the common law and legislation in existence in the area of theft. After its enactment it was determined that there was still a problem with the drafting of deception and therefore the Theft Act 1978 was enacted to resolve the problem. But by the 1990s major issues were still arising with deception and the Theft (Amendment Act) 1996 was enacted. Continuing issues around fraud and deception later led to the Fraud Act 2006.

The procedure for enacting a Public General Act sponsored by the government
Often before legislation begins its journey through Parliament the government will canvass the opinion of stakeholders in the community. It may publish a completely exploratory report asking for general views, which is bound in a green cover and referred to as a **Green Paper**. Or it may issue a discussion paper with an attached prospective bill to generate more specific comment. Bound in white, this is called a **White Paper**.

Government bills are drafted by the parliamentary counsel. The civil servants in the relevant government department promoting the bill instruct counsel and by a rather strange convention the ministers who are actually responsible for sponsoring the bill do not see the instructions sent to parliamentary counsel by the department.

Each bill has three readings in both Houses of Parliament. However the House of Commons can ignore the dissent of the House of Lords using the Parliament Acts 1911 and 1949. These Acts only allow the House of Lords delaying power, not a total veto. It does not matter in which House the process starts, although the majority of bills are introduced in the House of Commons as illustrated in Figure 4.5 and described below. Note that for statutory instruments, the parent Act usually specifies the procedure for enactment. Either Parliament can ignore it unless it wishes to negative it, or it is laid before Parliament for approval, or no approval by Parliament is required.

The procedure for the creation of legislation

The House of Commons

First reading: A formality. The title of the bill is read and a time set for a second reading which conventionally should not be before the passing of two weekends.

Second reading: A main debate and a vote. If a majority vote is obtained the bill goes to smaller groupings of committees.

Committee stage: The bill is usually discussed by a standing committee of 16–50 MPs. Votes are taken clause by clause, after detailed scrutiny.

Report stage: In the whole House amendments are considered. There may well be attempts to undo changes previously secured at the committee stage.

Third reading: Final debate on the contents of the bill, but there can be a motion for no debate and to proceed to vote.

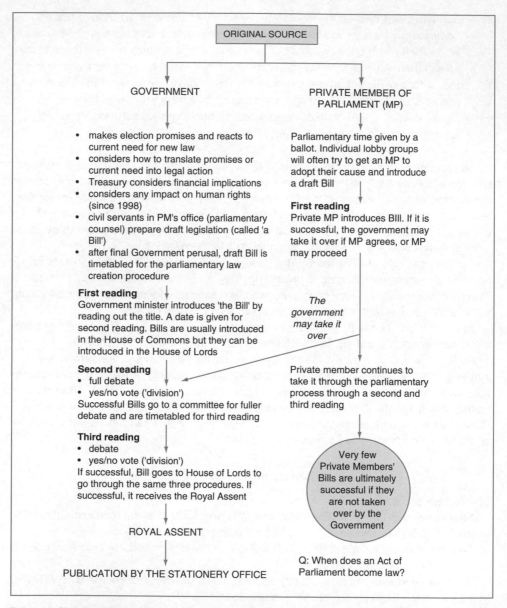

Figure 4.5 Standard procedure for the creation of legislation

The House of Lords

If the House of Commons votes in favour at the third reading, the bill is tied with green ribbon and sent to the House of Lords requesting their agreement to the bill. The procedure in the House of Lords mirrors that in the House of Commons.

The House of Lords has delayed and refused consent on several notable statutes in recent years including the Sexual Offences Amendment Act 2000 and the Hunting Act 2005.

Royal Assent

Even if the bill receives agreement from the House of Lords and the House of Commons it cannot become law until the monarch has assented to it. There is no legal rule that states the monarch must assent but by convention the monarch does always consent. The last time the monarch refused to assent to an act was in 1707. The Royal Assent Act 1967 provides for formal assent by notification and there just needs to be a formal reading in both Houses of the short title of the Act signifying assent.

Date in force of Act

Unless the statute states anything to the contrary an Act becomes law on the day it receives Royal Assent, and for the avoidance of doubt the whole of that day is included.

The date in force is an important aspect of legal method and you should carefully check in *Halsbury* or the UK Statutes Database the current position of individual sections in the statute. It may be the case that the whole of a statute has a delayed in force date (for example, the Equal Pay Act 1970 did not come into force until 1975) or that individual sections have delayed and different dates for coming into force. The statute itself may just contain a general permissive section stating that various parts of the legislation come into force on a day to be set by the minister by order.

The internal layout of legislation: a statute

There is a standard method of laying out statutes which, when recognised and understood, becomes a great help for analysis or evaluation. Most large statutes will be divided into **Parts** for ease of reference. Each Part will deal with different aspects of the overall collection of rules and their meanings. Each Part contains **sections** (often abbreviated as 's' (singular) or 'ss' (plural)) which give more details in each area. Where appropriate, sections will deal with definitions. Sections can be further divided with the use of arabic numerals into **subsections** (abbreviated as 'sub-s' (singular) or 'sub-ss' (plural)). Subsections are capable of further division, with the use of roman numerals, into **paragraphs** (abbreviated as 'para' (singular) or 'paras' (plural)). Paragraphs can be further divided with alphabetical ordering into **subparagraphs** (abbreviated as 'sub-para' (singular) or 'sub-paras' (plural)).

At the end of the statute, there will often be **Schedules** (a capital 'S' is always used) and these are numerically divided as well. These deal further with matters raised in the various parts. Schedules can only relate to previous sections in the Act. Schedules too

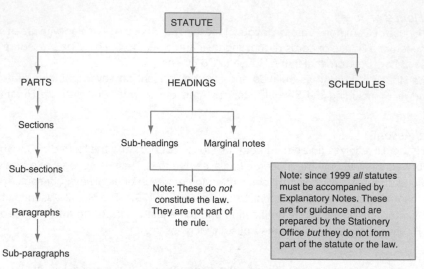

Figure 4.6 The general layout of a Public General Act that has been divided into its various elements

can contain Parts. They cannot create anything new without an anchoring in the main body of the statute. Statutes also contain marginal notes, headings and sub-headings. These organising devices, however, are said not to form part of the law.

Correct understanding of the relationship between parts, sections, subsections, paragraphs, subparagraphs, marginal notes, headings and Schedules enables the general layout of the Act to be ascertained. Assistance is also obtained from the 'long title' of the Act, (which looks more like a long sentence describing the area covered by the Act). Central to the analysis of statutes is the ability to understand how the statute is structured as a whole, and what the relationship is between the different areas of the statute. In more technical language we can say it is important to understand the intratextual (within the text) relationships. Figure 4.6 sets out the general layout of statutes and Figure 4.7 presents an annotated first page of the HRA 1998.

When approaching a statute as a new law student the most difficult task is understanding at a basic macro-level what the statute as a whole is striving to do *and* at the micro-level what each section is saying. As you gain proficiency in handling statutory rules you will find that it is not usually necessary to deal with the entire statute. The overall statute can be briefly contextualised and only relevant sections need to be extracted for detailed consideration, analysis, or application. However, knowing how the part fits into the whole, and being aware of connectors between sections, will make it easier to comprehend what is going on.

We will now look at a short case study to show the importance of combining English language and legal skills to obtain foundational understanding.

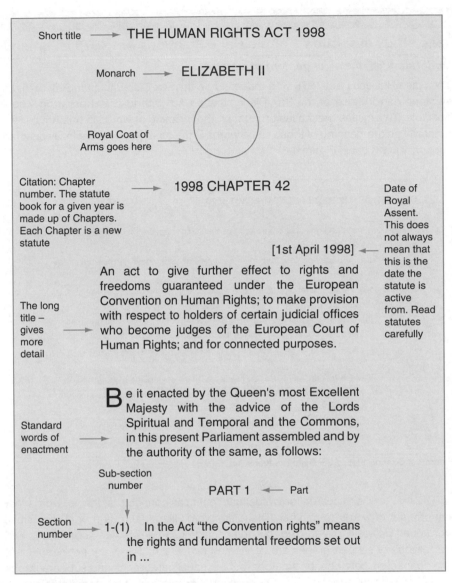

Figure 4.7 Annotated first page of the Human Rights Act 1998

CASE STUDY

A case study of section 1 of the Race Relations Act 1976 as amended

Understanding the arrangement of a statute

The Race Relations Act 1976 was modelled on the Sex Discrimination Act 1975. Its sections mirror those of the Sex Discrimination Act with identical phrasing where possible. This means that cases brought on the meaning of words in one Act can be authority on the meaning of those same words in the other Acts. As originally enacted section 1 is set out in Figure 4.8.

SECTION 1 (1) OF THE RACE RELATIONS ACT 1976

(1) A person discriminates against another in any circumstances relevant for the purposes of any provision of this Act if—

    (a) on racial grounds he treats that other less favourably than he treats or would treat other persons; or

    (b) he applies to that other a requirement or condition which he applies or would apply equally to persons not of the same racial group as that other but—

        (i) which is such that the proportion of persons of the same racial group as that other who can comply with it is considerably smaller than the proportion of persons not of that racial group who can comply with it; and

        (ii) which he cannot show to be justifiable irrespective of the colour, race, nationality or ethnic or national origins of the person to whom it is applied; and

        (iii) which is to the detriment of that other because he cannot comply with it.

Figure 4.8 Section 1 (1) of the Race Relations Act 1976

The first task is to search for words functioning as connectors, that is, words that link one set of words to another. These are words like *if*, *and*, and *or*. These small words can be easily overlooked, but they enable us to see which subsections and paragraphs or subparagraphs are connected and which, if any, are not connected. The connectors between the sections, subsections, paragraphs and subparagraphs reveal the type and function of the connection. For example, if the connector is '*or*' it is clear that the connector is indicating that *two* things are in the **alternative**. Or indicates an either/or situation. If the connector is '*and*', it is equally clear that the connector is indicating that two things **both** have to be present. There is a major difference between saying '1 or 2', or saying '1 and 2'.

Consider the connectors between sections, subsections, paragraphs and sub-paragraphs in Figure 4.8. If we write down a list of the sections, subsections and

Section 1 (1) ... if
(a) ... or
(b) ... but
(i)   ... and
(ii) ... and
(iii).

Figure 4.9 Linguistic connectors used in s 1 Race Relations Act 1976 as originally enacted

paragraphs, setting out only the connectors we obtain a pattern as shown in Figure 4.9. This linear format may not suit the understanding of everyone, but placed in a tree diagram with arrows indicating the flow of reading, the relationship between the section areas becomes more apparent. An example is shown in Figure 4.10.

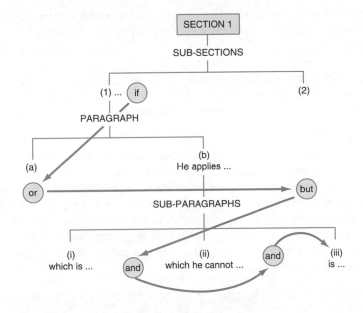

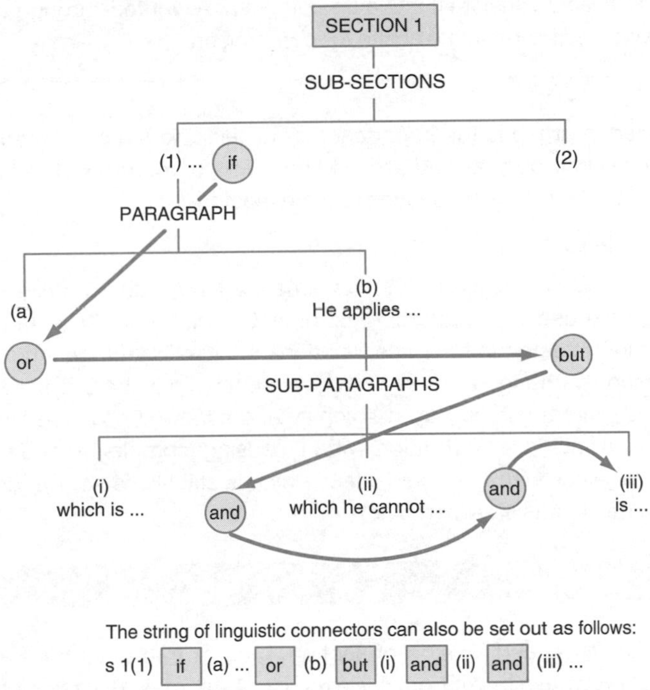

The string of linguistic connectors can also be set out as follows:

s 1(1)   if   (a) ...   or   (b)   but   (i)   and   (ii)   and   (iii) ...

Figure 4.10 Tree diagram of the connectors used in s 1 Race Relations Act 1976 as originally enacted

Look at the two figures and consider what can be ascertained from the seemingly abstract pattern, or the linear listing in text form. You should be able to draw the following connections:

- something in section 1(1) will be the case *if* something in paragraph (a) *or* (b) is the case;

- paragraph (b) is tied to subparagraphs (i), (ii), and (iii) by the connector '*but*';

- subparagraphs (i), (ii) and (iii) are all tied together by the two connectors '*and*' which occur at the end of subparagraphs (i) and (ii). This indicates that whatever is stated in (i) (ii) and (iii) all have to be present.

We have only focused on one section of the Act here but it is possible to represent an entire Act by virtue of a tree diagram as illustrated in Figure 4.11.

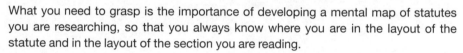

ACTIVITY 4.1: REPRESENTING AN ACT AS A TREE DIAGRAM

Take the HRA and translate it into a tree diagram. A worked-through version is available on the companion website for comparison.

What you need to grasp is the importance of developing a mental map of statutes you are researching, so that you always know where you are in the layout of the statute and in the layout of the section you are reading.

Amendments to statutes

Section 1 of the Race Relations Act was amended in a rather complex manner in 2003 through the use of a statutory instrument (a piece of secondary legislation made by authority vested in the Race Relations Act itself). And the amendment was made necessary by changes required by our membership of the EC. The amendment itself is a good example of the way in which amendments in English legislation occur. Text is inserted into the legislation, often causing complex renumbering. This amendment together with the original text which is still law is set out below Figure 4.12 (the inserted text is shown in bold).

ACTIVITY 4.2

Translate the amended version of section 1 into a tree diagram – and then review what you have learnt from this exercise. A full worked version of the tree diagram can be found on the companion website.

A further case study for breaking into statutes can be found on the companion website. It is annotated and will enable you to consolidate the work that has so far been done on domestic legislation.

THE UNFAIR CONTRACT TERMS ACT 1977 C50

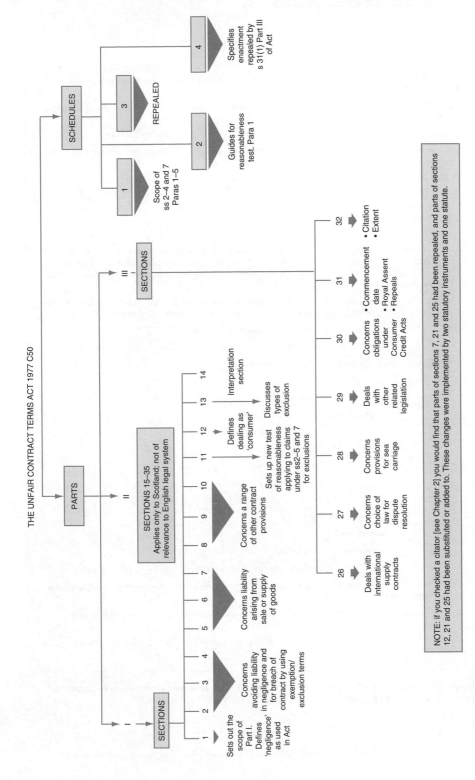

Figure 4.11 The layout of a statute

Section 1(1) of the Race Relations Act 1976 as amended by the Race Relations Act 1976 (Amendment) Regulations 2003

(1) A person discriminates against another in any circumstances relevant for the purposes of any provision of this Act if—

(a) on racial grounds he treats that other less favourably than he treats or would treat other persons; or

(b) he applies to that other a requirement or condition which he applies or would apply equally to persons not of the same racial group as that other but—

(i) which is such that the proportion of persons of the same racial group as that other who can comply with it is considerably smaller than the proportion of persons not of that racial group who can comply with it; and

(ii) which he cannot show to be justifiable irrespective of the colour, race, nationality or ethnic or national origins of the person to whom it is applied; and

(iii) which is to the detriment of that other because he cannot comply with it.

[(1A) A person also discriminates against another if, in any circumstances relevant for the purposes of any provision referred to in subsection (1B), he applies to that other a provision, criterion or practice which he applies or would apply equally to persons not of the same race or ethnic or national origins as that other, but—

(a) which puts or would put persons of the same race or ethnic or national origins as that other at a particular disadvantage when compared with other persons,

(b) which puts that other at that disadvantage, and

(c) which he cannot show to be a proportionate means of achieving a legitimate aim.

(1B) The provisions mentioned in subsection (1A) are—

(a) Part II;

(b) sections 17 to 18D;

(c) section 19B, so far as relating to -

(i) any form of social security;

(ii) health care;

(iii) any other form of social protection; and

(iv) any form of social advantage;

which does not fall within section 20;

(d) sections 20 to 24;

(e) sections 26A and 26B;

(f) sections 76 and 76ZA; and

(g) Part IV, in its application to the provisions referred to in paragraphs (a) to (f).

(1C) Where, by virtue of subsection (1A), a person discriminates against another, subsection (1)(b) does not apply to him.]

(2) It is hereby declared that, for the purposes of this Act, segregating a person from other persons on racial grounds is treating him less favourably than they are treated.

Note: S. 1(1A)-(1C) above were inserted by The Race Relations Act 1976 (Amendment) Regulations 2003 (S.I. 2003/1626), Regulation 3.

Figure 4.12 Section 1(1) of the Race Relations Act 1976 as amended by the Race Relations Act 1976 (Amendment) Regulations 2003

THE EUROPEAN INFLUENCE ON UK LAW

The European context of law is becoming increasingly important in the English legal system. The detailed content of these important European influences and sources of English law will be discussed in detail in other courses you will study. There are two main areas of major influence on UK law:

■   Since 1972, and the enactment of the European Community Act, large swathes of law in legislative form created by the institutions of the EU have legal effect in the English legal system because of our initial membership of the EC (set up in 1957 by the Treaty of Rome and joined by the UK when the government signed that Treaty in 1972). Now that community is the legal and political core of the broader creation – the EU.

■   Since 1998, and the enactment of the HRA, English courts must bear in mind the decisions of the European Court of Human Rights when deciding cases in the UK based on the articles in the ECHR. The UK government was a signatory of the ECHR in 1951 but it only achieved legal effect within the UK with the 1998 HRA. Before then individuals with claims under the ECHR had to pursue them at European level through the European Court of Human Rights: a costly and time-consuming procedure.

As you should note from reading the above, both of these separate sources of law spring from European treaties signed by the UK government. Subsequent to signature aspects of these treaties have then achieved legal effect in the UK through the enactment of UK (or domestic) legislation.

Not only has the incorporation into English law of these treaties changed the face of the law, it has also had an impact on standard English legal method with regard to interpreting legislation and case law. It has particularly impacted the judiciary, who have made changes to their standard methods of interpretation of statutes. In those areas where the courts have to consider the case law from the European courts they confront a major difference. There are not dissenting – or a plurality of – judgments; there is one determination of the court. In addition, European courts note decisions but do not give the detailed rationale for those decisions. It is both customary and necessary to note the rationale for decisions in English courts. This does not mean that English courts do not themselves give reasons in cases dealing with EU law or the ECHR but the cases it receives from the European level have to be incorporated into their decisions and these cases come from a different tradition where the detailed rationale for decision is not expected or required.

The template of European legislation and case law is very different to that of the English legal system. It is not based on rigid adherence to precedent. At the level of treaties and legislation within the EU there is a greater use of more open, textured language which allows much leeway to the court in individual cases. Again these matters are considered in detail in your other courses. But it is necessary to be aware of these changes and challenges to standard English legal method when dealing with the European dimensions of the law.

In order to appreciate properly the European dimension of the domestic legal system you need to be able to navigate your way around treaties, understanding their standard legal effect, their layout and the methods for allowing changes to a treaty, or for allowing a signatory nation state to sever its relationship with a treaty.

This part of the chapter is divided into three sections considering:

1.   reading and understanding treaties. This will ensure that you properly follow the discussion in the following sections;

2.   understanding the ECHR 1951 and the law relating to human rights;

3.   understanding the EC and EU treaties and legislation.

Reading and understanding treaties

Many students of English law encounter difficulties with the vast number of unfamiliar terms used when they turn to a consideration of the European influence on English law. Often, students do not appreciate the international nature of treaties and their normal effect, and confusions creep in. This section is therefore designed to provide a straightforward introduction to the general purpose and format of treaties.

Definition of a treaty

A treaty is a political agreement between two or more states. Treaties, conventions, charters, codes and agreements are in fact all treaties as defined by the Vienna Convention (despite the differing terms used). The sole difference between a convention and an agreement is that an agreement is usually signed by heads of government with no intention that it should be subsequently ratified by the state (for the meaning of ratification and the significance of signing, see below). A bilateral treaty is made between two states, a multi-lateral treaty is concluded between more than two states.

Legal effect

A treaty signed by the government is only subject to international law and has no effect on the English legal system. The nation states signing it are called contracting states and the treaty may, depending on its nature, be enforceable against contracting states under international law.

If there is the political will to translate all or part of the treaty into English law this has to be specifically by enacting domestic legislation. This primary legislation usually makes provision for later changes made necessary by the treaty obligations to occur through the use of statutory instruments which often use a quick method of making changes (usually referred to by the technical name of 'fast-track').

Naming a treaty

Every treaty has a formal name (which is usually abbreviated) and in addition many treaties are by custom referred to by the place where the treaty was signed, as shown in Figure 4.13.

1. The **Treaty on European Union 1992** (this is the treaty that established the European Union)

> Formal name: Treaty on European Union 1992
> Abbreviation: TEU 1992
> Place of signing: Maastricht. It is therefore also called the Treaty of Maastricht.

2. The **Treaty on European Union 1997**

> Formal name: Treaty on European Union 1997
> Abbreviation: TEU 1997
> Place of signing: Amsterdam. It is therefore also called the Treaty of Amsterdam.

3. The **European Convention on Human Rights and Fundamental Freedoms 1951** (despite the term 'convention' this is still an example of a treaty)

> Formal name of treaty: The European Convention on Human Rights and Fundamental Freedoms
> Also tends to be called 'The European Convention on Human Rights' or just 'the Convention'
> Abbreviation: ECHR
> Place of signature: London, but this is never used to describe the treaty.

Figure 4.13 Treaty naming complexities

The subject-matter of treaties

The potential subject-matter of treaties is unlimited; they can be about anything over which the government has authority. Treaties tend to contain two types of provision:

■   specific obligations that states agree to follow and enforce;

■   statements about ideals and expression of joint hopes, standing as statements of good intention.

An example would be the expressed desire of states to cooperate in co-ordinating developments in a specific area (for example, the treaties setting up the EU to cooperate in a range of areas).

The process of formalising agreement to be bound by a treaty

Once the matters to be included in the treaty are settled, the text is drafted, approved by all prospective states to the treaty and then officially 'opened for signature'. Such signature will be that of the head of government, or other authorised person, from each state and this person is the 'signatory'.

The signature is only an **expression of interest** by the relevant state. The whole government, or legislature, or people of each signatory state, in the usual manner for that state, has to agree to the treaty, allowing **ratification** of the treaty to take place. This marks the formal agreement by the state to be bound by the treaty as signed. An example of this two-stage process is Norway's application to join the EC in 1973. The government of Norway signed an accession treaty joining the EC. However, the people of Norway were not prepared to support joining and the government lost a referendum (a ballot put to the people). The government, therefore, could not ratify the treaty and Norway did not join the EC.

Exceptionally in the UK a referendum was held prior to membership of the EC and the 'Yes' vote obtained. At this point the treaty was ratified for the UK, consented to by the government and became one of the UK's international obligations. Ratification does not have any effect on the domestic law of the UK. Our constitutional arrangements do not allow this to occur and as we noted above separate domestic legislation has to place the treaty or part of it inside English law for it to have domestic legal effect.

The methods to minimise dissent in the negotiation process

When a treaty is being negotiated by a group of nation states it may well be the case that whilst one state may be in favour of most of the treaty there are matters under discussion which they find unsatisfactory and cannot at that time agree to. Rather than risk the whole treaty failing to be negotiated, which could be an international political disaster, methods have been devised to get round these potential serious problems.

Derogation

If the nation state agrees with the core of the treaty but does not wish to be bound by certain aspects of the treaty they can make this clear by entering what is called a **derogation**. They agree the treaty with the unsatisfactory item 'taken away': the state opts out of that aspect. A written record of the derogation is drawn up, signed by the state concerned, and attached to the treaty.

Reservation

If a state is potentially sympathetic to an aspect of the treaty but for political reasons (perhaps lack of support in the nation as a whole for that particular item) does not wish to agree that aspect at that time the state can formally say that they want to consider the treaty or modify it slightly, delaying agreement to a later date. This is done by the state recording a written **reservation** in relation to the operation of that part of the treaty in that state. As with derogations a written record of the reservation is drawn up, signed by the state concerned and attached to the treaty.

Changing a treaty

Treaties can be changed in several ways as indicated in Figure 4.14.

Cancelling an agreement

If a state wishes to cease to be bound by a treaty, it may sign an instrument cancelling its agreement. This is known as an **abrogation** and it is attached to the original treaty.

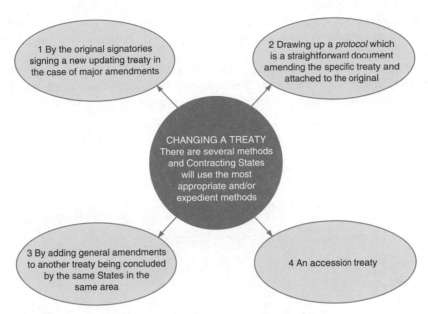

Figure 4.14 Changing a treaty

Official records of treaties

The Secretary General of the Council of Europe is the depository for European conventions, agreements and treaties[5]. The Secretary General keeps all of the originals and usually presides over their signatures. He or she also keeps the written records (instruments) of ratification or accession (joining other states to a treaty that has already been negotiated and ratified). These European documents are also registered with the Secretary General of the United Nations[6].

How do obligations entered into through treaties become part of English law?

If the UK government wishes all, or part, of a treaty, to become part of English law it must *specifically incorporate* the treaty, or part of it, into the English legal system via legislation. This legislation goes through the same procedures as other legislation. If the government expects the treaty to give rise to a range of other measures over time it will usually place sections in this legislation delegating the authority to make later legal changes to others (such as the minister of appropriate government departments). Whilst future changes are still the subject of parliamentary debate, an essential **fast-track procedure** is set up.

There is always the possibility that Parliament may refuse to enact the legislation, which would leave the government in an extremely difficult situation. However, the UK Parliament

---

5   The Council of Europe was established in 1949 in the aftermath of the Second World War to consider ways to improve and protect human rights and work towards greater unity in Europe. It is an entirely separate institution from the EU and is discussed later in this chapter. It promulagated and ratified the European Convention on Human Rights and Fundamental Freedoms 1951.

6   After the First World War (1914–1918) the League of Nations was established to promote peace and security and to protect human rights. After the Second World War (1939–1945) the League of Nations was superseded by the United Nations which was set up and in 1948 it adopted the Universal Declaration of Human Rights.

is usually controlled by the political party forming the government. The government would not risk the embarrassment of failure but would gauge its position in Parliament prior to signature of a relevant treaty.

Some treaties have a life at the level of international law only, as shown in Figure 4.15. The figure indicates that EC, EU and ECHR treaties and protocols have an effect at the level of international law and within the domestic legal system, hence the arrows going from

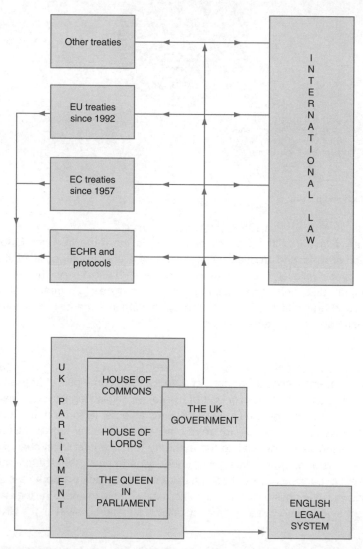

Figure 4.15 The relation of treaties to international and English law

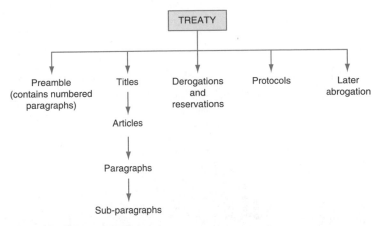

Figure 4.16 The standard layout of a treaty

these three boxes through parliamentary processes and then into the English legal system. The box labelled 'Other treaties' however, has not been incorporated into English law and only has an effect at the level of international law.

The standard layout of a treaty

A treaty, like English legislation, has a standard format, as shown in Figure 4.16. At the beginning of the treaty is a preamble setting out the main goals of the treaty and the aspirations of the parties. It is divided into clusters of items dealing with similar matters. Each cluster is called a title (which roughly equates to the parts within an English statute). Titles contain numbered items called articles, each one setting out a basic rule or principle. Articles can be divided into paragraphs and subparagraphs. The numbering system is Arabic and it is not as dense and complex as that used in English statutes.

Figure 4.17 summarises the matters that should be taken into account when handling treaties and Figure 4.18 shows how to break down an essential complex treaty, using the Treaty on European Union 1992. From the information given in this chapter you should now be able to construct similar diagrams for the Treaty on European Union 1997 (the Treaty of Amsterdam) and the Treaty of Nice 2000.

Understanding the European Convention on Human Rights and Fundamental Freedoms 1951

In 1998 the UK enacted the HRA. This Act made it possible for UK courts to hear cases concerning the breach of a large number of articles in the European Convention for the Protection of Human Rights and Fundamental Freedoms 1951 (a treaty that tends to be referred to as the European Convention, or as here, the ECHR). The ECHR was initially drafted and opened for signature in 1950 and ratified in 1951 by many members of the Council of Europe. In 1965 the UK government eventually gave UK citizens the right to take their grievances to the European Court of Human Rights to be heard under European law.

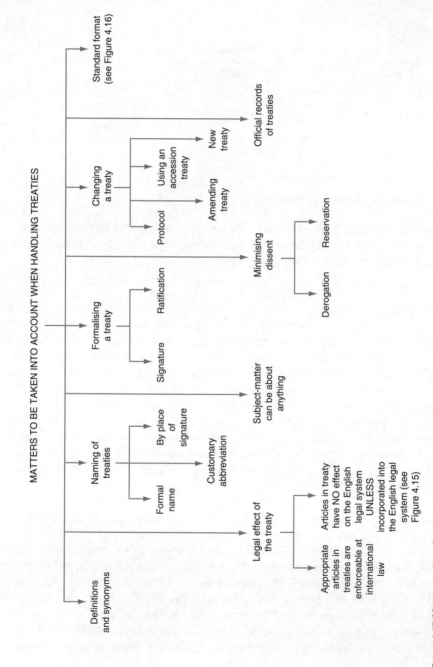

Figure 4.17 Matters to be taken into account when handling treaties

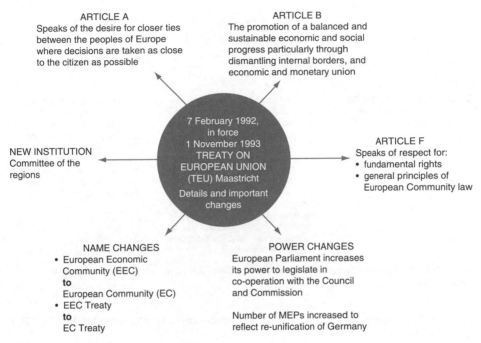

ARTICLE A
Speaks of the desire for closer ties between the peoples of Europe where decisions are taken as close to the citizen as possible

ARTICLE B
The promotion of a balanced and sustainable economic and social progress particularly through dismantling internal borders, and economic and monetary union

NEW INSTITUTION
Committee of the regions

7 February 1992, in force
1 November 1993
TREATY ON
EUROPEAN UNION
(TEU) Maastricht
Details and important changes

ARTICLE F
Speaks of respect for:
• fundamental rights
• general principles of European Community law

NAME CHANGES
• European Economic Community (EEC)
  to
  European Community (EC)
• EEC Treaty
  to
  EC Treaty

POWER CHANGES
European Parliament increases its power to legislate in co-operation with the Council and Commission

Number of MEPs increased to reflect re-unification of Germany

Figure 4.18 Breaking down a complex treaty

But the decisions of this court, whilst embarrassing for the government, had no legal effect on the government or between the parties, and at international law there was no provision for executing a judgment on the UK.

The rationale behind the ECHR is the protection of a series of agreed rights considered core to life, such as the right to life, to a family, to privacy, and to freedom from slavery. As the ECHR has developed through protocols, the ideology of rights now also includes economic, social and cultural rights and the right to economic and political determinism for states and indigenous peoples.

You will be referred to its force in a number of courses including public law, English legal system and criminal law.

The Council of Europe

The Council of Europe was established by the Treaty of London 1949 by Belgium, Denmark, France, Ireland, Italy, Luxembourg, Netherlands, UK, Norway and Sweden. Over time these founding states have been joined by nearly all the other European nations, with a current membership of 47. Any European state can be a member of the Council of Europe if certain basic minimum standards of conduct, particularly in relation to the observation of human rights and fundamental freedoms, are observed. In addition to setting up the ECHR 1951 which came into force in 1953, the Council established the European Court of Human

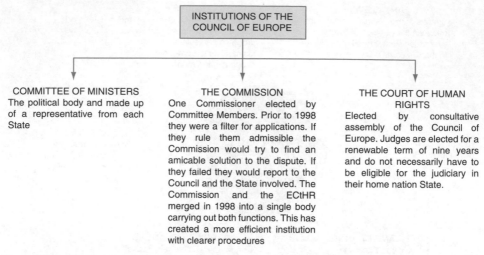

Figure 4.19 Institutions enforcing the European Convention on Human Rights and Fundamental Freedoms 1951

Rights in Strasbourg 1950 to ensure observance of obligations under the ECHR by member states.

The Council of Europe originally set up three institutions: the Committee of Ministers, the Commission of Human Rights (EComHR) and the European Court of Human Rights (the ECtHR), as set out in Figure 4.19. The last two were merged in 1998 to create a more efficient system for dealing with cases brought under the ECHR[7].

Although the Council of Europe has a working relationship with the EU it is not an institution of the EU. It should not be confused with the EU institutions of the Council of Ministers, or the Council of the European Union.

Relationship between the Convention and English law

As an international treaty the ECHR initially had no force within the English legal system and Convention rights were not enforceable in English courts. However, the UK government could be taken to the European Court of Human Rights by individuals. Between 1975 and 1990, 30 cases were brought against the UK and in 21 of these the European Court found that the government had violated the ECHR.

Although the ECHR had no force in the English legal system at the time, it was not ignored. English courts were indeed influenced by it. Judges in the House of Lords stated that they would presume that Parliament did not intend to legislate contrary to the ECHR. Therefore, when judges in court needed to choose between two possible interpretations, one conforming with the ECHR and one not, the interpretation in conformity with the ECHR was generally preferred[8]. In its judicial opinions, however, the House of Lords was careful to

---

7   For current information the official website of the Council of Europe (http://www.coe.int) is an excellent way of finding your way around this important institution.

8   See *R v Secretary of State for the Home Office, ex p Brind* (1991) 1 AC 696.

stress that it should not be assumed that such an interpretation *must* be applied, as judicial discretion remained.

By 1997, when the Labour government came to power, the number of successful applications against the UK in the European Court of Human Rights had risen to 50. One of labour's election promises was to incorporate the ECHR rights into English law, and in 1998 the majority of the rights in the ECHR were made capable of enforcement in UK courts because of the domestic HRA 1998. The HRA 1998 was enacted with an 'in force' date for the majority of its sections of October 2000. UK citizens can now bring actions under the ECHR in domestic courts.

The Act sets out the ECHR rights incorporated into the English legal system in Schedule 1. Not all of the articles in the ECHR have been put into the HRA The enforcement procedures and processes in the ECHR were *not* incorporated, *only* the majority of rights. A major omission is article 13 of the ECHR which places a duty on every member state to provide an effective remedy in national courts for infringement of the ECHR.

Section 4 of the HRA allows judges to issue a declaration of incompatibility with the ECHR but they cannot invalidate primary legislation. This limit seems problematic, and is directly caused by the decision not to incorporate article 13 which requires every state to ensure that there are appropriate and effective remedies in the national courts.

Consider the text of section 1 of the HRA, set out in Figure 4.20 and note the process used to lay out what is, and what is not, included in the Act. The long title of the Act gives an indication of the purpose of the Act.

Before the Act, UK citizens could go straight to the European Court of Human Rights. Now they must bring their action in the domestic UK courts. Article 35 of the ECHR states that individuals can only go to the European Court if all domestic remedies have been exhausted.

The remedies under English legislation allow for the following:

1. English courts and tribunals MUST take account of cases in the European Court of Human Rights and other relevant courts and decide cases accordingly.

2. English courts can note whether legislation is incompatible with the ECHR and if so issue a declaration of incompatibility. They have no power to declare primary or secondary legislation invalid, although they do have a power to invalidate secondary legislation *if* the primary legislation that it is based on does not forbid it. This severely limits the power of the judges to enforce the ECHR rights.

3. *If* Parliament decides that the incompatibility should be dealt with there is a fast track procedure for delegated legislation to deal with the speedy removal of the incompatibility allowing a 'remedial' order to be enacted.

4. Public authorities can be fined for contravention of the Act.

5. Courts must act in a manner compatible with the Act.

Author notes	An Act to give further effect to rights and freedoms guaranteed under the European Convention on Human Rights; to make provision with respect to holders of certain judicial offices who become judges of the European Court of Human Rights; and for connected purposes [9th November 1998].
This is the short hand term that will be used throughout the statute and is set out immediately and given a precise definition. In other States Convention rights mean all of the Convention rights but this statute narrows it to a specific meaning set out in paragraphs (a), (b) and (c) sub-section (1).	1(1) In this Act 'the Convention rights' means the rights and fundamental freedoms set out in –
Note Articles 1, and 13 and 15 are not referred to. *This list gives all the rights now to be claimed in UK courts.* *Protocols are late additions and these related to education, property, elections and death penalties.*	(a) Articles 2 to 12 and 14 of the Convention, (b) Articles 1 to 3 of the First Protocol, and (c) Articles 1 and 2 of the Sixth Protocol, as read with Articles 16 to 18 of the Convention.
'Opt outs'. *Time out to consider.*	(2) Those Articles are to have effect for the purposes of this Act subject to any designated derogation or reservation (as to which see sections 14 and 15).
	(3) The Articles are set out in Schedule 1.
Section 1(4) gives power to minister to make delegated legislation.	(4) The Secretary of State may by order make such amendments to this Act as he considers appropriate to reflect the effect, in relation to the United Kingdom, of a protocol.
Finalised.	(5) In subsection (4) 'protocol' means a protocol to the Convention – (a) which the United Kingdom has ratified; or
It is interesting that the minister has the power to create delegated legislation even if protocol NOT ratified (but this is qualified by s 1(6)).	(b) which the United Kingdom has signed with a view to ratification.
	(6) No amendment may be made by an order under subsection (4) so as to come into force before the protocol concerned is in force in relation to the United Kingdom.

Figure 4.20 Annotated text from section 1 of the Human Rights Act 1998

6.   All statutes must carry a declaration of compatibility with the HRA 1998 signed
     by the minister responsible for the original bill stating that the legislation is not
     incompatible or if it *is* incompatible that the government intends the legislation to
     be incompatible.

ACTIVITY 4.3: INTERPRETING THE HUMAN RIGHTS ACT 1998

1.   Obtain a full text copy of the HRA 1998 and set the text out as a tree diagram,
     using the method demonstrated above in relation to the parts and schedules of
     the Race Relations Act 1976. You can do this most quickly and efficiently by
     looking at the menu of parts and sections at the beginning of the statute, but
     note the HRA has no parts. You will have to decide how you wish to deal with
     the detail of the attached relevant articles of the ECHR and its protocols (found
     in the Schedules to the Act). You will also need to find a way of clearly indicating
     derogations and reservations noted in the ECHR and protocols.

2.   Consider the written text of the statute and your tree diagram. Which do you
     find the most useful when trying to understanding the areas covered by the
     statute? What in particular is more easily clarified by one method than the other?

3.   Now visit the companion website, where you will find a tree diagram of the
     HRA 1998. Compare your diagram with this version and note any differences.
     Do you understand why there are differences?

4.   Look closely and you should begin to see the interconnections, just from an
     appreciation of the basic headings of each section and Schedule. Although the
     Act has no parts, it does contain four Schedules, one of which lists all of the
     incorporated ECHR rights.

5.   Remember that matters referred to in Schedules only have legal effect in so
     far as the content of the Schedules is referred to in the sections of the
     statute. Look carefully to see what the relationship in this statute is between
     the Schedules and the sections of the main body of the statute. Recall that the
     excerpt from s 1(1)(a)–(c) of the HRA 1998 set out in Figure 4.20 lists these
     rights. In this particular statute you will find that one role of the Schedules
     is to set out the articles in the ECHR. Another role is to set out the protocols,
     derogations and reservations.

6.   Now amend your diagram as necessary.

We will be turning next to consider the EU. It is important to note that while the EU and the ECHR interact, the ECHR and the institutions remain firmly separate from the EU. These interconnections and interrelationships are shown in Figures 4.21, 4.22 and 4.23.

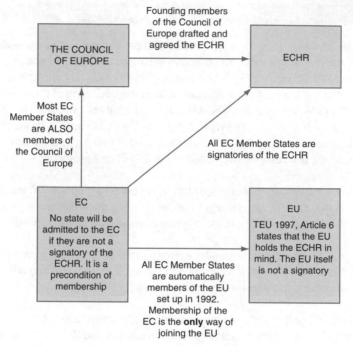

Figure 4.21 Interconnections between the ECHR, the EC and the EU

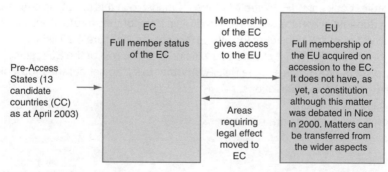

Figure 4.22 The links between the EC and the EU

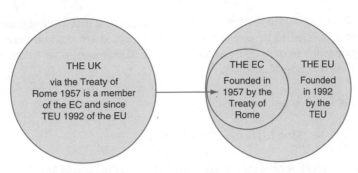

Figure 4.23 The interrelationship between the EC, the EU and the UK

Understanding the European Communities and European Union treaties and legislation

The relationship between the English legal system, and the terms EU and EC is relatively easy to explain. Three treaties concluded between the six founding nations (France, West Germany, Belgium, Italy, Netherlands and Luxembourg)[9] in the 1950s established three distinct European communities with a range of distinct and shared institutions:

■ The European Coal and Steel Community 1951 Treaty of Paris;

■ The European Atomic Energy Community (Euratom) 1957 Treaty of Rome 1;

■ The European Economic Community (EEC) 1957 Treaty of Rome 2;

The motivation behind the communities was joint ownership of resources and closer union in the aftermath of the Second World War.

In 1965 The Merger Treaty merged the institutions of all three communities although each community remains distinct. But references to the EC were, and still are, used to include all three. The main treaty remains the treaty setting up the European Economic Community (The Treaty of Rome No 2 1957). This treaty creates a legal order, the *acquis communautaire*, and, unusually for a treaty, demands that the law of the EC becomes law in each member state. In the UK this required specific legislation through the European Communities Act 1972. When a member state joins the community the technical term is that it accedes to the Treaty of Rome through a separate accession treaty.

The EU was firmly established by the member states of the European communities by the Treaty of Maastricht (1992) and the Treaty of Amsterdam (1997). These treaties are formally referred to as the Treaty of European Union 1992 and the Treaty of European Union 1997. The EU covers a range of areas of collaboration and cooperation between member states, as well as areas where member states have legal obligations imposed by the Treaty

---

9 Five of these were co-founders of the Council of Europe. The UK, whilst a co-founder of the Council of Europe, and instrumental in the moves to closer union in Europe, was not keen to join the communities. Instead it set up the European Free Trade Area (EFTA) with Austria, Denmark, Norway, Sweden and Portugal. When the UK did finally decide to join in 1961 France successfully blocked membership for just over ten years.

of Rome No 2 and other later treaties. It has been suggested that this cooperative element allows potential policies to be considered before decisions are made to make them legal obligations under the *acquis communautaire*. Now all references are to the EU. But it is important for you to understand that:

■   the EU only exists because of the EC;

■   the legal order of the EU is the EC legal order;

■   states can only become members of the EU by first acceding to the European communities, and then they automatically become part of it.

There are three main areas of collaboration and cooperation within the EU. These are customarily referred to as the three pillars of the EU, as shown in Figure 4.24. The architectural term 'pillar' is used to indicate a supporting structure. Activity in all three areas collectively makes up the EU. However political and legal power resides in the first pillar, containing the three original communities and the sole law-making powers.

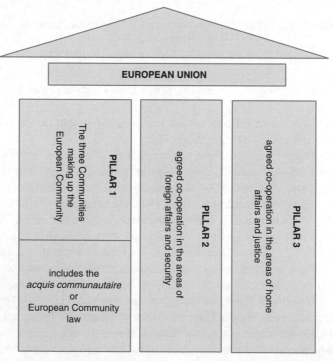

EUROPEAN UNION

PILLAR 1 — The three Communities making up the European Community — includes the *acquis communautaire* or European Community law

PILLAR 2 — agreed co-operation in the areas of foreign affairs and security

PILLAR 3 — agreed co-operation in the areas of home affairs and justice

Figure 4.24 The three pillars of the European Union

Clearly the EU is a much larger entity than the EC. The EC remains intact, but as one of three different spheres of activity. Remember, however, that the law-making powers of the EU are concentrated in the EC.

The EU is joined together not as a federal system of states (as in the US), nor as a range of states contracting at only a political level. The EU is a supra-national (that is, above the nations) union of states agreeing to be bound together in part politically, in part cooperatively and socially, and in large part through the unique legal order, the *acquis communautaire* ('community patrimony') or 'Community law'. This legal order has effect by being incorporated into the legal systems of every member state, and the English legal system is no exception.

It is the nature of the legal order that makes the EU unique. For, although the EU is established by treaties, it is not just governed by international law and political relationships based on agreement at intergovernmental level.

For all public intents and purposes, there is now only the EU. The official website[10] only refers to the EU and within its legal pages speaks of EU law. However, it remains true to say that to use that term is technically incorrect. The EU has no law-making powers outside those conferred by the founding treaties of the EC, so the appropriate phrase is Community law or EC law, not EU law.

Multiple names and dealing with changes in numbering of treaties
As you can see a variety of names can be used to describe the:

■ phenomenon that is the Union;

■ law in this area;

■ nature of the relationship between the nation states.

Some texts prefer the term 'Community', others use 'Union', or 'European Union'. With regard to the law different texts refer to 'Community law', 'European Union (EU) law' or 'European law'. The technically correct name is European Community law, or community law, but all of these terms are interchangeable and synonymous.

For the avoidance of doubt in the rest of this section the following terms will be used as follows:

---

10 http://www.coe.int accessed 16 April 2009.

■   'Union' when referring to the European Union;

■   'Community' when referring to the European Community;

■   'Community law' or 'EC law' when referring to European Community law generally;

■   EC legislation or EC case law when referring to a specific sub-division of Community law.

Another potential difficulty for students relates to the numbering of the articles in the key European Community Treaty – the Treaty of Rome 1957 (No 2). The articles in the founding Treaty of Rome have had their numbering changed, as the Treaty of Amsterdam sought to regularise the changes brought about by various amendments (including alphabetical amendments made by the TEU 1992). Articles in the Treaty of Rome use the following method. References in source materials therefore use the following protocols to denote numbering changes:

■   the *new* number of the article in the newly named treaty is given, with the *old* article number in brackets immediately following. For example, article 249 (189) EC Treaty;

■   in some cases the texts will only refer to the EC Treaty as EC.

These naming and numbering changes are summarised in Figure 4.25.

The treaties setting up the Community and the Union
Having given a basic introduction to the Union we will now turn to consider in brief the treaties that are important for the setting up of the Community and the Union. These have been chronologically listed in Table 4.1 and arranged via type and function in Figure 4.26. Currently there is one treaty awaiting ratification by all member states, the Treaty of Lisbon, which was signed by all member states in December 2008. There have been problems with two of the member states.

The institutions of the Community and the Union
The Treaty of Rome set up a range of institutions to make the Community function. It is relevant to consider this as many of them are able to pass legislative acts. The institutions which play essential roles in the law-making process, either as initiators of legislation or with the authority to make law, are shown in bold in the list below. The number of institutions has steadily increased in the intervening decades, as shown in Figure 4.27. Some of the most important and relevant for your purposes are the:

■   European Parliament;

■   European Commission;

- Council of Ministers;

- European Council;

- European Court of Justice;

- Court of Auditors;

- European Central Bank (ECB);

- European Investment Bank (EIB).

TABLE 4.1 IMPORTANT TREATIES IN THE SETTING UP OF THE EUROPEAN COMMUNITY AND EUROPEAN UNION (BY DATE)

Year	Place of treaty	Formal title of treaty	EC provision	*Abbr	EU provision	Type of treaty
1951	Paris In force 27/7/52	Treaty establishing the European Coal and Steel Community	Sets up the European Coal and Steel Community	ECSC	Pre-dates Union	Founding treaty
1957	Rome In force 1/1/58	Treaty establishing the European Atomic Energy Community	Sets up the European Atomic Community	Euratom	Pre-dates Union	Founding treaty
1957	Rome In force 1/1/58	Treaty establishing the European Economic Community	Sets up the European Economic Community	EEC Treaty now EC Treaty	Pre-dates Union	Founding treaty
1965	Brussels In force 1/7/67	Treaty establishing a single Council and Commission of the European Communities	The institutions of the three Communities are merged but the Communities remain distinct	Merger Treaty	Pre-dates Union	Merger treaty

Year	Place of treaty	Formal title of treaty	EC provision	*Abbr	EU provision	Type of treaty
1973	– 22/1/72	Accession Treaty	Ireland, Denmark, UK join the three Communities	–	Pre-dates Union	Accession treaties
1980	Athens In force 1/1/81	Accession Treaty	Greece joins the three Communities	–	Pre-dates Union	Accession treaty
1985	–	Accession Treaty	Spain and Portugal join the three Communities	–	Pre-dates Union	Accession treaty
1986	London In force 1/2/87	Single European Act	Paves the way for a closer economic union for the single currency	SEA	Pre-dates Union	Amending treaty
1990	–	Accession Treaty	GDR joins the three Communities	–	Pre-dates Union	Accession treaty
1992	Maastricht In force	Treaty on European Union	Sets up the Court of Auditors	–	Establishes the Union and idea of the European citizen	Founding treaty of the Union and amends EC
1997	Amsterdam In force	Treaty on European Union	–	TEU	Continues the establish-ment of the Union	Amending treaty
2000	Nice	Treaty of Nice Amending the Treaty on European Union, the Treaties Establishing the European Communities and Certain Related Acts	–	–	Working towards establishing a charter of fundamental rights and paving way for the European constitution	Amending treaty

(1) The European Economic Community was renamed the European Community.

(2) The founding treaty of the EEC, the Treaty of Rome 1957 that had come to be called the European Economic Community Treaty (or EEC Treaty as customarily abbreviated) was renamed the European Community Treaty (or EC Treaty as it is now customarily abbreviated).

(3) Sometimes you will find references to articles (such as 10EC) when the author has dropped the word 'treaty'.

(4) TEU 1992 inserted articles in the Treaty of Rome. This was mainly effected by using the alphabetical indicators A, B, C and so on, with subdivisions within the ALPHA runs. Textbooks published prior to 1993 refer to the old numbering; textbooks published later either refer to the new numbering with the old in brackets or to only the new numbering. Make sure you check the publication date of your text!

(5) Major numbering changes to the Treaty of Rome were introduced by the Treaty of European Union (TEU 1997), also known as the Treaty of Amsterdam 1997. The numbering of the articles of the Treaty of Rome was completely revised. Books and articles tend at present to use the new number with the old in brackets.

For example,
• 10EC (formerly 5) represents: Article 5 of the Treaty of Rome 1957 or the European Economic Community Treaty as amended by TEU 1992 (the name changes) and TEU 1997 (the number changes).
• 10 (5) EC Treaty could also be used instead of 10EC (5).

(6) Confusion can be caused when reading cases in the ECJ and books prior to the number and name changes. Remember that:
• The European Council is the name given to the meetings of the heads of government of members of the European Union. It was renamed The Council of the European Union in 1992.
• The Council of Ministers is the name given to the permanent body of government representatives that changes according to the issues debated (for example, agriculture, free movement of workers or taxation).
• The Council of Europe is the body established to protect fundamental rights of peoples. It has **no** connection to the European Community or the European Union. Those States who are members of the Council of Europe are also members of the EC and the EU, but there are also members of the Council of Europe who are not members of the EC and EU.

(7) In addition some names have been substituted by custom and practice rather than clear statement. For example, the institutions of the EU are the same as the institutions of the EC. Often they now refer to themselves as institutions of the EU carrying out their EU competency. For example, if you look again at the Race Directive in Figure 4.30 it states it is commissioned by the Council of the European Union. But it is secondary law with the legal competency of the EC, so the reference of the directive is Council 2000/43/EC.

Figure 4.25 Name and numbering changes introduced by the Treaty of European Union (TEU 1992), also known as the Treaty of Maastricht

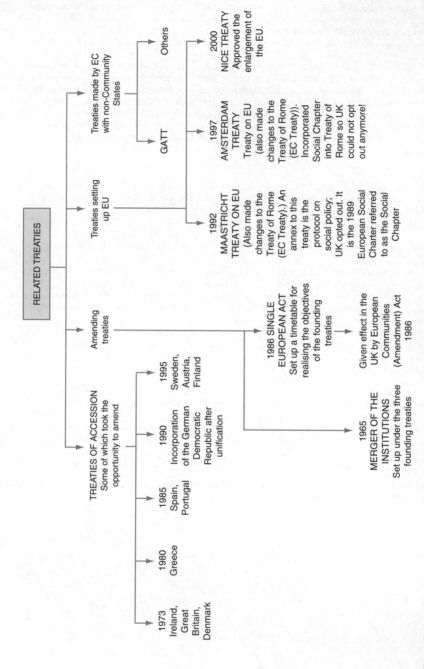

Figure 4.26 Important treaties in the setting up of the European Community and European Union (by function)

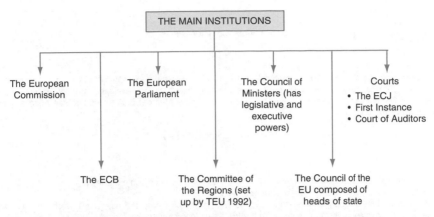

Figure 4.27 The main institutions of the European Union

Types of European Community law

There are several types of EC law each with *different* legal consequences. Some of the law developed in the Community immediately becomes part of the English legal system by virtue of the European Communities Act 1972. Other laws state a goal to be achieved within a timescale of three to five years and the governments of the member states are free to decide how best to comply with that law.

Perhaps the choice of available types of law is one of the most difficult to understand when approaching the area for the first time[11].

The main characteristics of EC legislation are that it:

■ is of several types;

■ is produced by different partnerships between the institutions;

■ has varying degrees of legal effect and legal consequences;

■ operates at the level of states but can also give individuals enforcement rights;

■ often immediately and automatically becomes part of the English legal system.

We will explore each of these attributes briefly below. As you read through these sections, bear in mind the tips in Figure 4.28.

European Community law is of several types

EC law can be divided into two main types: primary law (certain articles – not all – in the various treaties) and secondary law (EC legislation and EC case law). The Community's primary law was created by founding treaties and the source of all forms of secondary

---

11 You can read guides to the creation of legislation, and copies of all legislation and case law for the Union going back to the 1950s, on the Union website at http://www.europa.eu accessed 16 April 2009.

European Community Law

IS NOT

international law as NORMALLY understood or obligations between governments of states regulated by international law because Community law has the consequence that there is a limited transfer of sovereign rights from Member States to the Community, and the citizens of Member States also become citizens of the European Community.

European Community Law

IS

- a distinct legal order that every Member of the Community is bound by on membership.
- a legal order known as the *'acquis communautaire'*.
- a legal order that is specifically referred to in the TEU 1997 (the Treaty of Amsterdam) which clearly states that the Union is committed to maintaining the full *acquis communautaire*.

Figure 4.28 What European Community law is, and what it is not

Community law is derived from these treaties. The European Court has stated that one could consider the founding treaties together with appropriate changes in the related treaties as a 'constitution', because these treaties represent the supreme internal source of primary law and the facilitation of secondary law making.

Although this is the superior form of law, you should note that not all of the articles in a treaty constitute primary law. The EC Treaty lays out procedures to be adopted to determine when an article can be deemed to be primary law, and the European Court of Justice has also laid down guidelines. If a treaty is considered to be primary law, this becomes part of the law of the UK. Legislation is the secondary source of law along with ECJ case law as shown in Table 4.2.

Secondary legislation includes:

■ **regulations** addressed to all member states;

■ **directives** addressed to all member states (which can appear as framework directives giving quite detailed guidance for changes to a large area);

■ **decisions** addressed to named member states and/or individuals and organisations;

■ **recommendations** (not legally binding);

■ **opinion** (not legally binding).

as summarised in Figure 4.29.

TABLE 4.2 MAIN SOURCES AND TYPES OF LAW IN THE EUROPEAN COMMUNITY

Primary	Source	Effect on member state	Effect on individuals if criteria of precision, clarity, and lack of member state action
Articles EC in treaties	Member states	Directly applicable	Direct effect
Secondary legislation	**Source institution**	**Effect on member state**	**Effect on individuals if criteria of precision, clarity, and lack of member state action**
Regulations	Council and Commission in consultation with the European Parliament	Article 249 (189) EC Treaty says regulations are directly applicable and binding in their entirety	Direct effect
Directives including framework directives	Council and Commission in consultation with the European Parliament	Article 249 (189) refers to directives but does not provide for them being directly applicable. Binding only as to outcome, with states given a certain timescale of two–five years	Capable of direct effect after the timescale for action by the member state has been taken. This is referred to as indirect effect!
Decisions, including framework decisions	Commission	Article 249 (189) states they are directly applicable to those to whom they are addressed	Capable of direct effect
Recommendations	Commission	Article 249 (189) makes provision for them. Non-legally binding	No direct effect
Opinions	Commission	Article 249 (189) makes provision for them. Non-legally binding	No direct effect

Note: regulations, directives and decisions adopted under article 234 (189) must be signed by the President of the European Parliament and the Council of Ministers or the European Commission. Although they are published on the Union website, the published

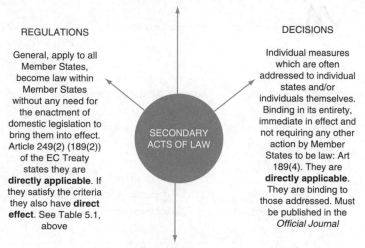

DIRECTIVES

Ask for a specific result within a timescale of one to three years. Addressed to **all**, **one** or **some** Member States. Member State has to take such action as it considers is necessary to ensure that the desired result is achieved. Binding in so far as it prescribes an outcome within a timescale. Not **directly applicable** (Art 249(3) (189(3)) of the EC Treaty). They can have **vertical direct effect** when timescale for government implementation has passed. TEU 1992 amended Art 191(2) of the EC Treaty and directives must now be published in the *Official Journal*. Article 169 of the EC Treaty allows Commission to commence enforcement proceedings for default

REGULATIONS

General, apply to all Member States, become law within Member States without any need for the enactment of domestic legislation to bring them into effect. Article 249(2) (189(2)) of the EC Treaty states they are **directly applicable**. If they satisfy the criteria they also have **direct effect**. See Table 5.1, above

SECONDARY ACTS OF LAW

DECISIONS

Individual measures which are often addressed to individual states and/or individuals themselves. Binding in its entirety, immediate in effect and not requiring any other action by Member States to be law: Art 189(4). They are **directly applicable**. They are binding to those addressed. Must be published in the *Official Journal*

RECOMMENDATIONS AND OPINIONS IN RELATION TO THE OPERATION OF COMMUNITY LAW

These have no immediate legal force. May be persuasive. The ECJ however has said that Member States should take them into account when deciding issues such as ambiguity in domestic law. Article 211C (formerly 155)

Note: Article 190 EC Treaty now requires that each legally binding Act contains a statement of reasons on which the law is based. It is possible for there to be inter-institutional disagreement on the basis of the law!

Figure 4.29 The different types of secondary laws in the European Community

version is produced in the *Official Journal* (OJ). For an example drawn from a directive, see Figure 4.30 and note the signatories.

Secondary case law comprises the decisions of the European Court of Justice set up by the Treaty of Rome No 2 (as amended) to deliberate on individual cases and on matters referred to it with regard to the appropriate interpretation of the Treaty of Rome. The legal authority for this power is found in article 234 (originally 177) of the Treaty of Rome. This is the situation when a court in a member state needs to have a word or a phrase in the treaty

COUNCIL DIRECTIVE 2000/43/EC

of June 29th 2000

implementing the principle of equal treatment between persons irrespective of racial or ethnic origin

ThE COUNCIL OF THE EUROPEAN UNION

Having regard to the Treaty establishing the European Community and in particular Article 13 thereof,

Having regard to the proposal from the Commission

Having regard to the opinion of the European Parliament

Having regard to the opinion of the Economic and Social Committee

Having regard to the opinion of the Committee of the Regions

Whereas

(1) The Treaty on European Union marks a new stage in the process of creating an ever closer union among the peoples of Europe

(2) In accordance with Article 6 of the Treaty on European Union, the European Union is founded on the principles of liberty, democracy, respect for human rights and fundamental freedoms, and the rule of law, principles which are common to the Member States, and should respect fundamental rights as guaranteed by the European Convention for the Protection of Human Rights and Fundamental Freedoms and as they result from the constitutional traditions common to Member States, as general principles of Community law.

[Another 26 general paragraphs follow]

CHAPTER 1

GENERAL PROVISIONS

Article I   Purpose

The purpose of this Directive is to lay down a framework for combating discrimination on the grounds of racial or ethnic origin, with a view to putting into effect in the Member States the principle of equal treatment ...

Article 16 Implementation

Member States shall adopt the laws, regulations and administrative provisions necessary to comply with this Directive by July 19th 2003 or may entrust management and labour, at their joint request with the implementation of this Directive as regards provisions falling within the scope of collective agreements ...

Article 18 Entry into force

This Directive shall enter into force on the day of its publication in the Official Journal of the European Communities.

Article 19 Addressees

This Directive is addressed to the Member States.

Figure 4.30 Specimen EC directive

defined and it will pause the relevant case before it and seek the ECJ's view on the appropriate interpretation of that word or phrase. The technical word for such referral is 'preliminary reference' and for the outcome of the court 'ruling on the preliminary reference'. When the reference is received the case in the member state continues. Its caseload has expanded and it is now assisted by the Court of First Instance and the Court of Auditors.

European Community law is produced by different partnerships between the institutions

EC law can be produced by the European Council, the European Commission or the European Parliament as well as institutions with the authority to act alone. These include the European Council and the European Court.

European Community law has varying degrees of legal effect and legal consequences

The legal effect and consequences differ depending on whether you are dealing with primary or secondary law.

With regard to secondary legislation, it depends on what type of secondary legislation it is. Some types of secondary legislation (directives) request that member states ensure a goal is achieved within a timescale, leaving it up to the state to determine how the goal should be achieved. These types of legal rules are said to be binding as to 'outcome'. Other types of secondary legislation (regulations) immediately place legal obligations directly into the legal system of all member states. These are binding in their entirety and said to be directly applicable. Still other types place legal obligations directly upon certain named states, individuals and organisations.

European Community law operates at the level of contracting states but it can also give individuals enforcement rights

Community law does not directly state that it gives individuals rights that they can enforce in their national courts. The legal rules are addressed in the first place to the Union and the member states. Yet under the founding treaties, member states are expected to enforce the rights, liabilities and powers that are a consequence of membership in national courts.

The ECJ has developed the concept of direct effect which describes EC primary or secondary law that gives individuals rights that are enforceable in their national courts. Direct effect is easier to prove in relation to regulations than it is in relation to articles and directives. The collective case law from the ECJ indicates that before any primary or secondary rule of EC law can give an individual the right to bring a legal claim (that is before any EC legal rule can be held to have direct effect) set criteria have to be held to apply as follows:

■   the legal rule to be the source of the claim does not require any action from the state (and directives do); and

■   the right to be enforced is clear and precise and the rule can be activated without recourse to the state (which is not the automatic case in relation to articles in a treaty concluded at state level or a directive issued to the state demanding certain outcomes within a timescale).

However, articles and directives considered on a case-by-case basis by the European and national courts have been held to give individuals rights.

European Community law can immediately and automatically become
part of the English legal system

Much Community law is immediately and automatically part of the English legal system as soon as it is enacted by virtue of authorisation for this being contained in the UK European Community Act 1972 as amended. A major difficulty is caused by the lack of uniformity of the use of the terms *directly applicable* and *direct effect*.

Directly applicable is the phrase used in article 249 (189) of the EC Treaty to refer to the process by which EC law of certain types is immediately and automatically part of the legal system of member states as soon as it is created in the Community.

The term *Direct effect* does not occur in any of the treaties. It is a phrase developed by the ECJ and consistently used in two different senses. It can describe both:

■   the process by which individuals acquire rights they can enforce in national courts, either against other individuals (known as horizontal direct effect) or against the state itself (known as the vertical direct effect);

■   the process by which EC law is immediately and automatically part of the legal system of member states as soon as it is created in the Community.

This *is* confusing, especially as some community law created by article 249 (177) of the EC Treaty is not said in the Treaty to be directly applicable in the sense of immediately and automatically becoming part of the legal system of member states. Yet the ECJ has held that such law can, if certain criteria are present, have direct effect. In fact, they have gone one step further and constructed a new concept, that of 'indirect effect'. It is indirect precisely because the law is not directly applicable but nevertheless an individual can enforce it in a national court.

From a pragmatic point of view there is a need to accept this confusion, and seek to derive the meaning of the phrase from its context. Some legal academics advise forgetting the issue, but this is like running away and will only create further confusion. The courts use the phrase synonymously. The EC Treaty, however, remains silent about individual rights in national courts and only uses the term 'direct applicability' to refer to the process by which EC law is immediately and automatically part of the legal system of member states as soon as it is created in the Community.

For the purposes of explaining some of the issues surrounding EC law, this text will assume an artificial distinction between direct applicability and direct effect, choosing to use the terms such that:

■   'directly applicable' applies to the process of automatic assimilation into the legal systems of member states.

■   'direct effect' refers to individuals deriving rights from EC law enforceable in national courts.

Principles of European Community law

Like all legal systems the legal order of the Community has developed certain principles that inform the interpretation and, to a certain extent, the creation of law. These principles are set out in diagrammatic form in Figure 4.31.

Legislative competency of European Community law

The institutions of the EC only have the power to make law in the areas given to it in Treaties. These are known as its areas of legal competency, and are set out in Figure 4.32.

The effects of European Community law on the English legal system

Now that you have a basic but reasonably secure understanding of the Community it is appropriate to turn to a discussion of the particular legal and constitutional changes to the English legal system and the English constitution caused by the political act of the UK joining the Community in 1973.

Article 10(5) of the EC Treaty stated that member states of the Community had to ensure compliance with EC law. Much of it was also intended to have an immediate effect in member states as soon as it was created in the institutions of the Community (remember the same institutions now serve the Union). Article 10(5) states that member states must:

> take all appropriate measures, whether general or particular to ensure fulfilment of the obligations arising out of this treaty or resulting from action taken by the institutions of the Community. They shall facilitate the achievement of the Community's tasks.

In other words, such law should automatically enter the legal system of member states. Article 10(5) was a major problem for the English legal system as it has no mechanism for this to occur.

The EC Treaty provides that the breach of any article by a member state can result in action brought in the ECJ either by any other member state, or by the European Commission. *Costa v ENEL* (Case 6/64)[12] (a landmark case) stated in no uncertain terms that:

> The treaty has created its own legal system which, on entry into force of the treaty, became an integral part of the legal systems of the Member States and which their courts are bound to apply. [A phrase that is known as the '*Costa* principle'.]

Furthermore in the leading EC case of the *Commission v Italy* (Case 48/71)[13] the ECJ declared that:

> if a national law is incompatible with European Law then all national bodies and national courts in the relevant Member State are to automatically cease to enforce that law.

---

12 *Costa v ENEL* (Case 6/64) [1964] ECR 1125; CMLR 425.
13 *Commission v Italy* (Case 48/71) [1972] ECR 527; [1972] CMLR 699.

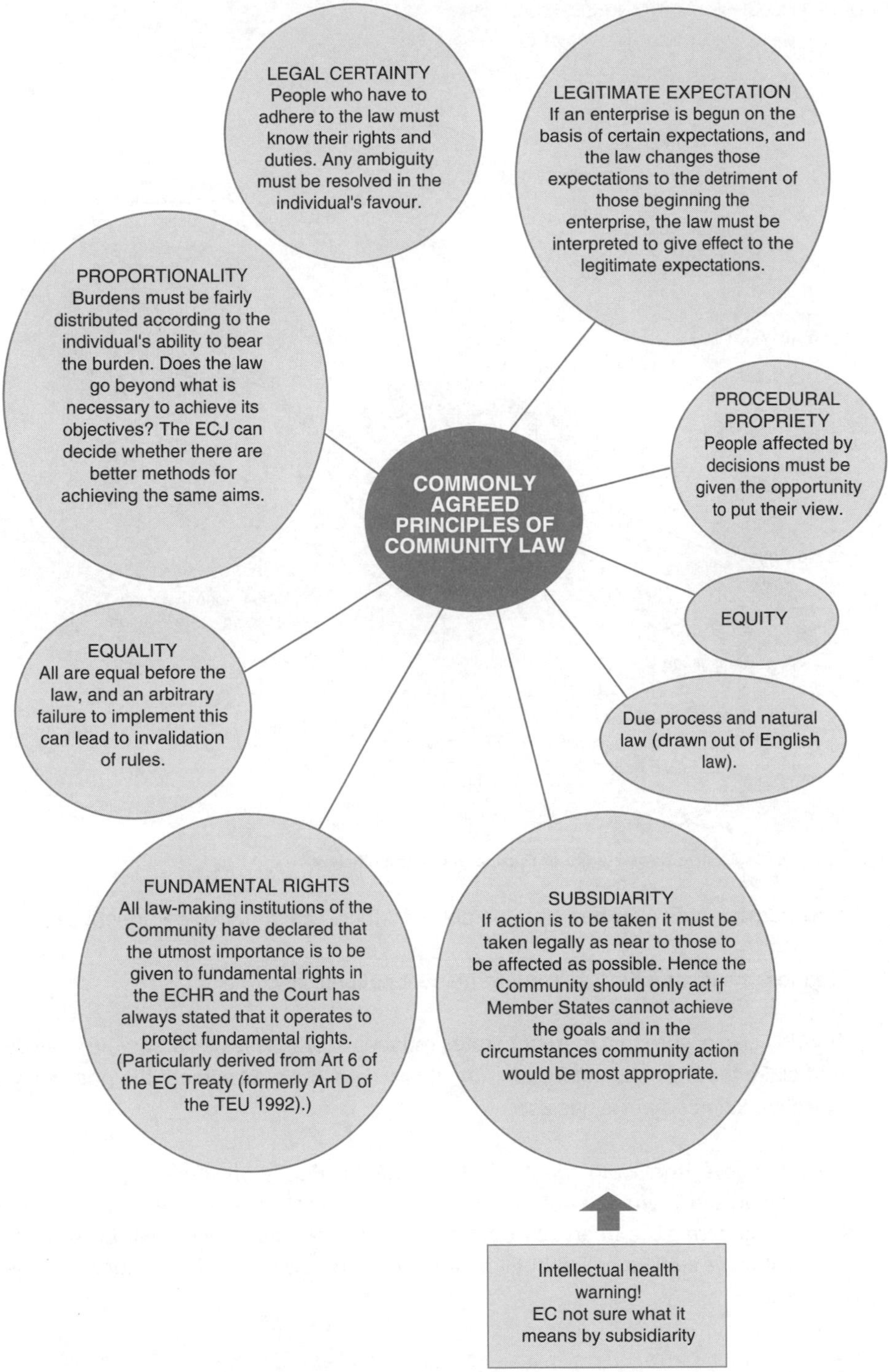

LEGAL CERTAINTY
People who have to adhere to the law must know their rights and duties. Any ambiguity must be resolved in the individual's favour.

LEGITIMATE EXPECTATION
If an enterprise is begun on the basis of certain expectations, and the law changes those expectations to the detriment of those beginning the enterprise, the law must be interpreted to give effect to the legitimate expectations.

PROPORTIONALITY
Burdens must be fairly distributed according to the individual's ability to bear the burden. Does the law go beyond what is necessary to achieve its objectives? The ECJ can decide whether there are better methods for achieving the same aims.

COMMONLY AGREED PRINCIPLES OF COMMUNITY LAW

PROCEDURAL PROPRIETY
People affected by decisions must be given the opportunity to put their view.

EQUITY

Due process and natural law (drawn out of English law).

EQUALITY
All are equal before the law, and an arbitrary failure to implement this can lead to invalidation of rules.

FUNDAMENTAL RIGHTS
All law-making institutions of the Community have declared that the utmost importance is to be given to fundamental rights in the ECHR and the Court has always stated that it operates to protect fundamental rights. (Particularly derived from Art 6 of the EC Treaty (formerly Art D of the TEU 1992).)

SUBSIDIARITY
If action is to be taken it must be taken legally as near to those to be affected as possible. Hence the Community should only act if Member States cannot achieve the goals and in the circumstances community action would be most appropriate.

Intellectual health warning!
EC not sure what it means by subsidiarity

Figure 4.31 Commonly agreed principles of European Community law

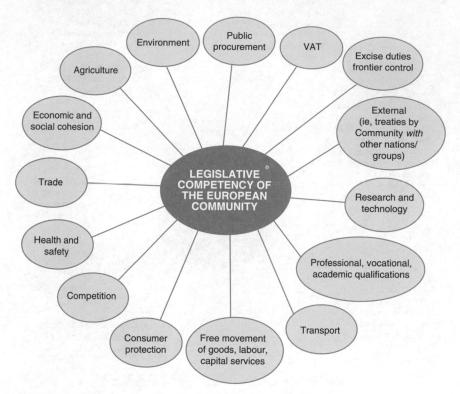

Figure 4.32 The legislative competency of European Community law

The supremacy of EC law has been established therefore from two perspectives:

■   treaties ensure that EC law is supreme over national law;

■   treaties also ensure that member states must have *processes* whereby the individual can claim the protection of EC law. (In other words, the right without the possibility of effective enforcement is useless.)

As noted above, the wording of article 10 of the EC Treaty (formerly article 5) is uncompromising and in order to comply with it the UK enacted the European Communities Act 1972 to incorporate the Treaty of Rome into UK law. The details of this will be studied in detail in substantive subject areas, but it is worth looking now at the key section, s 2, which provides that:

> where Community treaties give rise to rights, powers, liabilities, and obligations these shall be recognised in UK courts along with any remedies and procedures

provided by the treaties. Provision is made for the Queen by an Order in Council (or a minister by regulation) to make provisions for implementing Community obligations.

Note the delegation to a minister and the use of statutory delegated legislation signalled by the phrase 'Order in Council'. This means that the full parliamentary procedure for the enactment of legislation does not have to be involved, it is fast tracked[14]. No such fast-track power is given in the area of taxation, delegated legislation, creation of new criminal offences with certain punishments, or retrospectivity (making lawful action unlawful and backdating the operation of the law). In these cases, Parliament itself must enact legislation.

Community law impinges in several ways on our reading of English law, as shown in Figure 4.33. It is expected, for example, that in certain situations an English court, or any domestic court, considering an important point of EC law will refer to the European Court for a preliminary ruling as to the correct interpretation of the treaty. Under article 234 (177) of the EC Treaty, courts from which there is no recognised national appeal *must ask* for a preliminary ruling from the ECJ. Other courts where there is an appeal *may ask* for a preliminary ruling. This gives an important power to the ECJ to ensure uniformity in the development of EC law and the official interpretation of the treaties.

Having considered the standard definition and layout of treaties, and the complex relationship between domestic and European legislation it is now appropriate to turn and consider the relationship between the judges and domestic and European legislation when it arises for consideration in court and where the judges engage in statutory interpretation.

STATUTORY INTERPRETATION: CONSIDERATION OF LEGISLATION BY THE COURTS

The majority of law cases deal with the legal rules created by Parliament, as well as law created by delegated parliamentary authority. Although Chapter 5 will address reading law cases in detail, it is useful to introduce here the question of the role of the judiciary in determining the meaning of statutory words or phrases.

Given the discussion in Chapter 3 concerning the flexibility of language and the problems of interpretation, it should be no surprise to note that issues of tremendous importance can be raised when a problem about the meaning of a statutory provision goes before a court. How do judges interpret statutes? The ability to have the final say in this manner gives unelected judges unprecedented power to determine the meaning of words in legislation enacted by the democratically elected parliament[15]. Remember that, unlike politicians, judges are not democratically elected to their positions by local electorates but are appointed.

---

14 Similar fast-track procedures are in place under the HRA 1998.
15 It is also worth noting here that if a given parliament has a substantial government majority (that is, there are a large number of government MPs compared with representatives from other parties) then it is the government of the day that gets through the legislation that it wants, which may not be a democratic representation of the will of the majority of the people.

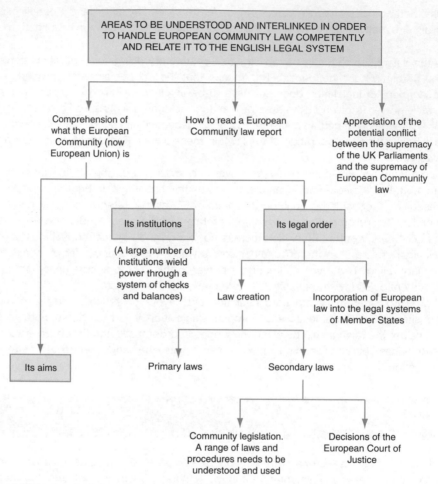

Figure 4.33 Areas to be balanced when engaging with European Community law

When judges engage in statutory interpretation they have to:

■   apply legislative rules to various fact situations;

■   decide the meaning of words and phrases used in the statute (of course words can mean many things, and that meaning can change over time);

■   deal with judicial disagreement over the meaning of words.

A range of so-called rules of interpretation have been developed over time by the senior judiciary for use in court.. There are three *known* rules of statutory interpretation:

■   the literal rule;

■   the golden rule;

■   the mischief rule.

We will now look at each in turn.

The literal rule

Essentially this rule states that words should always be given their ordinary, plain and literal meaning. If the words are clear those words state Parliament's intention. Judicial decisions going back over 100 years agree that this rule is important for preserving the intention of Parliament and ensuring the democratic parliamentary will is imposed by judges in courts.

One of the more interesting cases to demonstrate the literal rule is *Whiteley v Chappel* (1868)[16]. This is a criminal case where Whiteley was charged with impersonating a 'person entitled to vote'. The person that Whiteley had chosen to impersonate was dead. The argument put forward in court was that a dead person could not vote, or more strictly according to the wording of the legislation was not 'entitled to vote'. Thus, as the defendant had therefore impersonated someone who was not entitled to vote the offence had not occurred. The judges agreed with this argument.

On a literal interpretation of the words of the offence of impersonating a 'person entitled to vote' this causes no problems. But is it not equally clear that if Parliament had been asked if they had intended the offence to cover the circumstances of the case against Whiteley they would have replied 'Yes!' Indeed it is unlikely they would have said 'No'. This case demonstrates the ways in which it is impossible for a literal interpretation to clearly cut across the intention of Parliament. You may of course think that the legislators in Parliament should have been more careful with their use of words in the legislation, to ensure that it covered all possibilities. But here is the dilemma. Should the judges, in deciding cases to their satisfaction in court, fill in gaps in legislation or is that the job of the legislator? If they can fill in gaps in specific cases that would mean that one of the parties to the case received a result that they not only dislike, but that they know Parliament did not intend. Which is the correct path for justice and for interpretation?

Drafting legislation is not a scientific art and there will always be mistakes when the generalised words of a section in a statute do not cover all the specific instances it should cover. In *Whiteley*, the statute was designed to stop fraudulent voting at elections by people pretending they were someone else. Parliament only wished those entitled to vote to do so. Whitely was not entitled to vote. But, as the statute did not list the specific

---

16 *Whiteley v Chappel* (1868) LR 4 QB 147.

scenario of his case, he was acquitted[17]. What do you consider to be the best way out of this situation if it arose in court?

The golden rule

Keep the facts of *Whiteley* in your mind, and consider whether it would have been useful to apply the second rule of statutory interpretation: the golden rule in the case. This rule states that the literal rule should be followed except on those occasions when to apply the literal rule would lead to absurd results or go against public policy. Would you argue that the decision in *Whiteley* led to absurdity? Much would depend on your view of the role of the courts to fill in gaps in the legislation. You may think that the decision was in keeping with the section stating the offence and that as there was not another section covering the situation Whiteley should have been acquitted and Parliament should amend the legislation to cover the situation if they so wished. Another may say that it is absurd that Whiteley was acquitted. One person's absurdity may be another person's correct interpretation.

Another classic case illustrates the golden rule in operation: *R v Sigsworth* [1953] Ch 89. Sigsworth had murdered his mother who had died without making a will. This situation was covered by the Administration of Estates Act 1925 which provided that in the case of a person dying without making a will (the technical term is 'intestate') the possessions and lands of the person go to the next of kin. In this case, the next of kin was the son, Sigsworth. The court ruled that in a case such as this it would be absurd to allow the son who had murdered his mother to profit from her death. It refused to allow him to inherit. However, there was also another principle of law in operation here as well, that a person cannot benefit from his own wrong.

ACTIVITY 4.4: CHECK YOUR UNDERSTANDING OF LAW CASE CITATIONS

1. Why is the year in the citation for *Whiteley v Chappell* in round brackets (1868) and the year in the citation for *R v Sigsworth* in square brackets [1953]?

2. Where in the hierarchy of law reports is the case of *R v Sigsworth*? (Hint: what does Ch 89 mean?)

If you need reminding, go back to Chapter 2.

The mischief rule

Think of the *Whiteley* case again, as we move on to discuss the last of the three main rules of statutory interpretation: the mischief rule. This rule in fact predates the previous two, finding its source in *Heydon's* case (1584) 3 Co Rep 7a.

---

17 The Law Commission 21 stated very forcefully that the main problem with the literal rule was that it places 'undue emphasis on the literal meaning of the words of a provision' and this in turn 'assumes an unattainable perfection in draftmanship'.

ACTIVITY 4.5: CHECK THE CITATION

Can you remember which law report series this is now in, and who the author referred to by the abbreviation 'Co' is?

If you need reminding, go back to Chapter 2.

The mischief rule states that if conditions of doubt arise the judge can look to the purpose of the act and the mischief (the wrong) that it was supposed to remedy or prevent. The initial rationale for legislation was to correct weaknesses in the existing common law. So if a problem with interpretation arose in the court the judge chose the interpretation that best remedied the weakness in the common law. However, it was also extended to cover later legislation and new legislation dealing with mischiefs.

A more recent statement, made in 1980 by Lord Diplock in the case *Jones v Wrotham Park Settled Estates* (1980)[18] made clear the usefulness and current status of this rule.

In his judgment Lord Diplock took the opportunity to state that three questions should be answered in the affirmative to enable a court to operate the mischief rule when interpreting legislation:

1.   Can the court precisely ascertain the mischief the Act was intended to remedy?

2.   Is it apparent that the Act failed to deal with it?

3.   Is it possible just to state what additional words read into the Act would rectify the situation?

Would this have been of use in *Whiteley v Chappell*? The court could have answered 'Yes' to questions 1 and 2 above. And no doubt a few words aptly inserted into the relevant section would have resolved the situation. Why do you think they did not themselves think of applying the mischief rule?

ACTIVITY 4.6: CHECK THE CITATION

What court is this case decided in? **Hint:** You can tell from just the citation.

If you need reminding, go back to Chapter 2.

The mischief rule has been used in an extremely important case relating to an issue raised by the Royal College of Nursing (RCN) as to the correct interpretation of the phrase 'registered medical professional', particularly as used in abortion legislation. Does it refer

---

18 *Jones v Wrotham Park Settled Estates* (1980) AC 74.

just to a doctor or could a nurse be a valid 'registered medical professional'? The RCN took the Department of Health and Social Security to court over the issue. The court held by a three to two majority that operations by nurses alone were lawful as the purpose of the Act was to stop back street abortions by medically unqualified persons[19].

The purposive approach

The mischief rule has been developed into the 'purposive approach', which locates a suitable interpretation that gives effect to the general purpose of the legislation. It is an approach of increasing importance and was recognised by Lord Steyn relatively recently in the House of Lords case of *R (Quintavalle) v SS Healh* [2003] 2AC 687. During the course of his judgment, Steyn stated:

> The pendulum has swung towards purposive methods of construction. This change
> . . . has been accelerated by European ideas . . . the shift towards purposive inter-
> pretation is not in doubt.

The three main rules are summarised in Figure 4.34, below.

The teleological approach

One can also refer to a fourth possible rule, described as the teleological approach. This asks for a further leap in interpretation from the more narrow constraints of locating the mischief the Act is designed to remedy, of the locating of its purpose, to looking at the *spirit* of the Act. This approach takes a much broader view of the legislation and is useful when considering EC law, which presents particular problems for the English courts as it is drafted by the legislator in much broader terms than is the style of English legislative drafting. European law refers to broad principles, leaving the courts a great deal of leeway relating to interpretation. Indeed, the courts must make use of this leeway as they cannot find the information they need in the detail of the words in the law.

When Parliament enacted the European Communities Act 1972, s 2(4) it bound UK courts to take into account all legal rules arising from treaties or other forms of European law and to interpret cases in court (within the areas under the jurisdiction of our member-ship of the Union) in accordance with EU law. Often it is necessary for courts to take into account issues such as socio-economic policy. There are many examples of this happen-ing particularly in relation to sex discrimination, racial discrimination and more recently age and religious discrimination, in the workplace.

There are other rules of interpretation developed by judges. For example presumptions, linguistic rules and intrinsic (inside the text) and extrinsic (outside the text) aids or rules to interpretation[20]. We will now briefly consider these.

Presumptions

Presumptions represent the accepted judicial view of a range of circumstances that have been predetermined to be the way in which every manifestation of those circumstances will

---

19 *The Royal College of Nursing v DHSS* [1981] 1 All ER 545.
20 There are also probably many *unknown* rules. For example, the '*gut-feeling rule*'!

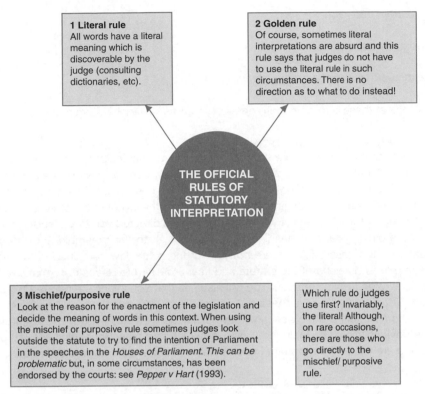

1 Literal rule
All words have a literal meaning which is discoverable by the judge (consulting dictionaries, etc).

2 Golden rule
Of course, sometimes literal interpretations are absurd and this rule says that judges do not have to use the literal rule in such circumstances. There is no direction as to what to do instead!

THE OFFICIAL RULES OF STATUTORY INTERPRETATION

3 Mischief/purposive rule
Look at the reason for the enactment of the legislation and decide the meaning of words in this context. When using the mischief or purposive rule sometimes judges look outside the statute to try to find the intention of Parliament in the speeches in the *Houses of Parliament*. *This can be problematic* but, in some circumstances, has been endorsed by the courts: see *Pepper v Hart* (1993).

Which rule do judges use first? Invariably, the literal! Although, on rare occasions, there are those who go directly to the mischief/ purposive rule.

Figure 4.34 The official rules of statutory interpretation

be viewed, until any evidence to the contrary is produced. These tend to arise from theoretical and practical principles of the law. Examples of presumptions are:

■ legislation does not intend to change the common law unless this is clearly expressed;

■ legislation does not have retrospective effect (it cannot make unlawful lawful behaviour that occurred prior to the legislation being enacted);

■ Parliament does not intend to bind the Crown by law if this is not clearly expressed;

■ legislation does not intend to prohibit judicial review unless this is clearly expressed.

Linguistic rules

Linguistic rules apply to the way in which judges will approach the language of legislation in certain circumstances. These rules are known by their Latin tags as:

- *ejusdem generis;*

- *noscitur a sociis;*

- *expressio unius est exclusio alterius.*

You will look at these in rules in more detail in your English legal system course.

Intrinsic aids to interpretation

Intrinsic aids to interpretation are the signposts *within* a particular piece of legislation to assist the reader to make sense of it (often referred to as aids being within the four corners of the legislation). Taken to its logical conclusion this suggests that the whole of the statute needs to be referred to for meaning. If you look back to the layout of the statutes shown at the beginning of this chapter you will note that arrows directed you to the short and long titles, to marginal notes and headers (such as Part 1), to the preamble and of course punctuation. All of these devices are *not* part of the actual law contained in the statute but they point to divisions of the statute and its words, and to issues of formatting. They are, as such, aids to interpretation. You will also see that Schedules are referred to as well as Parts. Not all statutes have these but when they are present there may be a separate interpretation section, or such a section may be included in the main body of the statute. All of these devices should be included. Unlike other intrinsic aids, Schedules are part of the statute and are extremely important in determining the meaning of words or phrases.

Extrinsic aids to interpretation

Extrinsic aids to interpretation are the signposts *outside* a particular piece of legislation which assist the reader to make sense of it. These are of several types. There is a generic interpretation statute, the Interpretation Act 1978 that gives a definition of words commonly found in statutes. For example it states in section 6 that words referring to the masculine gender include the feminine (and vice versa). But be warned: any statute can give a different interpretation to these words. Additional extrinsic aids are described below.

Reference to earlier statutes using the same word

Courts are able to look at the use of some words in earlier statutes for guidance on the meaning of a word, as long as it is clear that the use of the word is about the same matter. The Latin term *in pari materia* is used to denote this condition.

Dictionaries

If a word has no recognisable legal meaning the court is permitted to consult a dictionary[21]. However, since words can change their meaning over time, different editions of dictionaries may include different definitions. Obvious words whose meanings have changed would include, for example, 'gay'. Each dictionary could also give a different perspective on a word. Which is the 'right' one?

---

21 The companion website exercises connected to Chapter 2 refer to exercises based on a reading of the case of *Mandla v Dowell Lee* [1983] 2 AC 803 which concerned ascertaining the meaning of the word ethnic, and there is a good demonstration of the problems of dictionaries and the meaning of the word in the judgment of Lord Denning in the Court of Appeal.

Travaux préparatoires

In many European legal systems working from variants of Roman law within civil code systems, courts are able to study public materials produced during the course of the journey from a draft to finalised legislation. These documents are referred to as preparatory works or *travaux préparatoires*.

Hansard

Traditionally UK judges were not permitted to look at documents produced before the Act was drafted (for example, government reports, recommendations or other policy documents), or at any proceedings in Parliament as the Bill was going through its journey to becoming an Act. These latter documents are recorded verbatim by Hansard. The underlying rationale for not allowing access to this material is the fact that Article [IX] of the Bill of Rights 1689 allows MPs to say what they wish within Parliament, stipulating that 'Parliament ought not to be . . . questioned in any court of law or place outside Parliament'. This had been widely interpreted to mean that it was not even permissible to look at Hansard, the verbatim record of the debates and committees in Parliament.

However, a change was signalled in the case of *Pepper v Hart* [1993][22]. The judges in the House of Lords were of the opinion that Hansard could be referred to if:

■ the legislation that is the object of the statutory interpretation is ambiguous, obscure or leads to absurdity;

■ the document relied on relates to statements by the minister or promoter of the legislation, together with any other parliamentary documents as necessary to understand such statements;

■ the statements relied upon are clear.

The House said that this should only happen in rare cases, not as a matter of course. Six judges were in agreement with this course of action but one, Lord Mackay, dissented. He argued that the practicalities involved would be tremendously expensive. Lord Bridge considered that the court would not use its power very much, although he was initially proved wrong. However, concurrent with the greater use of this freedom, drawbacks became apparent. Exactly how much ambiguity sufficed to open Hansard, and how clear must the minister's statement be? By 1996 the House of Lords was voicing concern about the use of *Pepper v Hart*[23]. Lord Steyn[24] has even severely criticised *Pepper v Hart* in non-judicial situations such as after-dinner speeches or public lectures. The main issue is that, of course, any word in a statute can in certain contexts be thought ambiguous. Opening up Hansard for discussion and determination by the judges raised the possibility that understanding concerning the meaning of words and phrases could be completely overturned.

---

22 *Pepper v Hart* [1993] 1 All ER 42 (HL).
23 Brown Wilkinson LJ was one of the majority judges in *Pepper v Hart*, but in *Melliush (Inspector of Taxes) v BMI (No 3)* [1996] AC 454 said that the ministerial statement had to be directed to the very point that is the subject of doubt in the current case.
24 Steyn J 'Pepper v Hart' A Re-examination' (2001) 21 Oxford Journal of Legal Studies 59.

In 1995 a practice direction was issued relating to the usage of Hansard material for the purposes of statutory interpretation[25]. This was repeated in a later consolidating practice statement in 1999 covering the Court of Appeal (Civil Division)[26] and then later the criminal courts[27]. If a party to a case wishes to rely on Hansard, they must serve copies of the extract and a short précis of their argument on the other party or parties at least five working days before the hearing.

The decision in *Pepper v Hart* has had a mixed reception from the judiciary, and judges speaking extra-judicially have been highly critical of it. It remains an important mark of a paradigm shift with regard to interpretation.

Explanatory notes

The department of state sponsoring bills now issues explanatory notes in important areas of law to guide the reader. They do not form part of the statute, are not authorised, and have no legal effect. But such notes do have their uses, particularly as an aid to understanding the aim and intent of the drafter of the legislation. Those aims and intentions, however, can of course change during the act of interpretation.

Which rules should be used, when, and in what order?

The rules of interpretation that have been so far identified are not, themselves, legal rules but guidance rules. And you will not be surprised to learn that no legal rules exist that state which rules of interpretation can be used. What we should consider, however, is how judges choose the appropriate rules of interpretation applicable to the job in hand, and how they explain that choice. Some might say judges merely want to be seen to have a method so that they are not accused of just creating law, but you would be better off thinking of statutory interpretation as allowing the use of a range of styles of interpretation. Everyone is different and individual judges prefer and use different styles of interpretation.

Nearly 50 years ago, long before the development of cases such as *Pepper v Hart*, Karl Llewellyn[28] noted that judges in fact have two styles of interpretation: the grand style and the formal style. The formal style is quite rigid in its deference to tradition, doctrine and the view that judges should not and do not create law. The grand style is used by judges who are more creative and flexible in their use of interpretation[29].

Statutory interpretation and secondary legislation

It is not just primary legislation that calls for statutory interpretation. There are thousands of pages of secondary legislation published each year, and these too can become central to legal disputes prompting a need for interpretation. More or less the same rules apply as those that we have already briefly noted, but with secondary legislation there are also extra tasks and issues that require consideration:

---

25 Practice Direction (Reference to Extracts from Hansard) [1995] 1 WLR 192; 20 December 1994.
26 [1999] 1 WLR 1059.
27 [2002] 1 WLR 2870.
28 K Llewellyn, *The Common Law Tradition* (Little Brown, Boston Mass 1960).
29 An excellent case study of Llewellyn's observation can be found in the case of *Davis v Johnson* [1978] 1 All ER 841 (CA) affd [1978] 1 All ER 1132 (HL). It is also the subject of an excellent case study by Twining and Miers, *How to Do Things With Rules* (1999). An informative and interesting summary of this area is also contained in Holland and Webb, *Learning Legal Rules* (6th edn OUP, 2006).

■ The regulations containing the secondary legislation have to be read in conjunction with the parent Act. The Interpretation Act 1978 states in section 11 that words used in the secondary legislation must be interpreted to have the same meaning as words used in the parent Act. But, as we know by now, the parent Act could itself be vague. Then the court will probably have to consider the meaning of both!

■ Whilst primary legislation has hierarchical standing over common law, secondary legislation does not. The courts, therefore, will not wish to apply an interpretation that dislodges established common law.

■ Whilst courts cannot declare a primary Act invalid they may declare a secondary Act invalid if the powers delegated have been overstepped.

CONCLUSION

■ Domestic legislation comprises the law made by the authority of Parliament (a primary source of law) and law created by a person or group to which Parliament has delegated the power to create legislation (a secondary source of law).

■ Treaties are concluded between contracting nation states. States wishing not to be bound by certain articles can enter a derogation, and states wishing more time to consider being bound by particularly contentious articles can enter a reservation.

■ Since the enactment of the HRA 1998, English courts have to decide cases based on articles in the ECHR by considering cases in the European Court of Human Rights.

■ Since the enactment of the HRA all bills, prior to debate in Parliament, have to be certified as compatible with the HRA.

■ Since the enactment of the HRA UK courts can issue a declaration that legislation is incompatible with the ECHR; this has no legal force.

■ The UK's decision to join the Union in 1973 resulted in particular legal and constitutional changes to the English legal system and the English constitution.

■ Some EC law is immediately incorporated in the body of English law, by virtue of existing powers in the European Communities Act 1972 as amended. Some types of EC law have to be specially enacted by Act of Parliament.

■ Competent English language skills are an integral part of understanding both domestic and EC legislation.

■   This chapter provides a firm foundation for skills introduced later in the book concerning the interpretation of legislation by judges (in Chapter 5), and the essentials of argument construction (in Chapters 7 and 8).

FURTHER READING

Those of you who are interested in exploring domestic legislation will find the following two books of great interest.

J Holland and J Webb, *Learning Legal Rules* (6th edn OUP, 2006) which also contains an excellent chapter on European legal method.

W Twining and D Miers, *How To Do Things With Rules* (4th edn CUP, Cambridge 1999).

READING AND UNDERSTANDING LAW REPORTS

5

" In almost every case except the very plainest, it would be possible to decide the issue either way with reasonable legal justification."

Lord Hugh Macmillan

CHAPTER SUMMARY

This chapter will discuss law reporting, the ranking of law reports as official, unofficial and specialist, the mechanics of the doctrine of precedent, and most importantly *how to read* a law report in its appropriate contexts. Where appropriate the chapter will point to detailed case studies and exercises on the student companion website. These will help you to break down the language and argument of law reports and take a step-by-step approach to reading them.

INTRODUCING LAW REPORTS AND PRECEDENT

The few legal disputes that cannot be resolved by negotiation between lawyers or last-minute settlements outside the court are determined by judges in the trial courts and, in even fewer cases, by the senior judiciary in the appellate courts. The word 'few' must be stressed here because a law student surrounded by law reports may think that the entire English legal system is composed of nothing but law reports. This is not the case: only about 4% per cent of all formally commenced disputes reach a hearing in court and many of these settle at the doors of the courtroom.

The decisions of judges are delivered orally in court, when the judge may read a pre-written judgment or speak from notes. The words spoken and recorded in writing constitute the words that contain any legally binding rules. At the time of delivery, they are usually recorded verbatim by the court stenographer. In addition, law reporters, employed by one of the private law report publishers, are in court taking shorthand notes. The record of all judgments will be kept by the court. But some decisions, thought to be important to the development or understanding of the law, will also be published in one of the privately published series of reports of decisions in law cases in courts and tribunals. A case that is chosen for publication in this way is called a law report. Each publisher will structure their reports differently, perhaps adding footnotes or summaries, but the words attributed to the judge have to remain a true and accurate record of the words actually spoken. The reports given the highest regard are those that allow the judge concerned to check the accuracy of the written record before publication.

Usually, judges in the civil courts and the appellate courts (both criminal and civil) will reflect upon the case before reaching a final decision. They therefore hold back, or reserve, judgment until a later date. In criminal cases the judge may sentence immediately after the jury has reached a verdict in the trial court, or call for reports and sentence at a later date.

What judges say in their judgments is of immense importance, not only for the litigants, but for the development of the law. The phrase 'common law' has different meanings according to the context in which it is used. One of its meanings relates to the legal rules developed by senior judges when deciding law cases in the appeal courts (the Court of Appeal and the House of Lords). Common law when used in this sense relates to legal rules that are not created by the authorisation of Parliament but through the decisions and judgments of the most senior judges in the English legal system[1]. The English legal system is unique in its public insistence that cases must be decided in keeping with the reasoning process used by judges reaching decisions in similar previous cases of the same court or higher. This process of deciding a case in accordance with past judicial reasoning in similar cases is known as the *doctrine of precedent*. The doctrine is referred to by the use of a Latin phrase which is usually shortened to:

Stare decisis = *let the decision stand*

Often, the whole doctrine *and* the specific legal rule created in the case is referred to by an even more abbreviated Latin term:

ratio

The practice of keeping to such a strict reading of previous cases is not a legally imposed requirement but one that has been developed as a matter of custom and practice in the higher courts since the nineteenth century. And it is a practice enforced by the senior judiciary with a rigour unknown in other legal systems, although most legal systems have some notion of previous decisions being taken into account when new cases are decided. This rigour therefore makes the English legal system unique among *all* others because of the manner in which courts maintain the doctrine of precedent.

It is generally argued that, among other virtues, the doctrine of precedent:

- gives certainty to the law;

- curbs arbitrary decisions;

- maintains equality;

- provides a rational base for decision making.

However, some argue that the doctrine brings disadvantages, because it can:

- make the law inflexible;

- force legal change to be slow and convoluted;

- encourage tedious hair-splitting tendencies in legal argument.

---

1   There has been, and continues to be, much argument among legal philosophers as to whether judges actually *make* or *create* law 'out of nothing' through their reasoning, or merely *declare* what the law has always been. Many judges state that they do not make the law, they discover it and thus *declare* what it has always been. This latter viewpoint is referred to as the *declaratory theory* of law making.

Whatever your view, it is important to appreciate fully these basic issues about precedent before reading and ultimately evaluating law reports. It is also important to understand the relationship between cases and legislation. If the law created by the authority of Parliament (legislation) is in conflict with the common law developed by judges, it will *always* overrule common law.

Hierarchy of the courts

Flowing from the close adherence to the doctrine of precedent comes the important question of when any given court is bound by a previous case. As you may expect everything depends upon the court's position in the hierarchy of courts, with lower courts being bound by the decisions of higher courts. The House of Lords, as the highest Court of Appeal, and the most senior court in the English legal system, is often referred to as the 'apex' of the court hierarchy. The further up the hierarchy one goes, the fewer cases the court deals with and the longer the cases will last. This hierarchy is set out in Figure 5.1.

The development of law reports

As we only know what judges say because of the reports issued after the conclusion of the law case, it is essential to have a system of accurate reporting of legal cases. If you cannot trust the reporting, then you cannot trust the law. Whilst the litigants have to accept the decision of the court at the time it is given, that is the court's determination of the decision between the parties; the detail of the *precedent* in the case is worked out after the case, in the next case that arises calling for discussion of the previous case. Of course editors of law reports, academics and judges may all publish articles and commentaries on cases describing how they consider the case has developed the law or created a new precedent but it is only in the reasoning in later cases that these views can be tested against what the judiciary consider to be the situation.

The competent production of volumes of reports of past cases is indispensable to the operation of the doctrine. Reliable law reports have only been available in England since 1865 although there are a range of fragmentary law reports going back to the twelfth century, known as *Yearbooks*. Reports existing in the *Yearbooks* cover the period from the late twelfth century to the early sixteenth century. However, it is not always possible to discover if the report is of an actual case or a moot (a fictional argument contest between lawyers). The detail given and the quality of the reports also varies considerably, making them an unreliable source. Some reports record outcome, but not facts, others record facts and outcome, but give no reasoning process. Reports also exist in the nominate (named) reports[2] dating from the late fifteenth century to 1865. By the nineteenth century, a court-authorised reporter was attached to all higher courts and his reports were published in collected volumes by name of reporter. By 1865, there were 16 reporters compiling and publishing authorised reports. They were amalgamated into the Incorporated Council of Law Reporting and the reports were published in volumes known as the *Law Reports*. These reports are checked by the judges of the relevant case prior to publication and a rule of citation has developed that, if a case is reported in a range of publications, only that

---

2   Reports classified according to the name of the reporter, such as Coke's reports.

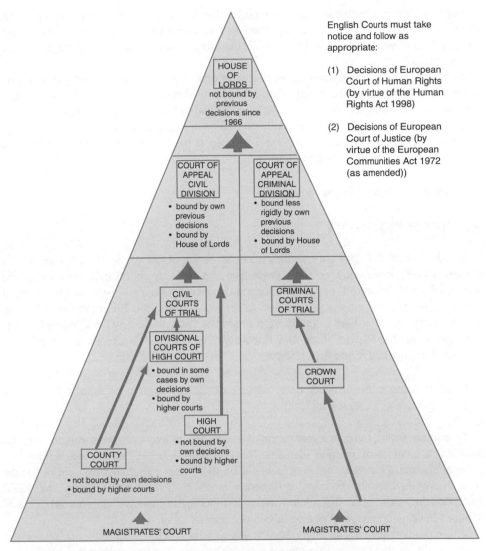

English Courts must take notice and follow as appropriate:

(1) Decisions of European Court of Human Rights (by virtue of the Human Rights Act 1998)

(2) Decisions of European Court of Justice (by virtue of the European Communities Act 1972 (as amended))

Figure 5.1 The hierarchy of courts in the English legal system[3]

version printed in the *Law Reports* is cited in court. However, the accuracy of reports pre-dating the setting up of the Incorporated Council of Law Reporting in 1865 cannot be guaranteed.

Surprisingly, there are no *official* authoritative series of law reports in England to equate with the Queen's Printers copy of an Act of Parliament. The Stationery Office is responsible for publishing revenue, immigration and social security law cases. However, traditionally, law reports remain in the hands of private publishers. Today, there are numerous, often

---

3 By virtue of the Constitutional Reform Act 2005 the House of Lords will have its jurisdiction transferred to the new Supreme Court of the United Kingdom from October 2009 if current planning stays on track.

competitive, private publishers of law reports. The full range of available law reports is shown in Figure 5.2. Do not forget that there are law reports deemed by the courts as the most authoritative and you need to know this hierarchy. These were discussed and referred to in Chapter 2.

Although there are no official series of law reports, the courts do respect some reports more than others, as we have already discussed in Chapter 2. A long-established, conventional rule is that a law report, if it is to be accepted by the relevant court as an authority, must be prepared by and published under the name of a fully qualified barrister.

Given that the *Law Reports* only cover 7 per cent of the cases in the higher courts in any given year, it can be interesting to consider:

■   **who** selects which cases to report?

■   **how** are they selected?

Editors select the cases for inclusion in the series of law reports. These are highly trained lawyers, well acquainted with precedent and the likely importance of cases. Some law reports are annotated, particularly for the use of practitioners, others are left without annotations or introductions. In addition to reported cases, the Supreme Court Library contains thousands of files of unreported cases. In 1940, the Lord Chancellor's Department prepared *The Report of the Law Reporting Committee*. The Committee considered that, after editors had made their choices:

> What remains is less likely to be a treasure house than a rubbish heap in which a jewel will rarely, if ever, be discovered.

Of course, today, there is a vast range of electronic retrieval systems for accessing the details of thousands of unreported cases. This has caused its own problems and there has been a legitimate concern that courts would be inundated with cases that did not really contain any new law. In the case of *Roberts Petroleum Ltd v Bernard Kenny Ltd* [1983] 2 AC 192, the House of Lords took the step of forbidding the citation of unreported cases of the Civil Division of the Court of Appeal without special leave.

When reading any law report you should ask whether it is the most authoritative version available. Or are there more authoritative versions? You should also consider whether there is any other case that is only recorded electronically that may be of authority. But note that the courts have strict rules about admitting as authoritative, cases where only electronic versions are available.

You could also ask yourself if there might be any unreported case that could be more authoritative than the law report you have located. This would only be a task you would undertake for research or professional purposes.

It is important to note that just because a case has not been reported, or if it is only

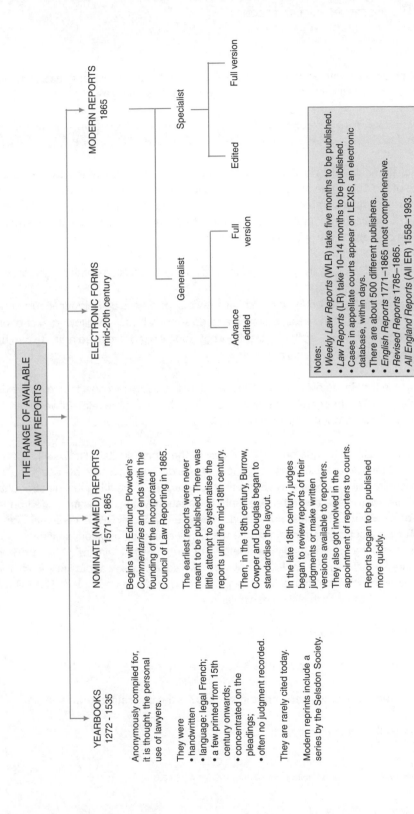

THE RANGE OF AVAILABLE LAW REPORTS

YEARBOOKS
1272 - 1535

Anonymously compiled for, it is thought, the personal use of lawyers.

They were
• handwritten
• language: legal French;
• a few printed from 15th century onwards;
• concentrated on the pleadings;
• often no judgment recorded.

They are rarely cited today.

Modern reprints include a series by the Selsdon Society.

NOMINATE (NAMED) REPORTS
1571 - 1865

Begins with Edmund Plowden's *Commentaries* and ends with the founding of the Incorporated Council of Law Reporting in 1865.

The earliest reports were never meant to be published. There was little attempt to systematise the reports until the mid-18th century.

Then, in the 18th century, Burrow, Cowper and Douglas began to standardise the layout.

In the late 18th century, judges began to review reports of their judgments or make written versions available to reporters. They also got involved in the appointment of reporters to courts.

Reports began to be published more quickly.

ELECTRONIC FORMS
mid-20th century

Generalist

Advance edited

Full version

MODERN REPORTS
1865

Specialist

Edited

Full version

Notes:
• *Weekly Law Reports* (WLR) take five months to be published.
• *Law Reports* (LR) take 10–14 months to be published.
• Cases in appellate courts appear on LEXIS, an electronic database, within days.
• There are about 500 different publishers.
• *English Reports* 1771–1865 most comprehensive.
• *Revised Reports* 1785–1865.
• *All England Reports* (All ER) 1558–1993.

Figure 5.2 The range of available law reports

reported in electronic format, it does not mean it *cannot* be an important case. You would need to access court transcripts yourself to determine these matters.

UNDERSTANDING PRECEDENT

Many legal theorists and practitioners have attempted, over the years, to give precise definitions of the English doctrine of precedent. Unfortunately for law students there are no simple shortcuts to understanding the practical everyday working of the doctrine. However, a few theoretical groundrules can be established, which at least place the operation of the doctrine of precedent within a context. For instance:

■   judges at all levels of the court hierarchy *must follow* decisions of the higher courts;

■   judges in the higher courts *must follow* previous decisions of their own court or that of a higher court if the case is similar, and does not fall into any allowed exceptions. It is accepted, however, that in the Court of Appeal a more relaxed attitude can be taken in relation to criminal appeals;

■   judges in the House of Lords have the freedom to decline to follow their own previous decisions[4]. This freedom is exercised sparingly, but in a more relaxed way in its criminal jurisdiction than in its civil jurisdiction.

In practice, much depends on the definition of the word 'similar'. How similar must a previous case be before it becomes a precedent to be followed in a current case? The facts of cases usually vary in some way. Sometimes, counsel for the litigants will strenuously argue that previous cases are not precedents because they can be distinguished on their facts. In other words, they are not similar. There are no definitions of similar for the purposes of the doctrine and this is where the judge can bring subjective influences into the decision-making processes. He or she can determine what 'similarity' is. In this way extremely subtle 'differences' are found between two cases. Law is about life and life rarely replicates itself exactly, but trends and degrees of similarity can be noted. The following questions are important to the issue of similarity:

■   must the law be similar now as then?

■   what happens if there are small factual differences?

■   what if there are a range of small differences? Is the case sufficiently similar?

■   how can the reason for the case be extracted?

---

4   As given in *Practice Direction (Judicial Precedent)* [1966] 3 All ER 77.

Cases defined as similar must be decided in accordance with the same *reasoning* process, since the actual doctrine as it has developed refers to keeping to the *reasons* for deciding past cases. But how does one find that reasoning? Wambaugh[5], a theorist working in America in the late nineteenth century, suggests that one way of ascertaining the reason for the decision (the *ratio decidendi*) is to look for a general rule of law in the judgments and test whether it is foundational for deciding the case by translating it into the negative form. You can then see if the case would have been decided differently. This negative method of finding the *ratio* or rule is illustrated by the flow chart in Figure 5.3.

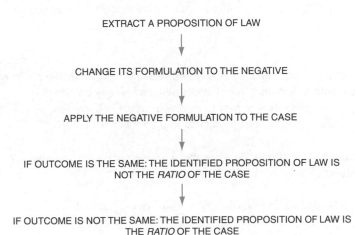

EXTRACT A PROPOSITION OF LAW

↓

CHANGE ITS FORMULATION TO THE NEGATIVE

↓

APPLY THE NEGATIVE FORMULATION TO THE CASE

↓

IF OUTCOME IS THE SAME: THE IDENTIFIED PROPOSITION OF LAW IS
NOT THE *RATIO* OF THE CASE

↓

IF OUTCOME IS NOT THE SAME: THE IDENTIFIED PROPOSITION OF LAW IS
THE *RATIO* OF THE CASE

> Problem: this method is designed to work only with one
> proposition of law. Cases can have more than one
> proposition.

Figure 5.3 Wambaugh's method for finding the *ratio*

Another famous legal theorist, Goodhart, wrote an influential article *Determining the Ratio Decidendi of a Case* which refers far more to the *principle* in the case than the *ratio*[6]. Goodhart emphasises the consideration of facts:

■   what are the material facts as found by the judge?

■   what is the judge's decision?

■   unless there is a new material fact (or there are some missing material facts) a future court, depending upon its place in the court hierarchy, and thus its obligations under the doctrine of precedent, must follow it.

---

5   E Wambaugh, 'The Study of Cases 1894' cited in R Cross and JW Harris *Precedent in English Law* (Clarendon Press, Oxford 1991) 52–3.

6   A Goodhart, *Determining the Ratio Decidendi of a Case* (1959) 22 MLR 117.

Goodhart provides a thorough discussion on finding the principle of a case, which revolves around the tension between a range of issues. He is also clear about occasions where he considers the principle *cannot* be found. A major problem with Goodhart's suggested method is his emphasis upon the facts. Although it can be said that reading a judgment in the light of the facts of the case is a core requirement of the doctrine, attention also needs to be paid to the way that the case is:

■   argued;

■   pleaded (exactly how have the lawyers formally lodged the complaint?);

■   reasoned

in relation to other precedents. Every judgment has to be read in the light of previous cases and, if relevant, with a view as to how subsequent cases may be affected.

Wambaugh and Goodhart's methods are summarised in Figure 5.4. Even when considered together, there are still problems. In particular:

■   what should an interpreter do when there is a decision without reasons? Can the *ratio* be inferred?

■   what can be done with the diversity of forms of judgments?

While it is true to say that the *ratio decidendi* of a previous case comes from the language of a judge, the interpreters themselves can bring new meanings. In the appellate courts, depending upon the importance of the case, three, five or seven judges can sit. Each can give judgment, although often a judge says 'I concur with my learned colleague, Lord Bridge' or some such similar phrase. At times there may be one or more judgments disagreeing with the majority view that a certain litigant should win the case. In such cases, there is no doubt that each reasoned judgment has a *ratio*. But can it be said that there is a *ratio* of the court? There is, of course, no problem where it is clear that the majority agree with the same statements of the application of the law. But what if the different judges agree on outcome and disagree on reasons for the outcome, as shown in Figure 5.5?

Lack of agreement among judges in relation to the reasoning process can weaken the precedent value of the case, because judgments in cases can result in different scenarios. Consider, for example, these two different scenarios:

1.   The majority of judges agree to dismiss/allow the appeal on one ground. A minority of judges agree with the majority as to outcome, but base their decision on a

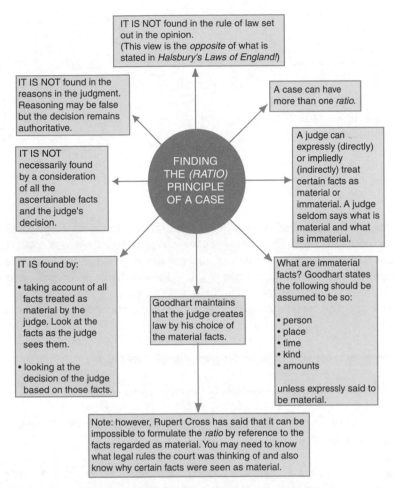

Figure 5.4 Finding the ratio of a case (ideas from Wambaugh, Cross and Goodhart)

different ground. In this situation, the *ratio* of the majority is binding and strong. The *ratio* of the minority may become the object of weighty consideration in a future case.

2.   The majority agree to dismiss/allow the appeal but there is no common ground as to why the appeal has been dismissed or allowed. In this situation, there is no clear majority in favour of any *ratio*. The case, therefore, lacks authority for the narrowest interpretation of the *ratio*. It is impossible to state clearly how such a case is viewed other than to treat it as a weak authority.

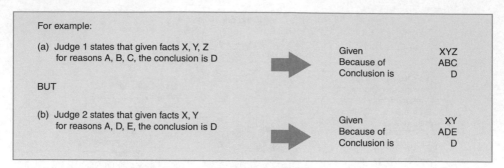

For example:

(a) Judge 1 states that given facts X, Y, Z
     for reasons A, B, C, the conclusion is D

BUT

(b) Judge 2 states that given facts X, Y
     for reasons A, D, E, the conclusion is D

Given	XYZ
Because of	ABC
Conclusion is	D

Given	XY
Because of	ADE
Conclusion is	D

Figure 5.5 How different reasoning can deliver the same outcome

When there is a strong original *ratio* that is wide, there is the most scope for later inter-pretation to mould the law. If, for example, case A has just been decided, the *ratio* for which the decision is binding being found in the actual opinion of the judge, in a later case (case E) which seeks to interpret and apply case A, the judge may have to interpret case A in the light of the new set of facts before him and also interpretations given by subsequent cases B, C and D. In practice, when a judge is considering case E currently before the court, he or she:

■   states what is considered to be the *ratio* in the earlier case A;

■   then considers that *ratio* in the light of the facts in case A;

■   also considers the observations made by judges in later cases B, C and D concerning case A;

■   ultimately formulates a rule of law based on a number of cases (the original case A and cases B, C and D) and applies this composite reasoning to case E before the court.

It is difficult if not impossible to come up with a clear formula that will always work for ascertaining the *ratio* of a case. But a reasonable idea of the difficulties in ascertaining the *ratio* is a necessary and revealing step for any interpreter. Ignoring these difficulties will ultimately lead to simplistic and inadequate construction of legal arguments. If an argument is being made on weak, tenuous or stretched grounds, it is better to know that it is. Deciding whether a case is a precedent involves consulting a wide range of sources and using a broad range of skills. Figure 5.6 outlines a simplified version of the process. It asks some of the questions necessary in deciding whether a previous case constitutes a prece-dent to be followed in a current case.

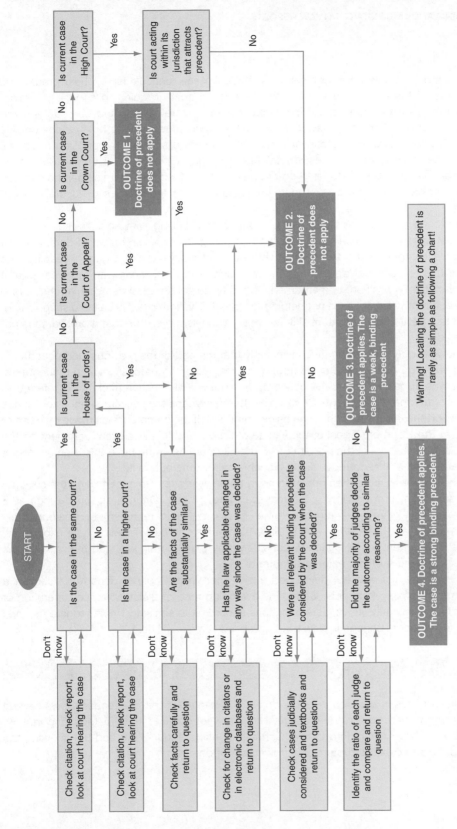

Figure 5.6 Flow chart to assist in locating the *ratio* of a case.

At times, lawyers have to research previous cases meticulously to help predict the outcome of the current case. After all, there is no point in going to court if the exact point the client wishes to make has already come before a court and been determined to his detriment. Part of the lawyer's particular expertise is knowing how to look quickly through past cases to find relevant decisions either supporting or opposing a client's case. The location of materials is relatively easy given the range of on-line databases available. Unfortunately, students do not have unlimited access to training in how to use such databases, so there is a need to rely on one of the citators to locate relevant cases.

Searches can be made, first, to pinpoint cases dealing with specific legal rules. A range of cases with similar facts can then be pulled from this first trawl of data. Each of these cases then needs to be carefully read and analysed. After careful reading, the lawyer has to construct detailed arguments concerning similarities with other cases that help the client's position, and arguments need to be constructed demolishing the potential precedent value of cases not helping the client. This latter skill is called *distinguishing*, and it is a particularly important skill for those who wish to ensure that a precedent is not followed.

A lawyer may need to argue convincingly that the part of the previous judgment that is being relied on by an opponent is not part of the reasoning process leading to judgment; that it was an 'aside' comment, based on a hypothetical situation (technically referred to as an *obiter dictum* comment). On the other hand, perhaps the only argument a lawyer has to support the client's position is an aside comment. If the comment was made by a senior judge in the Court of Appeal or the House of Lords, and it is a relevant comment on the exact circumstances of the present case, then it could be argued that this is an important indicator of what that court would do if such a case came before it.

Where there is more than one judgment, the lawyer's task in ascertaining the strength of a precedent in a previous case may be more difficult. Often a dissenting judgment can eventually, through a range of other cases, come to represent the majority view of an area of law. If the judge who is dissenting has a particular reputation for excellence, then the judgment will be seriously considered by those coming to read the case for the precedential value of the majority judgments.

English law, as created, developed and refined in the courts, does not resemble a straight line of development. Rather, it is a winding road of distinctions, consideration of majority and minority views, determinations according to similarity, more judgments, then more distinctions. Change is slow but English law remains flexible.

HANDLING LAW REPORTS

When law cases in any area are considered, it is important that the reader knows several things about the case for future usage. These are set out in Figure 5.7. Most importantly, law reports have a standard layout. Carefully consider Figures 5.8 and 5.9 showing the front page and overall structure of a typical law report.

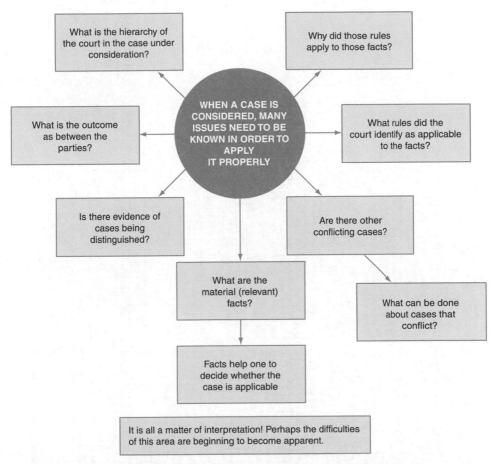

Figure 5.7 Issues to be taken into account when properly applying a case in legal reasoning in court

Law reports are complex pieces of written English and, therefore, of double difficulty to students in terms of their legal content and, generally, in terms of their sophisticated English usage. It can also be useful to consider the law report not just as an official public document but also as a literary text[7]. The illustrations and aside comments made by judges in their judgments may be complex and relate to politics, history, art, religion, literature and so on. Quotations may be given in different languages and reports can sometimes be liberally peppered with Latin legal maxims.

All judges express themselves in different ways but they all share seniority within their respective courts in the English legal system. Seniority is matched to the hierarchy of the

---

7   In the past decade a growing number of scholars have become interested in exploring law as literary text and in exploring literary texts as mirrors of the law (see Chapter 3). A particularly fascinating text is T Ziolkowski, *The Mirror of Justice: Literary Reflections of Legal Crisis* (Princeton University Press, 2003). For a now classic work of fiction exploring the ideology of law you may be interested to read F Kafka, *The Trial* (Random House Press, New York 1956). It is also available as an e-book, free according to licensing conditions from Project Gutenberg http://www.gutenberg.org accessed 18 April 2009. The Further Reading section in Chapter 3 also directs you to reading in this area.

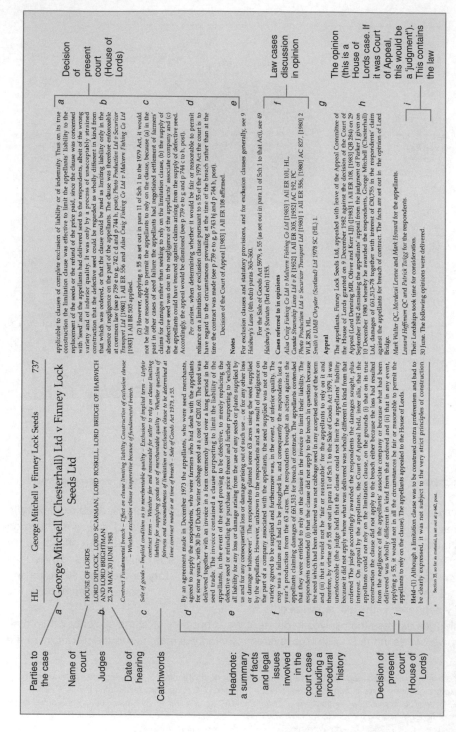

Figure 5.8 First page of law report showing range of sections and subdivisions

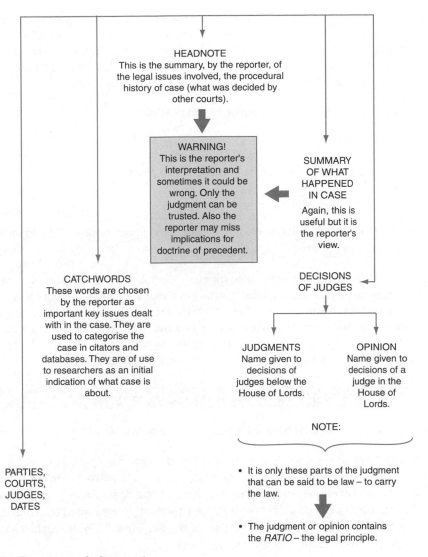

Figure 5.9 The anatomy of a law report

court, with judges in the House of Lords being the most senior. Therefore judges in the House of Lords and the Law Lords are more senior than judges in the Court of Appeal, the Lords of Appeal Ordinary.

Unlike other jurisdictions there is no such concept as the career judge. Promotion to the 'Bench' occurs as recognition of years of proven ability, usually, as a barrister. However, lower ranks of the judiciary are now appointed from successful solicitors. Therefore, although law students are very new to the enterprise of law, they are called upon to engage in sophisticated evaluation of the highly competent analysis of the English legal system's most senior judges, who combine years of successful practice with excellent skills in language usage and technical substantive law ability. These judges may discuss several complex issues simultaneously, applying and interpreting the law to the facts of specific disputes. Students need to develop their skills in order to be able to obtain:

■   a good grasp of the relevant area of substantive law;

■   an appreciation of issues relating to language usage;

■   an understanding of the doctrine of precedent in practice;

■   a familiarity with statute;

■   a sound foundation in the mechanics of argument construction in order to make initial sense of the text.

Judges are social actors with their own preferences who attempt to act fairly in judgment, despite themselves and their natural inclinations. However, at root a judgment is a subjective text and a student's or a lawyer's interpretation of that text is also subjective. Any interpretation should be tested against the text and evaluated to see if it is a plausible reading. As noted in Chapter 3, the language of the law tries to be injected with scientific objectivity, but flounders because of the imprecision of language.

READING CASES

Law reports at appellate level of cases in court, can be of two broad types:

1.   Those cases where the judge(s) have extracted a 'new' legal rule out of close consideration of previous cases in order to give a legal claim that had not before been known or certain, in that there may have been a general agreement that there was such a rule but no such rule had been specifically constructed by an institution with the power to do so (the court or, of course, Parliament). These can be described as law reports of cases that are sources of law.

2.   Those cases where the judge(s) are grappling with the meaning of legislative words and phrases in order to determine the case. These are law reports of cases involving statutory interpretation, that is, judicial determination of the meaning of words and/or phrases in a statute.

The majority of cases fall into category 2 above, where the courts have, as one of their most important tasks, the application of legislative rules to various fact situations. They must decide whether these legislative rules apply to given situations.

Many people need to apply statutory rules. Often this application will be purely routine but sometimes doubts will arise. Such doubts may, or may not, reach court. How do judges set about deciding the meaning of words? Already in this text there have been several illustrations of words not meaning what they appear to mean. Despite the supposed certainty of statutory rules, rules in 'fixed verbal form', words can change their meaning over time, and courts will disagree over the meaning of words. Choices of meaning, not perceived by the drafters, may lie latent in the words and be drawn out in court in a manner defeating intention and narrowing, extending or making meaningless the ambit of the rule. A discussion of the three rules of statutory interpretation (the literal, the mischief and the golden rules) took place in Chapter 4. These rules are, however, rules of practice not rules of law. Do judges really use the rules of statutory interpretation? If so, which rule do they use first?

Judges rarely, if ever, state that they are applying a certain rule of interpretation. Often, judges look to see if there can be a literal meaning to the words used in the disputed statutory rule. However, there is no rule that states that they must use the literal rule first. Holland and Webb[8] quite correctly assert that perhaps the better question relates to what style of interpretation judges use. Interpretation is more a question of judicial style than the use of interpretational rules. Indeed, should you attempt to use the rules of statutory interpretation as a guide in the interpretation of a statutory word or phrase, the uselessness of the rules as an interpretational tool will become immediately apparent. However, as a justificatory label they may have a function. As you gain experience in reading judgments you will notice vast differences in judicial styles. Some judgments seem to be based on a blow-by-blow analysis of precedents and previous usage of words, others seem to be based on tenuous common sense rationales.

Decisions based on the *external* context of the statute will be identified as such. This covers situations where judicial decision-making appears to be based on issues of public policy, a particularly favoured device in the 1960s and 1970s. Reliance on public policy rationale can be referred to as the 'grand style' or the 'teleological' approach. Cases may also turn on the *form of* the statute itself, that is, its *internal* context. Judges who rigidly adopt the internal approach are often referred to as *formalists*. Such judges say that they do not create law, they find it. They find it by following the pathways of the rules of statutory interpretation, by moving *within* the statute document. A closer consideration of the simplest definitions of the rules of statutory interpretation enables the classification of the literal rule as the *formalist* approach and the mischief rule as the *teleological* approach. The golden rule, of course, allows one to ignore the formalist approach of the literal rule. It is most likely to result in a teleological approach as the judge, through the golden rule, is released from formalism!

---

8   J Holland and J Webb *Learning Legal Rules* (6th edn Oxford Univeristy Press, 2006).

CASE STUDIES

The chapter now turns to two practical demonstrations relating to reading cases:

- A case study of *George Mitchell (Chesterhall) Ltd v Finney Lock Seeds Ltd* [1983] 2 AC 548. This gives a detailed account of a paragraph by paragraph reading to enable you to track through the analysis of a case dealing with relatively complex issues of common law and the interpretation of statutory rules. It is also used to demonstrate the art of writing case notes.

- A case study concerning some of the aspects of the case of *Mandla v Dowell Lee* [1983] 2 AC 548. It is a case exclusively relating to statutory interpretation.

You will also find an additional detailed case study on the companion website.

A case study of *George Mitchell (Chesterhall) Ltd v Finney Lock Seeds Ltd* [1983] 2 All ER 732–44

This practical exercise involves reading a relatively short law report (about five pages of A4) in depth, in order to demonstrate one method of reading, note taking, evaluating and using a case to construct arguments. You can locate the full case in your library's print or electronic collection, and you will need to do this if you wish to engage in the companion website exercises for this case. However, the practical exercise in this book only requires you to read the leading opinion of Lord Bridge, which we have printed at the end of this chapter. Its paragraphs have been numbered in square brackets to cross index with our own analysis.

Initially you will be required to approach the case as a person engaging in a sophisticated English comprehension exercise. This will demonstrate how far you can get by meticulous reading in the absence of detailed knowledge of a particular area of law (in this case, the law of contract). No assumptions will be made concerning your knowledge of the law.

This exercise requires your active engagement and asks for certain tasks to be carried out. You will be given the context of the case, so that you are not working completely in the dark (if you already have a good grasp of the law of contract you can ignore this), before being guided through four stages of reading. Stage 1 involves skim reading, stage 2 involves checking the skim reading and making a first note of Lord Bridge's opinion, stage 3 spends time considering the issues in the case and stage 4 outlines a paragraph-by-paragraph summary of the opinion. This stage also involves a 'statutory diversion' looking at the statutory references brought up in the case. Finally you will be asked to write a brief case note of the case.

The context of the case

Whilst you do not need any pre-knowledge for this exercise if is, of course, useful if you understand the legal context of the dispute in a case. For this reason, the basic framework of the law of contract is set out in Figure 5.10. The triangles denote the

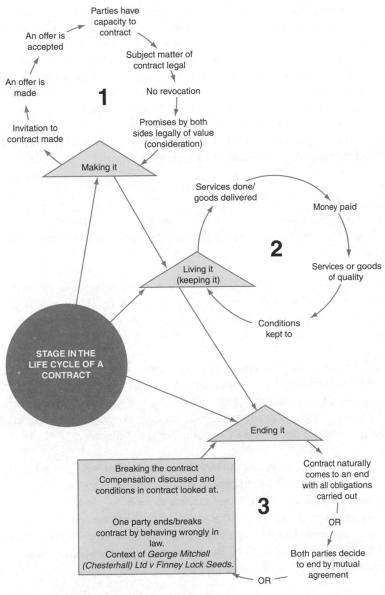

Figure 5.10 Stages in the life cycle of a contract

basic stages of making a contract, living or keeping it, and ending it. The events which occur in *George Mitchell* are summarised in the square by the triangle labelled 'Ending it'. This is not a case of mutual agreement to end the contract, or it coming naturally to an end; one of the parties is accused of breaking the contract and compensation is requested.

Usually, contracts contain provisions that lay down the compensation payable to one party if the other party breaks the contract by not doing what he, or she, says will be done. The contract in *George Mitchell (Chesterhall) Ltd v Finney Lock Seeds Ltd* is no exception. However, the party selling put a special clause in the contract called a limitation clause which stated that damages payable if the contract was broken would be limited merely to replacing the goods purchased (seeds). No other damage would be compensated, for example, for loss of profits.

This case is particularly interesting because it is also concerned with a situation in which common law rules created by the judges in previous cases are operating alongside statutory rules created by the legislature.

Stage 1: The basic reading

To fully ascertain what the main issues are in the case it has to be broken into with some determination. If you can understand the methodology used here, you will be able to use that methodology to break into other cases. Stage 1 has three basic tasks:

1. Access the opinion of Lord Bridge on the companion website which has been numbered for you by square brackets on left, eg. [1]. Read it as quickly as you can and time yourself. If this takes you more than 60 minutes you need to work on your reading strategies generally.

2. As you read, note in particular how each paragraph begins and ends. You will often find signposts to meaning at the beginning and end of paragraphs, and they often contain indicators of the progression of discussion or argument. Be aware of the use of any technical language. Look up words you do not understand in a good English dictionary or law dictionary.

3. Give a summary, in no more than 200 words, of what this case is about. Remember that the binding aspect of the judgment is the *ratio decidendi*: 'the reason for deciding'. Knowledge of facts alone does not give you a clue as to the precedent; knowledge of the applicable rules alone does not give you the precedent; knowledge of legal rules and facts does not give you the precedent. Only the reasons why those rules applied to those facts gives you an understanding of the precedent created.

INTELLECTUAL HEALTH WARNING!

Do not proceed any further until you have quickly read the case and engaged in tasks 1–3

Now look at your summary and see if you picked out the issues discussed in the following paragraph.

This is a case about a buyer of seeds wanting compensation because he was sold the wrong seeds and suffered financial loss. Furthermore, the buyer made it clear which seeds he wanted but the wrong seeds were accidentally sent. However, this is far too general a description of the issues in the case. If you only note that the House of Lords decided that the decision between the parties was that the seller/supplier of seeds had to pay compensation to the buyer for the delivery of the wrong seeds, this may well be correct but it does not give you any useful information for future use. It certainly does not give the precedent of the case.

Stage 2: Checking the basics

If you only have the basic facts you will not be able to *use* this case. It is essential to understand why the buyer won the case. So let us go back to the case and engage in a second reading. Stage 2 includes six tasks (numbered 4–9 below):

4.   Look again at the opinion, check you have a clear idea of the facts in the case and note them down.

5.   Are any of the facts disputed by the parties or are they agreed? Note your answers.

6.   What are the specific issues in this case? State them in list form.

7.   What is the procedural history of the case? What other courts has this case been heard in and what did the previous courts decide?

(Answering questions 4–7 properly enables you to follow the development of arguments.)

8.   Go back, carefully read the opinion again and make notes on:

    a)   the procedural history; where the case was heard and the decisions made before the case came before the House of Lords;

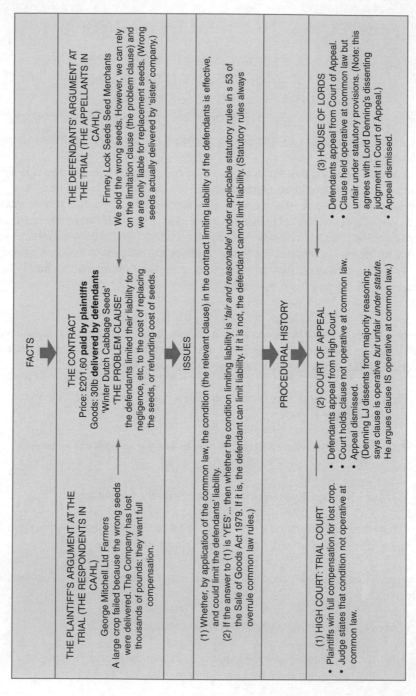

FACTS

THE PLAINTIFF'S ARGUMENT AT THE TRIAL (THE RESPONDENTS IN CA/HL)

George Mitchell Ltd Farmers

A large crop failed because the wrong seeds were delivered. The Company has lost thousands of pounds: they want full compensation.

THE CONTRACT

Price: £201.60 **paid by plaintiffs**
Goods: 30lb **delivered by defendants**
'Winter Dutch Cabbage Seeds'

'THE PROBLEM CLAUSE'
the defendants limited their liability for negligence, etc, to the cost of replacing the seeds, or refunding cost of seeds.

THE DEFENDANTS' ARGUMENT AT THE TRIAL (THE APPELLANTS IN CA/HL)

Finney Lock Seeds Seed Merchants

We sold the wrong seeds. However, we can rely on the limitation clause (the problem clause) and we are only liable for replacement seeds. (Wrong seeds actually delivered by 'sister' company.)

ISSUES

(1) Whether, by application of the common law, the condition (the relevant clause) in the contract limiting liability of the defendants is effective, and could limit the defendants' liability.

(2) If the answer to (1) is 'YES'... then whether the condition limiting liability is *'fair and reasonable'* under applicable statutory rules in s 53 of the Sale of Goods Act 1979. If it is, the defendant can limit liability. If it is not, the defendant cannot limit liability. (Statutory rules always overrule common law rules.)

PROCEDURAL HISTORY

(1) HIGH COURT: TRIAL COURT
- Plaintiffs win full compensation for lost crop.
- Judge states that condition not operative at common law.

(2) COURT OF APPEAL
- Defendants appeal from High Court.
- Court holds clause not operative at common law.
- Appeal dismissed.
(Denning LJ dissents from majority reasoning: says clause is operative *but unfair under statute.* He argues clause IS operative at common law.)

(3) HOUSE OF LORDS
- Defendants appeal from Court of Appeal.
- Clause held operative at common law but unfair under statutory provisions. (Note: this agrees with Lord Denning's dissenting judgment in Court of Appeal.)
- Appeal dismissed.

Figure 5.11 Facts, issues and arguments in the *George Mitchell* case

b)   the reasoning in the opinion of Lord Bridge;

c)   any words and phrases that you do not know (check them out in a dictionary or in the text for sense).

9.   Make a full summary of the opinion in no more than 300 words making sure you include the discussion of issues.

DO NOT CONTINUE UNTIL YOU HAVE COMPLETED TASKS 4–9

Check your answers and summary against the details in Figure 5.11, which was constructed by a careful reading of the opinion. Did you find all the facts and issues? Did you correctly ascertain the procedural history?

Stage 3: Finding and beginning to understand the issues in the case
Having labelled the limitation clause that the case is about as 'the relevant condition', Lord Bridge identifies the two issues in the case in paragraph [3] of his opinion as shown in Figure 5.12. Note that he gives the two issues shorthand labels:

1.   the first issue is the '(common law issue)';

2.   the second issue is the '(statutory issue)'.

> 1 The first issue is whether the relevant condition, on its true construction in the context of the contract as a whole, is effective to limit the appellant's liability to a refund of the price of the seeds (the common law issue).
> 2 The second issue is whether, if the common law issue is decided in the appellant's favour, they should nevertheless be precluded from reliance on this limitation of liability pursuant to the provisions of the modified s 55 of the Sale of Goods Act 1979 which is set out in para 11 of Schedule 1 to the Act and which applies to contracts made between 18 May 1973 and 1 February 1978 (the statutory issue).

Figure 5.12 The issues in the appeal as set out by Lord Bridge in paragraph [3] of his opinion

Finding and understanding what these issues are as a matter of basic comprehension is not easy. It may not be too difficult to locate the specific sentences where the judge says what the issues are. Unfortunately, it does not necessarily follow that you will be able to understand the issues just by reading the sentences. You may have to work extremely hard to reach a place of understanding, as the judge may have used unfamiliar vocabulary, unfamiliar legal references, complex grammatical structures and dense, perhaps boring, text.

A first strategy is to remember that each paragraph is connected to the one above and the one below it on the page, or the computer screen. This is useful to remember if you are stuck on your reading. Reading the paragraph above the one you are struggling with and the paragraph below may be enough to resolve your difficulty.

A second strategy for breaking into paragraphs where you find the language difficult is to set them out with spaces, as demonstrated in Figure 5.12, before reading it carefully and annotate it with your own notes, thoughts and definitions. The language of paragraph [3] is annotated for you in Figures 5.13 and 5.14. Figure 5.13 deals with the first issue, and Figure 5.14 deals with the second issue. This activity will reveal where you lack understanding, highlight the areas of interconnection and help you to identify words and phrases that need defining. Remember that where a statute is concerned the actual words are *fixed* in law by the statute. When dealing with a judgment any common rules contained and constructed in the judgment do not fix rules with specific words. It is said that the decisions of judges state rules in an *unfixed* verbal format.

We have been considering the complex issues at the heart of this case. Now, before moving on to explore Lord Bridge's opinion in detail, it is useful to ensure that you understand the procedural history of this case. You may find it useful to glance

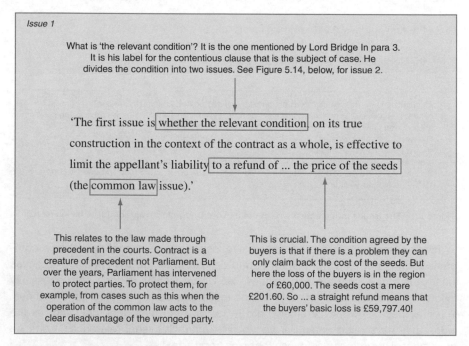

Figure 5.13 Issue 1 from Lord Bridge's opinion annotated

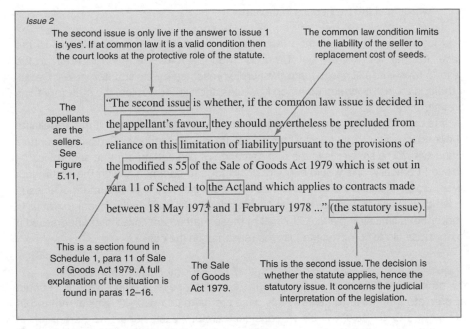

Figure 5.14 Issue 2 from Lord Bridge's opinion annotated

back to Figure 5.11 and note the basic information given there concerning the procedural history. This will enable you to obtain an appreciation of the differences in opinion by the various judges who have considered the case before its arrival in the House of Lords.

Initially the case was won by the buyers of the seed, in the trial court (the High Court). The buyers were the original claimants[9], George Mitchell (Chesterhall) Ltd. The sellers of the seed, Finney Lock Seeds Ltd, (the defendants) in the High Court immediately appealed to the Court of Appeal, where they become the appellants, and they again lost. This did not deter them and they appealed to the House of Lords, where they also lost. There was a lot of money at stake: the difference between the £201.60 that the seeds cost as awarded by the Court of Appeal or the £90,000+ that the trial judge awarded.

Now take time to consolidate the information we have considered so far before moving on to stage 4, actually breaking into Lord Bridge's opinion. We have already considered the:

■   procedural history;

■   facts;

■   operative rules of law;

---

9   Although at the time of this case in 1983 they would have been called plaintiffs.

■   wording of the two issues in the case,

It is known that both common law rules and statutory rules are relevant to the case. Further, it is known that if the common law rules are found to apply in the seller's favour he still has to jump the hurdle presented by the statutory rules. Recall, if there is a clash between common law rules and statutory rules, the statutory rules prevail.

It is clear that Lord Bridge will argue through each of the issues. If the appellants succeed in issue 1 they may still fail overall if they fail over issue 2. (Can you understand why? The answer is in the first sentence of text setting out 'the second issue' above.) Logically, one would expect Lord Bridge to commence with the arguments over issue 1, the common law issue, as this is the gateway to an argument over issue 2, which will only take place if issue 1 is decided in the appellant's favour (and this is contentious limitation clause). Until all of these matters are linked and understood it is not possible to comprehend fully the reasoning in the case.

Stage 4: Breaking into Lord Bridge's speech

By now you will have read Lord Bridge's opinion several times and you should appreciate that the arguments in this case are quite complex. The initial method of breaking into the text will be to consider carefully each numbered paragraph in square brackets. Paragraphs are intended to convey a new idea. So each paragraph represents an idea or a cluster of ideas. Writing a précis of each paragraph helps you to understand each of the different ideas. When you are skilled at reading law texts you will not have to write down your précis. Instead, you will automatically take in the contexts and signals in each paragraph, only occasionally writing down an idea or proposition in an argument.

Each paragraph is a stepping stone, leading the reader to the end of the text and the conclusion of the argument. As paragraphs relate to each other you should not skip any paragraphs. If you do not understand something in a paragraph, read the paragraphs before and after it to help clarify the issues. If you find references you do not understand cast your eyes back to see if this has already been clarified.

Very early on in his opinion, at numbered paragraph [2], Lord Bridge organises the disputed limitation clause by saying that 'the issues in the appeal arise from three sentences in the conditions of sale' and are part of the terms of the contract. To make things easy he numbers these as 1, 2 and 3. He then states that he will call each sentence a clause as shown in Figure 5.15. Note he uses 'cll' to mean 'clauses'.

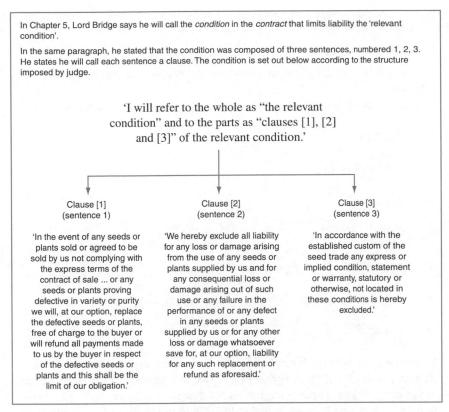

In Chapter 5, Lord Bridge says he will call the *condition* in the *contract* that limits liability the 'relevant condition'.

In the same paragraph, he stated that the condition was composed of three sentences, numbered 1, 2, 3. He states he will call each sentence a clause. The condition is set out below according to the structure imposed by judge.

'I will refer to the whole as "the relevant condition" and to the parts as "clauses [1], [2] and [3]" of the relevant condition.'

Clause [1] (sentence 1)	Clause [2] (sentence 2)	Clause [3] (sentence 3)
'In the event of any seeds or plants sold or agreed to be sold by us not complying with the express terms of the contract of sale ... or any seeds or plants proving defective in variety or purity we will, at our option, replace the defective seeds or plants, free of charge to the buyer or will refund all payments made to us by the buyer in respect of the defective seeds or plants and this shall be the limit of our obligation.'	'We hereby exclude all liability for any loss or damage arising from the use of any seeds or plants supplied by us and for any consequential loss or damage arising out of such use or any failure in the performance of or any defect in any seeds or plants supplied by us or for any other loss or damage whatsoever save for, at our option, liability for any such replacement or refund as aforesaid.'	'In accordance with the established custom of the seed trade any express or implied condition, statement or warranty, statutory or otherwise, not located in these conditions is hereby excluded.'

Figure 5.15 Paragraph [2] of Lord Bridge's opinion

Lord Bridge's opinion consists of 22 paragraphs and, as noted above, these have been numbered in square brackets [1] for you in the text of Lord Bridge's opinion set out at the end of this chapter. These square bracketed numbers allow you to cross reference the paragraph numbers set out in Table 5.1, which contains a summary of each of the paragraphs in Lord Bridge's opinion.

You will be asked to summarise each paragraph for yourself, then read the summaries in Table 5.1. By comparing your summary to the one in Table 5.1 and cross referencing back to the full text of the opinion you will begin to understand how to break into difficult texts such as this one. As you acquire expertise in reading such texts, you will be able to make the summaries in your head with only a few paragraphs noted in rough.

ACTIVITY 5.1: SUMMARISING LORD BRIDGE'S OPINION

1. Read Lord Bridge's opinion from paragraphs [1]–[22]

2. As you read, consider whether you understood the original text. If not, why not?

3. Try to classify the function of each paragraph under headings such as:

■   descriptive;

■   setting out facts;

■   procedural;

■   conclusion;

■   proposition or point in an argument;

■   inference;

■   evidence.

Internally identifying the function of individual paragraphs and then clusters of paragraphs is part of the way that one is able to organise a text in terms of its arguments and its proofs. Paragraphs build argument by laying out propositions and evidence (proofs). You should be able to clearly see the arguments and how the text builds up to a final decision.

4. Summarise each paragraph giving only the essential detail. If you do not understand what the paragraph is saying remember the strategy of looking at paragraphs above and below to search for understanding and sense.

5. When you have a summary of the opinion of Lord Bridge with *each* paragraph summarised and numbered in accordance with the numbers in squared brackets in the original text at the end of the chapter it, turn to Table 5.1. Check each of your summary paragraphs against the table and ask yourself whether:

■   your summary contains *all* of the same information;

■   you missed anything;

■   the summary paragraphs are easier to understand in Table 5.1 (if so, consider why this might be?).

TABLE 5.1 A PRÉCIS OF THE OPINION OF LORD BRIDGE IN
*GEORGE   MITCHELL (CHESTERHALL) LTD AND FINNEY LOCKE
SEEDS LTD*

Para nos	Summary of paragraph
[1]	Facts set out. The seller delivered the wrong cabbage seed to the buyer who, as a consequence, had a failed crop with grave financial consequences. The contract of sale limited the seller's liability to a refund of the price of the seeds.
[2]	Issues arise from three sentences in the conditions of sale. These are set out and identified.
	Lord Bridge states he will call the contentious limitation clause 'the relevant condition', and will refer to each sentence as a clause, so clauses 1, 2, 3. If a student reads carelessly this important explanation will be overlooked then the phrase 'relevant condition' and 'clauses 1, 2, 3' will cause confusion when they are used later in the text to refer to his divisions of the contentious limitation clause.
[3]	Sets out the two issues as the common law and the statutory issue. Gives details of relevant legislation.
[4]	Discusses the finding of the trial judge that under the common law the 'relevant condition' could not be relied upon by the sellers. The reason being the seed delivered was 'wholly different'. (As we have already noted issue 2, the statutory issue, need only be dealt with if issue 1 is decided in favour of the sellers.)
[5]	Discusses the finding of Denning LJ in the Court of Appeal. Denning LJ thought the common law issue should be decided in favour of the sellers. He said that the wording of the condition was sufficient to cover the situation. Kerr and Oliver LJJ decided the common law issue against the sellers.
	Kerr LJ's reasoning was that the condition would only cover them for *defects* in the '*correct*' named seeds. Not for delivery of the wrong seeds. Oliver LJ's reasoning was that the condition did not cover the breach because it only happened through the negligence of the seller.
[6]	The Court of Appeal, however, was unanimous in deciding the statutory issue against the sellers.
[7]	Discusses the way that Denning LJ traced the history of the court's approach to such conditions. The conditions being ones that 'limit' or totally 'exclude' a contractual party's liability for any damage caused.
	Lord Bridge picks out two relevant cases (*Photo Production Ltd v Securicor Transport Ltd* [1980] 1 All ER 101 and *Ailsa Craig Fishing Co Ltd v*

TABLE 5.1—Continued

Para nos	Summary of paragraph
	Malvern Fishing Co Ltd [1983] 1 All ER 101) and uses these to explore the common law issue. Note that the judge is beginning to deal with cases decided previously and commenting upon them in relation to whether he is bound by the doctrine of precedent.
[8]	Lord Bridge brings up the phrase 'fundamental breach'. The word 'fundamental' suggests an important breach or break of the contract. The essence of the points made is that: – the *Photo Production* case made it clear that, even if there is a finding of fundamental breach of contract by one party, like the seller here, this finding does not stop a party, the seller, relying on limiting or excluding conditions in the contract; – the *Ailsa Craig* case drew distinctions between: limiting clauses; exclusion clauses. Basically, limitation clauses should not be judged according to the strict principles applied to exclusion clauses, although they remain to be construed *contra proferentem* against the party claiming their protection (*contra proferentem* means construed strictly/against the party relying on it).
[9]	Lord Bridge criticises the trial judge, Parker J, and the Court of Appeal judge, Oliver LJ, for trying to go back to the position. Before the *Photo Production* case, Lord Bridge said a fundamental breach *does not* stop a party relying on exclusions or limitation clauses.
[10]	Lord Bridge points out that the condition applies to seeds sold and indeed seeds were sold! Lord Bridge says that the condition unambiguously applies to the present situation.
[11]	Lord Bridge says that Kerr LJ (in the Court of Appeal) in finding for the seller had in fact misinterpreted what Lord Fraser had said about *The Canada Steamship v R* [1952] 1 All ER 303 in the *Ailsa Craig* case! This is an excellent paragraph for demonstrating the way in which judges argue about other cases, following, distinguishing, overruling or stating the precedent or a case erroneously. Lord Bridge decides the common law point in favour of the sellers in agreement with Lord Denning in the Court of Appeal.

Para nos	Summary of paragraph
[12]	Lord Bridge turns to discuss the 'statutory' issue. We now begin to understand the reference to 'the Act' in issue (2) as set out by Lord Bridge at paragraph [2]. The modified s 55 of the Sale of Goods Act 1979 is set out. The Sale of Goods Act 1979 was a statute that was pure consolidation. (This means that it merely collected together the existing law and put it in one place.) Modified s 55 preserves the law between 18 May 1973 (the date that the Supply of Goods (Implied Terms) Act came into force) and 1 February 1977 (the date that the Unfair Contract Terms Act 1977 came into force).
[13]	Section 55, sub-ss (1), (4), (5) and (9) are set out. Students need to study s 55 carefully to ensure that they understand what it is providing for and that they can follow the discussion of it by Lord Bridge.

An aside: A consideration of the statutory rule of the modified s 55 of the Sale of Goods Act 1979

This is an appropriate moment to look in more detail at s 55 of the Sale of Goods Act 1979 and to experiment with ways of breaking into it. To understand properly the development of the reasoning of the court on the statutory issue, it is vital to spend time understanding the basic layout, interconnections and effect of the provisions. Often, students do not pay sufficient attention to such matters and then wonder why they cannot understand discussions!

The purely textual explanation is complicated and needs to be read in conjunction with the statutory provision. Two diagrams will follow:

- the first, Figure 5.16 sets out s 55 in its entirety similar to the way we have broken into section 1 of the Race Relations Act in Chapter 4. This enables the relationship between differing subsections and paragraphs to be seen. It will be annotated.
- The second, Figure 5.17 is a précis version of s 55, identifying the most relevant sections according to the facts of the case. This has been done by indicating whether the relevant section applies to this case, does nor apply or whether it is unknown whether it applies.

Section 55 is highly complex and it is necessary for you to put personal comprehension time in before we return to the rest of Table 5.1. and the judge's deliberation. But more generally it is often vital for readers to stop and check their understanding, or to check their view against that of the judge and this reflection begins the process of evaluation.

Please study both diagrams carefully until you understand them.

TABLE 5.1—Continued

SECTION 55 OF THE SALE OF GOODS ACT 1979

Words circled = connectors
Words boxed = key phrases

SUB-SECTIONS

(1)

(2) and (3) not referred to ...

Where a right, duty (or) liability would arise under a contract of sale of goods by |implication of law| |it may be negatived (or) varied by express agreement| ... (but) the preceding provision has effect subject to the following provisions of this section.

Note: Lord Bridge at para 12, says "the statutory issue turns on the words in s 55(4), "fair and reasonable" and here they are in context. It is clear these words can only be construed in the light of s 55(5), paras (a)-(e).

(5)

In determining for the purpose of sub-s (4) above |whether| (or) no: reliance on any term would be fair and reasonable, regard shall be had to all the circumstances of the case (and) in particular to the following matters:

Note: does this sound familiar? It should – wording closely mirrored by s 11(2) of UCTA 1977. See Figure 3.12, above, in Chapter 3.

PARAGRAPHS

(a)

the strength of the bargaining positions of the seller and buyer relative to each other, taking into account, among other things the availability of suitable alternative products and sources of supply;

(b)

whether the buyer received an inducement to agree to the term (or) in accepting it had an opportunity of buying the goods or suitable alternatives without it from any source of supply;

(c)

whether the buyer knew (or) ought reasonably to have known of the existence and extent of the term having regard among other things to any previous course of dealing between the parties;

(d)

where the term exempts from all (or) any of the provisions of section 13, 14, 15 above if some condition is not complied with whether it was reasonable at the time of the contract to expect that compliance with that condition would be practicable;

(e)

whether the goods were manufactured processed or adapted to the special order of the buyer.

(9)

(4)

In the case of a |contract| for the sale of goods, |any term| of that (or) any other contract| exempting from all or any of the provisions of sections 13, 14, 15 above |is void| (in) the case of a |consumer sale| (and) is (in) any other case, not enforceable| to the extent that it is shown that it would not be |fair| (and) |reasonable| to allow reliance on the term.

Any reference in this section to a term exempting from all (or) any of the provisions of any section of this Act is a reference to a term which purports to exclude or restrict, (or) has the effect of excluding or restricting the operation of all (or) any of the provisions of that section, or the exercise of a right conferred, by any provision of that section, (or) any liability of the seller for breach of a condition or warranty implied by any provision of that section.

Figure 5.16 Layout of the modified s 55 of the Sale of Goods Act 1979

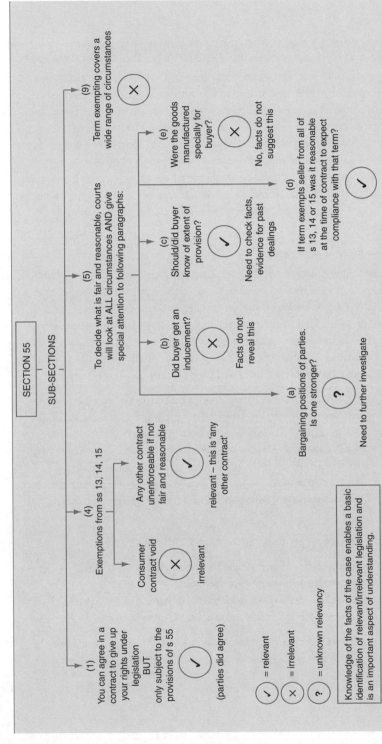

Figure 5.17 Revised diagram of section 55

SECTION 55

SUB-SECTIONS

(1)
You can agree in a contract to give up your rights under legislation BUT only subject to the provisions of s 55

✓

(parties did agree)

(4)
Exemptions from ss 13, 14, 15

Consumer contract void

✗

irrelevant

Any other contract unenforceable if not fair and reasonable

✓

relevant – this is 'any other contract'

(5)
To decide what is fair and reasonable, courts will look at ALL circumstances AND give special attention to following paragraphs:

(a)
Bargaining positions of parties. Is one stronger?

?

Need to further investigate

(b)
Did buyer get an inducement?

✗

Facts do not reveal this

(c)
Should/did buyer know of extent of provision?

✓

Need to check facts, evidence for past dealings

(d)
If term exempts seller from all of s 13, 14 or 15 was it reasonable at the time of contract to expect compliance with that term?

✓

(e)
Were the goods manufactured specially for buyer?

✗

No, facts do not suggest this

(9)
Term exempting covers a wide range of circumstances

✗

✓ = relevant
✗ = irrelevant
? = unknown relevancy

Knowledge of the facts of the case enables a basic identification of relevant/irrelevant legislation and is an important aspect of understanding.

Q: What do ss 13, 14 and 15, say? If you were studying contract you would already know. However, from a comprehension perspective, Lord Bridge does discuss them – you can work it out as a matter of comprehension. At para 14, he says, '... cl 3 of the relevant provision is to exclude, *inter alia*, the terms implied by ss 13, 14, 15. Statute law, while accepting that all common law parties can agree to any legal contract, provides that, in some areas, "protective" terms will be "read into" [implied into] the contract even if, in reality, they have not been written in or spoken'.

TABLE 5.1—Continued

Hopefully you now have a clearer picture of section 55. What you have just done is to read complex information in diagrammatic form. Often, students continue reading text when it is clear to them that they do not understand what they are reading. It is not always viable to draw a diagram. But you should never go on reading when you know that you do not understand what you are reading. You should instead stop and return to that last point in the text when you did understand and re-read – slowly and carefully until you do understand, or at least have a partial understanding that stands a chance of growing as you read on. In texts discussing complex issues, tiny connectors, if missed, rob the reader of understanding. A paragraph-by-paragraph reconsideration will often restore comprehension.

Para nos	Summary of paragraph
[14]	Lord Bridge observes that the contract in question is not a consumer contract but 'any other contract': This information is obtained by a careful reading of s 55(4) plus knowledge of what a consumer sale is; look back at Figure 5.16 and re-read s 55(4). This contract is not a consumer contract and therefore falls under the second heading in s 55(4).
	Lord Bridge further observes that cl 3 of the relevant condition exempts the seller from liability for breach of ss 13 and 14 of the Sale of Goods Act.
	– This is a good example of the need to have an active dialogue with the text. Clause 3 is the third sentence of the relevant condition and the relevant condition is the condition limiting liability.
	– How is this known? Because in paragraph [2] of his opinion Lord Bridge states (see précis above): issues arise from three sentences in the conditions of sale. These are set out and identified. He states he will call this the relevant condition, and will call each sentence a clause, so cll 1, 2, 3.
	Lord Bridge goes on to say that ss 13 and 14 provide that:
	items sold by description should correspond to the description; items sold should be of merchantable quality, and that cll 1 and 2 substitute for the full protection of the legislation the limited obligation to replace seeds or refund price of seeds.
	Lord Bridge sums up that the statutory issue depends on whether cll 1 and 2 are 'fair and reasonable' according to the criteria as set out in s 55(4) and (5).

Para nos	Summary of paragraph
[15]	Lord Bridge gives some general guidelines about how the judiciary should respond to the powers given to it in s 55. He says that one of the reasons that the case is important is that for the first time the House of Lords is being asked to consider a modern statutory provision that gives the court power to decide to override contractual provisions limiting or excluding liability that have been agreed between the parties at common law. This is a far reaching power to interfere with the freedom of individuals to contract. The court can say 'no', you cannot freely agree this, because, in our opinion, it is not fair and reasonable. The actual decision in this case specifically regarding s 55 is of limited importance (as we are told s 55 is protecting the contracts made between 18 May 1973 and 1 February 1978) and, as such, would soon outlive its usefulness. *However*, the wording of s 55 is substantially replicated in s 11 and Schedule 2 of Unfair Contract Terms Act 1977, which Lord Bridge predicts will be of increasing importance. He discusses the fact that the exercise of any power to decide what is fair or reasonable will involve legitimate judicial differences and that the courts should refrain from interfering with the decision of the previous court unless they feel that there was a clearly wrong decision or that the case was decided on some clearly erroneous principle.
[16]	Lord Bridge turns to a question of construction, of the meaning of words used in the statute. The onus is on the respondents to show that it would not be fair or reasonable to allow the appellant to rely on the relevant condition. Appellants said the court must look at the situation at the date of the contract, but Lord Bridge said that the true meaning of the phrase in s 55(5) 'regard shall be had to all the circumstances of the case' must mean that the situation at the time of breach *and* after breach must be taken into account.
[17]	Lord Bridge discusses another issue of the meaning of words used in the statute. The meaning of the words 'to the extent' in s 55(4). Lord Bridge asks: 'Is it fair and reasonable to allow partial reliance on a limitation clause, to decide . . . that the respondents should recover say, half their consequential damage?' Lord Bridge goes on to say that he considers that the meaning of the phrase 'to the extent' is 'in so far as or in circumstances in which'. He suggests that the phrase does not 'permit the kind of judgment of Solomon illustrated by the example'. The reference to Solomon is typical

Para nos	Summary of paragraph
	TABLE 5.1—Continued
	of the literary/religious referencing that one often finds in cases. Solomon was an Old Testament king accredited with much wisdom in his judging. When confronted with a baby claimed by two mothers he suggested cutting it in half so each could have half. The false mother agreed, the real mother said no, the other mother could have the baby. Thus, he located the real mother.
[18]	Lord Bridge goes on to say that his answer in relation to the question is not necessary for the outcome of this case and declines to answer one way or the other! It is interesting to note that if he *had* categorically answered the question, yes or no, it would be a clear example of an *obiter dictum* statement in a strong case by a senior judge and may well have been used in argument in a later case where this issue is at the core of the case.
[19]	Eventually, Lord Bridge turns to the 'application of the statutory language' to the case. He states that only s 55(5)(a) and (c) are relevant. (This is the moment to reread s 55(5)(a) and (c) above, if you do not remember the provisions. Otherwise, one loses sight of the argument!) As to s 55(5)(c), he says of course the buyer knew of the condition as it was standard throughout the trade.
[20]	As to s 55(5)(a), he states that there was evidence that similar limitations had never been negotiated with representative bodies. Witnesses for the appellant said that it had always been their practice in genuine justified claims to settle above the price of the seeds but that, in this case, settlement had not been possible. Lord Bridge said 'this evidence indicated a clear recognition . . . that reliance on the limitation of liability imposed by the relevant condition would not be fair or reasonable'.
[21]	Lord Bridge concluded, therefore, that wrong seed was supplied due to the negligence of the applicant's sister company. Seedsmen could insure against the risk of crop failure caused by the wrong supply without materially increasing the cost of seeds.
[22]	Lord Bridge felt no doubts about the decision of the Court of Appeal over statute. Lord Bridge refers to an earlier point in paragraph [15] that it is wise to 'refrain from interference' in matters of legitimate judicial difference.

Para nos	Summary of paragraph
[23]	'If I were making the original decision, I should conclude without hesitation that it would not be fair or reasonable to allow the appellants to rely on the contractual limitation of their liability.'
Decision	Appeal dismissed

A quick review of the paragraphs begins to show the patterns of argument delivery. Re-reading the paragraphs while looking at the statutory diagrams 5.16 and 5.17 allows the argument to be reviewed whilst looking at the entire provision. The paragraph approach has also allowed the common law issue and the statutory issue to be isolated. Reviewing Figure 5.11 above, dealing with the facts, issues and procedural history enables you to appreciate the differences between the reasoning in the Court of Appeal and the House of Lords, although both courts reached the same decision.

It should be possible at this stage to identify the precise rationale behind the court's view of the common law issue and the statutory issue. In relation to the statutory issue, it should be possible to pinpoint precisely the statutory areas of relevance and how the court dealt with the issue. A summary of this information has been put into diagrammatic form in Figure 5.18.

As proficiency is developed, it will be possible to read carefully and move straight to a diagrammatic representation, although, ultimately, a brief conventional textual note should be made to supplement the diagram. Brief, as you will have seen, does not mean easy or simple!

Constructing a usable case note

One of the most important tasks of a law student or legal professional is the ability to read a case and make a usable record of it. This is technically called a 'case note'. The cases that are reported are invariably important as non-important cases remain as court transcripts.

The point of a case note is to record, in a quick and accessible form, all of the important issues for the later use of the case. That later use will invariably include deciding whether to apply the case to the facts of another legal problem. You may do this if you consider that it is relevant because it sets a precedent that must be followed, marks a change in law (perhaps only at the level of the dissenting judge) or gives a clear interpretation of the meaning of words in legislative rules created or authorised by Parliament.

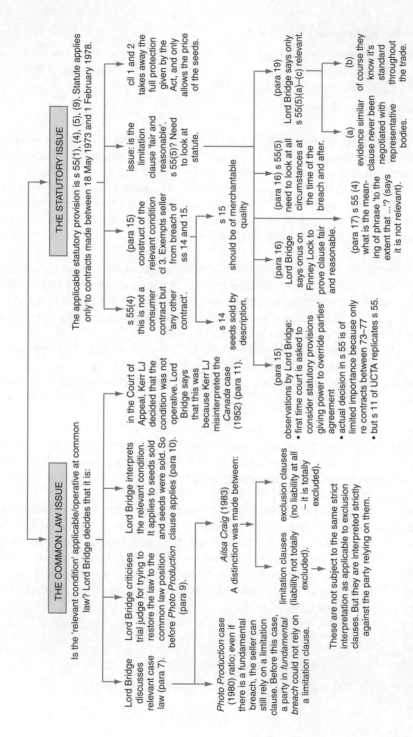

Figure 5.18 Statutory areas of relevance for the *George Mitchell* case

A case note can only be made when you have read and re-read the case under consideration, made notes for yourself and obtained a thorough understanding of the case and the inter-relationships between the legal rules discussed, the facts of the case, and the reasoning of the court. There are differing ways of listing the information that should be included in a case note. Invariably the ordering will be similar to the following:

■ date of court and formal citation of law report;

■ hierarchy of court, judges;

■ facts;

■ issue(s) before the trial court;

■ identification of applicable legal rules;

■ issue(s), before appellate court(s);

■ procedural history of the case;

■ the record of judicial reasoning as to why those rules applied to those facts in that way. Each judge's reasoning should be indicated separately;

■ decision of the court on the appeal (the outcome between the parties).

A case note cannot be used if it only records the facts and the issues before the court but not the rationale for the decision; or if it records the reasoning and not the facts. Everything in law depends upon the legal reasoning which occurs through a careful analysis of the facts of the case in light of the specific legal point before the court for adjudication. By the time a case reaches the appellate court the dispute will be quite narrow and in many ways very different from the dispute on the facts between the parties in the previous trial court, or previous appellate court if it is now in the House of Lords and it previously went on appeal to the Court of Appeal. For example, in a discrimination case the original argument between the parties when the case is first heard will be that one of them has been discriminated against and the other in relation to a section in the Race Relations Act 1976. The point on appeal could, however, be concerned simply with the appropriate meaning of a word or a phrase in a section, subsection, paragraph or subparagraph of the legislation. Several important cases under the Race Relations Act for example have turned on the meaning of the word 'can'. You can only properly use your case note in legal argument when the reasoning of the court is both known and understood by you and stated in your note together with the relevant facts, the legal issues before the court and the applicable legal rules considered.

It is often not even necessary to rehearse the facts of a case in an argument in which the case is used. What is important is that you know the facts and therefore know the points of similarity and difference between the two sets of facts. Then you can apply the reasoning in the earlier case to the later situation. But you cannot know the points of similarity and difference between facts if you do not properly record the facts of the case. The facts are no more and no less than the story of the dispute that reached the courts initially. The facts do not record court decisions; these are placed in the procedural history.

If strenuous efforts have been made to understand a law report thoroughly, the case note will contain all the ingredients to enable it to be competently applied to any problem question or incorporated into any relevant essay. In addition you will have obtained a thorough understanding of the topic.

ACTIVITY 5.2: CONSTRUCTING A CASE NOTE

You have worked through the opinion of Lord Bridge. However, now is the time to refer to the entire case and read the other opinions. If you look back to Figure 5.8, you will see that in addition to Lord Bridge of Harwich (his full title) there were three other Law Lords hearing the case: Lord Diplock, Lord Scarman and Lord Roskill.

1. Using the bullet point list above as headings write a case note of the case of *George Mitchell (Chesterhall) Ltd v Finney Lock Seeds Ltd*. Each of the Law Lords' opinions must be part of your final case note.

2. What precedent(s) come(s) out of this case?

3. Consider the reasoning for the decision by all four Law Lords – would you consider that this case is a strong or a weak precedent?

Once you have written your own case note, you can check the companion website for the completed case note of *George Mitchell v Finney Lock Seeds*, as well as answers to Questions 2 and 3 above. If you carefully complete this exercise and find that your answers are similar in most respects to the model answers on the companion website you have the basic skill of reading law reports in place. Now all you have to do is practise!

Lord Bridge's judgment is set out in full on the companion website.

A case study of *Mandla v Dowell Lee* [1983] 2 AC 548

Mandla v Dowell Lee is a case concerning statutory interpretation where the judge must grapple with the meaning of legislative words and phrases in order to determine the case.

ACTIVITY 5.3: COMPLETE BEFORE READING FURTHER

Locate and read the House of Lords' judgment of Lord Fraser in the case of *Mandla v Dowell Lee* [1983] 2 AC 548. You may choose to read it on one of the law report databases to which you have access, or from a hard copy in a law library. Lord Fraser's judgment gives the facts of the case and considers the judicial decisions in the Court of Appeal. Then read and reflect on the following discussion based upon the reading of the judgment as giving examples of formalism and a teleological approach. The case turns on the interpretation of two sections of the Race Relations Act 1976: section 3 and section 1(1)(b),(c).

The case of *Mandla v Dowell Lee* involved the interpretation of legislative provisions in the Race Relations Act 1976 and went through both appellate courts (the Court of Appeal and the House of Lords) surrounded by much publicity. The crux of the case concerned whether Sikhs constituted a racial group under section 3 of the Act and could therefore claim the protection from racial discrimination provided by various parts of the Race Relations Act 1976. The Court of Appeal decided that Sikhs did not constitute a racial group and could not claim the protection of the Race Relations Act. It was an unpopular decision, taken two days before Lord Denning MR's retirement as Master of the Rolls (the senior judge in the Court of Appeal). At a pace quite unusual in the English legal system it was subject to a quickly listed appeal and a reversal of the Court of Appeal's decision by the House of Lords.

The particular contentious legislative provisions were sections 1 and 3 of the Race Relations Act 1976. Section 3 was the gateway provision. If this section gave Sikhs protection, then the gate to the Act was open, the Act applied to them and the claim under section 1(1)(b) for indirect discrimination could be made. It defined the meaning of racial group by a list, which *inter alia* included 'ethnic origins'. A racial group can be defined by 'ethnic origin'.

When reading the case, however, you will see that in fact the entire case revolved around the interpretation of just three words:

■   'ethnic' in section 3;

■   'can' in section 1(1)(b)(i);

■   justifiable' in section 1(1)(b)(iii).

The case is a good example of the movement from theoretical rules to their inter-pretation and application in reality; a movement from rules in books to the legal construction of reality. It is also a good illustration of the power of the appellate court to determine the meaning of legislation.

The facts of the case were that Mr Mandla, a Sikh, wanted his son to go to a private secondary school. The child was offered a place which was subsequently revoked when the father informed the school that the child would not remove his turban as school uniform rules required. The headmaster stated that the rules concerning uniform were rigid and that other Sikh pupils removed turbans during school hours. Mr Mandla reported the matter to the Commission for Racial Equality (CRE) who took up the case. The CRE alleged that the son had been unlawfully discriminated against, either directly or indirectly, on racial grounds, in that he had been denied a place at the school because of his custom of wearing a turban.

The meaning of the word 'ethnic' in section 3 of the Race Relations Act 1976
This issue was of tremendous importance to the Sikh community as it determined whether they could claim protection from discrimination under the Race Relations Act 1976. The Race Relations Act states that it is unlawful to discriminate against another on racial grounds in the areas covered by the Act. One of these areas is education. To bring an action, it had to be proved that Sikhs were a racial group.

Section 3 of the Act defines racial grounds as:

> . . . a group of persons defined by reference to colour, race, nationality or eth-nic or national origins.

The main argument centred around whether Sikhs fitted into the word 'ethnic', as other words and phrases in the list in section 3 were accepted as not applicable. The trial court found that Sikhs were not a racial group and the appellant appealed to the Court of Appeal and came before Lord Denning.

The Court of Appeal had two choices. It could take the teleological approach, looking at the wider context, and consider the history behind the legislation, the mischief that it was designed to rectify. This would involve using the mischief rule of statutory interpretation and the purposive rule. Or it could choose a formalist approach, considering the text, the word or words, and their possible meanings in a more literal sense. That is they could apply the literal rule of statutory interpretation[10]. Lord Denning had always, in essence, taken a teleological approach. He had, for much of his legal career as a senior judge, fought against blind literalism. He had always fought for the right to 'fill in the gaps' left in legislation. Indeed, his career was often based on the right to take the broader teleological view rather than the narrow, literalist view. Surprisingly, he chose, in this case, to take the formalist approach, to stand by the literal meaning of the words. He discussed the history, or etymology, of the word 'ethnic'. Certainly, the etymology of the word is fascinating, but why did the

---

10 Recall the discussion of these rules in Chapter 4.

legislators choose to put in the word 'ethnic'? Did they do so after scanning its etymology? Of course, it is not known. Yet, the imposition of an interpretation based on the history of a word obviously presumes that, yes, the legislators did consider the etymology of the word when they chose to use it. Otherwise, there is no point in the court doing so.

When constructing legal rules in *fixed* verbal form, language is of the utmost importance. Thought is given to the best words to be used to 'fix' or 'stick' the rule, so that contrary interpretations cannot be reached by courts, and so that the mischief to be tackled is tackled. However, as noted in Chapter 3, the flexibility of language will not allow it to be permanently fixed. The choice of words is often determined by a desire to:

■ make it impossible for judges to change the meaning;

■ make a major policy change as uncontentious as possible;

■ compromise, or a need to compromise, to ensure that major aspects of the draft statute get through the legislative process, and are not blocked by the opposition within, or external to, the government.

In the Court of Appeal in *Mandla v Dowell Lee*, Lord Denning looked at the history of the word 'ethnic', charting its meaning and usage through three editions of the *Oxford English Dictionary*. In the past, he had always argued that words do not and cannot have a literal meaning and yet, here, in a highly contentious case, he traced the history of words.

In Lord Denning's judgment in the Court of Appeal case[11], he noted that, in its original Greek form, 'ethnic' meant 'heathen' and was used by the translators of the Old Testament from Hebrew to Greek to mean non-Israelite, or gentile. He identified the first use of 'ethnic' in English as describing people who were not Christian or Jewish, referring to the 1890 edition of the *Oxford English Dictionary* to confirm this. He then referred to the 1934 edition, stating that its meaning had, by then, changed to denote 'race, ethnological'. This is hardly surprising as the great anthropological expeditions of the 1920s and 1930s introduced the idea of ethnography as the descriptions of unknown groupings of people. His Lordship stated that the 1934 version indicated that 'ethnic' meant 'divisions of races' and, as far as he was concerned, this was right. This is, of course, a highly dubious and subjective viewpoint. But a judge has the power, via language analysis, to make a choice between what is, and what is not, right. Indeed, this is the judge's task.

Finally, he referred to the 1972 version of the dictionary, which gave a wider definition of 'ethnic'. It was this definition that was relied upon by the plaintiff's counsel. Here, 'ethnic' was defined as relating to:

---

11 [1983] QB 1 at 8–10.

... common racial, cultural, religious, or linguistic characteristics, especially designating a racial or other group within a larger system.

Lord Denning then turned to discuss 'origins'[12] for, as used in section 3 of the Race Relations Act, 'ethnic' appears in a small phrase including the word 'origins' ('or ethnic or national origins'). Turning again to the dictionary, noting its usage with parentage, he decided that it meant, as in previous case law, 'a connection arising at birth'. 'Origin', he said, therefore meant a group with a common racial characteristic. His Lordship reconsidered the entire phrase as used in section 3:

... a group of persons defined ... by reference to ... ethnic ... origins.

He concluded that the group must be distinguishable from another by a definable characteristic. Re-reading his judgment in the Court of Appeal, it is noticeable that he constantly used the words he is supposed to be defining in the definitions[13].

Having defined ethnic origin, the next task was to apply that definition to Sikhs to consider whether they could be said to be 'people defined ... by reference to ... ethnic origins'. Lord Denning launched into a potted history of the word 'Sikh' and the people who follow the teaching of Guru Nanak[14]. Again, in a subjective manner, Lord Denning decided that:

1.   Sikhs can only be distinguished by religion, and therefore

2.   they are not defined by 'ethnic origins', and therefore

3.   they are not a racial group, and therefore

4.   it is not illegal to discriminate against Sikhs.

He went on to criticise the CRE for bringing the case, stating that schools should not be interfered with when they properly manage their affairs.

Oliver LJ in the same court said that the dictionary shows 'ethnic' to be a vague word and he doubts whether only the most general assistance can be obtained from dictionaries[15]. Can one discern a community in a loose sense among Sikhs, he asked rhetorically? Without providing evidence, he says no, customs among Sikhs are so disparate they cannot be said to be members of an ethnic group. However, the essence of the discrimination legislation is that the 'man in the street' is the one to discriminate. The court concluded that Sikhs were not an ethnic group. The CRE appealed to the House of Lords.

The House of Lords reversed the decision of the Court of Appeal, allowing the appeal. The House of Lords found that, to be an ethnic group, a group must be

---

12 *Ibid*, at 10.
13 You may find reading the whole of Lord Denning's judgment in the Court of Appeal instructive as he adopts a highly censorial tone towards the CRE for supporting the action.
14 [1983] QB 1, at 11–12 fn 11.
15 Ibid, at 12 fn 11.

regarded by itself and others as a distinct community with, for instance, a shared culture, history, language, common descent or geography, customs, religion. Not all of these factors need be present. The leading (main) opinion given was by Lord Fraser. He discussed the views of Lord Denning and Oliver LJ in the Court of Appeal. He dispensed with the dictionary arguments and the suggestion that ethnic denotes race by saying, in favour of a teleological approach:

> My Lords, I recognise that 'ethnic' conveys a flavour of race but it cannot, in my opinion, have been used in the Act of 1976 in a strictly racial or biological sense. For one thing, it would be absurd to suppose that Parliament can have intended that membership of a particular racial group should depend upon scientific proof of biological characteristics (if possible to prove). It is clear that Parliament must have used the word in a more popular sense. 'Racial' isn't a term of art, either legal or scientific. No, 'ethnic' today has a wide populist meaning denoting common factors of shared history, etc. It would include converts, etc. So by birth or adherence one can have an ethnic origin.

He finds support for his views in a line of New Zealand cases[16] which maintain that it is important to consider how a group regards itself, and is regarded by others. He says that, not only does he like this definition, but:

> . . . it is important that courts in English-speaking countries should, if possible, construe the words which we are considering in the same way where they occur in the same context.

He concludes that, applying his broader definition of ethnic origin, Sikhs are a racial group on ethnic grounds.

This opens the gateway for the court to consider if indeed the boy had been unfairly discriminated against by the school. (You may find it useful at this point to reread the consideration of sections 3 and 1(1)(b) given in Chapter 4.) As the House of Lords found that they were included in section 3 within the idea of ethnic then the details of the indirect discrimination case under section 1(1) could be argued. After the study of s 1, both in terms of connectors and substance, it is appropriate to return to the discussion of the meaning of the words 'can' and 'justifiable', which were the subject of deliberations in the House of Lords. and the judgment of Lord Fraser.

The meaning of the word 'can' in section 1(1)(b)(i)

Mandla argued that the school had indirectly discriminated[17] against his son because they supported a school uniform rule which stated there could be no deviation from the uniform. Because his son wore a turban, which was not permitted under the

---

16 New Zealand has a case-based system and uses the idea of precedent but not as rigidly as in the English legal system. Because of the past close ties to the Commonwealth and the adoption of the English system, cases from commonwealth countries can be used as persuasive precedents in English cases – but they are not binding.

17 Direct discrimination is covered by the Race Relations Act 1976 s 1(1)(a).

school uniform rule, he could not satisfy the requirements of the rule. Therefore he could not attend the school, therefore a condition was applied to him that it was more difficult for him and others like him to comply with. The actual phrase was 'can comply'. The issue turned into a discussion of the meaning of the word 'can' in that subsection.

The school's argument was that 'can' simply meant that someone could do something physically. Equally therefore they could choose not to, and of course that is their choice. So, of course, it is always physically possible to remove a turban. However, this simplified argument neglects the religious, cultural and psychological dimensions of behaviour. If the Race Relations Act 1976 is to have any impact, it cannot be the object of such simplistic interpretation. Lord Fraser stated that 'can' does not merely mean 'can physically comply'. 'Can' means 'can comply' in practice, given the constraints of ethnic origin. If restrictive interpretations were to be placed on a word as seemingly innocent as 'can', it would be possible to undermine the entire purpose of the Act. Herein lies the power of the interpreter of language which, at root, will always remain flexible.

The meaning of the word 'justifiable' in section 1(1)(b)(ii)

Subparagraph (ii) of subsection (b) in section 1 maintains that a condition is discriminatory if it cannot be justified on grounds other than race. The school argued that it wanted total equality among its pupils in all areas including dress. Therefore, the 'no turban rule' was a necessary aspect of uniform, discipline and equality. The school insisted that it was non-sectarian yet the headmaster also maintained that the school wished to project 'a Christian image'. Therefore, by implication suggesting that the turban was also said to be a challenge to the Christian faith. The headmaster also objected because it was a manifestation of the appellant's ethnic origins.

Lord Fraser found that the school could not justify the condition on grounds other than on ethnic origin and that this was illegal under the Act. In addition, Lord Fraser stated that Lord Denning's criticism of the CRE was completely unjustified.

This brief discussion reveals the different approaches to statutory interpretation that can occur as one case travels through the judicial system. Interpretation occurs but the rules of statutory interpretation that a judge is applying are not referred to by the judiciary. Context and perhaps judicial attitudes dictate the rules used. Indeed perhaps the best indicator of what is going on is a careful consideration of what is being said and what 'styles' of interpretation seem represented by the tone of the written opinion of each judge. Each judge does indeed have a personal style. You should begin to be aware of these styles, preferences and differences.

Interpretational problems can never be solved by the neat application of interpretational rules. Even worse, perhaps, the rules do little or nothing to solve problems. Perhaps all they do is justify solutions. There is rarely one right answer, only a range of more plausible and less plausible outcomes, varying according to interpretational styles. Judges use their creativity in working out a solution according to criteria which must be rational either in reality or in argument. They invariably go beyond the text when constructing answers. Lord Denning, for example, moved from dictionary definitions to subjective assertion. Often, judges say no more than 'this is the answer because I say so'.

Judges, as previously noted, can be classified as formalists or contextualists. Knowing this it may sometimes be possible to guess which rules the judges think they are using, though sometimes you may not understand what they are arguing. At times, judges themselves are wrong and not too sure themselves of the appropriate outcome. This is what makes comprehension of the methods of statutory interpretation, and the use of precedents, so difficult. It is essential to realise the limits of a supposed scientific approach and the limitless possibilities that open up when the illogical bridges from one set of rationales to the next are located.

As judges engage more with the European dimensions of interpretation they are being forced to engage more often with the teleological approach used in European cases. As discussed in Chapter 4, the Human Rights Act 1998 states that judges deciding cases on the enforcement of European Convention rights *must* have regard to the case law and jurisprudence of the European Court of Human Rights. In addition, by virtue of the European Communities Act 1972 (as amended) English courts are required to take notice of the decisions of the European Court of Justice. It is highly likely that this consistent engagement will result, over time, in a profound change in the tradition of statutory interpretation within the English legal system.

ACTIVITY 5.4

Do the exercises on the web companion part 2 relating to the Court of Appeal and House of Lords law reports of the case of *Mandla v Dowell Lee*. These will reinforce your reading of cases, writing case notes, breaking into and critiquing the judgments[18] and opinions[19] of the senior judiciary.

How to handle European Community law reports

It is also important that you are able to understand how to read European Community law reports. Whilst all legal systems have some appreciation and acknowledgment of precedent, we have noted the way in which the English legal system has a far more rigid adherence to the idea of precedence than other systems. The Community legal order or *acquis communautaire*, is an artificially created legal system that draws on the legal systems of the Member States for the establishment of approaches to interpretation and law making in relevant areas.

---

18 The decision of the judge in the Court of Appeal is called a judgment.
19 The decision of the judge in the House of Lords is called an opinion.

However the majority of Member States operate from a Civil Code legal system unlike the UK's preference for a common law system. Because of the familiarity of most Member States with civil law systems and the fact that all of the founding members were nation States with civil law systems, the European Community's legal system is deeply embedded in the civil system.

In the English law's common law tradition, the legal theory underpinning the practical approach to decision making in the law courts is the declaratory theory. This states that when a judge in court is deciding a case he declares in his decision what the law *is*. The case can then become an important precedent, as it states the law and determines when other courts must follow it. One case can determine and preset the law within the limits of the doctrine of precedent.

In civil law systems codes are used to organise areas of law. All civil systems are based in different ways on Roman law where the legal theory position is that when a judge in a court makes a decision about the law, that decision is *evidence* of the law. The European Court of Justice (ECJ) not surprisingly, when setting up legal principles that apply across all member states and cases, drew upon the legal experience of all Nation States, but the minority approach of the English legal system is not the approach in the Community legal order as there were 15 years of development of the legal system before the UK joined.

The English common law system decisions of the courts are the law, rather than evidence of what it is thought to be. Through the system of precedent in the English legal system, previous court cases and law cases are presented to the court as precedents.

But this is not the case in the ECJ where arguments consider other cases and other documents and practices in order to present what may seem appropriate principles of the law.

It may seem odd that there is a lack of precedent in the ECJ. But the ECJ has a determination to carefully develop and keep legal principles which do give a great deal of consistency and coherence to Community law. Commentators have noted that it has now become normal and accepted for courts to refer to earlier cases and use these earlier cases as the rationale for decisions, which begins to feel like precedent. However, even given these suggestions of openness to the concept of precedent there is no suggestion that the ECJ would ever reach a decision that it did not want to purely because of other cases deciding matters differently. The reverse could, however, occur in the English legal system.

When you read ECJ reports – unless you are reading them in French – you will be reading a translation, for French is the working language of the court and the French judicial style is the commonly accepted model. You will find short sentences with facts, arguments and final conclusions. The language is formal and characterless in contrast to English judgments, which take on the linguistic style of the particular judge. No conflicting judgments are published – only one judgment reflecting the opinion of the Court. Indeed, judges are sworn to secrecy over disagreements!

Instead of reading a judgment that is conducting a reasoned argument one tends to find the listing of ultimate conclusions as assertions.

To assist you to begin to understand the differences of approach and construction of European law reports a case study of a leading case *Van Gend en Loos v Nederlandse Tariefcommissie* (case 26/62) [1963] CMLR 105 has been placed on the website companion.

You will be 'talked' through it in a similar manner to the case of *George Mitchell.*

CONCLUSION

■   The doctrine of precedent means English judges, when deciding cases in court, must refer to similar prior decisions of the higher courts, and keep to the *reasoning* in those cases.

■   Much depends on the definition of the word 'similar', and this is determined by the judges in the court.

■   Locating the *ratio* or principle of a case can be difficult and there may be dissenting views among the judges hearing the trial or the appeal.

■   The practice of the doctrine of precedent in the English legal system requires a system of accurate reporting of legal cases.

■   Law reports are reports of important cases (for example cases where the judge has extracted a 'new' legal rule and/or cases involving statutory interpretation).

■   A paragraph-by-paragraph reading approach is the best way to gain an in-depth understanding of the law report of a case.

■   A case note must include date of hearing, citation, court, procedural history, the facts of the case, the legal issues before the court, legal rules discussed, the judicial reasoning of each judge for the decision reached, the outcome between the parties.

FURTHER READING

As already mentioned, if you are a law student the ground covered by this chapter will also be covered in English legal system courses and constitutional or public law courses. Coverage of reading cases can be found in the following excellent texts relating to both the theoretical and practical aspects of legal method.

C Sychin, *Legal Method* (2nd edn Sweet & Maxwell, London 1999).

W Twining and D Miers, *How To Do Things With Rules* (4th edn CUP, Cambridge 1999).

READING TEXTS ABOUT LAW

" Reading is to the mind what exercise is to the body. It is wholesome and bracing for the mind to have its faculties kept on the stretch."

Augustus Hare

LEARNING OUTCOMES

After reading this chapter and the relevant reading you should be able to:

- develop a reading strategy for secondary texts based on your purpose for reading;

- competently use different methods of reading;

- quickly identify whether a secondary text is relevant to your needs;

- identify the main and subsidiary issues in a secondary text;

- identify the main argument(s) in a secondary text, outlining both propositions and evidence;

- combine and compare arguments from several sources to effectively answer an essay question;

- gain confidence in reading and using secondary texts.

CHAPTER SUMMARY

At the beginning of this book, the distinction was made between primary texts of law and secondary texts about law. While the core of legal studies is, or should be, the primary legal text, it is also vital to handle competently secondary legal texts: textbooks, academic journal articles, official publications, and so on. Articles and books about law are consulted, in panic or at leisure, for a range of reasons. For example, you may wish to obtain:

- a general grasp of an area of law;

- a description of a topic;

- a range of different views about a case, statute, area, theory or method;

- a sophisticated analysis of a topic or case;

- historical or political data on law.

Usually, this information is being sought to provide the raw material for use in answering an essay question, writing a project, or answering a problem question. The ultimate answer will only be as good as your ability to:

- understand the assessment or seminar task;

- competently undertake the research required;

- identify the arguments in the material;

- understand the arguments in the material;

- evaluate the arguments in the material;

- compare the arguments in the material;

- differentiate between information, description and argument;

- write a good conclusion to an assessment.

This chapter briefly introduces a general reading strategy that can be used to identify, understand, evaluate and compare arguments in the material you read. The strategy will be demonstrated by applying it to the reading of a short article by JHH Weiler, 'The European Union belongs to its Citizens: Three Immodest Proposals' (1997) 22 EL Rev 150–56.

Chapter 2 has already discussed the various types of secondary text available. In this chapter we will focus on breaking into texts and understanding the article or book chapter. The chapter is also complemented by Chapters 7 and 8 which consider argument construction and legal reasoning.

READING EFFICIENTLY

Once they have realised they have to read, the burning question for most students is how to read efficiently. So much reading is required on a law degree that you need to acquire good habits very quickly, and know how to adapt your reading to suit the type of text and the purpose for which it is being read. For each text located, vital decisions have to be made:

■   is this text relevant?

■   is it necessary to skim read and/or scan, and/or close read?

■   what is/are the argument(s) of the text?

Just as it is vital to have a research plan, and a strategy for assessing the authority and the reliability of retrieved texts, it is absolutely essential to have a plan for reading your retrieved materials. Reading in the context of studying always implies reading for a purpose. The parameters of the problems before you have to be carefully thought out before you start reading. All too often students see reading as passive, moving their eyes from one line to the next without necessarily stopping to join the words into sentences and derive meaning from those sentences. Some readers researching books do not write notes, nor consider how they will remember everything of relevance in the absence of notes. Strategies for note-taking have to be competent as well.

As a law student you may be given a problem question to research, or an essay to write. With both types of assessment activity, it is vital that you correctly identify the limits of the question. For example, the facts of problem cases are often set in the areas between decided cases where there is an area of 'unknown', an area that the student is expected to talk about confidently. The competent identification of the issues from the outset often determines the quality of the answer. These matters are explored in greater detail in Chapter 9.

The care given to the reading of cases and statutory provisions has *also* to be brought to the reading of secondary explanatory, interpretative or evaluative texts. Reading with an idea of why the text is being read, and a view of what you hope to do with the extracted information, will help you devise an appropriate reading and note-taking strategy. Ask yourself: 'Am I reading this for description, information or analysis?'; 'Am I seeking to find out basic things about the topic or am I trying to support propositions in my argument?'.

The most important issue is to grasp that reading can never be a purely passive act, because a writer always seeks to engage the reader in active dialogue with the text. No one writes in order not to be read, and no one wishes to be read passively without thought entering into the reading process. Try to develop an inner dialogue between yourself and the text as you read. You should be continually processing, reflecting, considering, agreeing or disagreeing with the information. If you become frustrated or bored with the text, stop. Are you scared, threatened, annoyed with the text? If so, why?

Not allowing enough time to read a text can be fatal to understanding. This causes stress. Often students have an over-optimistic view of how long it takes to read and understand an article or set reading from a book. This means that they rarely get to a point of understanding the article properly and getting the most out of it. If you only allow thirty minutes to read an article that takes two hours to read properly you are setting up the conditions for your own failure. To assist you to get to grips with this issue please complete task 1(a), task 1(c) and task 4 in Activity 6.1 to get a grasp of your reading speed. Task 1(b) is important but you can do it another time. Task 2 is particularly important, but needs to happen the day after you complete the other tasks, so come back to it tomorrow.

Everyone is of course different, and reading speeds will dramatically change. Even fast readers can be slowed down by complex ideas, unfamiliar technical vocabulary and unfamiliar standard English vocabulary. So this first activity is just designed to obtain a very broad idea of your reading speed for academic purposes.

ACTIVITY 6.1: FINDING YOUR READING SPEED

Time yourself reading work for your academic degree course and:

1. Make a note of your start time – note exactly how long it takes you to do the following:

    (a) Read five pages in a focused way for detailed understanding *without* writing notes.

    (b) Read a *different* set of five pages in a focused way for detailed understanding, this time writing notes.

(c)   Read a third *different* set of five pages quickly to get a general sense of what is being said without writing notes.

When you know how long each of the above standard tasks take then you can know how long a reading task will take you no matter how many pages you are given.

2.   The next day return to re-read task 1(a) and task 1(c) above. Then write down what you can remember from your reading the previous day.

3.   From the above exercise in 1 & 2 did you realise that you have at least two academic reading speeds: focused and quick?

4.   Were you able to complete task 2 or had you forgotten everything? This is the most likely outcome. It is essential to take notes for focused reading and sometimes basic notes for quick reading can be of assistance. You will slowly learn the best strategies to adopt.

There are four main stages to any reading enterprise:

1. Preparation prior to reading:

■   locating texts;

■   ascertaining purpose for reading.

2. Methods of reading:

■   skimming;

■   scanning for key words;

■   in-depth focused reading.

3. Understanding what is being read.

4. Critically evaluating what is being read.

These are deceptively easy stages to set out but much harder to utilise for the first time, especially if you have any already established ill-disciplined approaches to reading. Each of the above stages can be split into sub-stages, as the following strategy for competent reading demonstrates.

TABLE 6.1 THE FOUR STAGES OF READING

STAGE 1

Preparation prior to reading

Reading intention:
- why am I reading this text?
- what do I hope to get out of it?

Reader prediction of use and content of text:
- this involves a consideration of what the writer is saying. This can be judged from the subject matter and the title;
- the very act of choosing a text involves prediction:

    that this text is relevant;

    that the text will begin to answer some of the questions that you have in your mind.

STAGE 2

Methods of reading

Skimming: read very quickly and generally through a text noting:
- publication date – for the study of law, it is particularly vital to know which edition you are reading; texts can go out of date due to changes in the law in a matter of months;
- index;
- foreword;
- any headings and sub-headings;
- author details;
- introductory paragraphs;
- the first sentence or two of paragraphs following introductions;
- look at concluding paragraphs.

This activity assists in deciding the potential relevance of the text.

Scanning:
- Unlike the general skim through, scanning involves quickly looking for specific words, phrases or information.

Detailed reading:
- Reading will allow attention to be given to secondary or subsidiary points in the text. Here, the reading is slower and careful. Check unfamiliar vocabulary. Some words and phrases become clear as more text is read.

    Note the type of language used:
        technical;
        figurative;
        journalistic;

academic;

personal (you must . . .);

impersonal (one must or it is therefore);

intimate;

distanced.

> Note how arguments are put together:
> - are points backed up by reference to evidence?
> - are points made left to stand alone without evidence?
>
> Details on argument are found in Chapter 7.

STAGE 3

Understanding what is being read

Guessing words that you do not know:

- Do not expect to know all the words read. Even as a more extensive vocabulary is acquired, there will be words that are not known.

Identifying main ideas:

- Many main ideas will have been discovered on a first skimming. A second reading begins the process of identifying the main points made by the writer. This aids in the acquisition of a deeper understanding of the arguments presented in the text.

Identifying subsidiary ideas:

- As the main points are identified, it is possible to organise the information and classify secondary, subsidiary points.

Identifying overall text organisation:

- Every writer has a different way of organising, classifying and structuring their work. This needs to be ascertained by any reader who wishes to break into the text successfully.

An initial issue is to decide whether the writer is: outlining an area;

- discussing a specific problem;
- proposing a solution to a problem;
- comparing and contrasting ideas;
- speaking of the present, future or the past.

STAGE 4

Evaluating what you are reading

Ascertaining the purpose of the writer:

- This is crucial.
- Does the writer want to inform you about something or try to persuade you of the correctness of a particular point of view?
- Often a writer will seek to both inform and persuade.

TABLE 6.1—Continued

Ascertaining the argument(s) of the writer:

- Some texts are said to be complex not because they use particularly difficult words or arguments but because, in order to understand the full detail of the writer's position, extensive knowledge of other areas within or outside the particular discipline will be required.

Ascertaining the attitude of the writer:

- Writers are usually biased towards a certain view in their writing, although on occasion a writer may be neutral.
- You must be able to gain skill in identifying a writer's attitude to the ideas he or she is discussing.
- You must at least know whether the writer is neutral or biased.

A STRATEGY FOR COMPETENT READING

Each of the four stages outlined above is interconnected as shown in Figure 6.1. We will now work through each stage.

Reading an article

Applying the reading strategy demonstrates that reading appropriately is a highly disciplined, complex and skilled process. The reading strategy will be applied to an article, 'The European Union belongs to its Citizens: Three Immodest Proposals' by JHH Weiler; the full text can be found on the companion website, along with answers to the activities. Numbers in square brackets in the article denote the paragraph and these are referred to by number in the diagrams and text in this chapter. The task we will undertake is outlined in Figure 6.2 on page 216.

Demonstration of the reading strategy

Stage 1: Preparation prior to reading

Identify your reading intention with the following questions:

- ■ Why am I reading this text?

    - ■ to learn *how* to read texts?

    - ■ or because this particular legal text happens to be the one chosen (by tutor or by self)?

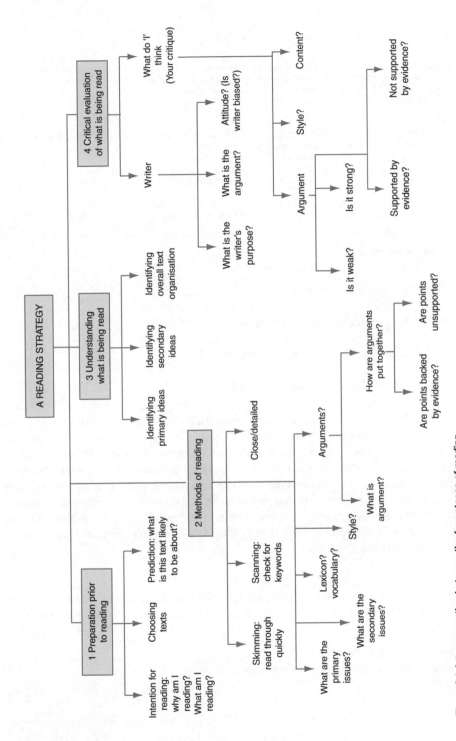

Figure 6.1 Interconnection between the four stages of reading

Task

The article to be read, 'The European Union belongs to its citizens: three immodest proposals', is a relatively uncomplicated article in terms of language usage and concepts introduced. This makes it ideal for current purposes to provide a short demonstration of the reading strategy and enable feedback.
The first task is for *you* the reader to participate.

You are asked to:
1 Study carefully the four stage reading strategy that has been set out above in both its narrative and diagrammatic forms. Make sure that you understand how each of the stages is interconnected. This may take any time from 20 minutes to an hour.
2 Then following each stage of the reading plan read the article. Make notes as appropriate.
3 Compare your notes of the reading with the demonstration of the reading strategy that follows immediately after this task.
   (i) Were there any major differences between your version and the version in this text?
   (ii) How did this occur? Where you have any gaps go back to the text to see how you missed them.

Figure 6.2 Reading strategy task

■   What do I hope to get out of it?

   ■   a strategy for competent reading?

   ■   or some new knowledge from the article?

■   What does the title of the article suggest?

It is about the European Union and it suggests that it 'belongs to its citizens'. The last phrase of the title is a deliberate play on words. Usually, an author would say 'I am making three *modest* proposals'. This author is being controversial and states 'three *immodest* proposals'. Usually, people will argue that they are only suggesting modest, small changes. Here the suggestion is that the changes are large and perhaps outrageous. The first part of the title sounds like a political slogan, a call to arms maybe. So the article is, or should be, about proposals relating to the concept of the Union belonging to its citizens. Did you pick up on the unusual usage of immodest? Or did you ignore the word and just read the title as 'three proposals . . .'?

Stage 2: Methods of reading

Different tasks require different kinds of reading. Initially you want to learn about the author, how old the article is and the structure of the article (which you can easily ascertain from any headings in it).

Skimming and scanning

Read very quickly and generally through the text noting:

- **Publication date:** 1997. The date gives a context to the article. Today you are reading this many years after it was written. Changes may have occurred in that time.

- **Headings and sub-headings:**

  - Introduction;

  - Proposal 1: the European Legislative Ballot;

  - Proposal 2: Lexcalibur – the European Public Square;

  - Proposal 3: limits to growth.

- **Author details:**

  - Name: JHH Weiler;

  - Title: Professor of Law and Jean Monnet Chair, Harvard University;

  - Job: Co-director, Academy of European Law, European University Institute Florence.

Note that Jean Monnet was one of the original architects of the European Community in 1957. Harvard is a prestigious American university with a renowned law school, so the job titles of this author add weight to the potential authority of the argument forwarded.

- **The introduction:** What does a skim read of the introduction tell us? We will note it is only eight paragraphs long. The introduction is usually where the author gives the map of the argument. Many academic articles come with an abstract summarising the article which greatly assists in determining whether it is relevant. Figure 6.3 provides a précis of these opening paragraphs.

ACTIVITY 6.2

Read the first sentence or two of the paragraphs following the introduction.

Also quickly read the *concluding paragraphs on the last page of the article*. The article does not have a signalled conclusion, but it does conclude with paragraph 30 stating:

ACTIVITY 6.2—Continued

The IGC[1] has proclaimed that the European Union belongs to its citizens. The proof of the pudding will be in the eating.

■ Did you note the use of the figurative language (proof of the pudding)?

■ What figure of speech is it?

■ What is the source domain of the metaphor?

■ What is the target domain of the metaphor?

■ What does it mean? What is the message that you the reader get from the metaphor?

Para 1	Asks the reader to recall days of the Maastricht Treaty. Notes who was for and who against and raises doubts about understanding.
Para 2	Talks of: – street reaction relating back to title; – disempowerment of the individual European citizen.
Para 3	Gives three 'roots' of disempowerment: (i) democratic deficit;
Para 4	states second root. (ii) ever-increasing remoteness, opaqueness and inaccessibility of European governance;
Para 5	third root: (iii) competencies of the Union.
Para 6	One sentence: don't be surprised by the alienation.
Para 7	Says proposals of IGC 'very modest', with those who gain being governments, and consumers losing out.
Para 8	Says the author will give three proposals that can make a difference without a political fuss.
The three proposals: • proposal 1: the European Legislative Ballot; • proposal 2: Lexcalibur – the European Public Square; • proposal 3: limits to growth.	

Figure 6.3 Skim précis of paragraphs 1–8

---

1   Inter-Governmental Conference.

This activity has assisted in deciding the potential relevance of the text. If the work in hand concerned the European citizen, enough has been gained by the introduction, headings and last paragraph to conclude that the article is relevant. Unlike a general skim through, scanning involves quickly looking for specific words, phrases or information. This approach could also be used to check for potential relevancy of any research materials retrieved for any academic task.

Detailed reading

A detailed reading will allow you to begin to identify primary and secondary or subsidiary arguments properly in the text. Here, the reading is slower and more careful. Do make sure that you check out unfamiliar vocabulary. Some words and phrases will become clearer as more text is read. In our article, you might question:

■   the word 'Lexcalibur'. What does it mean? Where does it come from?

■   the phrase 'the European public square'. What does it mean?

Neither the word 'Lexcalibur' nor the phrase 'the European Public Square' can be found in a dictionary. However, their meanings unfold as you read the article.

Note the type of language used. The most obvious language usage in the article is *figurative*. The writer uses short sentences, slogans, rhetorical questions, poetic language, metaphor and even invents words (for example, Lexcalibur, signalling the literary Excalibur sword of King Arthur and his noble Knights of the Round Table). Take a look at the break down of figurative language noted in Figure 6.4. Often readers, and particularly students, do not follow the signposts to argument located in the figurative language. They miss clues and connections and certainly do not take the opportunity to question the argument that is being formed, in part, by poetic language.

Stage 3: Understanding what is being read

There are a number of stages to work through to increase your understanding of the text, including:

■   **Guessing words you do not know.** Do not expect to know all the words read. Even as a more extensive vocabulary is acquired, there will be words that are not known. You may have singled the following out already: Lexcalibur, democratic 'deficit', 'competencies of the Union', 'specific gravity' and 'apocryphal statement'. The guessed meaning of words can be double-checked in a dictionary but remember that unusual combinations of words may bring with them meanings not caught in a dictionary. Here informed guesses followed by plausible interpretation may be all you have to go on.

■   **Identifying main ideas.** The main idea in the article is that a package of three proposals (a limited ballot by citizens concerning legislation, internet access to

Political imagery	the Mandarins heralded
Mathematical imagery	'what's-in-it-for-me?' calculus
Architectural/geological	shaky foundation
Nature imagery	roots of disempowerment
Scientific imagery	the specific gravity of whom continues to decline
Nature imagery	the second root goes even deeper
Religious imagery	an apocryphal statement
Food imagery	it is End of Millennium Bread and Circus Governance
Elemental imagery	could be shielded behind firewalls
Grand teleological style	ours is a vision which tries to enhance human sovereignty, demystify technology and place it firmly as servant and not master
Food imagery	• the European Court of Justice should welcome having this hot potato removed from its plate • the proof of the pudding will be in the eating

Figure 6.4 Examples of figurative language

European decision-making and establishment of a constitutional council), taken from research, initiated by the European Parliament, can make a real difference in increasing the power of the European citizen without creating a political drama.

■ **Identifying subsidiary ideas.** You should be able to identify that there could be potential clashes between the constitutional council and the function of the European Court of Justice.

■ **Identifying overall text organisation.** Every writer has a different way of organising, classifying and structuring their work. Here the author has clearly indicated structure through headings and has discussed the points in the order indicated. Overall, the writer is:

■ discussing a specific problem; and

■ proposing a solution to that problem.

Identifying the main argument
In chapter 7 we will be discussing general issues relating to argument and a specific definition will be given. The argument presented by the author in this article has been

divided into propositions (assertions, or statements building the argument) and the evidence supporting them, as outlined below. At this point it is essential to note that many readers do not differentiate between the two issues. This is a major error and leads to confusion and misunderstanding. A proposition is a statement being put forward. Strong propositions are given their strength by evidence supporting them. A weak argument has no or little evidence. Therefore you must always differentiate between the two.

1. **Proposition 1, located in paragraph 2:** The Maastricht Treaty was not the remarkable diplomatic achievement it was claimed to be.

Evidence: street reaction apathetic, confused, hostile, fearful:

(i)   Danes voted against it;

(ii)   French approved it marginally (1 per cent);

(iii)   commentators at the time said that if there had been greater scrutiny in Great Britain and Germany the outcome would have been uncertain;

(iv)   even those supporting it were just plain greedy.

2. **Proposition 2, located in paragraph 3:** There was a 'growing disillusionment with the European construct as a whole'.

Evidence: None given.

3. **Proposition 3, located in paragraph 3:** The *'moral and political legitimacy'* of the European construct is in decline.

Evidence: There is 'a sense of disempowerment of the European citizen' which has many roots, but three stand out: paragraph 4:

(i)   democratic deficit; paragraph 4;

(ii)   remoteness; paragraph 5;

(iii)   competencies of union. paragraph 6.

Conclusion: a package of three proposals taken from research, initiated by the European Parliament, can make a real difference in increasing the power of the European citizen without creating a political drama.

The summary of the argument as set out in the introduction (in paragraphs 1–3) is as follows:

The Maastricht Treaty was not the diplomatic achievement it was claimed to be. The European citizen continues to be disempowered. There remains a growing disillusionment with the European Union as a whole which is suffering from a decline in its moral and political legitimacy. However, a package of three proposals (a limited ballot by citizens concerning legislation; internet access to European decision-making; establishment of a constitutional council), taken from research, initiated by the European Parliament, can make a real difference to increase the power of the European citizen without creating a political drama.

Stage 4: Evaluating what you are reading

As you read you should ensure you:

■   ascertain the purpose of the writer. The writer wants to inform about something and indicate the correctness of a particular point of view;

■   evaluate the argument(s) of the writer.

The argument here is relatively easy to extract because the article is written in a punchy, journalistic style. What is clear, however, is that the detail that has been given in setting out the three proposals is not matched when indicating evidence to support propositions, perhaps because the writer feels that many of his propositions are self-evident. This would be a weakness of the article if you wished to use it for academic work.

Having ascertained the arguments, it is up to you to decide your view of the persuasiveness of the article, the strength of the argument and the evidence put forward supporting it. Your view of the argument of the writer will initially be limited by your lack of knowledge of the issues spoken of. But as you conduct more research, you will learn more about competing views and the area in general. Your view of the argument may then change or develop.

Sometimes you may need far more information before you can evaluate the writer's proposals concerning problems and solutions. You may not even agree with the problem itself. If a problem has been misdiagnosed, then the solution will not work. If the problem has been correctly identified, but the wrong causes attributed then, again, the solution will not work. In any text identifying problems and putting forward solutions in argument or description formats, the following questions need to be asked:

■   is it plausible to classify these circumstances as a problem?

■ is it plausible to maintain that these are the causes of the problem?

■ given the view on the above two questions, is it plausible to offer these solutions?

■ is this conclusion plausible?

■ do I agree with the conclusion to the argument?

■ if I do not, how do I attack it?

■ do I agree with all of the propositions that are the building blocks in this argument? Are the propositions strong or weak?

Try answering these questions in relation to the article on the European citizen. If there is any area of lack of understanding, ask yourself 'why?' Are there problems with the vocabulary, or the concepts, or is there too much pre-supposed information? What is the attitude of the writer? Writers are usually biased towards a certain view in their writing, although on occasion a writer may be neutral. You must be able to gain skill in identifying a writer's attitude to the ideas he or she is discussing. You must at least know whether the writer is neutral or biased.

Using the article with other texts

Having read the article, it is possible to represent the argument as shown in Figure 6.5. This is a useful method of viewing all arguments unidimensionally, which our brain cannot do quite so easily with text.

If you were marshalling evidence for an essay entitled 'Does the European Union Belong to its Citizens?', it would be possible to incorporate the views of Weiler, and other authors – we will call them X, Y and Z – into the essay by slotting them into your diagram, as shown in Figure 6.6. Here we have annotated in Figure 6.6 whether X, Y or Z agree or disagree with Weiler's argument and evidences. In addition, you would look in leading textbooks to see if those authors had anything to state.

Having noted the areas of agreement and disagreement between the authors on the diagram, a clear view emerges of strong and weak arguments. Then, it is possible for you to come to a personal conclusion. If you do not feel able to come to a personal conclusion, ask yourself the following questions:

■ is there enough information collected to properly cover the area?

■ have all of the arguments put forward been understood?

■ is there a lack of empirical/practical evidence to support theoretical positions?

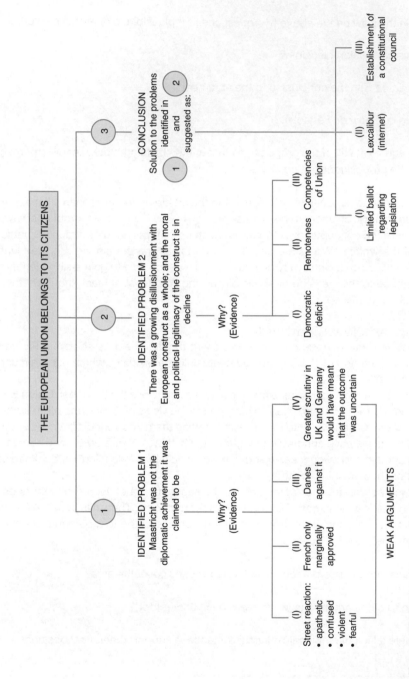

Figure 6.5 Weiler's argument in diagrammatic form

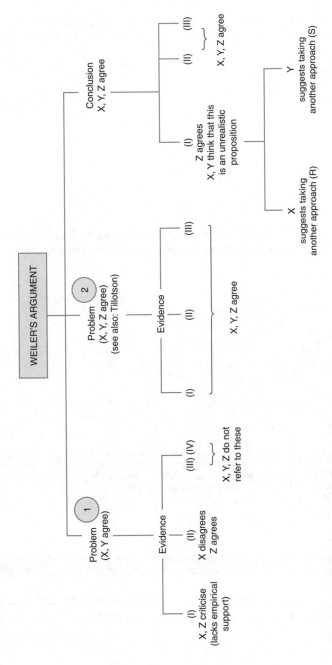

Figure 6.6 Comparing Weiler's argument with other texts

It is vital to decide whether there is enough information and this is often a subjective matter.

A brief conclusion to the above suggested essay is given in Figure 6.7. It centres on Weiler's articles and the imaginary authors X, Y, Z. Hopefully, it forcefully illustrates how:

■   identification;

■   organisation;

■   classification;

■   competent reading strategy and notes;

■   diagrams

can work together to bring clarity of thought and expression. Textbooks are not included here but if a textbook did comment on a theory or give useful insights, these could also be incorporated.

'The European Union belongs to its citizens.' Discuss.

Conclusion

Weiler (1997) argues that at present the European citizen does not exert power over policy and law making within the European Union. This indicates that the European Union certainly does not belong to its citizens. However, as noted above, he convincingly argues that with very little change the situation could be rectified. X (1997), Y (1998) and Z (1998), in large part, agree with Weiler, both in terms of the problems and solutions presented by him.

It is suggested that Weiler's argument is well set out and is essentially backed by supporting evidence and attainable solutions. It is further suggested that the evidence presented concerning proposition 1, that Maastricht was not the diplomatic achievement it was claimed to be, is weak. A point also noted by X (1997) and Y (1998).

Proposition 2 is strongly supported by the available evidence. If the governments of the Member States and the institutions of the European Community seriously consider the issue of the European citizen in terms of Weiler's problems and solutions, it may well be that, in the opening years of the new millennium, it will be possible to maintain that the European Union does belong to its citizens.

Figure 6.7 Conclusion for a sample essay question

CONCLUSION

■   Secondary texts are an important component of research for essays, problem questions and assessment. They should be read with as much care as primary sources.

■ Effective reading involves defining your purpose and acquiring the ability to adopt different reading strategies according to that purpose.

■ Reading and understanding arguments are linked. If you do not understand what an argument is and how it is constructed then reading a text may not be enough. With this in mind Chapter 7 concentrates upon the techniques of argument construction.

■ Consideration should be given to the standpoint of the author and the evidence provided (or not provided) to support their argument.

FURTHER READING

If you find that you are having trouble with reading, particularly in relation to your reading speeds or breaking into texts, it is useful to consult a general text dealing with issues of how to read effectively.

D McGovan, *Reading* (Prentice Hall, New York 1994).

A Northledge, *The Good Study Guide* (2nd edn Open University Press, 2005).

See Chapter 2 section 2 on reading (you have already been referred to this general study skills text in Chapter 1).

COMPANION WEBSITE

Now visit the companion website to:

■ work through the series of Part Two related exercises in Workbook Two;

■ tackle quiz questions on domestic and European legislation, General Treaties and statutory interpretation;

■ access the author's 'Talk through exercises', further explaining how to read a case through a case study on Van Gend en Loos, and how to read statutory interpretation through a case study on the Unfair Contract Terms Act 1977.

PART THREE:

ARGUING THE LAW – THE CONSTRUCTION OF ARGUMENT

"Imagination is more important than knowledge"

Albert Einstein

This section of the book develops your competency in identifying, constructing and critiquing arguments. The ability to construct an argument is a key skill in all disciplines and many professions. A good lawyer is not just a wordsmith, but also an 'argument-smith', a skilled producer of arguments. It takes knowledge, imagination and creativity to build an elegant argument. Could, as Albert Einstein says above, imagination even be more important than knowledge? What do you think?

You will need to deploy both legal and academic arguments in your legal study. It is therefore important to know what each looks like. Without the ability to argue you will journey less effectively to your destination of successful legal study, taking circuitous routes or dead-end paths because you have not made informed choices. With a good understanding of the basics, you will be able to continue learning about the nature of arguments throughout your academic, vocational and professional life.

Chapter 7: The anatomy of argument introduces the general characteristics of induct-ive and deductive arguments and their basic building blocks (propositions, evidence and conclusions). It also spends time considering the nature of rules and problems. This is important as you will spend much of your time as a law student identifying problems and applying rules to resolve problems.

Chapter 8: Legal Reasoning considers in particular the form of legal reasoning used in the English common law system and looks in detail at breaking down problem scenarios and applying law to facts. As such it concentrates unusually on fact management, the management of the facts of problems and how to attach them to the legal rule involved in a particular problem. This chapter provides the basic material for careful legal problem solution because in order to engage in legal analysis you need to be able to match facts to the elements making up a legal rule. If you cannot do this you will not understand how to apply law reports to problem questions to reach a solution and may not be able to apply a range of secondary academic texts and law reports to help you construct essay arguments. Once you have achieved competency in the area of basic argument construction you can move on to Part Four of this text, which discusses essays and problem solutions in detail.

Chapters 7 and 8 will introduce you to material that is particularly unfamiliar. However, if you take the time to read and understand them you will be rewarded with an increase in your competency to construct arguments. This ability will not only make a great difference to your university-based academic work, it will also stand you in good stead in employment and social settings.

THE ANATOMY OF ARGUMENT

7

" Logic is the anatomy of thought."

John Locke

LEARNING OUTCOMES

After reading this chapter you should be able to:

■ define argument and explain its general characteristics;

■ distinguish between inductive and deductive argument;

■ appreciate the importance of analogous reasoning in the English legal system;

■ appreciate the process of argument construction and the skills required to complete them effectively;

■ understand the relationship between the diagnosis of problems and the construction of rules to solve problems;

■ understand the relationship between facts, evidence and legal rules;

■ appreciate the limitations of logical reasoning and the necessity of legal judgments.

CHAPTER SUMMARY

Everyone argues at some point in their everyday life. You probably argue with family, friends, employers, work colleagues, fellow students and teachers. The tools used for arguments like this are usually not precise and are often driven by emotional responses to other people's behaviour, such as anger, frustration, anxiety, and even love. Despite their seriousness in terms of the potential consequences to relationships and status, these arguments are informal and non-academic. Argument in universities, where it is manifested as academic argument, and in the courtroom or negotiator's office, where it has a professional and punitive form, has a more formal definition.

Students and lawyers must be competent argument constructors and dismantlers. An ability to construct a good argument is the core of successful study in any area. The ability to identify someone else's argument, take it to pieces and cast doubt on its main propositions is also a key skill.

This chapter introduces the concept of formal, academic argument, and outlines the basic characteristics of argument and argumentative terms in order to enhance your ability to use properly the legal and academic source material that you will research for seminar work, assessments and exams.

The chapter considers the raw material of arguments, propositions, inferences, logic and also the role of argument in legal analysis.

WHAT IS AN ARGUMENT?

Formal and informal arguments all comprise a range of assertions and counter assertions that lead to a resolution of the argument to the satisfaction of one of the parties, if not both. It is useful to remember that 'to argue' is a verb and therefore argument is an action. There are always two sides to an argument even if one side seems passive. Take, for example, the essay question, where you are asked to discuss a stated question. In this 'one-way' argument, the side opposing the position you have taken, and which you must argue against in your answer, is passive.

The word argument has a range of meanings, all of which revolve around proving the validity of an assertion. Take a careful look at Figures 7.1 and 7.2, which illustrate the various meanings of 'argue' and 'argument'. Figure 7.1 gives three meanings of the verb 'to argue' (in Latin, French and English) and highlights the meaning now commonly used. From this, an argument offers reasons to support or deny a proposition or maintains that something is the case by bringing reasons to prove it. In this book we will use the following definition of argument:

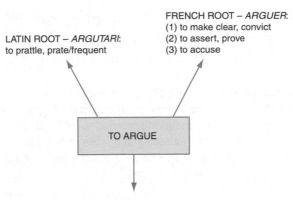

LATIN ROOT – *ARGUTARI*:
to prattle, prate/frequent

FRENCH ROOT – *ARGUER*:
(1) to make clear, convict
(2) to assert, prove
(3) to accuse

TO ARGUE

ENGLISH – TO ARGUE:
the root that acquired ascendancy in English is the French.
English meaning is now:
(1) to bring reasons to support or deny a proposition
(2) to maintain that something is the case by the bringing
    of reasons to prove that it is so

Figure 7.1 The Latin, French and English meanings of 'to argue'

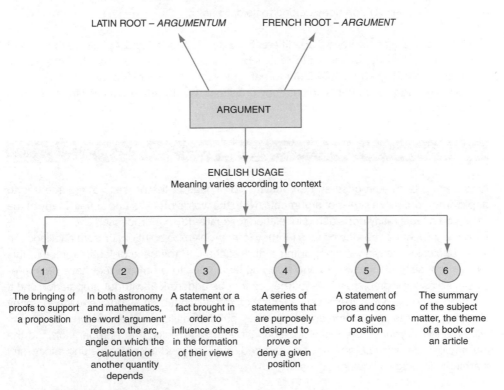

LATIN ROOT – *ARGUMENTUM*   FRENCH ROOT – *ARGUMENT*

ARGUMENT

ENGLISH USAGE
Meaning varies according to context

1	2	3	4	5	6
The bringing of proofs to support a proposition	In both astronomy and mathematics, the word 'argument' refers to the arc, angle on which the calculation of another quantity depends	A statement or a fact brought in order to influence others in the formation of their views	A series of statements that are purposely designed to prove or deny a given position	A statement of pros and cons of a given position	The summary of the subject matter, the theme of a book or an article

Figure 7.2 Different meanings of the word 'argument'

An argument is a series of statements, some backed by evidence, some not, that are purposely presented in order to prove, or disprove, a given position.

Figure 7.2 demonstrates that law is not alone in having argument as a core activity. It shows how various disciplines use the English meaning of argue, each with slightly differing meanings but all coming under the main idea of argument, as supporting or denying propositions or maintaining that something is the case by bringing reasons.

Our preferred definition of argument refers to supporting 'a given position'. Given positions in a legal context could be issues such as:

1.   Mary is guilty of theft contrary to the Theft Act 1968.

2.   Mary is not guilty of theft contrary to the Theft Act 1968.

3.   The European Union does not belong to its citizens.

4.   The European Union does belong to its citizens.

Note that statements 1 and 2 are different to 3 and 4. Whilst 3 and 4 could be the subject of a theoretical essay, or the topic of a debate, 1 and 2 are assertions that require the consideration of legal rules and facts to determine innocence or guilt, as in a court case.

However, good arguments for all four questions would share similar structures and characteristics.

DEVELOPING YOUR SKILLS OF ARGUMENT

Argument is both a process and an activity. To engage in the *process* of argument is to deploy methodically a *series* of arguments. Note the words *process* and *series*. Many of the skills you have already considered in relation to legal study are processes.

An argument can be viewed as a journey *from* problem *to* solution, or *from* an allegation *to* a conclusion denying or supporting that allegation. In the case of legal problems, this journey consists of interpreting and applying legal rules to problems that have been pre-classified as legal problems. This journey cannot be undertaken without preparation and if the preparation is not properly carried out then the destination may not be reached. Many students hate the preparation and the journey but the challenge of developing arguments will help refine your study, research, legal and language skills. If the preparation and the journey can be enjoyed, and not just endured, then the road is set for lifelong successful learning: learning that has good results.

The journey from problem to solution requires a map; a map others can follow, a map that allows the argument-crafter to take others precisely to the desired destination, a map that eloquently explains why it is not a good idea to take this side-road or that alternative route, a map that also explains how, if matters were different, another route could have been taken. To create a good map, you need a good balance of skills, as illustrated in Figure 7.3. An argument will only be as good as the ability of the person constructing it, and the skills they have.

Legal arguments take place through the mediating influence of oral and written language. We have already seen that language is a notoriously flexible and subjective medium of communication. The consideration given to statutory, European and common law rules, and the discretion language injects into the process of interpretation covered in Part Two demonstrates this. Language moulds the law and determines outcomes.

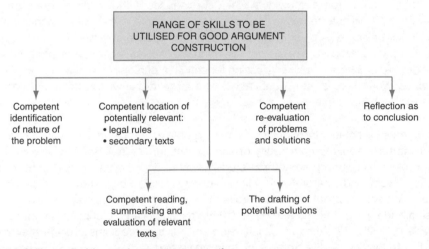

Figure 7.3 Skills required for good argument construction

PROBLEMS AND RULES

Before continuing to discuss the details of argument construction and the legal reasoning preferences of the English legal system it is useful to look briefly at the nature of problems and rules. Legal disputes use rules to resolve problems. Therefore a proper understanding of the interpretation and deployment of legal rules is essential to constructing a good argument. However, choices can always be made about which rules to apply, and how to apply them to specific legal problems.

The nature of problems

Problems are described in a variety of different contexts, including:

■   a difficult question put forward for an answer in scholastic disputation;

■   the question asked in the standard formal logic method of deductive reasoning;

■   in mathematics and physics, an inquiry or a question which, starting from a given position, investigates some fact, result or law.

Twining and Miers (1999)[1] give a more detailed description:

> A problem arises for an individual when she is faced with a puzzling question to answer, or a difficult choice to make, or some obstacle in the way of achieving a particular objective. A person is faced with a theoretical problem when she is confronted by a question calling for an answer that dissolves the puzzlement or solves the problem, without necessarily calling for action. A person is faced with a practical problem when there is some doubt about what to do. It is unwise to draw too sharp a line between theoretical and practical problems.

Of course it is not just individuals who have problems; problems can have a corporate or social impact requiring community or societal action. The real issue is how you move from problem to solution, something students often find difficult. If you can correctly identify, classify and interpret you will be able to begin the journey from problem to solution. But solving problems also requires imagination and solutions can even involve guessing and testing. Twining and Miers (1999)[2] have applied the concept of 'standpoint' to problems, with interesting results. They point out that problems change their nature according to the perspective from which they are viewed.

Even a seemingly simple problem can be complex for those seeking a solution. Many problems come not as single units but as a series of interconnected issues and problems. Problems, like so many other issues, are *processes*, often *complex processes*. If you do not understand the nature of problems generally, it can be difficult to understand the nature of legal rules, and the complexity of using legal rules as solutions to problems.

Solving problems

Problem solving and problem management are parts of everyday life and the skills you have developed automatically in these areas can help you turn your attention to more methodical approaches in dealing with complex legal problems. However, you may not always be aware of how you solve life problems, and some of the techniques you may use, like anger, fear, frustration or running away, would be unsuitable for academic work. Just as

---

1   W Twining and D Miers, *How To Do Things With Rules* (4th edn CUP, Cambridge 1999) 114.
2   Ibid.

legal problems themselves can comprise a series of interconnected issues and problems, their solutions are the end product of a series of complicated interrelated operations.

Effective problem solving involves accurately:

■ identifying that there is a problem;

■ classifying what type of problem it is (this determines much about the eventual solution);

■ presenting a solution to the problem.

Solutions can be aimed at *dealing* with the problem, or making the problem-solver *feel better*. Solutions aimed at making the problem-solver feel better could include doing nothing, removing themselves from the situation, or effecting a reconciliation and extraction of a promise not to repeat the behaviour.

In many disciplines, professionals use problem-solving models which enable users to check certain steps along the road to eventual solution. One of the best known and most useful problem-solving methods within legal education is the model set out in Twining and Miers (1999)[3]. Their seven steps aimed at problem solution are set out in Figure 7.4. They include issues of identification (steps 1 and 2) and classification (step 3) through to prescription and implementation of the solution (steps 6 and 7).

Many organisations and individuals can be too quick to jump to step 6 (prescription), before they have had an opportunity to diagnose the nature of the problem. This course of action is a classic government response to a crisis, and can also be seen in students when confronted with an essay.

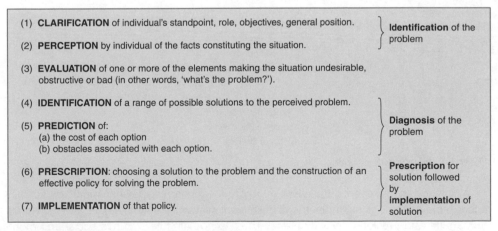

(1) **CLARIFICATION** of individual's standpoint, role, objectives, general position.	**Identification** of the problem
(2) **PERCEPTION** by individual of the facts constituting the situation.	
(3) **EVALUATION** of one or more of the elements making the situation undesirable, obstructive or bad (in other words, 'what's the problem?').	
(4) **IDENTIFICATION** of a range of possible solutions to the perceived problem.	**Diagnosis** of the problem
(5) **PREDICTION** of: (a) the cost of each option (b) obstacles associated with each option.	
(6) **PRESCRIPTION**: choosing a solution to the problem and the construction of an effective policy for solving the problem.	**Prescription** for solution followed by **implementation** of solution
(7) **IMPLEMENTATION** of that policy.	

Figure 7.4 Twining and Miers' problem solving model

3 Ibid.

Even when you try to follow a model or imagine all eventualities, solutions to problems can often cause more problems. If you search deeper into a problem, it is usually found to be a cluster of problems with a range of causes, and a range of potential solutions, each with a different set of obstacles and costs. This means lawyers tend to solve problems in a range of ways, mostly revolving around the application and meaning of legal rules.

The nature of rules

There are many meanings of the word 'rule'. A rule can be a principle or a maxim governing individual or group conduct in life or in a game. It can be a system that creates a way of life, like the rule of St Benedict that prescribes the actions of a monastic group. Some rules only have force within religious or social settings; others have effect within legal settings. Some rules only have force within a given academic discipline, such as philosophy, law or indeed legal method. Even language is subject to the rules of grammar, rules that literary luminaries like James Joyce have attempted to subvert. Figure 7.5 sets out a definition of a rule highlighting its constituent parts. Different rules share these general characteristics but vary in their consequences and in who has the power to create, interpret and break them.

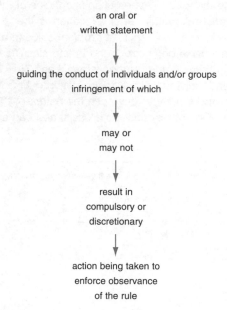

an oral or
written statement

↓

guiding the conduct of individuals and/or groups
infringement of which

↓

may or
may not

↓

result in
compulsory or
discretionary

↓

action being taken to
enforce observance
of the rule

Figure 7.5 The definition of a rule

A rule often represents the view of a group concerning lawful, moral or socially acceptable action. For example, the English legal system, like most legal systems, values human life and prohibits unlawful killing. The 'Do not kill' rule also has social and moral functions, backed by a range of religious or philosophical groups worldwide. To enable these functions to be enforced the rule has been given a legal base and infringement can lead to severe penalties. Figure 7.6 sets out the different classifications of rules that you might come across.

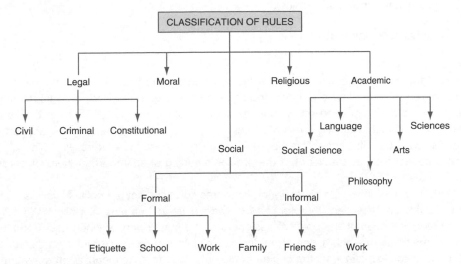

Figure 7.6 Classification of rules

Rules in general – and again legal rules are no exception – relate to people engaging in certain activities, either in thought, word or deed. Particular words are used to enforce this and some of these are set out in Figure 7.7.

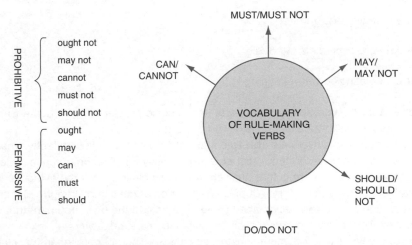

Figure 7.7 The vocabulary of rule-making verbs

Rules affect behaviour in a range of ways. They can:

■   stop action (**prescriptive** rules);

■   guide action (**normative** rules);

■   allow action (**facilitative** rules).

Legal rules

A rule that has not been created by the law-making process or accepted by those empowered to create law is not deemed to be a legal rule. In England, all legal rules are created by state-authorised procedures and are enforced by the full force of the state. Often, the difficulty with legal rules is that they are general and need to be applied to specific, particular situations. This means that legal rules need to be *interpreted*. That a rule seems applicable may be clear but the precise meaning of an important word or phrase may not always be.

Statutory rules in our simple majority democracy often reflect the political values of the party in power. They can, therefore, be described as instruments of policy. Whatever the original intention of the political designers of the statutory rule, when users of these rules come to interpret them, defects in design are always apparent because words can, so often, be made to mean what the originator did not intend them to mean: another reminder that language is flexible.

CONSTRUCTING ARGUMENTS

Now that a little thought has been given to:

■   the meaning of argument;

■   the nature of problems and rules;

■   the mediating power of language

it is hoped that the complexity of any attempt to solve problems by recourse to rules is better appreciated. Now we can consider *how* to argue.

It is essential that lawyers are able to construct arguments and use effective reasoning to resolve legal problems. Without that core skill, a lawyer lacks competence. One of the difficulties of legal argument is that answers are rarely clear cut. All the evidence will not necessarily have the same degree of plausibility, or be of the same strength. The law may be unclear, and all of these issues need to be ordered into the best argument that can be constructed. This is why argument involves imagination and creativity.

The good news is that argument construction utilises a number of preparatory skills with which you have already engaged:

- finding appropriate texts and choosing the most useful;

- summarising texts;

- researching and organising texts;

- critique and analysis;

- collecting appropriate materials in order to persuade the listener of the validity of the arguments presented.

Reasoning itself is analogous to a journey: it involves the:

- preparation and collection of information;

- ordering and organisation of information;

- working through the information once the 'direction of travel' that it supports is clear.

When people set out on a journey, they normally have an idea of where they are going. If they do not know where they are going, this is usually a matter of deliberate choice. When you begin to consider argument construction, you need to know where you are going: 'to begin with the end in mind.' If you do not know where you are going you may become exhausted and frustrated and end up arbitrarily writing in your essay or problem solution, words which imply 'therefore, this is the end'. It is not possible to craft a good argument by accident. Useful information to include as evidence for an argument may be uncovered accidentally. However, the argument can never be accidentally constructed. It is a technical ability that must be understood and practised knowingly.

Evidence

Legal argument is a delicate balance of propositions backed by evidence. Such evidence will depend on the context of the argument and could involve facts, legal rules and theories. If the dispute is a legal problem, argument construction will be concerned with the application of existing rules connected by reasoned comments to persuade the listener of the validity of adopting the outcome suggested. In the courtroom, both parties put forward arguments and the judge chooses the argument that is either the most persuasive or the closest to the judge's own belief concerning the outcome of the case. Evidence substantially increases the persuasiveness of an argument. An argument that is a series of propositions not backed by evidence is unlikely to succeed in any area of study or dispute resolution. On your course you will need to engage with tasks that require you to apply legal rules to hypothetical fact scenarios in legal problem solution activities.

Judgments

So far, in this text, there have been opportunities to read judgments and the judges have presented their decisions in the form of reasoned responses to the questions posed by the case. Much of the study of a lawyer revolves around the decisions of the senior judiciary in the senior appellate courts. Each case is based on particular grounds of appeal. One side succeeds because, in the opinion of the judges, theirs is the most persuasive argument.

The reasoning most valued within law demonstrates a consistency of approach and logic; consistency is highly valued. However, the law is not, and cannot be, a closed system like an automated software programme. Analytically there are always other possibilities, which makes a lot of legal decision-making contingent. In a civil court confronted with the real litigant the law expects the contingent nature of legal decision making to turn 'on a balance of probabilities'. In the criminal court it expects the contingent nature of legal decision to be based upon a jury or magistrate finding the minor premise 'proved beyond all reasonable doubt'.

Decisions as to correct action can only be made by people who are able to distinguish between competing arguments and determine that, in a given set of circumstances, one argument is more valid than another. Judges are, of course, the ultimate arbiters of the acceptable decision. Sometimes, this decision is quite subjective.

For the practising lawyer, a valid argument is of the utmost importance. In the class-room, you are constantly called upon to practise and refine your skills in legal problem solving by engaging in reasoning processes leading to full-scale argument construction.

It is now time to explore and apply the more formal aspects of general argument construction: logic, deduction and induction.

Logic

It is generally believed that academic and professional lawyers and, indeed, law students, are skilled in the art of legal reasoning. Furthermore, it is believed that they are people who argue 'logically'. To most, the term 'logical' indicates that a person can separate the relevant from the irrelevant and come to an objective view, based often on supposedly objective formulae. Colloquially, people sometimes accuse those who change their mind or who are emotional in their arguing, of allowing their emotions to get the better of them, of 'not being logical'.

The dictionary defines logic as the science of reasoning, thinking, proof or inference. Inference involves drawing a conclusion from something known or assumed using reasoning. Consider Figure 7.8 for a more visual description. Logic can even be defined as a science in its own right, a sub-branch of philosophy which deals with scientific method in argument and the uses of inference. The German philosopher Georg Hegel described logic as the fundamental science of thought and its categories. It can certainly claim to be an accurate form of reasoning: its root is found in the Greek word *logos* meaning reason.

Lawyers, like scientists, spend time supporting statements with evidence and considering how one might weigh evidence on a scale of weak to strong. What is it that is

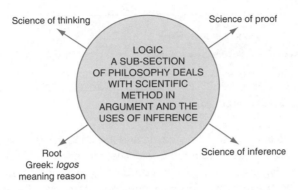

Science of thinking

Science of proof

LOGIC
A SUB-SECTION
OF PHILOSOPHY DEALS
WITH SCIENTIFIC
METHOD IN
ARGUMENT AND THE
USES OF INFERENCE

Root
Greek: *logos*
meaning reason

Science of inference

Figure 7.8 Definition of logic

actually proved by the evidence? However, lawyers deal in words, reports and reconstructions. Unlike scientists, lawyers are not present observing the wrong, the accident or the incident.

The logician, like the lawyer, deals in statements, or propositions, expressed in words and symbols. In the context of logic, the word 'proposition' can be most simply explained as a statement or assertion about something. More particularly it is a statement that is put forward as the basis of an argument that brings evidences for or against its validity. In the science of logic, the proposition takes on a more formal role as a particular type of statement in which something (the predicate) is affirmed or denied concerning something (the subject). Therefore each proposition must contain a predicate that is an assertion. In a formal argument it is expected that there is proof for the predicate in the proposition.

Essentially, logic is the study of propositions and how conclusions may be correctly obtained from them through the process of reasoned argument. There are two main types of logic: deduction and induction. Each of these will be discussed below.

Deduction

Deductive reasoning occurs in an extremely stylised manner and follows a standard procedure and structure. There is a first, major, statement, variously called a premise or a proposition that is a general or normative statement. For example, 'stealing is contrary to section 1 of the Theft Act 1968'. This is followed by a second, minor, statement that is quite particular: for example, 'Anna has stolen a book'. A third statement reaches a conclusion in a precise manner, drawing only on the two previous statements. For example, 'Anna has committed theft under section 1 of the Theft Act'. There is no permission to conclude by way of plausibilities or probabilities: the conclusion can only be extracted from the linguistic forms making up the major and minor statements. Therefore the conclusion is said to be *compelled*, and the reasoning system is *closed*.

Looking at the individual statements, they are each sentences, and each sentence is made up of a predicate and a subject. The rule in deductive reasoning is that the subject in the major premise or proposition becomes the predicate in the minor premise. In this case,

A major premise – which tends to state a generality

A minor premise – which tends to state a particularity

Conclusion

This form of argument is called a *syllogism*

Figure 7.9 The components of a deductive reasoning argument

the subject of the major proposition is stealing and this becomes the assertion or predicate in the minor proposition: Anna *stole* the book. The necessary, or compelled, conclusion is the only conclusion possible: Anna acted contrary to section 1 of the Theft Act. In deductive reasoning, the argument follows a prescribed form called a syllogism, as set out in Figure 7.9.

Deductive reasoning leaves no space for examining the truth or otherwise of the premises, and is therefore of limited use within a legal context. A deductive reasoning argument could be logically valid without being correct, since we do not know if the minor proposition is true. For example, we can verify that stealing is against section 1 of the Theft Act by checking the law books. But we need a full trial to discover if Anna did steal the book. The proof or otherwise of this premise is outside the remit of deductive reasoning but we will return to this example in Chapter 8. Analytically there are always other possibilities.

Deduction can, however, be a good way of testing whether a new legal rule clashes with any existing legal rule. It can also be useful when precedent is being teased out for the first time and logical consequences need to be tracked.

Induction

Inductive reasoning involves arguments that put forward a first particular proposition, or thesis, followed by a series of propositions relating to facts and evidences. The last proposition, or conclusion, is drawn out of the previous propositions. One of the most important differences from deductive reasoning is that the reasoning system is *open*, meaning it can be possible for more than one conclusion to be drawn.

As with deductive reasoning, the conclusions are based on propositions. However, in inductive reasoning, the conclusion reached extends beyond the facts in the premise. It is not compelled, it is *drawn out*. The supporting propositions make the conclusion probable but there is no one absolutely clearly correct conclusion as there is for deductive argument.

An inductive argument can, for example, have as an inference a generalisation, such as 'innocent people do not run away'. Different types of generalisations are set out in Figure 7.10. A generalisation can be quite easily challenged as it is usually constructed on flimsy arguments. But it is also worth remembering that no argument can ever be a hundred per cent sound. Remember our legal system requires less than perfect proof: balance of probabilities in the civil area and beyond reasonable doubt in the criminal law. So, accusing someone of not having a perfect argument is not in itself a good argument. No one has a cast-iron case.

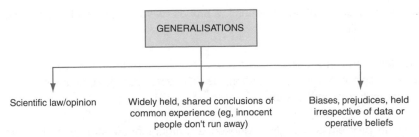

Figure 7.10 Types of standard generalisations which can find their way into inductive argument

Inductive argument is perhaps the closest to the everyday legal argument where decisions are made concerning which party to a legal dispute is accorded the privileging of their story in terms of the law's authority to provide a declaration of legal rights followed by the imposition of criminal sanctions or civil law remedies.

Like deductive reasoning, and from a purely scientific point of view, the logic of inductive reasoning has no interest in the actual truth of the propositions that lead to the conclusion. The court, on the contrary, is most concerned with establishing the probability that the conclusion is correct and that the propositions are correct. Just because a logical form is correctly constructed, it does not mean that the conclusion expressed is true. The truth of a conclusion depends upon whether the major and minor premises express statements that are true. The statements may be false. Much time is spent by lawyers in court attempting to prove the truth of statements used as building blocks in the construction of arguments.

A sub-division of inductive reasoning is reasoning by analogy or analogous reasoning. The Greek word 'analogy' means likeness, or similarity, and is used to describe the equality of ratios of proportions in mathematics. In logic it expresses the resemblance of attributes between two or more things. Analogous reasoning is used in the English legal system, where the courts argue from rules developed in previous cases according to the theory and practical implications of the doctrine of precedent. In doing this they reason from the general to the particular, applying abstract generalised rules from previous cases to the particular current case. We will cover more about analogous reasoning and the detailed construction of legal argument in Chapter 8.

CONCLUSION

■ An argument is a series of statements, some backed by evidence, some not, that are purposely presented in order to prove, or disprove, a given position.

■ Legal arguments are based around problems, rules and facts. They are undertaken through the mediating influence of oral and written language.

- Successful argument construction is a process which requires a balance of many different skills.

- Problem-solving models can help you work in order through the key steps (clarification, perception, evaluation, identification, prediction, prescription and implementation) on the route to reaching a solution.

- If a legal problem is wrongly diagnosed, any argument constructed will be as flawed as the erroneous diagnosis in the first place.

- Deductive reasoning is a closed system of logic in which the only possible conclusion is compelled from the major and minor propositions.

- Inductive reasoning is an open system of logic in which the probable conclusion is drawn out of the propositions. It can result in more than one conclusion.

- Analogous reasoning is the system of logic used in the English legal system. A specific type of inductive reasoning, it applies general rules from previous cases to the particular current case.

- Reasoning itself cannot always prove or disprove the facts of a case. This is why cases go to trial: to find the conclusion that is most likely on the balance of probabilities (in civil cases) or that is proven beyond all reasonable doubt (in criminal cases).

FURTHER READING

T Anderson, D Schum and W Twining, *Analysis of Evidence* (CUP, Cambridge 2005).

S Cotterell, *Critical Thinking Skills: Developing Effective Analysis and Argument* (Palgrave Macmillan, 2005). This is also referred to as a useful text for Chapter 1.

N Gold, K Mackie and W Twining, *Learning Lawyer's Skills* (Butterworths, London 1989).

W Twining and D Miers, *How To Do Things With Rules* (4th edn CUP, Cambridge 1999).

LEGAL REASONING

8

" The life of the law has not been logic; it has been experience. The felt necessities of the time, the prevalent moral and political theories, intuitions of public policy, avowed or unconscious, even the prejudices which judges share with their fellow men, have had a good deal more to do than the syllogism in determining the rules by which men should be governed. The law embodies the story of a nation's development through many centuries, and it cannot be dealt with as if it contained only the axioms and corollaries of a book of mathematics. "

Oliver Wendell Holmes, Jr.

LEARNING OUTCOMES

After reading this chapter you should be able to:

■ understand the difference between fact analysis and legal analysis and the connections between these activities;

■ basically define and then differentiate between inductive, deductive and abductive reasoning;

■ be aware of the need to develop critical thinking;

■ understand the way in which an argument relies on factual analysis, legal reasoning, persuasion and critical thinking;

■ construct a modified Wigmore chart and apply it for argument construction;

■ construct a competent argument in relation to a legal problem to be solved according to rules of legal reasoning acceptable within the English legal system;

■ construct a competent critical argument relating to theoretical aspects of the study of law.

CHAPTER SUMMARY

Law students tend to be taught through a method that emphasises law cases and relies heavily on the development of argumentative strategies to apply the law and facts to simulated legal problems. This chapter looks closely at the basics of reasoning and argument formation in English law. It builds on Chapter 7 as it turns its attention to concentrate on practical issues connected with argument construction. The chapter considers in detail the relationship between propositions, building an argument and proofs supporting propositions. It also explains how to produce a modified Wigmore chart, showing how it can be used as a learning tool for argument construction.

LEGAL ARGUMENT IN PRACTICE

Argument concerns not only laying out facts and rules, it also involves aspects of persuasion, and determination of where the weight lies in opposing arguments. Assessors in the court, judges or jurors, decide whether an argument is strong or weak, proved or unproved. In the final analysis, how does the court decide the criteria for the *evaluation* of an argument? Evaluation cannot be solely guided by rules. Ultimately, argument construction is also a personal thing. Different people will take different routes to evidence, and relate the evidence to the issues in different ways. Much depends upon an individual's ability both to imagine and reason; to imagine doubts, as well as links in proof. Nothing exists in the realm of methods to tell anyone what a strong link may be. We may be excellent at the processes of transmitting, storing and retrieving facts and information but we do not have similarly developed skills of obtaining defensible conclusions from these facts and this information.

The law as an institution has a vested interest in demonstrating that its trial procedures are fair and its legal rules are neutrally applied. In this context not only are pseudo-scientific approaches to decision making applied to the production of evidence but they are applied to the accepted methods of legal reasoning and legal argument construction. Emotion and passionate language from lawyers is not acceptable. Argument must be a dispassionate appeal to reason, an appeal based on argument constructed from the evidence (produced according to the rules of evidence) and applicable legal rules as applied to a set of facts. Of course, the majority of trials involve competing versions of the facts or of the meaning of words in legal rules (otherwise there would not be a contested trial).

Constructing argument pre-supposes competency in a number of complex skills groupings, such as:

■ the use of various methods of legal reasoning (deductive, inductive and abductive);

■ understanding logic and its limits;

- handling language well;

- interpreting and applying rules;

- understanding the nature of problems, and the use of rules to solve them;

- appreciating the concept of problem solving, or problem analysis;

- distinguishing between fact analysis and legal analysis;

- appreciating various definitions of argument;

- engaging with the concept of argument as a process and as a structure;

- understanding discrete terms such as propositions, evidence and inference which make up the constituent parts of argument.

At the academic stage of education the standard framework around which teaching takes place is that of legal analysis. Legal education is orientated towards the case method: how cases in courts are described and analysed. Your skill in understanding cases, how they have been argued and how the law has been applied, is tested by asking you to solve a hypothetical problem based on hypothetical facts. Often students are asked to present advice for one fictional party to a case. You will need to use the library (virtual or real) to search in books, journals and law reports to find similar, analogous cases, noting how these have been decided and why. You can then infer how the hypothetical case you have to argue will be decided, basing your inferences on the way applicable legal rules were applied in real cases. The legal analysis that students are trained to carry out, of course, involves basic analysis of the facts of the case. Which are the material facts? How can the facts as given be organised to make it clear that earlier cases apply? In the standard university problem question, the facts do not need to be ascertained, they are given as a neat, logically ordered, story. In real life, these stories are messier, the relevant facts are more difficult to extract, and the solutions are not so clear.

At the vocational stage of legal training, students are taught to engage in factual analysis and this provides the framework for the course. Students are also taught how to structure, organise and analyse a large amount of what is called 'raw data'. They learn how to draw out the probable story from clients, the inferences in the data and see how available evidence can support the argument on the case to be proved. Evidence is correlated to the relevant facts, the facts in issue (for example, that 'Anna stole a book'). The legal principles are assumed. Indeed this aspect of legal education reverses the university-education process of drawing out legal analysis. The legal principles here are not in issue, but are a given. In our example, there is no doubt that theft is against the law. The test of development for the student is to see how skilled they are in deciding whether the available factual data can be put into a structure that makes it possible to construct a viable argument. For example, constructing an argument that proves Anna is guilty of theft because enough evidence exists to prove the elements of the unlawful act according to the relevant standard of proof.

The common law model rests on assumptions that underlie both theory and practice and this will become clear as legal study is undertaken. It is said that in fact it rests on notions of the ideal type of rationalist tradition[1]. This model involves *the pursuit of 'truth' through rational means*. Can you make accurate present judgments based on reasoning in cases occurring in the past on similar facts? This is certainly what the doctrine of precedent demands. The English legal system has developed principles designed to draw out that past reasoning and use it in the present and to obtain consistent decision making. Such a pursuit has as a high, but not overriding priority, the securing of justice under law. The model of adjudication is instrumentalist in that the pursuit of truth through reason is only a means to achieving a particular type of justice: the implementation of substantive law.

The mode of legal decision making is rational not irrational and, because it is highly aspirational, its practice is often critiqued. As discussed in Chapter 7, the mode of reasoning used in the English legal system is inductive. Although there is room for constructing deductive argument, proof always needs to be by inductive means.

In reality the good lawyer needs to be competent in both legal analysis and factual analysis. Constructing argument requires careful attention to detail, planning and understanding, such that there is a close relationship between:

- cases of authority;

- language usage;

- logic and reasoning;

- planning;

- imagination

combined with excellent skills in critical thinking.

LEGAL REASONING

At this point it is worth restating the definition of argument discussed in Chapter 7:

---

1 See generally W Twining and D Miers.

An argument is a series of statements, some backed by evidence, some not, that are purposely presented in order to prove, or disprove, a given position.

Argument can also be described as the process of maintaining that something is the case, for example, that Anna stole the book, and of bringing reasons to support that case. If Anna were charged with a crime, the charge would note that 'Anna stole a book contrary to section 1 of the Theft Act'. This charge is an assertion or proposition where the subject (Anna) committed the predicate (stealing the book) contrary to the Theft Act. Tangible evidence, such as witness testimony, forensic evidence or documentary evidence, could provide reasons to support this proposition.

The process and dynamic act of reasoning can be described as a careful journey through various propositions. Each of these propositions can found its own argument with reasons being brought to support or deny it depending on your standpoint in the argument. As noted in Chapter 7 problems tend not to arise singly, they come in clusters. Arguments similarly tend not to arise as a one-off, but in clusters.

Argument by analogy

As noted in Chapter 7 argument by analogy is a form of inductive reasoning and the most common form of argument in law. Such an argument begins by stating that two objects are observed to be similar by a number of attributes. The conclusion then draws similarities between the two objects with respect to a third. The strength of the argument depends upon the degree of relationship between the objects.

Lawyers are advisers and they offer predictive advice based on how previous similar cases have been dealt with. All advice is based on the lawyer's perception of what would happen in court. This is usually enough to ensure that, in the vast majority of civil cases, matters between disputants are settled. A lawyer's perception is based upon his or her experience of how judges reason.

The English legal system operates a relatively rigid adherence to the doctrine of precedent that, like cases, must be applied consistently. Since argument by analogy looks for similarities between things it is ideally suited to the use of precedent in the English legal system. The lawyer confronted with a particular fact scenario and a doubt about the extent of a legal rule, or the meaning of words, will look at other previous cases in the senior courts (the Court of Appeal and the House of Lords). The strength of the precedent in a previous case is carefully considered to ascertain what it is and whether it is binding or only a persuasive precedent. Cases in the Privy Council are an example of persuasive rather than binding precedents, as the court only hears appeals from other jurisdictions. However, since the House of Lords judges sit in the Privy Council, their decisions are regarded as highly persuasive. Indeed their judgments can signal a change of policy in advance of a case arising in the English legal system that allows the House of Lords to implement that change.

The facts of previous cases setting precedents are also carefully scrutinised. Are they the same as the current case or different? If they are different, are they similar enough to be a 'like' case?

In the vast majority of cases, the conclusion will simply be an application of existing law to the facts. Occasionally, the decision creates a new law which may or may not be stated as a proposition of law. To ascertain whether a new law has been stated may require a comparison between the material facts implied within the major premise and the facts which make up the minor premise.

Reasoning by analogy is a process of reasoning by comparing examples in order to reach a conclusion in a novel situation. It involves three key stages:

1.   the similarity between the cases is observed

2.   the rule of law *(ratio decidendi)* inherent in the first case is stated. Reasoning is from the general to the particular (deductive reasoning);

3.   the general rule in (2) is applied to the case for decision. At this point, reasoning is from the particular to the general (inductive reasoning).

Figure 8.1 gives a graphic illustration of this.

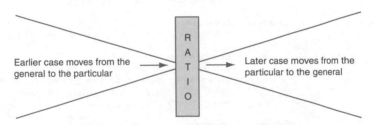

Figure 8.1 Reasoning by analogy

The building blocks of an inductive argument

The thesis

The first proposition in an inductive argument is, as you will recall, the thesis. It is particular not general. Our thesis is that Anna stole a book. We then proceed to build our argument looking first at the legal rule to see what is required to be proved and then returning to our facts. At present of course we do not have any facts.

The thesis makes a reference to the illegal act and to the law, by noting the action 'stole'. This is a good moment to look at the law relating to theft, (section 1 of the Theft Act 1968) and consider the issues of the *actus reus* and *mens rea*. The definition of theft is:

Theft Act 1968, s 1(1)
A person is guilty of theft if he dishonestly appropriates property belonging to another with the intention of permanently depriving the other.

This sentence includes five different elements that all need to be present for theft to be present, as shown in Figure 8.2. You will see that some of these relate to the act itself (the guilty *act*: technically in criminal law called the *actus reus*), others to the state of mind of the person (the guilty *mind*: technically in criminal law called the *mens rea*).

An argument involving a dispute about any legal rule will be a balance of legal analysis, matching the legal rule and case law on it, to the facts known in the new case, and engaging in factual analysis, organising the facts according to their evidential value and their relevance to the identified legal issues.

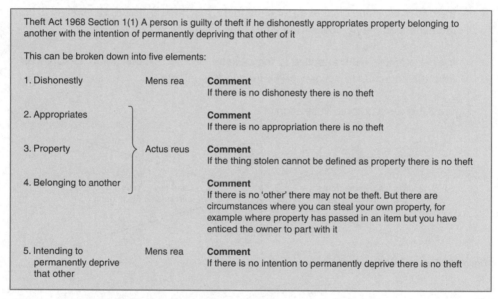

Figure 8.2 is a box containing the following content:

Theft Act 1968 Section 1(1) A person is guilty of theft if he dishonestly appropriates property belonging to another with the intention of permanently depriving that other of it

This can be broken down into five elements:

1. Dishonestly	Mens rea	**Comment** If there is no dishonesty there is no theft
2. Appropriates	Actus reus	**Comment** If there is no appropriation there is no theft
3. Property	Actus reus	**Comment** If the thing stolen cannot be defined as property there is no theft
4. Belonging to another	Actus reus	**Comment** If there is no 'other' there may not be theft. But there are circumstances where you can steal your own property, for example where property has passed in an item but you have enticed the owner to part with it
5. Intending to permanently deprive that other	Mens rea	**Comment** If there is no intention to permanently deprive there is no theft

Figure 8.2 The five required elements in the definition of theft

Factual analysis
We can now consider the types of evidence that may be needed to prove the *actus reus* or *mens rea* elements. For example, witness statements may show that a person was seen taking an item from a shop, that the item belonged to the shop and that it constitutes property. The item itself may also be put in evidence. The *mens rea* elements, the issues relating to the state of mind of the person, are more challenging. How does one prove dishonesty? Is it enough to say that the defendant walked out of the shop with an item? No, because there could have been a range of reasons for that action: she could have forgotten

she had it with her, she could have been going to check it out in the light, she might have been borrowing it with the intention to bring it back. Some of these reasons may negate the suggestion of dishonesty, others might negate the intention of permanently depriving.

Let us now suppose that we have three pieces of information relating to this case:

1.   An eyewitness saw Anna take a book from the shelf in the store and leave the store (the witness could be mistaken).

2.   Anna was stopped outside the store with the book by the store detective.

3.   That particular book had not been logged out of the store by the computer sales system, which still shows that it is on the shelf (has the system been operating well?).

From these statements we can infer that Anna took the book out of the store. This appears enough to prove the physical act (*actus reus*) of theft at the level of evidence. If Anna alleges that she did not intend to deprive permanently the owner of the book, or if there is no dishonesty then the *mens rea* remains unproved unless the prosecution can do so.

Legal analysis

The lawyer not only has to marshal all of the facts to prove the act, he or she must also know what law cases may affect the way in which certain words making up the legal rule have been interpreted in the statute or the cases. In this example, the lawyer ought to know that dishonesty has caused much concern in the law relating to theft and several cases deal with it. In addition the Theft Act makes clear that an intention to deprive permanently is not necessarily negated by saying that the item was only borrowed and the cases on this should also be considered. Similarly, whilst property has to belong to another there are a range of difficult cases where you can steal your own property because of the way in which the law has been developed.

In our suggestions so far, Anna has been accused of stealing a book from a shop. Figure 8.3 shows the relationship between deductive and inductive reasoning for the prosecution in this fictitious case. Note carefully how you can see immediately that the minor premise of the deductive argument becomes the thesis of the inductive argument.

ACTIVITY 8.1: FROM PROSECUTION TO DEFENCE

Rephrase the deductive and inductive reasoning set out on behalf of the prosecution in Figure 8.3 to provide inductive and deductive forms set out on behalf of the defence.

Hint: translate the minor proposition of the deductive argument and the thesis of the inductive argument into a form that is suitable for the defence.

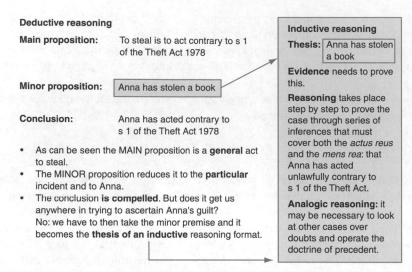

Figure 8.3 The deductive and inductive forms of the argument Anna has stolen a book

Inferences

It is important when setting up an argument that the potential dangers of inference are considered. You will perhaps remember from Chapter 7 that to *infer* means to draw a conclusion from something known, or assumed, or from evidence through the use of either deductive or inductive reasoning. An inference is therefore that which is inferred.

There are loopholes for error when dealing with the act of inferring, and one of the most common is overlooking the possibility of a plurality of causes or alternative explanations. For instance, each fact inferred as leading to an inference of Anna's guilt could provoke one of the following counter responses:

■   an explanation as to why the assertion is misguided (it could be explained away!);

■   a straight denial (denying the validity or existence of the evidentiary fact backing your inference);

■   a rival evidential fact is set up and asserted.

The important task is to identify possible alternative conclusions and test them out. The question then becomes 'which are the stronger inferences?' Does your favoured argument look strong or does a counterargument stand up? As we have already discussed, inductive reasoning is the closest to everyday legal reasoning because it involves putting forward a conclusion that seems strong, based on inferences that provide evidence in favour of one party.

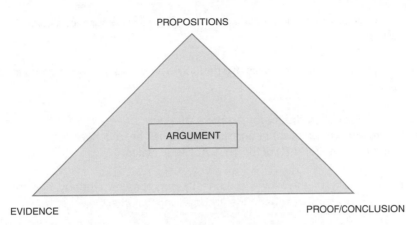

Figure 8.4 Arguments are based on propositions, evidence and proof

Your final argument will consist of a range of propositions or assertions that will invariably be backed by evidence from cases and statutes as well as forensics and witnesses. The relationship between these components is shown in Figure 8.4. Although the diagram looks simple it is necessary to bear in mind that the propositions may have alternative explanations and the evidence supporting these alternative explanations will need to be analysed. At the level of factual analysis, deductive argument requires extension by tracking through the process of inductive reasoning, starting with the minor premise of the deductive argument. For most law problems, a cluster of arguments may need to be set up dealing with separate issues. In assessing your final argument you should also have engaged in the process of predicting what the other party may be arguing and factor this into your argument and refute it.

Lawyers inevitably look at possible inductive reasoning that counters their own argument, to avoid being caught by surprise. You, as a law student, should do the same. This involves constructing opposing hypothetical theses. The evidence a lawyer has may suggest alternatives, and perhaps more plausible ones than his or her own proposition. The creative process which argues around the data based on hypothetical matters, rather than on matters known, is called abductive reasoning.

How do you critique a deductive or inductive argument?
So far we have noted the following:

■   the minor premise in a legal deductive argument becomes the thesis of inductive reasoning;

■   the conclusion of a deductive argument, although logically valid, may be wrong or untrue because either the major or the minor premise or both are incorrect or untrue;

- as the conclusion of a deductive argument is logically compelled, it cannot be attacked;

- the major or the minor premises of a deductive argument may be targeted for critique and attack.

Attacking the major premise of a deductive argument

The major proposition (premise) in our illustrations has been concerning theft. The legal definition of theft in section 1 (1) of the Theft Act 1968 states:

A person is guilty of theft if he dishonestly appropriates property belonging to another with the intention of permanently depriving the other.

The major proposition of the deductive argument as shown in Figure 8.3 was expressed as:

To steal is to act contrary to the Theft Act.

This could be expressed in a more specific manner and still remain general, for example as:

It is contrary to the Theft Act s 1(1) to appropriate dishonestly property belonging to another with the intention of permanently depriving that other.

The entire deductive argument can then be set out as shown in Figure 8.5.

Major premise (general)

- It is contrary to s 1(1) of the Theft Act to dishonestly appropriate property belonging to another with the intention of permanently depriving that other.

Minor premise (particular)

- Anna dishonestly appropriated a book the property of X store with the intention of permanently depriving the store of it.

Conclusion (compelled)

- Anna has acted contrary to s 1(1) of the Theft Act.

Figure 8.5 The deductive argument for Anna has stolen a book

How do we attack the major proposition in Figure 8.5?

One way of doing this is to check the interpretation of the words and phrases in section 1(1) of the Theft Act.

Looking at the premise, what do you consider to be the meaning of the phrases:

- dishonestly *(mens rea);*

- appropriates *(actus reus);*

- intention to deprive permanently (*mens rea*)?

These words and phrases may well become the focus of legal argument in the court. In order to explore their meaning, it is necessary to consult other cases where these words and phrases in the Theft Act 1968 have been discussed. This becomes a core task of legal analysis.

Figure 8.6 sets out the deductive reasoning on behalf of the prosecution stating that Anna stole a book and the two opposing inductive arguments by the defence and the prosecution. The prosecution argument affirms of course the central deductive argument and the defence argument sets out to deny it. This type of argumentative structure is the skeleton for the majority of arguments revolving around the use of facts and legal authority

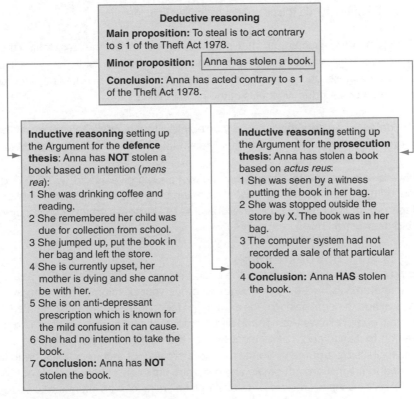

Deductive reasoning

Main proposition: To steal is to act contrary to s 1 of the Theft Act 1978.

Minor proposition: Anna has stolen a book.

Conclusion: Anna has acted contrary to s 1 of the Theft Act 1978.

Inductive reasoning setting up the Argument for the **defence thesis**: Anna has **NOT** stolen a book based on intention (*mens rea*):
1 She was drinking coffee and reading.
2 She remembered her child was due for collection from school.
3 She jumped up, put the book in her bag and left the store.
4 She is currently upset, her mother is dying and she cannot be with her.
5 She is on anti-depressant prescription which is known for the mild confusion it can cause.
6 She had no intention to take the book.
7 **Conclusion:** Anna has **NOT** stolen the book.

Inductive reasoning setting up the Argument for the **prosecution thesis**: Anna has stolen a book based on *actus reus*:
1 She was seen by a witness putting the book in her bag.
2 She was stopped outside the store by X. The book was in her bag.
3 The computer system had not recorded a sale of that particular book.
4 **Conclusion:** Anna **HAS** stolen the book.

Figure 8.6 **The inductive arguments for the defence and prosecution in *R v Anna***

to resolve legal disputes. To this skeleton lawyers add case law to strengthen the legal analysis, and strengthen factual analysis by ensuring evidence backs assertions of fact. Whichever party you act for in a legal dispute you should always predict your opponent's argument.

Both indicative arguments in Figure 8.6 are deliberately flawed:

■ The defence concentrates on intention, one of the two *mens rea* elements forming the penultimate *probanda*, arguing that Anna did not have the necessary *mens rea* for intention. But they should also discuss the other key element, the *mens rea* issue of dishonesty.

■ The prosecution concentrates on the *actus reus* but say nothing about the *mens rea* issues. Theft can only be proved if both the *actus reus* and the *mens rea* are present.

The run of the two arguments in Figure 8.6 on *mens rea* is as follows:

■ Point 6 of the defence thesis relates to the issue of intention.

■ The prosecution case argues that in fact Anna was seen in the store taking the book by an eye-witness and stopped and found with the book outside the store. This, argues the prosecution, demonstrates intention to deprive permanently (see points 1, 2 and 3 of the inductive thesis of the prosecution).

■ The defence counters this argument by pointing to personal circumstances that negate *both* dishonesty and intention (see points 2–7 of the prosecution thesis).

In this way we can see that the same information can give rise to two differing arguments based upon evidence unknown to the other party at the time. That is why it is always a good idea to try and predict counter-arguments to your own, so you can consider how you would deal with them.

Careful argument construction

You should now be able to appreciate the importance of careful construction of argument containing statements backed by evidence to prove your position (in addition, of course, one needs to add the legal basis for the arguments found in the authority of decided cases). The essential quality of a well-structured argument is that it takes the reader or listener from its beginning to its end and makes them hold to the opinion that the argument is correct or the most plausible argument. Sometimes, the process of argument uses bridges from one fact to another that are not backed by evidence but inferred from one set of facts to a proposition. For example, 'You are wet – so it must be raining' is an inference based on your observation of facts. However, the person you are looking at could be wet because they fell in a pond.

It is not wrong to assert a proposition that is not backed by evidence to prove it, but an adjudicating body is not compelled to accept the validity of an unproved proposition. It is difficult to refute a proposition backed by strong evidence but of course evidence is *not* always strong: it may be tenuous, or medium-strong.

You always consider the weak points in arguments. Most adjudicating bodies have elements of discretion and can accept the tenuous, but plausible, explanatory bridges from one proven fact to another fact that is not proven, as the argument progresses to conclusion. Much depends on the minor or major nature of the unsupported proposition asserted. If it is pivotal for the case, then it must be backed by evidence. Lawyers will tend to take the little jumps with plausibility and, hopefully, the big jumps with proven propositions!

At the everyday level of explanation, a legal argument tends to state:

- A book was stolen.

- The following law (Theft Act 1968) states that this behaviour, theft, is a criminal offence.

- These witnesses, these official documents, this forensic evidence prove that the book was stolen by Anna.

- It can be proved therefore that Anna stole the book.

- Anna therefore broke the law.

Argument construction is not difficult if there has been meticulous preparation of information. The argument will be basic or elegant depending upon the development of skills, understanding of the law, the level of preparation, thought and reflection that has gone into the argument construction. What one gets back is proportional to the quality of what has gone in. A strong argument may ultimately be rejected if there is a fair amount of discretion, but the person who has forwarded it will know it is good. Indeed, often an adjudicator, even when deciding against an argument, will compliment the argument-constructor on the art with which it was done.

THE WIGMORE CHART METHOD OF ARGUMENT CONSTRUCTION

The Wigmore chart method, created by the early twentieth-century American legal scholar John Henry Wigmore, is an extremely useful tool for understanding argument construction. A specimen Wigmore chart is set out in Figure 8.7. It uses symbols, numbers and key lists to allow simultaneous consideration of evidence and facts to enhance factual analysis

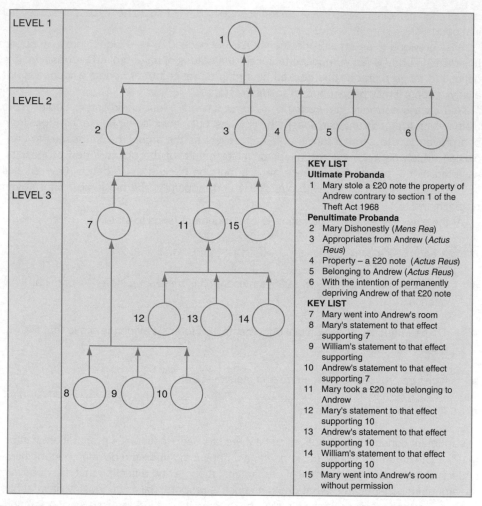

LEVEL 1

LEVEL 2

LEVEL 3

KEY LIST
Ultimate Probanda
1   Mary stole a £20 note the property of Andrew contrary to section 1 of the Theft Act 1968
Penultimate Probanda
2   Mary Dishonestly (*Mens Rea*)
3   Appropriates from Andrew (*Actus Reus*)
4   Property – a £20 note (*Actus Reus*)
5   Belonging to Andrew (*Actus Reus*)
6   With the intention of permanently depriving Andrew of that £20 note
KEY LIST
7   Mary went into Andrew's room
8   Mary's statement to that effect supporting 7
9   William's statement to that effect supporting
10 Andrew's statement to that effect supporting 7
11 Mary took a £20 note belonging to Andrew
12 Mary's statement to that effect supporting 10
13 Andrew's statement to that effect supporting 10
14 William's statement to that effect supporting 10
15 Mary went into Andrew's room without permission

Figure 8.7 Specimen demonstration of a Wigmore chart

and ultimately impact legal analysis. Do not be concerned by its appearance of complexity. It is a clear, manageable system of notation which can help you further develop the skills already discussed in this chapter.

Charting evidence and proof

John Wigmore wanted to restore an imbalance in the approach to evidence to be used in trial. He first unveiled his views in an article published in the *Illinois Law Review* in 1913[2] concerned with issues surrounding the law of evidence. The law of evidence, as it is normally considered in university courses and in practice, is particularly concerned with

2   JH Wigmore, 'The Problem of Proof' (1913–14) 8 Illinois Law Review 77–103.

what type of evidence is admissible in court to prove the case of the parties. We have already referred to it several times. It is also concerned with the procedures that need to be followed to ensure that admissible evidence is not rendered inadmissible due to procedural and avoidable mistakes by those dealing with it before it reaches the courtroom – this covers the field of forensic science as well as witness testimony. Wigmore, however, believed that while the admissibility of evidence and the following of procedures are important aspects of the law relating to evidence, there was another *more* important area that had been completely ignored. This was the aspect of proof itself. What is the *effect* of the admissible evidence? How does it build to a finding of case proved *for or against* one party? Can it be said that there is a science of proof? Here of course issues relating to evidence and the construction of argument begin to merge.

Wigmore saw proof in terms of the proving of points in argument persuading judges and juries of the outcome of a case. He argued:

> . . . there is, and there must be, a probative science – the principles of proof independent of the artificial rules of procedure[3].

He developed his charting method to lay out and evaluate the individual and cumulative strength and likely *effect* of evidence on judges. It is a method based on logical principles of relationship between propositions asserted and was designed to be able to:

- deal with all *types* of evidence;

- include all evidential data of relevance to an individual case;

- show the relationship of *each* evidential fact in the case;

- present data in a simultaneous scheme;

- be full but not too complex;

- distinguish between fact as alleged and fact as believed.

One interesting issue here is that the data includes assertions or argumentative propositions (she had the motive, she stole the book), as well as evidence relating to the act of theft (the book was not logged as sold on the sales system, the coffee-shop assistant saw Anna take the book).

Wigmore's method also allows these different types of data to be viewed simultaneously, to allow for a more precise evaluation of the persuasive proof of that evidence. Simultaneity also assists us in ordering our argument because the method is the evaluative means to the end of presenting a persuasive argument. Order is important and can affect outcome.

---

3   Ibid 77.

The last condition above can be considered by returning to our earlier proposition for the prosecution and adding a second variant:

| Proposition 1 | Anna stole a book | FACT ALLEGED |
| Proposition 2 | I believe Anna did steal the book | FACT BELIEVED |

Can you see the difference in the two propositions, and can you understand why they are qualitatively different?

Between propositions 1 and 2, which we now assume are part of the same argument, there is a transitional point when the movement is from **allegation** to **belief** in the truth of the allegation or belief in the **probable** truth. Law is about probability: 'I believe beyond reasonable doubt Anna stole a book'. The transitional point between assertion and belief is often implicit inference. It is important to remember that the chart can only show what the user now *believes* and how they got there. It *cannot* show what the user *ought* to believe.

Symbols and conventions

Wigmore's chart recorded symbols translated in a narrative key list. Each symbol in the chart stands for a type of evidentiary material, or a proposition of argument, and is given a number. The key list briefly relates the number to the proposition and/or evidentiary data it represents.

Wigmore gave two symbols for evidence. These are set out in Figure 8.8. A small horizontal line denotes defence; the symbol without a horizontal line denotes plaintiff or prosecution. Similar rules apply for symbols for circumstantial evidence.

The removal of a line in the square or the opening of the circle represents the negative impact of testimonial or circumstantial evidence, as seen in Figure 8.9.

Information placed vertically in the chart is hierarchical. Facts supporting other facts are placed below the fact to be supported and linked by a line, as shown in Figure 8.10.

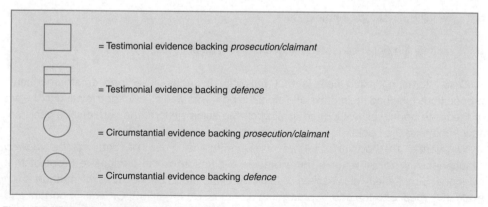

Figure 8.8 Wigmore's symbols relating to evidence

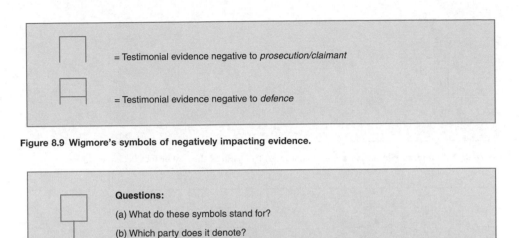

Figure 8.9 Wigmore's symbols of negatively impacting evidence.

Questions:

(a) What do these symbols stand for?

(b) Which party does it denote?

(c) Is it affirming or negating evidence?

(d) How many symbols are there?

Figure 8.10 Two facts with a possible connection

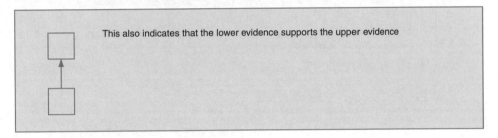

This also indicates that the lower evidence supports the upper evidence

Figure 8.11 Two facts with a firmly believed connection

If one fact as explained corroborates (backs up) another, it is connected by a line to the fact corroborated. As soon as we believe the fact to be true the connecting line is changed to an arrow pointing in the direction of the proof, as shown in Figure 8.11.

If we are uncertain about the link we remove the arrow and place a question mark against the connecting line. If we come to doubt the truth of the testimonial evidence itself we place a question mark in the symbol, as shown in Figure 8.12.

Wigmore also used closed and open dots placed inside symbols to denote belief of individual pieces of evidence, as shown in Figure 8.13.

Each symbol on the chart is numbered and relates to a list setting out brief narrative labels for the evidence represented by the symbol, as shown in Figure 8.14 relating to part of our earlier example.

Figure 8.12 Two facts with an uncertain connection. The truth of the higher fact is also in doubt.

Figure 8.13 Symbols for belief and unbelief

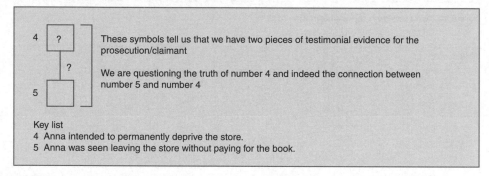

Figure 8.14 A Wigmore chart questioning the *mens rea* of the Anna stole a book case

Analysing the chart

Constructing the chart is only the means to the ends; the last stage is analysis. As the full chart is considered links between propositions and evidence can be more clearly seen. The simultaneous juxtaposition of the evidence, facts, assertions, etc should ultimately lead to a single, finally believed, outcome. The process of reaching the outcome is the argument, and the outcome is the conclusion of the argument.

Wigmore had many additional symbols denoting explanation, weak and strong inferences, the movement from doubt to belief, unsupported and supported inferences. He had symbols denoting object as opposed to person testimony, symbols for denials, rival assertions, generalisations and so on. His charts were extremely complicated matters taking many hours to construct, which is probably why his methods were not widely taken on board in criminal practice.

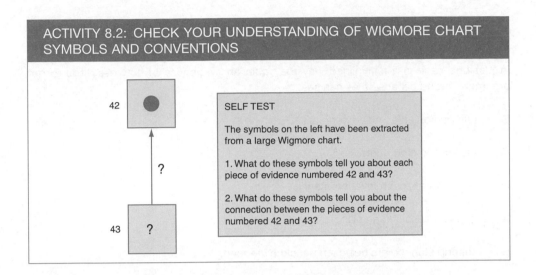

ACTIVITY 8.2: CHECK YOUR UNDERSTANDING OF WIGMORE CHART SYMBOLS AND CONVENTIONS

SELF TEST

The symbols on the left have been extracted from a large Wigmore chart.

1. What do these symbols tell you about each piece of evidence numbered 42 and 43?

2. What do these symbols tell you about the connection between the pieces of evidence numbered 42 and 43?

Uses and limitations of the Wigmore chart method

The complex symbolic networks used in the chart may appeal to some individuals, particularly visual thinkers or learners, but many people can be put off by what appear to be complex mathematical structures. The chart in its full form is also extremely time consuming to create and for that reason may be of extremely limited use to busy practitioners.

However, it has great potential as a learning tool for argument construction and the relationship between different types of data making up a legal argument. Indeed, Wigmore used it for over 40 years with his own law students and it was its educational value that caught the serious attention of Anderson and Twining (see below). The chart method develops awareness about the nature and construction of argument and as a result students recognise how arguments are constructed using relations between propositions supported by proof. This awareness is not often directly encouraged within the parameters of legal education. The chart therefore brings argumentative structure out into the open as an object of consideration. Judgments can be made subsequently about its probative and persuasive force.

Anderson and Twining's modification of the Wigmore chart method

In an excellent book, *Analysis of Evidence*, Anderson and Twining[4] take the time to discuss the uses and limits of Wigmore charts as a tool for legal education. They also note their use in other areas that require investigative tools. They recount a story that demonstrates the far-reaching applications of the method: when David Schum[5] asked a group of computer analysts in the 1980s to guess when Wigmore's chart method had been invented, the earliest date given was 1970 (more than 50 years after its actual invention). In the 1990s

---

4   T Anderson, D Schum and W Twining, *Analysis of Evidence* (2nd edn CUP, 2005).

5   DA Schum, 'Alternative Views of Argument Construction from a Mass of Evidence' (2001) 22 Cardozo Law Review 1461–502.

David Schum and others have effectively applied Wigmore's methodology to intelligence analysis, and other complex inferential systems such as weather forecasting.

Twining absolutely correctly says that if a student goes through the process of analysis in just one case in a disciplined way they gain an awareness of how easy it is to get argument wrong because they can see:

■   reliance on unidentified generalisations;

■   fallacies in argument;

■   presentation of irrelevant material;

■   gaps in reasoning and illogical jumps being taken;

■   shifting standpoints being left unacknowledged;

■   propositions not supported.

If there is a gap or a doubt in your argument it is better to find it yourself and work on it. Then you can at least connect gaps in reasoning by propositions that are unsupported and *know* that you have done this and thus be in control of your argument.

Anderson and Twining suggest there are in fact seven stages to a developing a chart:

1.   clarification of standpoint (why is the chart being constructed);

2.   the formulation of UP (ultimate *probanda*);

3.   the formulation of PP (penultimate *probanda*);

4.   formulation of the IP (interim *probanda*);

5.   formulation of the key list. The chart and the key list are the *means* to analysis;

6.   construction of the chart not the *end*;

7.   completion of the analysis.

Each of these seven stages will now be briefly described.

(1) Clarification of standpoint

Schum noted that standpoint affects inference network construction. How can an audience assess the chart without an insight into the standpoint of the creator? The greater the detail in the chart, the greater the extraction and/or revelation of conditions of doubt in relation to inference networks. So, it is important constantly to ask oneself 'Where are we in the process?', 'What are my objectives?' and to be aware that one's standpoint can change in the execution of one project. Basically, we can say that standpoint is the function of three variables:

- **Time and location**: Wigmore had in mind the trial arena. We will have different times and locations depending on the exercise. Usually, however, it will be post-trial. We will often be asking: was the court right on the evidence presented? Was there another story that was more probable? We may also set exercises presenting as pre-trial.

- **Objective purpose**: It can be within an organisation, or evaluative, or for advocacy, or as here, educational.

- **Role:** Here it is usually as student, or student in role play as prosecutor or defence at academic stage of training.

(2) The formulation of the ultimate probanda (UP)

Probanda is the Latin term for 'proposition' but the Latin word is very flexible, allowing a number of meanings to be implied. The Latin term is therefore retained. The ultimate *probanda* (hereafter UP)is the touchstone of relevancy controlling the relationship of *all* other propositions in the chart. It is the substantive law proposition – the elements of the crime or the civil wrong. It is also the matter to be proved. Once proved, there is no more to say on the point. This is the minor proposition (or premise) of a deductive argument which, as we have already seen, inevitably becomes the *thesis* of the necessary inductive argument. Figure 8.15 recaps this.

Deductive argument

Main proposition: Theft is contrary to s 1 of the Theft Act 1968
Minor proposition: Anna stole a book ⟶ *Thesis* of inductive argument
Conclusion: Anna is guilty of theft

Figure 8.15 The deductive argument

Look back to Figure 8.7 (the specimen chart). You will note that in the left-hand column are the headings level 1, level 2, level 3. Level 1 equates to the UP. The proposition is particularised to a named defendant, Mary. The symbol for this proposition is a circle ○. The circle is numbered 1. Looking to the key list you will see the narrative of the UP under entry number 1, under the heading UP.

In our ongoing example of Anna, the standard UP would be

Anna stole a book – contrary to the Theft Act.

(3) *The formulation of the penultimate* probanda (PP)

The law determines the specific elements that must be proven to a certain standard (standard of proof) to prove the UP. Looking at the UP above, it is that 'Anna stole a book contrary to the Theft Act', so we need to know the elements of the legal rule prohibiting theft. We have already broken section1 of the Theft Act into its five constituent elements. Each of these now becomes one of the penultimate probanda (hereafter PP). The numbering begins at 2 because the UP is number 1.

PP 2: dishonestly;

PP 3: appropriates;

PP 4: property;

PP 5: belonging to another;

PP 6: with the intention of permanently depriving that other.

The number of PPs that you will have in any chart will depend on the elements of the legal rule with which it is concerned.

Each PP has to be proved and if the prosecution fails to prove one element the entire prosecution fails as the UP cannot be proved. The PPs are the proofs of the UP.

Look back to the demonstration of the chart in Figure 8.7. The level 2 circles numbered 2–6 are the PP and the key list proves them to be the five elements of theft as defined in section 1 of the Theft Act.

(4) *The interim* probanda (IP)

The propositions linking the evidence to the UP and PP are called interim *probanda* (hereafter IP). These set up the inferences between evidence and UP. The IPs are the types of data available to add strength to the PP – clusters of facts, opinions and evidences leading to support each of the PP.

These provide the source of our claims about the strength or weakness of the final argument. If these are placed appropriately on the chart we can assess the evidence and test our argument, identifying any gaps and doubts. Indeed we can see all the raw material at our disposal and can assess how to structure our argument. Look back once more to the demonstration chart in Figure 8.7. Level 3 is the range of IPs, each numbered circle being translated in the key list. This is the most complex part of the charting process as you move data around, position it in the best place and ensure each alleged fact is supported by evidence. It may well be the case that one fact supports several PP and then you need to place it under each of the PPs it is relevant to. Similarly your evidence, eg a witness statement, may be evidence of more than one fact, or PP, in which case it should be entered under each fact and/or PP it supports.

It is at this point one comes to the main deviation in Anderson and Twining's presentation of the Wigmore chart method. They conclude most correctly that students, as well as practitioners, find the time required for a whole chart too much to be contemplated. However, since it is the juxtaposition of the types of data rather than the construction and the symbols themselves which are important, the person constructing a chart could equally well use their own symbols. Anderson and Twining did just that, vastly simplifying the range of symbols and aspects included in the body of the chart.

(5) The construction of the key list

The chart as a series of symbols is designed to show us the links between our facts, legal rules, generalisations and evidence. The chart and symbols alone are meaningless if we do not know the specifics of what the numbers represent. The key list is important because it translates our chart and its collection of symbols into narrative form. Then we can read the links. It must be placed on the same page as the chart for ease of reference.

(6) The chart

The final formulations of the UP, PP and IP together with the key list are placed on the chart. It is a series of linked numbered symbols translated through a narrative key list: connected by lines and identified by number. The chart records the propositions that lay out all evidence being considered and all IPs, PPs and UPs. The synthetic element of the chart is the link patterns. This is the place for the creative imagination and rigorous attention to detail of the chart-maker.

(7) Completion of the analysis

Again it is necessary to remember that the chart and key list are not the end of the process but the means of engaging in analysis. The end of the chart is the beginning of argument construction. Nothing in this process should suggest that it is a mechanistic process. In so far as it allows the construction of argument it teaches how an argument is constructed, but it cannot decide how important each item, or the accumulation, of evidence is. The user has to make this decision, evaluating strength, persuasive value, credibility, or positive or negative effect. The chart cannot determine issues such as whether the evidence assembled is admissible. The chart orders material and shows relationships between data and gaps in the proof of the PP. The chart does not solve problems. If there is a gap the user has to decide how to deal with it at the moment of analysis and argument construction.

The human element in handling, locating, ordering, analysing evidence and constructing argument remains an act of knowledge, experience and imagination. Each inference requires an evaluation of its persuasive operation. Then the user needs to come to a view concerning the persuasive effect of the *total* mass of evidentiary facts. Toulmin notes that

'Logic is concerned with the soundness of claims we make, with the solidity of the grounds we produce to support them, the firmness of the backing we provide for them'[6].

What is the objective? For a process model it may be solving a diagnostic model or increasing understanding of complex topics or for knowledge acquisition. Schum describes Wigmore's analytic methods as 'a conceptual microscope that allowed me to examine many subtleties in evidence'[7].

The important point is to show alternative conclusions and test them out. Do they, or your counter-argument, stand up? All counter-responses to your argument can be categorised as having one of the following effects:

- explains it away;

- denies the existence of the evidentiary fact;

- offers a new rival evidential fact.

Hanson's modification of the Wigmore chart

This book uses aspects of Anderson and Twining's modification of the Wigmore chart method to demonstrate how propositions, evidence supporting propositions, and relationship between propositions work together with forms of deductive and inductive legal reasoning to allow outcomes to be reached in relation to factual and legal analysis. Further, it allows a demonstration of the ways in which critical thinking applied to the outcome of such factual and legal analysis allows competent and valid conclusions to be reached on either side of an argument (for or against a specific party).

This book has in fact narrowed the symbols used and the information placed on the chart even further. This serves to simplify the process for you while retaining the educational value of the chart in demonstrating the processes of argument construction. You may have noted that earlier figures were differing shapes. In this book one symbol is used to denote all additions to the chart: a circle.

In our examples, the chart is only constructed for one party at a time, not both, as envisaged by Wigmore and Twining and Anderson. The chart therefore shows less information, but remains useful. The range of symbols we will use are set out in Figure 8.16.

Creating a Wigmore chart: *R v Mary*

We will now apply our adapted version of the Wigmore chart to a reasonably simple criminal law scenario (*R v Mary*) to show how the specimen chart in Figure 8.7 was actually constructed from three witness statements and a definition of the law. It is an important demonstration because you are carefully guided around the construction of the chart and you obtain a detailed understanding of the construction of legal argument. At the academic level of study this exercise can be used to allow you to see far more easily the issues to be teased out at the level of legal analysis, which would take place after the construction of the chart.

---

6 Stephen E Toulmin, *The Uses of Argument* (2nd edn CUP, 1958) 7.
7 DA Schum, 'Alternative Views of Argument Construction from a Mass of Evidence' (2001) 22 Cardozo Law Review 1461–502.

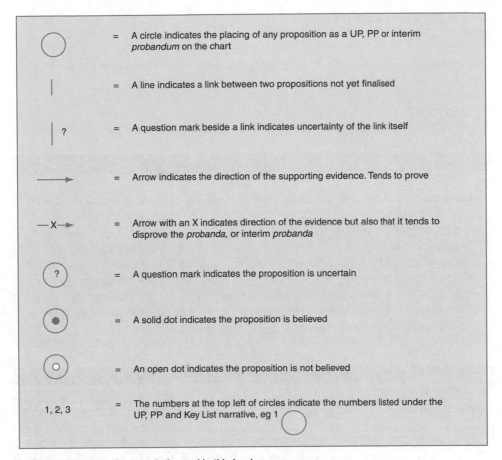

Figure 8.16 Wigmore chart symbols used in this book

The case of R v Mary

We will begin our consideration of *R v Mary* by considering three types of information:

1.   the charge;

2.   the governing legal rule(s);

3.   evidence.

(1) The charge

Mary has been charged with theft under section 1 of the Theft Act 1968. Specifically, Mary has been charged with stealing a £20 note from William, one of her flatmates.

(2) The governing legal rule

Section 1 of the Theft Act 1968 states that:

> A person is guilty of theft if he dishonestly appropriates property belonging to another with the intention of permanently depriving the other of it.

(3) Evidence

Three witness statements have been given to the police by Mary and her two flatmates:

STATEMENT 1: WILLIAM

I share a flat with Andrew and Mary. I came home on Saturday afternoon and Mary asked me if she could borrow £20 because she wanted to buy a skirt. I didn't want to go out and get her money from the cash machine so I said no. She asked me if I thought Andrew would mind if she borrowed the £20 note in his emergency funds jar. Andrew was away. I said I couldn't speak for him. I didn't know. He is generous but can be difficult about his personal stuff. He wouldn't lend me his football shirt the other week. It just did not seem a good idea and I told her so. I saw her go into his room and she came out with the jar. She took out the £20 note which was all that was in it, and left a note saying she would pay it back Monday.

STATEMENT 2: ANDREW

I came home late on Sunday night to the flat I share with William and Mary two good friends. I was extremely tired. When I walked into the kitchen at about midnight I saw my emergency funds jar in the kitchen. There should have been a £20 note in it and it should have been in my bedroom. It had no money in it just a note from Mary which said: 'Sorry – I had an emergency, need a skirt for my interview Monday, I'll put it back Monday night'. I was really angry – the money is mine for my emergencies. Mary knows that I don't like anyone walking into my bedroom. As far as I am concerned she stole my money. I don't believe she can pay it back Monday, or at all. She is unemployed and in debt. Perhaps if she had asked me personally I would have lent her the money to buy a skirt for her interview but she didn't.

STATEMENT 3: MARY

I share a flat with Andrew and William who are good friends with me. On Saturday I heard I had an interview for a clerical job on Monday. I have been unemployed for six months and really needed a job. I thought it would be a good idea to get a new smart skirt for the interview. Andrew and William have been great about helping me out and even let me pay less rent. I was down to my last £10 on Saturday. I get unemployment money every Thursday. I thought that William might lend me some money but he wouldn't go down to the cash machine for me. Andrew is never like that he always lends me money when I have asked him. I knew that if he was here he would give me the money. I decided to take the £20 in Andrew's emergency fund jar. William did say it wasn't a good idea. I took it from Andrew's room and put a note in it saying: 'Sorry – I had an emergency, need a skirt for my interview Monday, I'll put it back Monday night'. I left it in the kitchen so he would know it was gone. I couldn't get anything. So I went to the cinema instead and brought home a take-away and rented a video for me and William. When Andrew came home late Sunday he was unreasonable and shouted at me that I was a thief. He was furious I had gone into his room. But he goes into mine to get stuff he wants. I am really fed up with Andrew.

We will now track through the seven stages of charting already identified in this chapter.

(1) Clarification of standpoint

In our scenario of Mary and Andrew there are two possible main, opposing assertions

1.   that Mary has stolen £20 belonging to Andrew [the prosecution assertion];

2.   that Mary has *not* stolen £20 belonging to Andrew [the defence assertion].

The only information we have are the three statements, the legal rule and any other relevant case or statutory term more fully explaining the interpretation of section 1 of the Theft Act 1968. Therefore whatever question we are called upon to determine, our answer will use the facts as set out in the three statements, which constitute the evidence (a witness statement properly taken is testimonial evidence in court), and the legal rule that determines the elements that constitute theft. The law student also needs to be aware of the particular definition of words or phrases in section 1 of the Theft Act given:

■   in other sections of the same statute;

■   as the result of statutory interpretation in a law case.

An essential aspect of the ultimate legal analysis is the application of case law to your argument.

Your stating point is to fully understand the legal rule and most importantly its elements. It is the legal rule that determines both the construction of the UP (the final assertion, proof of which determines the case) and the PP (proof of which enables the UP to be proved). When the legal rule has been considered, and converted into the UP and PPs then you can move on to analyse witness statements and any other available evidence. These determine the lines of the IP, the pieces of assertion, backed by evidence, that form the argument for each of the PP.

It is now possible, working from the split into *actus reus* and *mens rea*, to begin the construction of the top end of the Wigmore Chart: the UP and PP followed by the IP.

(2) The formulation of the ultimate probanda

This is the matter to be proved to decide the issue. It can be expressed as a simple statement of a given position. It is dependent on the legal rule and the facts so that you can construct it appropriately. We will consider the law when looking at thePP below. For now it is sufficient to say we are taking the role of the prosecution and in this case our UP is:

> Mary stole a £20 note, the property of Andrew contrary to section 1 of the Theft Act 1968.

The individual symbols relating to this first statement are set out in Figure 8.17 and then inserted into the chart in Figure 8.18.

Description	**Symbol**
It is our first entry on the chart and is therefore given the number 1.	1
The symbol we are using to signify the entry is a circle.	
We will be attaching further entries to the chart and will therefore link this symbol with an arrow in the direction of the penultimate *probanda*, the elements of the offence.	
At the top of the key list, number 1 has the heading UP and it is our statement, our inductive thesis.	Mary stole a £20 note the property of Andrew contrary to s 1 of the Theft Act 1968

Figure 8.17 The Wigmore chart symbols for the ultimate *probanda*

LEVEL 1	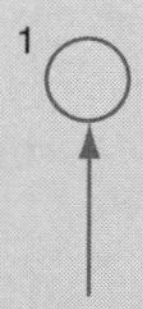
KEY LIST	**KEY LIST** **UP** 1. Mary stole a £20 note the property of Andrew contrary to section 1 of the Theft Act 1968

Figure 8.18 Wigmore chart for *R* v *Mary* with UP stage and key list

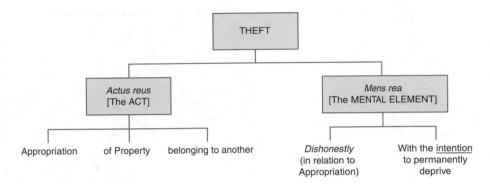

Figure 8.19 Section 1 Theft Act

(3) *The formulation of the penultimate* probanda

The second level, as we are working backwards, is the PP, the elements that have to be proved to show that the UP is correct (in other words, the elements of the legal rule, in this case of section 1 of the Theft Act 1968).

As we discussed earlier, each separate element of the *actus reus* and the *mens rea* must be proved to the satisfaction of the court, which means that most of these elements have to be backed by evidence beyond all reasonable doubt. The provision of an item of proof is not by itself sufficient, it has to be of a certain strength that can be said to be proof beyond all reasonable doubt.

Since we have already worked on this, we know that each of the five elements of section 1 becomes a PP displayed horizontally, as shown in Figure 8.20. As they are the second

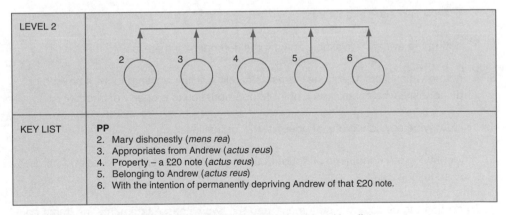

Figure 8.20 The penultimate *probanda*: chart detail showing level 2 and key list

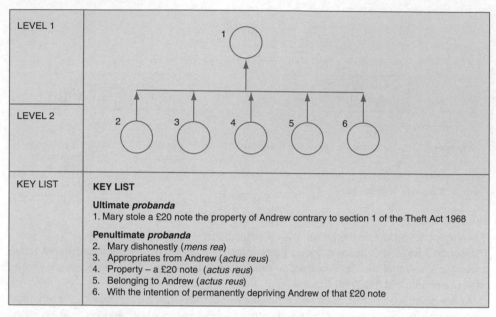

LEVEL 1	
LEVEL 2	
KEY LIST	**KEY LIST** **Ultimate *probanda*** 1. Mary stole a £20 note the property of Andrew contrary to section 1 of the Theft Act 1968 **Penultimate *probanda*** 2. Mary dishonestly (*mens rea*) 3. Appropriates from Andrew (*actus reus*) 4. Property – a £20 note (*actus reus*) 5. Belonging to Andrew (*actus reus*) 6. With the intention of permanently depriving Andrew of that £20 note

Figure 8.21 Wigmore chart for *R* v *Mary* with PP stage and key list

item to be determined we could consider them to be level 2. Level 2 is of course attached to level 1, as shown in Figure 8.21.

(4) The formulation of the interim probanda

Now it is necessary to deploy the evidence in terms of its support or denial of the PP by:

1.   assembling the relevant facts;

2.   noting the evidence available against the defendant, if there is any;

3.   noting which facts match the elements of relevant law, eg what facts, if any, point to dishonesty, what facts, if any, point to appropriation of property of another;

4.   identifying any conditions of doubt at the factual level;

5.   identifying any conditions of doubt at the legal level (meaning of words and phrases used in legal rule).

To do this the defendant's statement, and the two witness statements, as items containing evidence, have to be broken down. This requires thought, decisions and creativity. For the purposes of this exercise we will assume that the three statements provided contain all the information available and that the three statements were produced in ways not calling into doubt their admissibility or credibility. This means therefore that we only have to concentrate on their probative value (asking ourselves what they prove).

When these activities have been undertaken it will be possible to construct the next stage of the chart and the final part of the key list for use by the prosecution.

ACTIVITY 8.3: ANALYSING WITNESS STATEMENTS

So that you can appreciate the levels of analysis go back to the three boxed statements in the case of *R v Mary* set out above and highlight the key words and phrases that begin to allow you to break into them and locate the story, and the law. Then try to give answers to the following questions:

1. What are the relevant facts?

2. What key phrases in the statements give you clues as to the application of the law?

3. Can you construct the deductive argument for the prosecution?

4. Can you construct the inductive argument for the prosecution?

5. Can you construct the opposing inductive argument for the defence?

6. Are there any conditions of doubt in your mind surrounding the wording of section 1(1) of the Theft Act which may apply (for example questions surrounding the presence of both *mens rea* and *actus reus*)?

Hint: you may wish to know what is meant by 'dishonestly'.

By considering the three statements of Andrew, William and Mary in Figure 8.22 as they have been annotated evaluate your findings for items (1)–(6) in Activity 8.2. What did you get right? What did you miss? Why did you miss it? Ensure that you understand the issues. Read the comments in boxes A–F carefully and make sure that you can follow them.

Once the evidence has been particularly considered we can insert arrows, and indicate the status of the testimony, using the symbols shown in Figure 8.23.

If you have carefully considered the statements and worked through Activity 8.3 you are in a good position to finalise the placing of the IP on the chart. Having identified the facts from the statements and selected your evidence from the statements, you will have a good idea concerning what is at issue at the level of fact and evidence.

Statement 1: William I share a flat with Andrew and Mary. I came home on Saturday afternoon and Mary asked me if she could borrow £20 because she wanted to buy a skirt. I didn't want to go out and get her money from the cash machine so I said no. She asked me if I thought Andrew would mind if she borrowed the £20 note in his emergency funds jar. Andrew was away. I said I couldn't speak for him. I didn't know. He is generous but can be difficult about his personal stuff. He wouldn't lend me his football shirt the other week. It just did not seem a good idea and I told her so. I saw her go into his room and she came out with the jar. She took out the £20 note which was all that was in it, and left a note saying

FACT 3   FACTS 5 & 7

COMMENT BOX A: Facts emerging from statements 1– 3

1. Mary, William and Andrew share a flat and are good friends.
2. Saturday Mary takes '£20 note' from an emergency funds jar in Andrew's bedroom.
3. Andrew is away until Sunday.
4. Mary believes that Andrew would have given her money if she had asked.
5. Mary writes a note stating that she will return the money on Monday night.
6. Andrew returns Sunday night and angrily accuses Mary of theft.
7. William sees Mary take the £20 note from Andrew's bedroom and leave a note.

FACT 1
FACT 2
FACT 4

COMMENT BOX B:
Testimonial (Witness) evidence from William that Mary took the £20 from Andrew's room.

Statement 2: Andrew

I came home late on Sunday night to the flat I share with William and Mary two good friends. I was extremely tired. When I walked into the kitchen at about midnight I saw my emergency funds jar in the kitchen. There should have been a £20 note in it and it should have been in my bedroom. It had no money in it just a note from Mary which said "Sorry- I had an emergency, need a skirt for my interview Monday, I'll put it back Monday night". I was really angry - the money is mine for my emergencies. Mary knows that I don't like anyone walking into my bedroom. As far as I am concerned she stole my money. I don't believe she can pay it back Monday, or at all. She is unemployed and in debt. Perhaps if she had asked me personally I would have lent her the money to buy a skirt for her interview but she didn't.

Statement 3: Mary

I share a flat with Andrew and William who are good friends with me. On Saturday I heard I had an interview for a clerical job on Monday. I have been unemployed for six months and really needed a job. I though it would be a good idea to get a new smart skirt for the interview. Andrew and William have been great about helping me out and even let me pay less rent. I was down to my last £10 on Saturday.

I get unemployment money every Thursday. I thought that William might lend me some money but he wouldn't go down to the cash machine for me.

Andrew is never like that he always lends me money when I have asked him. I knew that if he was here he would give me the money.

I decided to take the £20 in Andrew's emergency fund jar. William did say it wasn't a good idea. I took it from Andrew's room and put a note in it saying, 'Sorry – I had an emergency, I need a skirt for my interview Monday, I'll put it back Monday night'.

I left it in the kitchen so he would know it was gone. I couldn't get anything. So I went to the cinema instead and brought home a takeway and rented a video for me and William. When Andrew came home late Sunday he was unreasonable and shouted at me that I

FACTS 2 & 5   FACT 6   FACT 3

COMMENT BOX C: If Mary gets paid on Thursday and was down to her last £10 on Saturday HOW could she pay the £20 back by Monday?

COMMENT BOX D: If Mary believes that Andrew would have lent her the money does this cast doubt on her 'dishonesty'? Does this mean she believed she had his permission to take the money and does that make any difference?

COMMENT BOX E: Admission by Mary that she took the £20 note from Andrew's room. This is an important admission of the one aspect of the *actus reus* – appropriation.

COMMENT BOX F: Mary's note and her statement states that she will give the money back on Monday (the next day). Does this cast doubt on her intention to 'permanently deprive'?

Figure 8.22 Annotated witness statements in the case of *R* v *Mary*

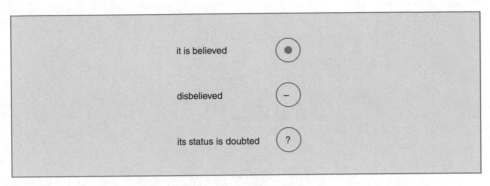

Figure 8.23 Symbols indicating belief, disbelief and doubt

Next we need to study PP 2–6 (which are of course the elements of theft), and we need to determine which facts and evidence support each PP. Do you know which facts from the statement you will insert here? How do we decide what supports the *actus reus* (3 of the PP) and what supports the *mens rea* (2 of the PP)? What might we as prosecutors be looking for? What might the defence be looking for? If you remain unclear look back at Figure 8.22.

Do not forget that earlier in this chapter we said that a good argument for one party always tries to predict what the other party might put forward so we need to bear this in mind.

As you will see in Figure 8.23 the arrows have now been placed on the chart with symbols for belief and uncertainty, as in Figure 8.25, which has a number of IP (items 7–15). Did you notice most of these when you first checked the statements? As can be seen by looking at Figure 8.25 the main areas of uncertainty concern PP2 and PP5. For each piece of evidence or each fact you will find it useful to ensure you note the origin on the chart as a symbol and on the key list, as shown in Figure 8.24.

Just producing a source of evidence is not enough: its source must be noted, and capable of being checked. Now it is possible to set out our final chart as in Figure 8.25. This is in fact our demonstration chart (Figure 8.7) from the beginning of the discussion of Wigmore charts.

(5) The key list
Draw up a careful key list and ensure all symbols are translated.

(6) The chart
We have discussed the creation of the chart alongside the formulation of the UP, PP and IP because we knew a lot about the area. In a new situation much time would be spent drawing up the UP, PP and IP on paper and then finally these would be placed on the chart.

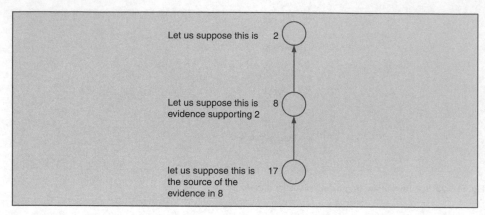

Figure 8.24 Origins of evidence

The analysis

Having laid out the chart as in Figure 8.25 (and this chart will be left at this point although there is more that could be done), you should be able to see two major problem areas. Because the chart is structured to lead to the UP through the PP (that is, the elements of the legal rule concerned), you should be able to see at once where there is strength and where there is not. If there is an element of the PP without support then it could be the end of the case.

There are major queries relating to PP6. This is the PP concerning intention, which in section 1(1) is one of the two aspects of the *mens rea* required to be proved. So, unless more certainty can be achieved in this area there is a problem. In addition, PP1 has a question mark indicating uncertainty. This is the element of the *actus reus* requiring the dishonesty, but Mary alleges she acted in the certainty that Andrew would have lent her the money: in other words she had his permission. We can see that there are many elements of strength stacking up under PP1 but a major issue is 15, going into Andrew's room without permission. Mary's statement of course notes that as far as she is concerned she had permission.

Having produced the chart and noted the strengths and weaknesses the next stage is to look at the law cases and engage in the legal analysis of the case law dealing with this issue. Immediately, however, one can ask a series of questions based on each PP, as outlined below.

PP2: Dishonestly (mens rea)

■   What is the legal meaning of 'dishonestly'? Does the Theft Act 1968 define 'dishonestly', and is the meaning of 'dishonestly' discussed in leading cases?

■   Does the legal definition include believing that you have permission to take something? Does the Theft Act deal with this aspect of honesty/dishonesty, and is this situation discussed in leading cases?

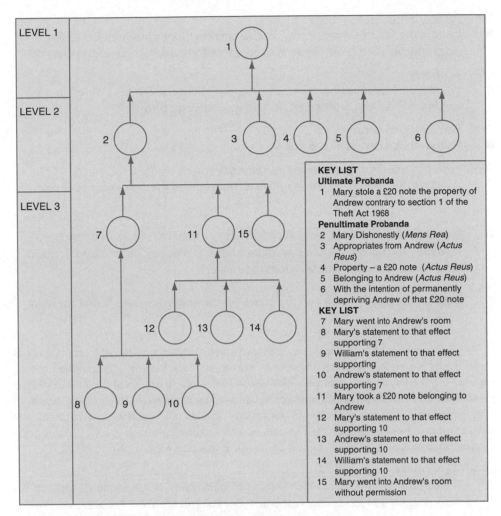

Figure 8.25 Completed Wigmore chart for the case of *R* v *Mary*

KEY LIST

Ultimate Probanda

1   Mary stole a £20 note the property of Andrew contrary to section 1 of the Theft Act 1968

Penultimate Probanda

2   Mary Dishonestly (*Mens Rea*)
3   Appropriates from Andrew (*Actus Reus*)
4   Property – a £20 note (*Actus Reus*)
5   Belonging to Andrew (*Actus Reus*)
6   With the intention of permanently depriving Andrew of that £20 note

KEY LIST

7   Mary went into Andrew's room
8   Mary's statement to that effect supporting 7
9   William's statement to that effect supporting
10 Andrew's statement to that effect supporting 7
11 Mary took a £20 note belonging to Andrew
12 Mary's statement to that effect supporting 10
13 Andrew's statement to that effect supporting 10
14 William's statement to that effect supporting 10
15 Mary went into Andrew's room without permission

■   What is the legal test (if any) for a reasonable belief that you have permission? Is it according to what other reasonable people would think (an objective test) or is it according to whatever Mary thought, no matter how unreasonable (a *very* subjective test)? Do the statute or cases discuss this situation?

■   Did Mary have conditional permission to take £20 for a skirt when she spent the money on something else? Does that matter? If she thought Andrew would give permission for the skirt does it matter that she went to the cinema and got a take-away meal instead? Do the statute or cases discuss this situation?

PP3: Appropriates (actus reus)

■ What is the legal meaning, if any, of 'appropriates'? Does the Theft Act define 'appropriates', and is the meaning of appropriation discussed in leading cases?

PP4: Property

■ What is the legal meaning, if any, of 'property'? Does the Theft Act define 'property', and is the meaning of 'property' discussed in leading cases?

PP5: Belonging to another

■ This is straightforward in this case.

PP6: With the intention to deprive permanently (mens rea)

■ What is the legal meaning of 'intention to deprive'? Do the statute or cases discuss this situation?

■ Mary said that she did not intend permanently to deprive Andrew of his money. However, she said she would pay Andrew back on Monday, yet she clearly would have no money until Thursday. Does this matter?

■ Does this suggest an intention to deprive permanently? Are there cases covering this?

As you can see whilst the chart is excellent at one task (factual analysis) it only highlights the areas for the equally important task of legal analysis. Which is why the charting process leads to legal analysis. Much of your skill will lie in the interpretation of the chart, and the identification of questions and issues of relevance to legal analysis. This is the moment to look for answers at the level of statutory sources and case law which we will do briefly. We will just make a few explorations to indicate how this matter can be pursued. But this book is about methods and skills – it is not a criminal law text and will not go into detail.

PP2: Dishonestly

■ The statute does not define the meaning of 'dishonesty' but in section 2 sets out three situations which are not dishonest. Section 2 of the Theft Act also makes clear that implied consent can negate a claim of dishonesty:

> 2(1) A person's appropriation of property belonging to another is not to be regarded as dishonest . . .
>   . . . (b) if he appropriates the property in the belief that he would have the other's consent if the other knew of the appropriation and the circumstances of it.

■ 'Dishonestly' has been held by the courts to be an ordinary word, to be interpreted by the jury or the judge as a matter of fact. It does not carry a technical legal meaning. The question is, was Mary as a matter of fact dishonest in the circumstances?

■ In *Gilks* [1972] 3 All ER 280, the jury was asked to place themselves in the shoes of the defendant and then ask 'was the defendant dishonest?' Was Mary dishonest in the circumstances of this case? The Court of Appeal thought that this was a reasonable question, agreeing that if the defendant held the belief he claimed, the prosecution had not established dishonesty. The defendant's belief applied, said the Court of Appeal 'not the standards of ordinary decent people, but the defendant's own standards, however deplorable'.

■ In *Boggein v Williams* [1978] CLR 242, the court held the defendant's belief in his honesty was essential.

■ In the leading case of *R v Ghosh* [1982] QB 1053 the Court of Appeal stated that whether a defendant is dishonest was to be determined by a two-part direction to the jury which is now referred to as the Ghosh test:

(1)   was what was done dishonest according to the ordinary standards of reasonable and honest people? If the answer is 'no' the defendant is not guilty as there is no proved dishonesty and a vital element of the *actus reus* is unproved. If the answer is 'yes' then the second question has to be asked;

(2)   did the defendant realise that reasonable and honest people regarded what he did as dishonest? If the answer is yes then the defendant is guilty.

■ In our case Mary may well find that the answer to the first question would come in as 'no' and she escapes liability. Should it not, the second question should be answered in the negative and she still escapes liability. Most reasonable and honest people would regard the taking of the money in the precise circumstances reasonable and not dishonest.

PP3: *Appropriates*

■ Section 3(1) of the Theft Act 1968 defines 'appropriation' as 'Any assumption by a person of the rights of an owner', which includes coming by property innocently but then assuming the rights of an owner.

■ In *Lawrence* v *Metropolitan Police Commissioner* [1972] AC 626 a taxi driver, when offered the wallet of a foreign passenger and told to take the fare, took too much. There was no implied consent to take money generally; the only implied consent was to take the fare.

■ The House of Lords in *Gomez* [1992] AC 442 stated that it is possible for there to be an appropriation even when the owner has consented to the taking.

■   Importantly for Mary, section 3(1) refers to the person who comes by property without stealing and later assumes the rights of an owner.

■   Mary believes she has permission to take the money for a skirt. Does that cover her later use of the money for entertainment? Or was the implied consent conditional upon the precise use the money was put to?

PP4: Property
■   Section 4 of the Theft Act defines 'property' and money is included under the general heading of property.

PP5: Belonging to another
■   This is defined in section 5(1) of the Theft Act. Possession, control and interest as well as ownership is included in the definition.

PP6: Intention to deprive permanently
■   This phrase is not defined and explored in the case law.

The real-life, every-day legal problem (which will be discussed in Chapter 9) is, of course, less obviously liable to provide the information required for the full factual analysis that we have engaged in here. However, in terms of knowing what to look out for at the level of facts and evidence, our discussion here will help you to develop a map of potential areas to be considered.

CONCLUSION

■   Argument by analogy is the most common form of argument in law. Such an argument begins by stating that two objects are observed to be similar, identifying the comparable attributes, with the conclusion drawing similarities between the two objects with respect to a third. The strength of the argument depends upon the degree of relationship between the objects.

■   Abductive reasoning is a creative process which argues around data based on opposing hypothetical theses. Some of these hypotheses may be more plausible than the argument-creator's own proposition.

■   Tools such as the Wigmore chart are useful ways of developing your skills or argument analysis.

■   The Wigmore chart is a means to an end and does not replace legal analysis, but in many respects it rests on our knowledge of legal analysis as well as clearing the ground for us to engage in legal analysis and critical thinking.

FURTHER READING

T Anderson, D Schum and W Twining, *Analysis of Evidence* (CUP, Cambridge 2005).

N Gold, K Mackie and W Twining, *Learning Lawyer's Skills* (Butterworths, London 1989).

W Twining and D Miers, *How To Do Things With Rules* (4th edn CUP, Cambridge 1999).

DA Schum, 'Alternative Views of Argument Construction from a Mass of Evidence' (2001) 22 Cardozo Law Review 1461–502 (contains a valuable set of references within the discipline of law and in other disciplines concerning arguments).

H Wigmore, 'The Problem of Proof' (1913–14) 8 Illinois Law Rev 77.

COMPANION WEBSITE

Now visit the companion website to:

■   work through the series of Part Three-related exercises in Workbook Three;

■   tackle quiz questions on the basic parts of argument;

■   test your knowledge and understanding with a flashcard glossary.

PART FOUR:

PUTTING IT ALL TOGETHER – LAST THINGS AS YOU ARRIVE

"We are approaching a new age of synthesis. Knowledge cannot be merely a degree or a skill . . . it demands a broader vision, capabilities in critical thinking and logical deduction without which we cannot have constructive progress."

Li Ka Shing

The final part of this book is concerned with your competent performance in written and oral assessment throughout the course, and your efficient revision and execution of examinations. It is called 'Putting it all together' because assessment and examinations test the whole range of your skills as you perform them in a series of one-off events.

The quality of your language and argument construction skills becomes paramount as these vehicles support your legal work. Your legal research skills allow you to locate the range of sources required for your work, but your skill in summarising, evaluating and critiquing those retrieved sources, and the demonstration of your critical-thinking powers, are equally important. Your ability comfortably to use legal and academic as well as occasional legal professional resources will also be evaluated in assessments and examinations.

Chapter 9: Writing the law demonstrates the differences between the two main types of written exercise you may be given for written assessments: the legal problem question and the essay question.

Chapter 10: Speaking the law focuses on oral skills work. Here you need to show competency in understanding the different purposes of the range of oral skills exercises that you might be given (for example, presentations, debates, mooting and negotiations). You need also to demonstrate that you understand the constraints of formal speaking and are capable of making the subtle shifts in emphasis and citation required in oral work as compared to written work.

Chapter 11: Exam strategies turns to understanding the requirements of the exam, pre-planning revision and the production of competent answers to problems and essay questions in the standard law exam.

WRITING THE LAW

" But words are things, and a small drop of ink, falling like dew upon a thought, produces that which makes thousands, perhaps millions, think."

Lord Byron

LEARNING OUTCOMES

By the end of this chapter you should be able to:

■ appreciate and apply the differences in approach to be adopted for essays and problem questions;

■ understand the importance of referencing, language usage and presentation;

■ confidently prepare for written work;

■ structure written work effectively;

■ bring together the skills of research, analysis and argument construction and demonstrate competency in writing.

CHAPTER SUMMARY

This chapter considers the differences and similarities in approach required to produce written work in the form of essays and answers to legal problem questions. It is necessary to take the time to get in control of the information gathered for written work. If you can consider the available material with a view to raising new issues for reflection, you will begin to move beyond the texts: beyond summarising, identifying and classifying and even beyond predicting.

The chapter begins with some general issues of relevance to essays and problem questions: language, presentation of written work, referencing, word limits, assessment criteria and what lecturers are looking for when marking. It then considers essay writing and suggests a method for constructing essays, before turning to the issue of answering legal problem questions and appropriate methods to use when dealing with their solution.

This part of the book is called 'Putting it all together' because your performance in written work, oral skills and exams depends on your stages of development in the whole range of skills.

INTRODUCING LEGAL WRITING

A competent approach to legal research skills, argument construction and legal writing will allow you to produce work that demonstrates your understanding of an area. If you can synthesise your skills and create argument rationally on the basis of existing theory, cases, statutes, and practice you should generate good results in the distinction category. Students who try to be creative but fail to produce any plausible evidence for their argument construct weak pieces of work that result in low grades.

Handing in work is not enough to complete the task you have been set. You need to demonstrate understanding by careful application, interpretation, prediction and creativity. If you are pushed for time and only engage in limited research for your written coursework, it can be tempting to focus on finding and summarising articles that obviously answer the question. Simply summarising a string of articles, texts and cases without presenting a serious argument supported by evidence will not attract a good mark for an essay or problem question. However, if your summaries are well prepared, they can provide a good basis for argument construction as part of your response.

In an exam situation, as well as in coursework, it is important to spend enough time thinking about what the question is asking, analysing the texts to be used and constructing an argument in answer to the question. Discussing the facts and outcomes of cases, or the description of argument in texts, without demonstrating an appreciation of the issues raised by the cases or their relevance and application to the question will not satisfy the examiner.

Of course, there are times when it is necessary to take a pragmatic approach to essay preparation. Making considered decisions about planning your time is one thing. Not taking the time to comprehend properly the task in hand is another matter. As we have said elsewhere, remember that academic writing is a time-consuming task, and the time has to be knowingly used!

It takes *time* to properly

- *understand* the basic issues involved in the writing task
- *appreciate* the interconnectedness of the texts
- *research* sources
- *compare* texts, and compare your view with the view of other writers
- *determine* your views
- *construct* an argument in answer to the essay or problem

STYLE, GRAMMAR AND LANGUAGE

Developing your written voice

For many students, finding their 'written voice' is difficult. When you speak to others you do not have to think how shall I sound, how shall I say this? You know. You automatically change your vocabulary, accent and tone of voice when speaking to different types of people, for example, a close friend, an acquaintance, your family, your lecturer. However, you may not be so accustomed to using and changing your written voice. It may be the case that you only write when you are being assessed in coursework or exams. Unlike the informality of emails, texting, instant messaging and Facebook, formal academic writing is a measured method of communicating, with clear rules of engagement that cover style as well as content. It has been described as a one-sided conversation with the reader. It can be difficult if you realise your writing does not sound right or you are told your style needs changing, especially if you do not understand why and how you can improve it.

Developing your written voice is exceptionally important. After all, it is the medium that will secure your degree. Take as many opportunities to write as possible, getting yourself used to the medium outside the assessment itself.

ACTIVITY 9.1: FINDING YOUR VOICE[1]

Stop now and find a piece of paper and pen. Start writing about anything for ten minutes, without worrying about style or grammar. When you have finished do not read it but put the paper to one side and keep on reading this book (or do something else). Later today or tomorrow return to the piece and see how your voice reads. Ask yourself:

■   Are there phrases you like or dislike?

■   What worked and why?

■   What did not work and why?

Keep trying this until you feel comfortable with the idea of writing. You should start to find your voice.

Legal writing requires the use of formal language, but not too formal. An objective style should be used, that does not in any shape or form refer to the person of the writer. This means you should avoid using the words 'I' or 'my'. This will take time to perfect but is well worth the effort. By objectifying you in effect describe to the reader what the essay, the object, will do. So instead of saying 'I intend to outline the issues involved in . . .' you translate it into descriptive language and say 'This essay will outline the issues involved in . . .'. This requirement to use objective language when communicating about the structure and content of your writing is not just about style. Whilst undergraduate students are expected to develop independent thoughts and views, in academic writing you should only express the views of those with authority (leading scholars and lawyers) on the issue. Any conclusion needs to weigh the academic and legal sources you have placed into your argument. Compared with these sources, your own views are not relevant.

Even when you are communicating the views of others, the language of your writing should not change. Rather than summarising each source separately and pushing it into your argument you need to review the words used and properly integrate all the sources into a coherent argument. *Your* written voice should be communicating the views of others.

There are many different ways to say what you want to say, and you can choose what you say and how you say it. One way to assess the quality of your writing may be to read it out aloud, so you can hear it and gain a different perspective on what you have written. Ask yourself:

■   Can you follow your argument?

■   Is there a flow to the language and the ordering of the points and evidences?

---

1   The idea for this exercise is taken from P Elbow, *Writing with Power: Techniques for Mastering the Writing Process* (Galaxy books OUP, New York 1981).

■　　Are the points in the best order?

■　　Is your movement from one statement, proposition or point to the next logical?

■　　Have you created any confusing moments?

■　　Or breaks in your argument?

■　　Are your paragraphs appropriate; does each new idea get its own paragraph?

Grammar and punctuation

The title of Lynne Truss' surprise bestseller on the subject of punctuation, *Eats, Shoots and Leaves*[2] shows the importance of correct grammar. Depending on where a comma is placed in the phrase, the sense changes. Truss described the story of a hapless panda who read in a book that a panda 'Eats, shoots and leaves'. This led to a tragedy as the panda went into a restaurant, ordered and ate a meal, took out a gun, began shooting and then left. The entry should of course have said that a panda 'Eats shoots and leaves', leading the panda to the park for a meal of leaves and shoots.

One of the things that makes English difficult to learn and use is a lack of precision generally about what the rules of English grammar might be. This is in part due to the fact that legal English is the result of many different language traditions. English also has a massive vocabulary, with extensive synonyms (words that mean the same thing). Even so, there are a number of conventions relating to grammar and punctuation that it is worth knowing, as shown below.

Apostrophes	These denote a missing letter or word or the idea of possession, for example: Peter's lunch (the apostrophe indicates the possession of the lunch by Peter); He hadn't eaten (the apostrophe is used to show the contraction of 'had not' by removing the letter o and combining the words together); It's and its are special cases: It's cold today (the apostrophe is used to show the contraction of 'It is' by removing the letter i); The dog scratched at its shoulder (there is no apostrophe as there is no missing word or letter, even though the shoulder is the possessive of 'it').
Articles	These are words like a, an and the. A is used when something is mentioned for the first time, for example: *He ate a bug*.

---

2   Truss, L. *Eats, Shoots and Leaves: The Zero Tolerance approach to punctuation* (London: Profile Books, 2003)

An is used when the article precedes a word that starts with a vowel, for example:

He ate an egg.

The is used when something is mentioned again, for example:

He ate an egg. The egg was boiled.

Conjunctions   These are words that join parts of speech, such as if and but. They are particularly important when interpreting statutes.

It is considered bad grammar to begin a sentence with a conjunction, since something that joins should not be at the beginning.

Prepositions   These are words used together with nouns or pronouns, denoting place, time, position and method. They include to, of, in, from, between, after, before.

They should not be used at the end of a sentence.

Pronouns   These are words used instead of a noun to refer to someone or something that has already been discussed. They include he, she, they, we, you, it, this.

For example:

Tom crossed the road. He wanted to get to the other side.

In the move away from sexist language, there is greater use of any, everyone and everybody instead of the classic gender pronouns she, he, him, her.

Sentences   Each sentence must contain a verb.

Paragraphs   Each new idea should be introduced in a new paragraph.

Choosing the right words

Although legal writing has a certain level of formality, you should not be excessively formal in the words you use. Lakoff[3] identified the concept of hyper-correct language in speakers who resort to long words and archaic terms because they feel uncomfortably out of their comfort zone. The classic scenario is the witness in court who says: 'I immediately apprehended that the person was moving his arm in my direction with a clenched fist and he made contact with my left cheek towards the area of the chin, and I experienced a rush of pain. I noted that I had been the victim of a battery!' instead of 'Then the defendant punched me in the face'. This can be most unconvincing in court and in written form.

It is of course the case that there are unusual phrases and words used in the law. Some remain in legal documents because they are the product of a time during which those words were thought to be best practice. Latin is used but there is a growing tendency to move away from it. There are still a reasonable number of Latin phrases which could be described as technical terms of art. For example, within criminal law the conduct and mental state elements of crime are still referred to as *actus reus* and *mens rea* respectively. However, many previously accepted Latin phrases have now been anglicised, such as an *ex parte* application which is now referred to as 'application without notice'. Latin phrases should always be written in italics.

---

3   R Lakoff, *Language and Women's Place* (Harper & Row, New York 1975).

A large number of perfectly ordinary English words have come to have a particular meaning within law, such as assault, battery, consideration, intention, reasonable, property, negligence, and reckless. It is wise not to use these terms except in their legal meaning to avoid any possible confusion in the mind of the marker about what you are saying.

You should also consider whether your writing style will be gender neutral. In the law, and often in the world at large, there is a convention that the masculine includes the feminine[4]. We are all accustomed to reading the male form as normal and it can be surprising if a writer discussing a hypothetical situation notes 'Let us consider the thief, she may . . .' rather than 'Let us consider the thief, he may . . .'. There are two schools of thought with regard to academic writing: either gendered language is discriminatory or it is not. You may choose your own style but it is worth finding out how your marker feels in case he or she is offended by non-gender-neutral language.

If you find language and style difficult, check to see if your university runs academic writing seminars.

Editing, formatting and referencing

Infuriatingly students often neglect the presentation aspect of written work[5]. In addition to finding your voice and refining your writing style and use of language, you should always allow time to edit and format your work. Make sure you read carefully for spelling, punctuation, grammar, and flow of your work through paragraphs. In addition:

- Follow your department's conventions on referencing (see the following section on notes and references).

- Follow your department's conventions on formatting. Your law department may require a certain font or line spacing to be used, and dictate whether you should only use one side of your paper.

- If you have a free choice of font, choose one that is easy to read (this will keep your marker relaxed and happy). A font size of 12 is recommended as 14 tends to be too big and 10/11 too small. Keep your line spacing to 1.5 or 2 lines, as this again makes reading easier.

- Cases and statutes tend to be formatted in order to make them stand out. Conventionally the names of cases are italicised. For example: *R* v *Briggs* [1977] 1 WLR 605.

- Be consistent in your use of headings and how they are displayed in your work.

- Number all pages.

---

4   Section 6 Interpretation Act 1978
5   One of my students many years ago managed to hand in work with a dried-up baked bean stuck to it.

Notes and references

We have already seen in Chapter 2 how citations describe the physical location of primary sources of law in volumes of law reports, collections of statutes or electronic sources. When you are producing written work there are very precise rules relating to the referencing of your sources. Law schools and the academic publishers of law use different methods of referencing sources. There are two main systems used: The Harvard Referencing System (Harvard) and the Oxford Standard for Citation of Legal Authorities (OSCOLA). You must use the method your law department insists upon and to fail to do so will lead to loss of marks. If there is no particular preference you should ensure that you never mix your styles in the same piece of work.

Both methods dictate the way in which references to sources should be set out in the body of the text of your work, in footnotes or endnotes, or in bibliographies. Table 9.1 sets out the main conventions in relation to the two systems. It deals with only five sources, academic journals, books, law cases, handling quotations, statutes and the internet. There are guides in excess of 100 pages for both methods and if you use different sources to the ones listed you should consult them.

TABLE 9.1 REFERENCING USING OSCOLA AND HARVARD: A QUICK GUIDE

Source	OSCOLA referencing	Harvard referencing
Journal articles	• Author's surname • Author's initial(s) • Title of the article in single quotes • Year of publication • Volume number if appropriate • Journal abbreviation • Page number on which the article begins • Page number on which the specific quote or idea is discussed if it is a specific reference **Example** Hanson, S, 'The Secularisation Thesis: Talking at Cross purposes' (1997) 12(2) JCR, 191 at page 200	• Author's surname • Author's initials(s) • Year of publication in round brackets • The title of the article in single quotes • The name of the journal underlined • The issue number • The date of that issue if given • Page numbers from the start to the end of the article **Example** Hanson, S (1997) 'The Secularisation Thesis: Talking at Cross purposes' <u>Journal of Contemporary Christianity</u>, Volume 12 Number 2, 191 at page 200

Source	OSCOLA referencing	Harvard referencing
Books	• Author's surname and Author's initial(s) • Title of the book in italics • Open brackets, then Edition • Publisher • Place of publication • Year then close brackets **Example** Hanson, S, *Legal Method, Skills and Reasoning* (3rd edn Routledge-Cavendish, London 2010) For specific pages state as follows: Hanson, S, *Legal Method, Skills and Reasoning* (3rd edn Routledge-Cavendish, London 2010) 22–37	• Author's surname and Author's initial(s) • Year of publication • Title of the book in italics or underlined • Place of publication • Publisher • Edition if there is more than one **Example** Hanson, S (2010) *Legal Method, Skills and Reasoning* London: Routledge-Cavendish 3e **In text** reference to surname, date in brackets and page. Hanson (2009:45) **Chapter in edited collection** • Author's surname • Author's initial(s) • Title of chapter • Name of editor(s) • Refer to editors next as 'eds' • Title of the book in italics or underlined • Place of publication • The publishers • Edition if there is more than one • Pages on which the chapter appears. **Example** Hanson, S 'The problem of referencing' in Hopeful Y and Careful N (2009) *All you ever wanted to know about referencing* Oaten Fantasy Books pp 1200–3000

TABLE 9.1—Continued

Source	OSCOLA referencing	Harvard referencing
Law Reports	**In your text** Names of the parties to the action (ideally in italics, or bold or underline) **In your footnote – the full citation** • Year of the law report in brackets (use appropriate round or square brackets) • Volume of the law report for the year • Relevant abbreviation for the law report • The page reference on which the report begins **Example** **In your text** *R v Briggs* . . . **In your footnote** [1977] 1 WLR 605	**In your text** Names of the parties to the action (ideally in italics, or bold or underline. Do not italicise the v) **In your footnote, or references or bibliography – the full citation** Give the full citation as per the Oxford method in the bibliography or references section but not in the main text of your writing. **Example** **In your text** *R* v *Briggs* [1977] . . . **In your footnote** *R* v *Briggs* [1977] 1 WLR 605
Quotations	The main format is • Short quotations of around three lines can be incorporated seamlessly into the body of your text. • Long quotations more than a couple of lines or sentences should be indented – these are referred to as block quotations: A short quotation is not too distracting as presumably it will be relevant to the paragraph. However a longer quotation, by virtue of its size will be far more problematic to accommodate in the text without a signpost that it is a quotation. Quotations should stand alone. Use whichever reference mark is required by system you are using • Adding or subtracting from a quotation: If you choose to add or subtract words from the quotation you should use the symbol of three dots (the ellipsis) . . . to show this.	

Source	OSCOLA referencing	Harvard referencing
Statutes	**The following conventions are acceptable in relation to both OSCOLA and Harvard** **The Statute**: Short title and year of Act : Race Relations Act 1976 **For specific sections** cite that section as 's' then short title and year: s 1 Race Relations Act 1976 **For several specific sections** cite ss 1, 2 and then short title and year: ss 1, 3 Race Relations Act 1976 **For subsections** cite the subsection in brackets (1) and then short title and year: s1(1) Race Relations Act 1976 **For Parts** cite the part followed by sections and short title of act and year: Part 1 Race Relations Act 1976 ss 1, 3 **For Schedules** cite as Sch followed by paragraph number in the Schedule. If you have already referenced the Act you do not have to repeat it every time you refer to a section etc. You can give it a standard abbreviation in your writing. For example, the Race Relations Act 1976 (this will be referred to as the 1976 Act). In this example you could also use RRA.	
Websites	**The following conventions are acceptable in relation to both OSCOLA and Harvard** If your source is also available in print then the print version must be cited. To include a website in your bibliography you must give its full URL and then the date of your accessing of the site.	

Harvard referencing

This American approach is an in-text method of referencing which uses the surname of the author and the date of publication. These are placed in brackets within the text, like this:

Research (Hanson 2004) has shown that students . . .

The name and date can be used to locate the full reference in an alphabetical bibliography at the end of the text. If you want to refer to a specific page, then the page number is incorporated after the date, like this:

Research (Hanson 2004:45) has shown that students . . .

If you mention the author in the main text you can shorten the reference to the date in brackets, like this:

As Hanson (2004) notes . . .

Where you have more than two authors you must cite all of them the first time you include the reference. Subsequently you can refer simply to (Hanson et al 2005). Two authors must always be quoted without truncations.

The Harvard method obviously requires a full set of references or a bibliography where the full citation of the book can be set out according to normal conventions. The role of a bibliography is to note for the reader in alphabetical order all sources consulted for the written work. The reference list just gives the full citation for all sources noted in the text using the Harvard methods. There is a degree of choice about how you refer to a case using the Harvard system: either the case name and citation in your text, or the case name alone with a list of citations in your references. If you put the citation in the text it need only be mentioned the first time.

OSCOLA referencing

In this English approach, the references are included as footnotes, with superscript numbers in the text relating to full references at the bottom of each page. Normally the footnoted number in the text is placed outside the punctuation, like this:

The superscript number can be placed outside the punctuation[6].

But more use is being made of them inside punctuation, which can be helpful if you wish to make a comment about an author which appears in the middle of a sentence, like this:

This was something that Hanson[7] said much about.

The general rule here is that you should use the full reference and any page number if relevant.

Notes

Footnotes can also be used to give a comment that is relevant but if placed in the text would be distracting[8]. Endnotes apply the same conventions as footnotes but appear at the end of a chapter or the end of a book.

Bibliography

Many lecturers will expect you to include a bibliography at the end of your work. This should include all the sources you have consulted, even if they are not referred to, as well as the sources in your text which are fully cited. Although, strictly, OSCOLA does not require one.

---

6   As you can see the superscript number above is placed outside the punctuation.
7   Here the reference is in the middle of the sentence.
8   For example it is worth noting here that I am not discussing referencing methods and their response to footnotes but am speaking generally. To place this above could break the sense of the discussion.

Word limits

Most coursework will have word limits imposed and there may be penalties for exceeding them. By one of life's strange ironies students often rush to finish their coursework as quickly as possible but struggle with word limits which do not allow them to say enough! Your lecturer will know what is required and will have set your work having determined that the word limit is sufficient to allow the work to be competently completed.

If your word limit is 2,500 words work out *before* you even start writing how many pages of your typing that amounts to. This will vary according to the font you use and whether you use double, single or 1.5 spacing between lines. Then you will know how many pages you are aiming for and you should not be surprised by finding yourself 1,000 words over the limit at 2am on the day work is due in.

Make sure you allow yourself enough time to edit your work before it is due. Otherwise you may end up deleting highly relevant information, and retaining irrelevant information, in a desperate attempt to reach the right number of words at the last minute.

If you often exceed the number of words, consider whether your style of writing can be improved. Perhaps you are saying very little, in a lot of words. Practising sticking to the word limit can help you to refine your work, reflect on your style and become more succinct in your expression.

WRITING ESSAYS

INTELLECTUAL HEALTH WARNING!

Often in an essay situation, many students spend pages describing facts of cases, outcomes of cases, describing at a textbook level a general area of law. Demonstrating by this, however, little appreciation of the issues raised by the books, articles or cases read, and little understanding of the question asked. This is not because they are not capable of understanding, but because they did not spend enough time thinking about *what* the question was asking and preparing the texts to be used.

What is an essay question?

In answering a law essay question students are required to produce a piece of work offering a sustained argument concerning a particular question. Generally speaking, essay questions are set in one of the following formats:

1.   A question is set consisting of several sentences requiring an answer.

2.   A quotation is given with the bland request to discuss.

3.   A quotation is given and there is a request to extract issues.

Usually an essay involves discussion in the formal sense of laying out an argument. In fact, the Latin stem of the English word 'discuss' is '*discutere*' which means to '*to* dash to pieces', a rather forceful way of describing argument. The more usual way of describing the meaning of the word 'discuss' is 'to investigate or examine by argument, to sift, and to debate'. The word is often wrongly used and understood to mean just idly talking. Reading many student essays does lead one to suspect that some students are idly and haphazardly just writing and wasting their hard work.

As a general rule an essay question tends to be set to test students' abilities in the following areas:

■   knowledge of the law or a law related issue;

■   ability to construct a sustained argument;

■   ability to apply primary legal texts and secondary academic texts to an issue;

■   knowledge of the grey areas of the law surrounding the cases decided in the given area under consideration;

■   knowledge of particular interpretational issues arising in the law under consideration;

■   ability to engage in critical reasoning.

Understanding the question

Essay questions can ask you to do many things and it is important to be aware of the range and meaning of the different tasks, as shown below.

Compare	Identify both similarities and differences between.
Contrast	Oppose two ideas, judgments or texts, and bring out differences.
Define (usually part of a two-part question)	Set out the meaning of a word or phrase; in law there may be competing meanings. Then you may be asked to give a view as to which is best.
Criticise	Identify arguments about theory or cases, look at hidden assumptions, question existing belief and make a judgment as to the better approach to an area as determined by the persuasiveness and authority of the sources you have located.
Evaluate	Determine the value of something.

| **Justify** | Look at evidence for or against in the sources. |
| **Review** (usually) part of a two-part question | Survey an area giving an overview of development. |

All essays involve critical thinking. It would be most unlikely to find a question that only asked you to describe, but you could have a two-part question asking you to 'Describe . . . and comment on . . .'.

To obtain an idea of how essay tasks can differ in what they ask and the way they are presented here are some examples:

ESSAY QUESTION 1

Critically assess the view that the Race Relations Act 1976, as amended, needs to be completely revised.

ESSAY QUESTION 2

'Damages are meant to put a claimant, so far as money can do it, in the same position as if the contract had been performed.'

Explain this statement and comment.

ESSAY QUESTION 3

'The English legal system is like a house that is not only too small, it is in need of repair. The question is do we build another extension and repair as necessary or pull the whole thing down and start again?'

Discuss the issues arising from this quotation.

ESSAY QUESTION 4   ?

'In *R v Secretary of State, ex p Factortame (No 1)* and *(No 2)* the English courts and the European Court of Justice made it clear that not only do English courts have the power to suspend Acts of Parliament conflicting with European Community law but that European law demands that the provisions of lawfully enacted Acts of the UK Parliament be overturned and the European Court can even dictate what national remedies should be available.'

Discuss solely by reference to the following texts:

(a)   extracts from *R v Factortame (No 1)*;

(b)   extracts from *R v Factortame (No 2)*;

(c)   extracts from J Tillotson *European Community Law: Text, Cases and Materials* (2nd edn Cavendish Publishing, London 1996).

As you can see, the style in which questions can be set for an essay can differ enormously.

Structuring your answer

Each type of essay question requires a different approach, but the same general structure is required, and the same store of information can be used, to answer each. This also holds true in relation to problem questions, which are discussed later in this chapter. The structure is likely to be one that you are most familiar with: an introduction followed by the main part of the essay and then a conclusion.

The introduction

The introduction lays out the brief details of the argument, describing succinctly the issues the essay will discuss (and why) and hinting at the conclusion. It is important to 'begin with the end in mind'. The introduction can be thought of as the road map to the essay, detailing to the reader where they will be taken. Do, however, make sure that in your conclusion you have taken the reader to the place you said you were taking them to! The introduction should be refined when the main body of the essay is finished and your conclusions are clearer. You will need to check that the roadmap in your introduction is carried out. Where you make changes you will need to go back and change your introduction. Often students forget the promises they make in their introduction and just do not deliver because they lost their way in the essay.

The main body

The main part of the essay is often referred to as the body of the text. Here, you will set out the propositions of your argument in a carefully pre-planned manner with each proposition supported by evidence from the texts, cases, etc that you have consulted. (You should be clearer about argument structure having worked through Chapter 7.) It is absolutely essential to refer to case law, legislation, and textbooks and articles as appropriate in this main part of the essay or you will have nothing but unsupported claims that do not constitute an argument. However, do remember that in assessed essays and exams you should be using primary legal texts and not academic texts.

The conclusion

The conclusion can do one of three things:

- answer the specific question asked;

- finalise your own decisions concerning the critique and review of information you have been given 'to discuss';

- present your final views on the issues you have been invited to extract for discussion.

It should align with your introduction and contain a *brief* survey of your argument and evidence as laid out in the body of the text, detailing strengths and weaknesses and then moving to your specific concluding response to the essay task.

Method for the preparation and construction of essays

In addition to the standard structure of an essay (introduction, main body and conclusion), it is also possible to lay out a standard method for the preparation and construction of an answer to an essay question. This chapter uses a straightforward method containing eight stages, very similar to the four-stage model for approaching reading used in Chapter 6. The process is shown as a quick reference diagram in Figure 9.1. Each stage is designed to help you see the ordering of breaking into the question, effectively researching the materials, thinking of argument construction and beginning to write. We will now take each of the headings in the figure and discuss the various issues in detail. As we track through each stage you may need to return to earlier chapters to recap on your skills.

Stage 1: carefully reflect on the question

This is an exercise in basic English comprehension and an intellectual act, requiring a considered and methodical approach. To draw out all of the possible issues raised you should ask questions of your essay question, such as:

- What is being asked?

- How many issues are raised?

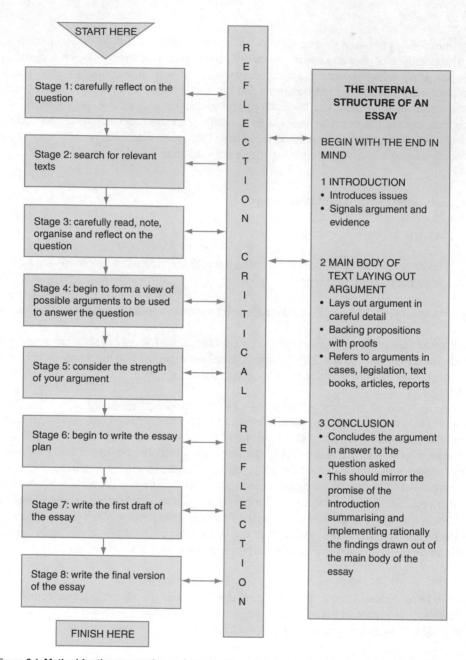

Figure 9.1 Method for the preparation and construction of essays

The actual essay question must be constantly borne in mind as texts are read and research is conducted. It is very useful to convert the question into a tree diagram that can be annotated as texts are collected.

Let us look at one of the essay questions we gave as an example above:

ESSAY QUESTION 3   **?**

> **The English legal system is like a house that is not only too small, it is in need of repair. The question is do we build another extension and repair as necessary or pull the whole thing down and start again?'**

Discuss the issues arising from this quotation.

Going back to the three types of essay question we defined at the start of this section, which type of question is this?

Hopefully you noted it is a hybrid 2 & 3 style question, that is, a quotation followed by a conventional request to discuss followed by a request to extract issues for that discussion. When trying to deconstruct the question you should bear in mind the metaphor. Remember we have considered metaphor in Chapter 3, and have a working definition of it as 'describing one thing in terms of another'. Here the house stands in for the English legal system and you should consider in terms of the metaphor what repair, extension and pulling down mean. The first thing to do is break down the metaphor into its parts. Then each one can be considered. You may have immediately understood that this is a question about reform and the nature of it, whether in parts or radical wholesale reform. If you did not do not worry. Draw out your radial diagram as shown in Figure 9.2 but leave the centre empty (this is the core which joins all of the outlying circles). When you have added the metaphor in those circles you may well have found the core issue.

There are a number of options referred to in the metaphor, you just need to check back to check that you caught them all. You may already know quite a bit about this area so you could move to each outlying circle and make it the centre of another diagram. When this is done it is time to move to stage two.

Stage 2: search for relevant texts
Another way of working out what the question is asking for is to actually annotate the words in it. This has been done in Figure 9.3 in relation to Essay Question 4. I have also taken the opportunity to put in a warning.

Once you have annotated the question you should look through relevant chapters in textbooks, lecture notes, seminar notes and any personal notes done. You may even find the source of the quote in this way. Make sure you have understood the material at the level

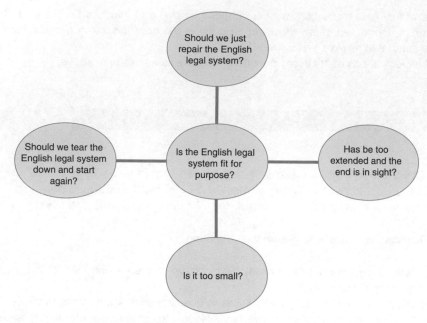

Figure 9.2 Radial diagram for Essay Question 3

you were dealing with it in class. Now turn to looking for academic and legal material on the subject of the reform being suggested. Locate as you consider appropriate:

■   legal rules;

■   legal discussion/decisions in: cases, textbooks, academic articles and practitioner articles (but these can never displace academic articles).

Remember the reading strategy discussed in Chapter 6. You are still scanning reading for location of texts from the print and electronic collections in your library.

Stage 3: carefully read, note, organise and reflect on the material collected
As you locate material that is relevant, photocopy it and highlight it, or make notes. Extract arguments presented and then *reconsider* the question. The first task is reading, asking the basic questions detailed below, whilst at the same time recalling the actual issues detailed in the essay question for which you are doing the research. Otherwise relevant details in your material could be overlooked.

Recall that you were introduced to the three reading techniques of skimming, scanning and detail in Chapter 6. Each of these techniques should be deployed as you approach

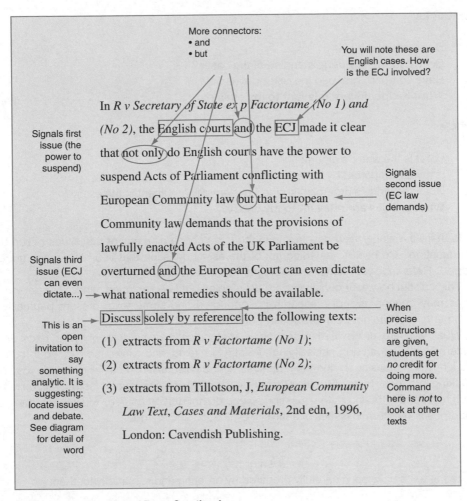

Figure 9.3 Annotated version of Essay Question 4

reading through your material. As you read texts you need to ask yourself questions which differ according to the text you are using, as shown below.

Law cases

■ What are the facts?
■ What legal rules have been applied and why?
■ How do the arguments presented assist in relation to the essay?
■ **What aspects of this case are relevant to my essay?**

Textbooks

- Do I understand?
- Does it fit with my understanding of the cases?
- Have I properly grasped the issues involved?
- **What textbooks are relevant to my essay?**

Articles

- What is the writer's argument?
- Is it well supported by the evidence?
- Does the writer's argument support or deny my argument in the essay?
- **What articles are relevant to my essay?**

Is there a majority view developing in the texts concerning any of the issues raised by the question? Go back to any diagram of the essay question that you have made under stage 1. Reference your texts on the diagram so a pattern emerges.

Think about how your own views are developing but keep an open mind. Your personal ideas may change as more research is conducted and some texts present persuasive arguments that had not been previously considered.

What you are doing in this section is methodically going through your texts and systematically organising, classifying, identifying texts and views and in your notes efficiently summarising. Using the strategies already discussed in earlier chapters you are breaking into these texts and sifting them ready for thinking about your answer. As you read each text keep returning to the question so you do not drift off course. You will then be in a good position to turn to issues of analysis, evaluation and critique.

Stage 4: begin to form a view of possible arguments to be used to answer the question

Once the texts have been carefully prepared by ordering and summarising, then:

- potential arguments can be reflected upon;

- arguments can be compared;

- differences of opinion expressed by judges and academics considered.

At this point, you can begin to have a personal view and to write about it. However the initial task is to:

- understand each text as much as possible in isolation;

- consider the interconnections between the texts.

Law cases and texts that conflict are as intimately interconnected as law cases that agree with each other. You should pull together:

■   cases and arguments that are the same;

■   cases and arguments that are different;

■   cases and arguments that are mixed in that in some areas they agree and some areas they disagree.

Chapter 7 on the anatomy of arguments demonstrates that no problem is ever a simple unitary matter; that problems come in bundles. Whilst questions posed may appear simple and unitary, they never are. Not only is there no such thing as a simple question, there is no such thing as a simple answer. All questions are complex and, of necessity, all answers are complex. It is never sufficient to give as an answer a purely descriptive commentary. No questions posed to test understanding will require only description. They will require evaluation and critique as well. You need to make choices. Decide what issues are most relevant; and what can, and what cannot, be discussed in the answer to the question.

Stage 5: consider the strength of your argument

This stage is important. You should by now have a reasonably clear idea of how your argument may look. You will know what supporting evidence you have and where you lack support. You do not have to throw out weak arguments if they serve to build a broader picture and support a broader argument. Look at all the diagrams and the argument constructed. Refine the argument. Look back now to the deconstruction of the question and deal with *each* assertion.

INTELLECTUAL HEALTH WARNING!

Texts which deny your argument are not to be ignored, they are to be dealt with. You can argue that they are unreliable (for example, you may argue that the argument is pure theory with no evidence to back it up); you can argue that it is one possible plausible interpretation but that you are presenting another equally plausible interpretation. If you cannot explain away an argument denying your view, then perhaps you should reconsider your view. How strong is your argument?

Your argument must be well supported; your lecturer will have thought carefully about the question set – knowing what texts are available and knowing what you should locate. The lecturer would not set a question that can only be the subject of weak arguments. Look at all the diagrams and the argument constructed. Refine the argument. Look back now to the deconstruction of the question and deal with *each* assertion. Ensure you have evidence supporting every proposition.

Stage 6: begin to write the essay plan

Now you are ready to write an essay plan. Look at:

■   the diagram of the question;

■   the notes of cases and other texts;

■   the notes of your personal ideas/argument.

Stage 7: write the first draft of the essay

Although you will have an idea of what you are doing and where you are going and indeed what your answer is, it is a good idea to start your detailed first draft in the body of the text.

■   Begin with the middle section;

■   Review everything for your conclusion;

■   Write the final version of the introduction last, ensuring that the body of the text and your conclusion does what your introduction says they will do;

■   Then finalise your conclusion;

■   Pay particular attention to the development of your argument – is it supported by evidence?

It is always worthwhile considering whether you need to search for any more texts. So allow time for this and go back and read the question again. As your understanding has developed through reading you may now spot issues in the question that you initially missed.

■   Revise and produce a second draft going through the same steps.

Stage 8: write the final version of the essay

Carefully review your second draft and:

- Consider whether there is a need to search for any more texts.

- Pay attention to the argument – does it clearly present itself?

- Pay particular attention to the conclusion and thoughts on the introduction.

- Review the argument. Is there evidence to back it up? Have opposing views been dealt with?

Then write the final draft and:

- Proof read it carefully.

- Double check all citations and references.

- Put it aside for a day if possible or a few hours if not and then carefully re-read and make any final changes.

WRITING PROBLEM QUESTION ANSWERS

It is now appropriate to turn attention away from essay writing towards the other major type of written assessment that is found on a law programme, the problem question. This section discusses in detail what the function behind problem questions may be and with that in mind, outlines a strategy for answering problem questions.

What is a problem question?
A problem question sets out a factual situation requiring the application of legal rules to move towards a solution. Look at the following selection of examples.

PROBLEM QUESTION 1   ?

Baby Dream (BD) plc manufacture disposable baby nappies. Baby's Little Friend (BLF) plc sent a telex to BD plc asking them to deliver 1,000 disposable nappies at a price of 8 p per nappy. BD plc agrees to do so by telex. However, 30 minutes later BD plc are offered 15 p a nappy by another wholesaler who has run out and is in crisis trying to fill a big order. BD plc therefore sends a telex to

BLF plc revoking their acceptance and meets the other order at the higher price. The managing director of BLF plc receives the acceptance telex and revocation telex at the same time. It is unclear which telex was read first.

Advise Baby Dream plc as to any legal liability they may have incurred.

PROBLEM QUESTION 2

Frieda, an auctioneer, sold a collection of miniature oil portraits on enamel by auction. Each portrait was described in the auction catalogue. When Frieda invited bids for Lot 35 – described as 'Portrait, artist unknown' – her assistant Timmy held up Lot 25 by accident. Lot 25 was described in the catalogue as 'Unknown girl', school of Bruett. However, Jake immediately recognised it as a lost masterpiece by Bruett himself. No other bidders noticed Timmy's error and Jake's bid of £30 was accepted by Frieda. When Frieda realised what had happened she refused to let Jake have the painting, which has been valued at £6,500.

Advise Jake. Consider, in particular, whether a valid contract for the sale of the painting has been created.

PROBLEM QUESTION 3

Mary has worked for 'The project' one day a week as a volunteer researcher since 1995. In January 1998 she had a child and continued to do her volunteer research from home. In October 1999 the project offered her financial remuneration for the use of her own facilities and they offered weekly payments of £60. Mary told them that this was too much. She was told to keep the rest as a deserved reward. She is paid when she is sick and during holidays. In December 2000 when she has a second child they allow her three months' payments without expecting work. In the period 2001–02 she is steadily pressured to extend her time to two days a week. She reluctantly agrees in December 2002. In April 2003,

Mary sends the project a bill for £1,466 representing six months' payments of an extra £60 a week for the extra day a week. The project reply they have no contractual arrangement to pay her.

Advise the project as to whether Mary has accrued any contractual rights and if so what type of contract she has entered into, and what their liability is.

PROBLEM QUESTION 4

Cedric, a 'coin' dealer, had a rare Roman coin for sale. He wrote to Dorothy, a collector who specialises in Roman coins, asking whether she would be interested in purchasing it. Dorothy wrote in reply: 'I am willing to pay £1,000 for the coin, I will consider it mine at that price unless I hear to the contrary from you and will collect it from your shop on Monday next week'.

Advise Dorothy as to the legal position:

a)   if Cedric ignored Dorothy's letter and sold the coin to Timothy for £1,200;

b)   if Cedric put the coin aside in an envelope marked 'Sold to Dorothy' but Dorothy decided that she no longer wished to buy it.

Problem questions can only be set around substantive law topics as they rely on the consideration of cases, common law, legislation and increasingly aspects of European Community law. These questions can also require knowledge of how an issue has been dealt with in another common law jurisdiction. Students are expected to handle rules competently using the doctrine of precedent in practice and applying legal rules to facts. It is possible for some examination papers to be 50–70 per cent problem questions, or perhaps even more. Even in courses that seem to be more discursive (such as English legal system) it is possible to construct some problem questions concerning police powers for example, and in constitutional and administrative law (now often called public law), there can be problem questions in relation to the administrative aspects of the course.

Understanding the question

A problem question has a range of functions many of which are shared with the function of an essay. The distinctive aspect of a problem question, however, is the purported simulation of real legal problems requiring the application of the law in the light of the doctrine of precedent and in full appreciation of any legal gaps, or doubts in the law. More specifically, problem questions can be said to be test your abilities in the following areas:

- knowledge of the law in a given area;

- ability to use a factual situation and apply the law to it;

- ability to apply case law and legislation;

- knowledge of cases (including the names, courts and dates of cases, and the sections, subsections and dates of legislation);

- understanding of the relationship between cases and statutes and the methods of arguing according to the doctrine of precedent;

- ability to organise the facts in a problem and systematically apply the law to those facts;

- ability to identify the legal issue or issues raised by the given factual scenario;

- knowledge of the grey areas of the law surrounding the cases decided in the given area under consideration;

- knowledge of available defences;

- knowledge of particular interpretational issues arising in the law under consideration;

- argument construction;

- ability to cite the law properly;

- ability to apply and understand precedent.

Above all, a problem question at the academic stage of education is looking for a highly competent ability to extract legal issues from fact situations and apply the law to them. Invariably you will be asked to discuss situations where there are conditions of doubt about facts, legal issues, or interpretation of the law.

Method for the preparation and construction of answers to problem questions

The key to answering a problem question successfully lies in spotting the 'clues' to the issues to be discussed. Many of these are purely linguistic. Figure 9.4 sets out a method for approaching problem questions similar to the model used for essays. We will now discuss each stage in this problem-solving method, using Problem Question 4 above as an example.

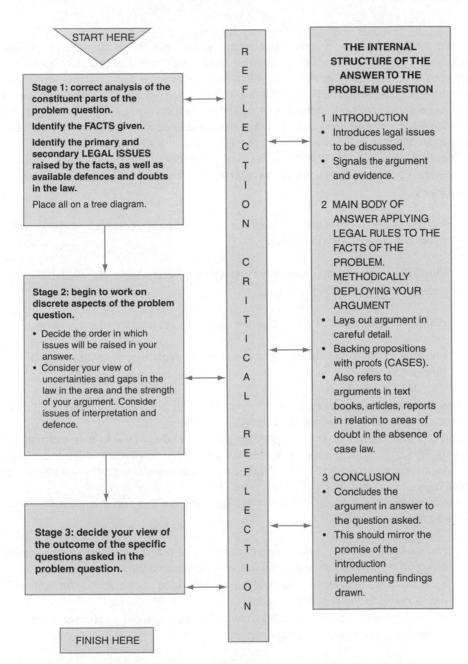

START HERE

Stage 1: correct analysis of the constituent parts of the problem question.

Identify the FACTS given.

Identify the primary and secondary LEGAL ISSUES raised by the facts, as well as available defences and doubts in the law.

Place all on a tree diagram.

Stage 2: begin to work on discrete aspects of the problem question.

• Decide the order in which issues will be raised in your answer.
• Consider your view of uncertainties and gaps in the law in the area and the strength of your argument. Consider issues of interpretation and defence.

Stage 3: decide your view of the outcome of the specific questions asked in the problem question.

FINISH HERE

REFLECTION CRITICAL REFLECTION

THE INTERNAL STRUCTURE OF THE ANSWER TO THE PROBLEM QUESTION

1 INTRODUCTION
• Introduces legal issues to be discussed.
• Signals the argument and evidence.

2 MAIN BODY OF ANSWER APPLYING LEGAL RULES TO THE FACTS OF THE PROBLEM. METHODICALLY DEPLOYING YOUR ARGUMENT
• Lays out argument in careful detail.
• Backing propositions with proofs (CASES).
• Also refers to arguments in text books, articles, reports in relation to areas of doubt in the absence of case law.

3 CONCLUSION
• Concludes the argument in answer to the question asked.
• This should mirror the promise of the introduction implementing findings drawn.

Figure 9.4 Method for the preparation and construction of answers to problem questions

Stage 1: correct analysis of the constituent parts of the problem question
The first task is to read the question and determine the topic. In our example, the problem chosen is contract. In an examination the speed with which a problem question is narrowed to a topic and then to issues within that topic can be of exceptional importance since time is of the essence. (Part of the technique is having engaged in consistent study techniques so you are up to date in your course study and your revision if an examination is involved.) You should have a clear idea of the areas of doubt where currently the law is unclear, as often this is the area in which problem questions will be located.

The first stage of analysis involves a combination of linguistic ability and legal knowledge. Look carefully at the question and consider the facts, legal issues and law that might apply:

- identify the facts given and list them in a flow chart as this gives a timeline as well as making it easier to pick out issues;

- identify the primary and secondary legal issues raised by the facts, available defences and doubts in the law;

- place the legal issues on a tree diagram. List the facts relevant to each issue;

- consider the law that might apply, for example legislation or common law and/ or European Community law.

The sources of law to be drawn on will vary according to the particular subject. Quickly list these under the issues on the tree diagram.

The problem question can be underlined and issues drawn out in a very simple first reading. This combination is demonstrated in Figure 9.5. The words that are the clues to the legal issues are boxed and arrows leading from these words begin to discuss the legal issues raised.

There are two things to note in a problem question like this one that comes with two labelled parts: (a) and (b):

- you must answer *both* parts unless instructed clearly that candidates are to answer *either* (a) or (b). Many students can fail here and assume there is a choice. Do not exercise a choice unless this is clearly given otherwise you could lose half of the marks going for the problem question;
- it is important to break the question down into its constituent issues, so that the context of (a) and (b) can be appreciated.

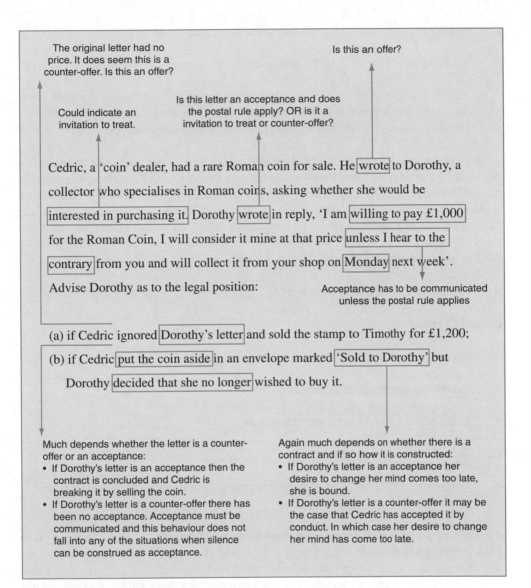

Figure 9.5 Annotated version of Problem Question 4

Stage 2: begin to work on discrete aspects of the problem question

Consider each aspect of the problem question, treating each potential liability and each potential party separately, and:

■   decide the order in which issues will be raised in your answer;

■   consider your view of uncertainties and gaps in the law in the area;

■   consider issues of interpretation and defence. A doubt about the interpretation of the law is not a defence, it is a doubt about the law. Make sure you do not make this mistake, as dealing with these doubts requires different approaches.

In our example, it should be apparent that you need to have a view as to whether a contract has been concluded between Cedric and Dorothy, and if so when, before (a) or (b) can be answered. The answer to this is dependent upon whether an offer and an acceptance can be located, and if so where they stand. The issues to be considered can also be set out as a narrative where you should consider the effect of each component:

Cedric writes to Dorothy to offer to sell the coin

■   Is it an offer or an invitation to treat?

Dorothy's letter

■   Is it an acceptance?

■   Do the postal acceptance rules apply?

■   Is Dorothy's letter a statement of intention?

■   Is Dorothy's letter an offer?

■   Can she waive the necessity for the communication of the acceptance if she so chooses?

Cedric's two suggested responses: that he ignored Dorothy's letter; that he put a sticker on it saying sold but Dorothy did not collect it.

The question therefore expects you to consider the facts and the uncertainties carefully, consulting case law and perhaps texts in areas touching on these matters. If a contract has been formed, then Cedric is in breach of this contract when he sells the coin to Timothy. With regard to case law and commentators it does seem highly likely that, in these circumstances, no contract has been formed with Dorothy and Cedric is free to sell the coin.

With regard to part (b), if Dorothy has made an offer, not an acceptance, then Cedric has possibly accepted the offer when he takes the step of setting aside the coin, as it is possible to show acceptance by conduct. If this is the case, a contract has been formed and Dorothy is obliged to buy the coin. It needs to be noted that there are flaws and weaknesses in this particular question. There are, however, significant weaknesses in reaching this conclusion. It should also be noticed that at present we have suggested issues but as yet we have no:

- argument by way of linked propositions;

- proofs (law cases) supporting or denying our propositions (or texts discussing areas where the law is unknown or uncertain).

Without a sustained argument backed by law cases there is no competent answer to the problem question.

Having used the word identification to sort out the legal issues they come down to the following.

(a) Is Cedric's letter an offer or an invitation to treat?

(b) The answer to (a) determines the status of Dorothy's letter – it is either a counter-offer or an acceptance.

How do we approach answering (a) and (b)? Much revolves around the issue of communication.

An offer must be communicated and be certain
Cedric's letter uses the words 'interested' in buying. It mentions no price. It is hard to see how this could be an offer. Because there was no offer Dorothy's letter cannot be said to be an acceptance. However, Dorothy is clearly interested and responds to the invitation to treat by putting in a counter-offer with a price and a method of acceptance. This counter-offer is clear and communicated and gives a price and constitutes an offer.

An acceptance of an offer must also be communicated
(a) Communication can be construed from conduct.

(b) Therefore if Cedric ignores the offer letter there is no contract.

(c) If Cedric puts the coin aside he can be said to communicate acceptance in the circumstances by his conduct.

For every proposition you make you must refer to a law case in support. You cannot assert without legal authority to support you. However, as you become proficient it may be the case that there is a persuasive precedent you could use for a small point, including from a minority or even dissenting judgment. But this is a level 2 or 3 activity rather than level 1.

We will not continue this demonstration as this is a legal method, not a contract, text, and enough has been set out to demonstrate the strategy of approaching problem

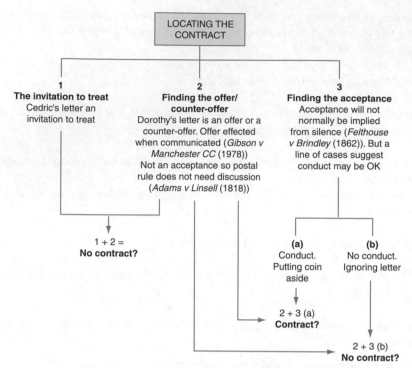

Figure 9.6 Locating the contract in Problem Question 4

questions and how, with the aid of diagrams you can be reminded to lay out propositions, produce supporting case law and know where the doubts are. In an area of doubt, for example, on some occasions it may be enough to make a decision and back it by the state of uncertainty and any case support no matter how tenuous. What the reader, who is also your marker, is looking for is your skill in dealing with such legal issues with certainty, competently demonstrating your knowledge of the area and the relevant cases, and competently applying that knowledge. Each subject area will have its own areas of doubt and uncertainty and these are the areas to concentrate upon: the rules, the exceptions to the rules and the doubts. Chapter 8 looked at the construction of legal argument and also referred to the issue of the use of case law. In addition Figure 9.6 begins to link propositions and cases.

Stage 3: decide your view of the outcome of the specific questions asked in the problem question

The facts in a problem question can give rise to many issues but all of these may not be necessary to resolve the specific question(s) set in your problem. Problem questions tend to ask you to do one of two main things:

■   discuss the issues raised in the problem scenario;

■   advise one of the parties.

Both types of problem question require the same knowledge to answer them successfully. However, your approach to the answers will differ. In response to a question about discussing issues in general you must raise all the issues without privileging one party. Where you have been asked to advise one of the parties you must raise all the issues but orientate your argument to the effect of those issues on the party you are asked to advise. This includes discussing in detail the likely chances of the other party being the successful party.

Figure 9.6 indicates a possible outcome to our example question that allows all eventualities to be explored but also makes a choice about when a contract may have come into existence.

CONCLUSION

■   Your performance in written work, oral skills and exams depends on your stages of development in the whole range of skills, particularly reading, writing and argument construction.

■   Whatever type of essay or problem question you are dealing with, the same type of information base is required for all questions. It is how this information, knowledge and understanding is drawn on to produce a particular written result that is important.

■   Following standard methods for the preparation and construction of essay or problem question answers can help you effectively order the different tasks involved.

■   Always allow sufficient time to be able to read and understand the question, research and study relevant materials, construct your argument and refine and edit your answer.

■   Good written work requires an effective written voice, excellent grammar and appropriate choices of words.

■   The referencing, formatting and presentation of your written work can be as important as the words you use.

FURTHER READING

There are two excellent texts to recommend to new students. Both are succinct guides to different types of legal writing:

S Strong, *How to Write Law Essays and Exams* (2nd edn OUP, Oxford 2006).

L Webley, *Legal Writing* (2nd edn Routledge-Cavendish, London 2009).

SPEAKING THE LAW

10

" Speak clearly, if you speak at all; carve every word before you let it fall."

Oliver Wendell Holmes

LEARNING OUTCOMES

After reading this chapter you should be able to:

■ develop personal confidence in public speaking in front of your peer group and teachers;

■ understand the specific personal skills of oral delivery, such as volume and tone of voice, body position, eye contact and speed of delivery, and how they equate with written skills;

■ appreciate the differing requirements of each type of oral skills exercise;

■ further consolidate the integration of a bank of skills, such as time management, legal research, note-taking, referencing and argument construction.

CHAPTER SUMMARY

Any form of rounded academic education should ensure that graduates leave University with excellent communication skills. Legal education at the academic stage provides you with several different opportunities to develop your oral skills. In addition, should you intend to pursue a career in law, the vocational stage of legal training majors on assessing students as they engage in a large number of oral exercises that test competency in communication, acquisition of correct legal knowledge and application of that knowledge. It is therefore essential that law students can perform well, not only during examinations and written assessments, but also during oral assessments.

This chapter covers four types of oral skills exercises that law departments often use to develop student competency: presentations, debating, mooting and negotiation. The first two are not unique to law and will be used in many degree programmes. Mooting, however, is unique to legal courses. If your department engages in national or international competitions in the areas of mooting and debating, or fields a team for the Client Counselling Competition, you may be able to further develop your competency in these fields outside the classroom.

Reading this chapter will help you develop a strategy for successful oral skills work but there are many additional places to locate more extensive general, and legal-specific, information on the oral skills exercises discussed here. You will be guided to these in the reading section.

INTRODUCING ORAL PRESENTATIONS

Oral presentations often cause students concern. Whilst some students are more reserved than others, and may not relish the thought of public speaking, others find it to be no problem. Whether you like or dread presentations, executing them can be a challenge. However, the same skills of careful research, thorough reading, good argument construction and clear introductions and conclusions required for written assessments or answering examination questions apply equally to oral presentations.

There are particular differences between the mediums of speaking and writing that need to be understood to ensure your oral skills exercises are performed well. A written piece of work, as explained in Chapter 9, requires editing until it is in its best format. The same is true for the script for an oral presentation, but you also need to practise and develop its delivery.

Oral skills exercises

The main types of oral skills exercises that you are liable to encounter on your law degree course are set out in Figure 10.1. Some of these will be individual tasks, others will require

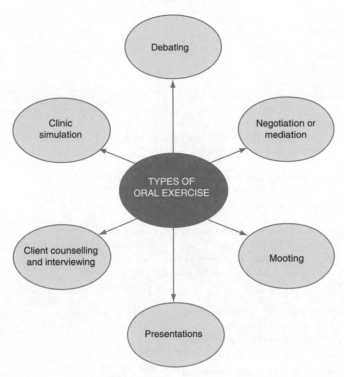

Figure 10.1 Types of oral skills exercises

group work. For the majority of these tasks, completing a successful exercise involves working on six key components:

■ understanding the nature of the task;

■ managing the task;

■ research;

■ content;

■ delivery;

■ teamwork.

Figure 10.2 summarises the nature of these six components while Figure 10.3 demon-strates how they are inter-related.

1. **Understanding the nature of the task**
   - Understanding the type of task
   - Understanding the requirements
2. **Managing the task**
   - Managing your personal time
   - Managing a team and managing the team's time
3. **Research**
   - Understanding the legal question posed by the task
   - Dividing the question into subsections for each separate issue
   - Researching the main issue and sub issues
4. **Content**
   - Ensuring relevance to the question and the argument constructed
   - Incorporating a rich range of sources supporting the argument constructed
   - Using appropriate referencing
5. **Delivery**
   - Delivering excellent personal and group performance of oral skills
   - Using appropriate and high quality audio-visual aids for the audience (the marker)
   - Deploying useful prompt cards for the presenters
   - Producing an accurate copy of the full text of oral delivery for the marker
   - Dealing with stress
6. **Team work**
   - Utilising different types of management and planning in the previous points
   - Managing team member performance
   - Managing the expectations of group members

Figure 10.2 Key components of oral skills exercises

The research and content aspects of oral skills exercises generally require skills that are no different from those of research and content with regard to written exercises. The main differences occur at the level of delivery in terms of style and language, and whether teamwork is involved.

The following sections work through each of the components in detail.

Understanding the nature of the task

There are several types of oral skills tasks and each has different requirements. We will cover the four main variants (presentations, debating, mooting and negotiation) at the end of this chapter.

You and your team (if there is one) must commit proper time to making sure you know exactly what the task is, what it is testing and drawing out all its issues. The type of analysis that you engaged in to understand written assessment tasks and questions in Chapter 9 can be reused here in this context.

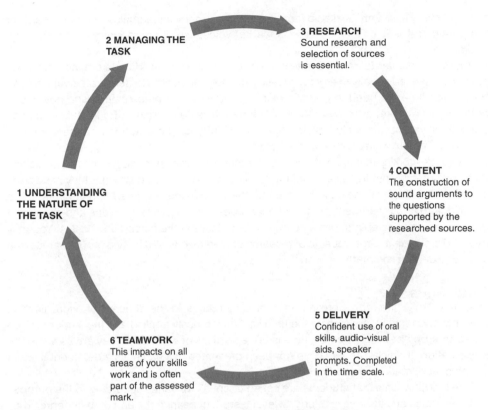

2 MANAGING THE TASK

3 RESEARCH
Sound research and
selection of sources
is essential.

4 CONTENT
The construction of
sound arguments to
the questions
supported by the
researched sources.

**1 UNDERSTANDING
THE NATURE OF
THE TASK**

5 DELIVERY
Confident use of oral
skills, audio-visual
aids, speaker
prompts. Completed
in the time scale.

6 TEAMWORK
This impacts on all
areas of your skills
work and is often
part of the assessed
mark.

Figure 10.3 The inter-related components of competent oral skills exercises

Managing the task

There are two levels at which it is important to manage the task: the macro-organisation of the order and timing of each sub-task that leads to the final product; and the micro-organisation of ensuring the time limit for actual delivery is met.

Overall task management

The degree of detail required by the oral skills exercise will be determined by the timescale you have been given. A 5-minute presentation cannot deliver the same level of detail as a 25-minute one.

Also, an assessed oral exercise will be treated somewhat differently to a non assessed exercise as it will be supplied with assessment criteria. These give details of what the marker is looking for in the finished exercise. You should ideally be given a copy of the marksheet that the assessor will use as well. The assessment criteria and the marksheet are important documents to consider because they tell you what you have to do and how this should be demonstrated. You should also check the marks allocations as you will find out how many marks are available for argument, how many for teamwork and how many for the purely oral skills of tone of voice, speed of voice, use of appropriate formal language and so on.

Working backwards from the date of the presentation you need to determine how much time you have realistically to engage in research, how much time to deliberate over content, how much time you need to practise delivery and edit your presentation, and how much time you need to prepare any audio-visual aids such as PowerPoints (though this should be done after you have decided on the final format of your presentation as otherwise your slides may be out of line with your final product).

If you are working in a team, it is important that everyone understands the timescale and that measures are put in place to deal with those who do not prepare what they have been asked to do. This is all the more important if there are marks allocated to teamwork. It is a good idea to appoint someone different each week to co-ordinate everyone and check that they are going to be able to produce the required tasks in the agreed timescales. You may need to decide that some aspects of research should be covered by two group members in case one cannot complete the work.

Time limits

The 'time limit' given for a presentation directly relates to the concept of 'word limit' in written work. In oral assessments the time limit is rigorously applied and the student will be asked to stop speaking when the time is up regardless of what point they are at within the presentation. If crucial matters have not been presented this can have a detrimental effect on the overall mark awarded for the work.

The length of time that students are asked to speak for varies according to the purpose of the exercise and the level of study. A level 3 student nearing the end of their degree may be asked to present for 25 minutes or longer. A level 1 student at the start of their studies may be asked to speak for 10 minutes alone, or to be a part of a group of students that in total only present for 10 minutes (so it is likely, depending on group size, that students speak for only 2–3 minutes each).

It is absolutely essential to practise the performance of the final presentation to ensure that it comes within the time limit. You will then have the opportunity to go for all of the marks available. It is not a good strategy to speak more quickly. This will mean that your audience and the marker will not properly hear or understand what you are saying and you will lose marks.

RESEARCH

Understanding the question

You must ensure that you have properly and thoroughly understood the question. Researching the right areas requires you to ascertain properly what the question is asking for. The issues here are no different to the type of investigations you were directed to engage in for law reports (Chapter 5), legislation (Chapter 4) and secondary sources (Chapter 6). Ask yourself what issues you think flow out of the question posed. Even if the topic is new to you, you can engage in prediction, as the reading strategy in Chapter 6 suggests.

Whatever the exact nature of your oral skills exercise you will be called upon to deploy argument. You can only hold a plausible given position (for or against a proposal) if you know *what* the question is asking. For example, you may have as a presentation topic the following question:

Should the English legal system allow cultural defence as a valid plea in relation to criminal offences?

This question asks you to reach a given position in a measured way. But it also requires certain issues to be explained. It splits therefore into discrete sections. Identifying the way that your question splits is important because it allows you to manage your time by deciding what has to be researched. If you are working in a team this will help you divide up tasks between you. Figure 10.4 sets out this hypothetical question so that you can see how the issues arise from it.

If a team is involved you should *all* concentrate on this first point. Several heads are always better than one – if *all* heads are thinking.

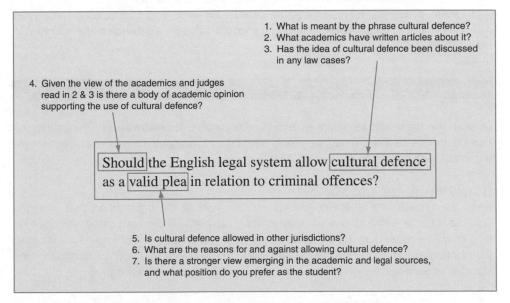

1. What is meant by the phrase cultural defence?
2. What academics have written articles about it?
3. Has the idea of cultural defence been discussed in any law cases?

4. Given the view of the academics and judges read in 2 & 3 is there a body of academic opinion supporting the use of cultural defence?

Should the English legal system allow cultural defence as a valid plea in relation to criminal offences?

5. Is cultural defence allowed in other jurisdictions?
6. What are the reasons for and against allowing cultural defence?
7. Is there a stronger view emerging in the academic and legal sources, and what position do you prefer as the student?

Figure 10.4 Questions flowing from a proper consideration of an oral skills question

Researching print and electronic sources

You must engage in focused and careful research through your institution's print and e-library collections. The depth of this research will be determined by the nature of the presentation. For instance, is it to start a seminar discussion, informing other members of the seminar group about descriptive issues? Or is it designed to demonstrate critical thinking? The depth of research will also be determined by whether the presentation is assessed or not. You must use judgment based on your understanding of the nature and purpose of the oral skills exercise.

If a team is involved, this is the point at which decisions are made concerning the allocation of certain sources to be researched. You need to have a risk assessment of the team and the likelihood of individuals executing any or all of the given tasks. If the team is arbitrarily put together then each student will have different skills and these should be discussed and borne in mind when tasks are being allocated.

Notes and sources

You should compile good notes, making sure that they are efficiently referenced so the original sources can be quickly located if needed. Of course, if it is an assessed presentation, your marker will also expect to hear your references. You should write notes according to the types of issues discussed about note-taking in Chapter 9.

Each team member should write legible notes and photocopy them for the group so that all information can be shared. Team members should be aware that each person's note-taking skills may be very different. Therefore your team time management should bear this in mind and allow a few days for rechecking notes if necessary.

If your presentation is split into several different topic questions and team members have been allocated one each, this will obviously determine the sources for note-taking.

CONTENT

Overall, you are aiming to create a considered argument. There are several things that you can do to ensure the content of your presentation is academically acceptable and the argument well-constructed.

Considering the question

Read your notes and reflect on the question in light of the information that you have collected. Understanding can sometimes occur instantly, like a light being switched on. It is, however, more likely for things to dawn more slowly, as you think about issues, read your notes, ask yourself questions and reflect on the points that you do or don't understand. If you are teamworking, these tasks should occur within the group.

Building arguments

Begin the process of building arguments based on your notes and your growing under-standing. Remember that the definition of argument given in Chapter 7 holds true for all arguments:

> An argument is a series of statements, some backed by evidence, some not, that are purposely presented in order to prove, or disprove, a given position.

It is also worth remembering that one piece of writing, and therefore one oral skills exercise, may require the setting up of several small arguments, the conclusion of each one going forward to form the overarching argument.

Let us now go back to our earlier question:

> Should the English legal system allow cultural defence as a valid plea in relation to criminal offences?

Your answers to the various questions posed in the 'Understanding the question' section above will help you begin to form a view. What is your view? Why have you reached that position? You may need to go back to your notes of the academic and legal position to answer that. Has any particular academic properly argued their case? What evidence have they used to back their proof of the correctness of one view and incorrectness of another view? This questioning process involves you in the exercise of critical reflection. You must substantiate your view of the stronger position, backing it by evidence drawn from your sources, and formulate your argument with a series of statements, each backed by evidence to prove or disprove a given position.

Your presentation of this question should then follow a standard format of introduction, body and conclusion as described below.

Introduction: mapping the terrain of your presentation and argument

Your introduction should clearly and concisely state:

- the question;

- the given position you have adopted;

- that your presentation will review the arguments on both sides of this issue;

- why your position is the more plausible to take.

You may decide not to give your position away initially, instead saying that you will review arguments for and against and finally indicate your preferred position based on the academic material.

Body of your presentation: the major landmarks on your way to your conclusion

The main body of your presentation should set out a series of statements that leads you to determine the position you have taken. When each statement is given, you should briefly refer to the academic and legal sources that support it and state why they are more acceptable than those sources that do not support your position.

Conclusion: your destination

In your conclusion you should sum up the points made in the body of your presentation, refer to any relevant points in your introduction and then explain your position and why it is preferred, based on consideration of the sources.

Again these steps are no different to the stages of essay preparation referred to in Chapter 9.

Quotes and references

You can use appropriate and relevant quotations to give interest to your presentation and demonstrate the academic credibility of your research. Where you have used texts for ideas and general information, you should reference sources even if you do not quote them.

DELIVERY

Your voice

Your oral skills exercise is a performance and your voice can be considered as an instrument. Your voice is your expression of yourself to the outside world. You use it to express pain, joy, fear, nervousness, excitement and more. You can slow it down, speed it up, make it loud, make it almost inaudible or utter many different levels of sound in between. Your voice comes with its own particular resonance and accent, giving you a unique vocal stamp.

Listeners have optimum levels of understanding for voices, but they can also be rather easily put off by the sound of a particular voice. This can mean that they do not properly listen to you, which could be a problem if you are being assessed. You need to use the right levels of audibility, changing your tone of voice to signal new ideas in much the way that you would signal a new paragraph in written work. Your body language should not be distracting, and you should not, as a way of dealing with nervousness, develop repetitive unconscious reactions, such as constantly flicking the same piece of hair out of your eyes or moving your hands too much. It is also possible not to move enough. Competent performance of language is a skill that needs to be acquired and this requires practice.

Think of times when you have listened to other people formally speaking: is it a problem if they speak

too quietly

or

too loudly?

Is it difficult to follow if their voice maintains a rather monotonous tone? Are you distracted by repetitive movements which are out of keeping with what the speaker is saying? Do you find it difficult to follow an argument if you are constantly drawn to irritating mannerisms such as foot-tapping or scratching?

It can be equally distracting and irritating for an audience to listen to vocal stutters, such as:

- errrrrrr;

- ummm;

- ahhhhh;

- errrr . . . ummmm . . . ah. . . .

Have you noticed that some speakers will say 'er' or something similar every few words?

> Well er, The title er of my er presentation today is er 'Theft – and ummmm. . . . Er . . . the problem with dishonesty'. Firstly I will er consider er the meaning of er . . . er dishonesty . . . errr and errrrrr dis – honesty ah no err . . . I mean honesty, ummm, um as, as those words are er um ummm er as used in the er the Theft Act 1978.

What the speaker is intending to say, and probably what she had in her prompts and script, is much clearer when tidied up:

> The title of my presentation today is 'Theft – and the problem with dishonesty'. Firstly I will consider the meaning of dishonesty and dishonesty (no, I mean honesty) as those words are used in the Theft Act 1978.

Unfortunately nerves probably intervened and she found herself at the mercy of 'er'. Often speakers are not aware of the impact of these verbal hiccups, but listeners definitely are. If you practise your oral skills exercise, asking fellow students or friends and family to listen, they will be able to assist you in eradicating these types of problems. The importance of such 'verbal editing' cannot be underestimated.

Part of the skill of speaking in public is to engage with the audience, and use your voice to supply the punctuation. This ensures your listeners maintain concentration and can understand. The tone of your voice should command the space given to you by others to speak. Even if you need to stop speaking to collect your thoughts, or to find a point in some notes, you need to command the silence. Do not appear to be embarrassed by stopping to check something. If appropriate, give an explanation of what you are doing, but do not apologise. Your tone should not in any way be condescending, too excitable, or indeed too obviously insecure or unhappy. You should speak at an appropriate speed. Recall times when you have been frustrated because you were unable to follow a speaker's point because they spoke far too quickly.

Regardless of the type of oral skills exercise, the aim of any communication is to actually communicate with the listener. You therefore need to plan both the argumentative layout of the content of your presentation and the way in which you will deliver it verbally for the listener. This can only come from practice, and from gathering feedback from others. If you ask people to explain constructively what was good and what did not work so well you will learn. Many universities have the facility for staff to video presentations. If you are videoed you may learn from watching yourself afterwards. Sometimes when we see mannerisms on screen that we think add to our effective communication it is clear that they add nothing and should be removed.

Oral performance

Try recording your presentation and listening dispassionately to your voice. Is your presentation delivered in a monosyllabic manner? Does your voice have emphasis? Is the delivery in a flat tone? Listen carefully to other students when they present. What do you like about how they communicate? Your task is to use your voice to carry your message successfully, letting it enhance your presentation. Above all make sure that you form your words carefully. Do not mutter or mumble. Speak loudly enough to be heard but not so loudly that your voice is distracting.

Learn to change the speed at which you speak, making accommodation for the listener. You should also maintain reasonable eye-contact with your audience to help maintain their attention.

Audio-visual aids

Presentations often require audio visual aids for delivery in the form of PowerPoint slides or handouts. Be sure to practise your delivery with PowerPoint and try and check out the room beforehand so that you see where the equipment is in relation to the audience. Your university webpages will have instructions on PowerPoint and its use.

Presenter prompts

Whilst you should have a good idea of what you are saying it is always sensible to have presenter prompts. For example, cards with trigger words on them so that if you forget something or lose your place you can easily find it again. Prompt cards allow you to glance down for a reminder of your next point. Be sure to write large enough to be able to read them from a distance.

Do not be tempted to read out your presentation. That is reading not presenting, and you will lose marks for it.

Managing nerves

You may always find speaking in public difficult, but you can find ways to do it without everyone else knowing you are nervous. When we are stressed, our mouths dry out, so it is a good idea to have a glass of water available. A quick note to your marker, explaining the situation, should be enough for that to be allowed. Breathing exercises can help steady your nerves too. You will also find that if you feel you are in control of the exercise, know what it is about and where you fit, this will lessen your nerves.

Body language

Slouching, leaning against furniture and putting your hands in your pockets can all be distracting. Do not let yourself down by using inappropriate body language for the circumstances.

Team issues

It is essential that a group presentation flows consistently. Ensure that you all have a copy of the whole presentation and work on making the moment where the next speaker stands and speaks as effortless and seamless as possible. Edit the presentation of the group as a whole unit, making sure each person knows what they have to do and by when.

TEAMWORKING

Oral skills exercises, whether assessed or non-assessed, will often involve team or group work. This brings into play another range of interpersonal skills and can be quite stressful, particularly if the exercise is assessed. Sometimes you will be allowed to choose your group, and sometimes (perhaps most often) your group will be neutrally allocated to you by your lecturer. Many of you will have experienced some degree of teamworking prior to university, and it may have been a good or a bad experience. The fact is that success in life is very much down to your ability to engage at the appropriate time in competent interpersonal skills and to work as part of a team. The development of interpersonal skills through teamworking is one of the essential skills of a competent graduate.

Many students working in teams or groups do not stop to consider the challenges of working with other people. It is important to note that everyone in the group may have different understandings of how to:

■ work with others as part of a team;

■ manage their own time;

■ make sense of the material collected;

- ■   make useful notes;

- ■   make sense of the question;

- ■   deliver an oral presentation.

Nothing can be more destructive to teamwork than self-appointed leaders inefficiently bullying others to do the work. The importance of commencing each team task as a group and considering what the task requires, how it will be managed and timed and who will do what, by when, cannot be over-emphasised.

PRESENTING, DEBATING, MOOTING AND NEGOTIATION

Now it is appropriate to describe briefly the four types of oral skills exercise you are most likely to encounter, looking at their similarities and differences.

Presenting

A presentation is a structured argument put forward by a student or a group on an aspect of a topic currently under discussion on the relevant course. Sometimes such presentations are assessed and sometimes they are not. Sometimes such presentations stand alone and on other occasions they are designed to aid fuller and deeper discussion of the topic within the class.

The presentation is usually posed as a question, such as our earlier example:

> ## Should the English legal system allow cultural defence as a valid plea in relation to criminal offences?

Debating

A debate is also a structured argument in relation to a given statement, likely to be drawn from an aspect of a topic currently under discussion. However, debates are usually posed as assertions rather than questions. For example, the presentation question above would be posed for a debate as:

> ## The English legal system should allow cultural defence as a valid plea in relation to criminal offences.

A debate is always composed of two teams each putting forward opposing views of the assertion. One team speaks in favour, ('For' it), and the other team speaks against, providing an excellent demonstration of the fact that there are indeed always two sides to an argument.

There are rules of engagement in a debate, such that each student is given a precise time to speak, and the ordering of speeches is determined by the allocation of those in favour and those against. You may be allocated a team and therefore find yourself forwarding views that you do not personally favour, but you should remember you are engaging in a formal academic activity. Each speaker is part of a team and the arguments forwarded must flow logically from each member of the group. It is essential that one speaker on the team does not contradict what another team member might say.

As with other oral exercises, each student is required to put forward a logical argument, backed by evidence, proving or disproving the assertion. All the usual analysis of sources and critique are required prior to speaking in the debate.

There are a number of excellent internet sites relating to legal debating. One of the most useful sources is that of the Oxford Union Debating Society.

Mooting

A moot is a structured argument on a narrow point of law. It is conducted as a form of role play unlike the presentation or the debate. The narrow point of law is posed as a question that has gone to an appeal court, either the House of Lords or the Court of Appeal. The mooting teams role-play as barristers representing their clients in the appellate court.

Our presentation question on cultural defence, which was translated into an assertion for the debate, would have an even narrower reference to the idea of cultural defence in an appeal court question of law. It could be set out as a question on appeal as follows:

> When a trial judge is directing the jury on provocation can he state that they must take into account the cultural characteristics of the defendant in deciding whether he acted reasonably?

As in debates, moots involve two teams presenting opposing views to a posed legal question. However, in a moot an extremely narrow, purely legal, point is taken as the object of legal argument.

Mooting also proceeds in a structured manner with rules of engagement concerning who speaks first, and how long each speaker has to speak. There are many rules to be observed when mooting, including issues relating to:

■ the etiquette between the students (role playing as barristers) and the marker (the judge). The forms of address used in court must be rigidly adhered to;

■ dress codes. These are rigid, usually set as smart dark clothing, preferably a suit, wig and gown;

■ timing. There are rules concerning the exchange of lists of cases to be used between the teams and the court;

■   law reports. There are rigid rules about the hierarchy of law report to be used. See Chapter 2 for more about this;

■   order of speaking. There is strict turn-taking between the students arguing in teams of two.

The judge can ask the participants questions during the moot. Time does not run for the space of the question and answer but students can still find this particularly stressful. The manner in which you respond to questions establishes your command and comprehension of the legal area and also tests how you withstand pressure. Listen carefully, think before answering and take your time when you do answer.

It is quite likely that the judge may deliberately put forward an interpretation of a point of law that you do not agree with. Whilst you must continue to treat the judge with respect, if you do not agree you are allowed to disagree, in the correct format. For example, you could say, 'Whilst I am of course much obliged to your [insert appropriate form of address] for drawing this to my attention, with great respect, I submit that the present case is distinguishable . . .' or 'If I may respectfully say . . .'. Even if you agree, you should be most polite in your agreement. Firmness and politeness is what is called for.

As well as developing valuable communication skills, mooting develops your ability to discriminate between arguments which are valid and those which are not. Your skills of argument construction are developed, as are your skills of fact management, the selection of legal rules and their application to fact situations. As moots always involve working with others, mooting also develops important teamworking skills.

Again there is an abundance of good information about mooting on the internet, with some law schools posting instructive videos of student moots.

Negotiation

Legal negotiation is a structured, formal discussion between legal advisors designed to explore the basis of a legal dispute between two clients, and to move towards a settlement that is intended to have legal force.

At the academic stage of legal education negotiation is, like mooting, conducted as a role play between two teams, who act as legal advisors for the respective clients in a fictitious legal dispute. Unlike mooting, however, the subject-matter of a negotiation can be far broader and conceptually different. Whilst mooting represents the litigation paradigm and the concept of court-based dispute resolution, negotiation introduces the ideology of alternative dispute resolution (ADR). This is the *alternative* to going to court or moving along the court process[1]. While the aim of a moot is to win (as is the aim of a court case), the aim of a negotiation is to reach a settlement with the other party.

As with mooting the discussion is conducted according to a range of agreed rules of engagement concerning who speaks first and appropriate turn-taking. However, the setting is less formal. Students are seated, usually around a table, and whilst the language is formal and respectful primary legal sources are not quoted and speeches are not given.

---

1   ADR encompasses not only negotiation but also further mechanisms of mediation (when a trained facilitator allows the parties to interact with each other and reach a resolution) and arbitration. You will learn more about it on your English legal system course.

There is a conversational dialogue between the two sides as each seeks to implement their pre-planned strategies for obtaining the best deal for their client in light of their client's instructions.

As you may by now expect negotiation requires you to integrate a large number of skills, including:

■   personal management of the task;

■   team management of the task and interpersonal skills;

■   research;

■   handling primary legal rules;

■   managing facts and instructions from clients, and other documentation;

■   competent note-taking;

■   writing pre-negotiation strategies;

■   competent reporting back to the team;

■   argument construction;

■   oral skills;

■   handling the unforeseen within the negotiation;

■   competent critical review post-negotiation.

Negotiation exercises are increasingly being used within the context of the academic stage of training because of their great value in allowing students to work within such broad skill sets. If you are able to engage in such exercises you will find that your understanding of these skills, your ability to handle legal rules and your ability to manage facts will be considerably enhanced. Since these skills are transferable, you will also be enhancing your understanding of other law subjects. You could even consider entering the national negotiation competition organised by the Centre for Effective Dispute Resolution (CEDR)[2].

A moot is always conducted in the same way, using the same methodology. A negotiation, however, can occur in one of two forms:

1.   Where both parties wish a settlement on purely financial grounds and do not wish to continue any relationship with each other. This is often referred to as **positional** negotiation which tends to be more confrontational.

---

2   This centre also trains practitioners in the areas of mediation and negotiation and it hosts an excellent website.

2.   Where both parties not only wish a settlement of the current dispute (which may be seen in financial terms), they also wish, or need, to continue a relationship. This requires a particular approach since the most amicable solution may not constitute the best financial solution for your client. For some clients the continuance of the relationship is more important than financial issues. This is often referred to as **principled** negotiation. By the nature of its aims, it tends to be more interactive and flexible in terms of outcome.

As you will appreciate you will probably need to adopt different stances in the two types of negotiations. You can determine which type of negotiation is called for from the information you are given for your exercise.

The skills you bring with you to negotiation

It is highly likely that you come to the exercise of negotiation with some naturally acquired skills relevant to the task. These will have been deployed and developed just by being in the world, as part of a group of friends or family, in school, university or in the workplace.

Consider the last time that you made a bargain with someone to get something that only they could give you. You probably gave something or offered to do something as an incentive to get what you wanted from the other person. Maybe you wanted time off from your part-time job but thought your boss might refuse. You will have carefully chosen your time to ask, and thought of what you could offer in return. Maybe there is a time in the week when your boss has trouble getting his staff to work. You might have suggested that if he gave you the time off that you wanted, then you would do one or two of those problem shifts straight away, or on your return to work. This situation would be a classic example of principled bargaining or negotiation because you need to continue your relationship with your boss.

All of this natural everyday activity involves flexibility. You need to think in advance about what barriers you might have to overcome before you get the 'yes', the object that you want. Often you may need to give something in order to get what you want. Usually you need to have an understanding of how the other person may be thinking, how they will view your request, what is it that you think they may object to, and how can you deal with this. All of this natural experience can be used to help you gain an understanding of formal legal negotiation.

Formal negotiation

You will not be surprised to be told that negotiation is a process. It begins before you and your team enter the room and continues afterwards. It is best viewed as a three-stage activity, as shown in Figure 10.5:

1.   pre–negotiation planning;

2.   in-negotiation strategy;

3.   post-negotiation critical review.

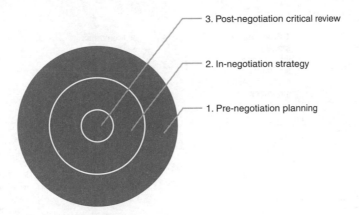

3. Post-negotiation critical review

2. In-negotiation strategy

1. Pre-negotiation planning

Figure 10.5 The three stages of negotiation

As you can see, the greater part of the work takes place before the negotiation.

There are several ways in which to set up a negotiation and a variety of 'paper trails' may be constructed for you. You may be given the time and opportunity to interview a live 'client' to extract the details of the dispute and their desired outcome for the negotiation. Or you may be given a written set of client instructions to work from. These written instructions should be relatively comprehensive, giving you all the information you require to look into the dispute. They may or may not be supplemented by other constructed documentation such as letters sent to your client or written by them, copies of any relevant contracts or copies of emails and file notes if your client is a business.

A typical negotiation

The next pages will take you briefly through the steps in a typical negotiation. As with other skills there is no shortage of good guidance available. If you *are* to engage in negotiation you will be guided through your exercise by your tutor.

Seen from a macro-level, the key steps for a negotiation are shown in Figure 10.6.

Pre-negotiation planning

The first task in any negotiation is to remember that you are part of a team. However, that does not mean you should not take responsibility for acquiring a general understanding of the area. The negotiation as an exercise, whether assessed or non-assessed, will succeed or fail on the basis of:

■ each individual team member's independent management of the task;

■ the overall team management of the task.

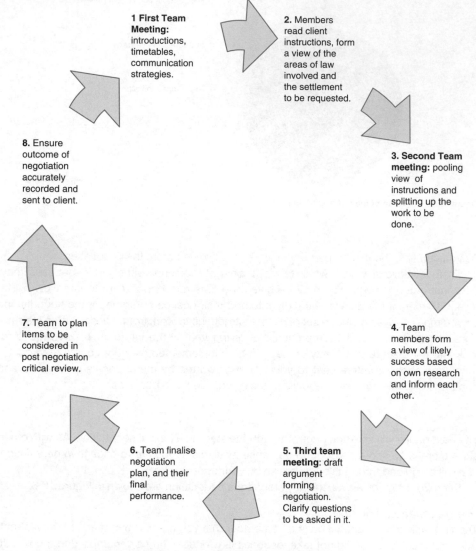

Figure 10.6 The basic macro-level of arrangements for the negotiation

First meeting with your team and becoming familiar with the client instructions

There are usually just two or three students to a team, and you may not know each other before the task. It is a good idea to meet briefly right at the start, so that introductions can be made. You should then arrange a time to meet to discuss the negotiation, once each of you has had the time to consider:

■   your client's written instructions, determining the area(s) of law involved and the
       potential issues raised;

■   your client's instructions concerning what settlement in resolution of the dispute they
       would find acceptable.

   Giving each team member proper time to consider the client instructions will avoid
jumping to conclusions. It is important that each team member comes to their own view
without being initially led by anyone else. This ensures that several minds have reviewed
the instructions. If there are uncertainties in the team, a debate can begin about relevant
issues.
   There is no reason why you cannot in your first brief meeting agree that you will meet
one or two hours later. The important issue is not to rush these important preliminary
stages.

Second meeting with the team and allocation of tasks

A good discussion should take place concerning the areas of law thought to be involved,
the nature of the dispute and the client's desired settlement. Ideally your team should reach
a preliminary view as to the areas of law involved and then you can all decide how you will
split the initial research between you. You all need to agree a timescale within which this
initial research will be concluded. This will be determined by the date of the actual negotiation or times given to you by your lecturer. You can then work on:

■   researching the area of law that is relevant to your part of your client's legal dispute.
       The best place to start is a textbook, to get an overview of the area. You can then look
       at primary legal sources as relevant. Follow any advice from your lecturer on this
       matter;

■   re-considering the facts of the dispute as set out by your client in light of your
       research and understanding of the general area of law;

■   considering, if you can at this point, the likely success of your client if the matter were
       to go to court, given your understanding of the law and the dispute.

Third team meeting and decisions concerning application of law, negotiating strategies and division of tasks in-negotiation

At the third team meeting you should:

■   Pool your research and discuss the likely success of your client, given your
       understanding of the law and the dispute, if the matter were to go to court. This
       information lets you know how advantageous it is for your client to settle. It also lets
       you know the likely response of the other side to your attempts to settle.

■ Consider your client's directions concerning their desires in relation to settlement. Is it solely a financial issue or are there other matters relating to relationship? Effectively, is this a positional or a principled negotiation?

■ Consider any incentives you can offer, such as continuing business relationship.

■ Draw up a plan for introducing issues during the negotiation. Decide which questions to ask, in which order and determine your best and worst acceptable outcome. Make a plan as to what to do if one of the team 'freezes' or begins to discuss a matter out of turn. Is there a leader who will interject?

■ Decide who is responsible for ensuring that at the end of the negotiation there is a clear note of the settlement (if there is one) or the next action to take (if there is no settlement). If there is a settlement your note of it should be compared to the other side's version. Make clear that any settlement has to be finally agreed by your client.

■ Ensure you have a proper strategy for good post-negotiation critical reflection.

As you discuss all of the matters above you will agree as a team what further meetings may be required and what written notes have to be made and circulated.

In-negotiation strategy

The negotiation itself is a dynamic event. You cannot control everything and you do not know if the other team is going to be competent, efficient or professional. You do not necessarily know what it is that they are going to say or what their plan is, but your team should have thought about their likely strategies and plan. What you do know is your team strategy, where you fit within it and what your job is. Keep to this strategy and your job. Do not jettison it in a panic: you could place your team in jeopardy in the middle of the negotiation.

As a team you need to respond to the other team as required. This could mean taking control of the negotiation at appropriate points to ensure your strategy is worked out when it is needed. You may also need to change your strategy in response to the other team's behaviour and strategy.

At the micro-level you also need to consider the language that each of you uses. It must be appropriate, formal, professional and not peppered with legal terms.

When you turn to the actual negotiation itself, no matter how much time you have given to planning you will be surprised by the speed with which your allotted time passes. You need to have a clear view of the micro-dynamics of the negotiation and the processes it moves through to ensure you reach your goals. These are set out in Figure 10.7.

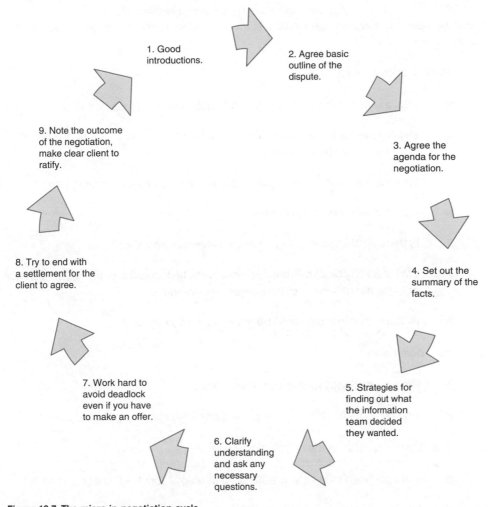

1. Good introductions.

2. Agree basic outline of the dispute.

3. Agree the agenda for the negotiation.

4. Set out the summary of the facts.

5. Strategies for finding out what the information team decided they wanted.

6. Clarify understanding and ask any necessary questions.

7. Work hard to avoid deadlock even if you have to make an offer.

8. Try to end with a settlement for the client to agree.

9. Note the outcome of the negotiation, make clear client to ratify.

Figure 10.7 The micro in-negotiation cycle

Post-negotiation critical review

Reviewing the negotiation after it has taken place is an important learning tool. Indeed critical reflection on any learning task is important as it allows you to achieve your full learning potential. Even if you felt the task went well, discussing the negotiation together as a team can help to tease out real problems and mistakes. You should take time to note which issues were the fault of the other team and which were down to you. However, mistakes by the other team might have caused you or your team to lose confidence. So it is important to discuss all of the issues.

Agenda for post-negotiation review

It can be useful to have an agenda to discuss the different aspects of the negotiation. It could include:

- Team-working issues

    - Was a sensible timescale set up and implemented at team level?

    - Did anyone fail to meet their obligations and cause a problem for the team? Could this have been avoided?

    - Was there a good set of in-team interpersonal relationships for the task?

    - How did you respond in the team?

    - Is there anything that could be done differently next time?

    - Was there any team mismanagement of the task in terms of timing, preparation or in the negotiation itself? If so was this inevitable?

    - Is there anything that could be done differently next time?

- Individual issues

    - Did you efficiently manage your own time?

    - Do you consider that you put in adequate time and energy to the team?

- The appropriateness of the negotiation strategy – pre-planning

    - Did your team follow the pre-planned strategy? If not, why not?

    - Was the pre-planned strategy extensive enough?

    - Did the team allow themselves enough pre-agreed flexibility?

    - Did the team set sufficient 'best' and 'worst' case agreed settlements?

    - Did the team set boundaries where they would not settle?

    - Did anything unexpected occur? If so how successfully did the team deal with it?

    - What would you and/or the team do differently next time re a strategy?

■   The negotiation outcome

    ■   How successful was the outcome – was it the one you had planned for?

    ■   If you did not want that outcome as a team is there anything that you or the team could have done differently to avoid it?

    ■   Was the outcome you achieved the best that you could have got in the circumstances?

Negotiation is a dynamic, creative activity that provides you with the opportunity to work with a range of skills to refine your understanding of law. It refines your communication skills and teamworking skills, and continues to develop your argument construction skills. Your success in negotiation also depends on your research and analysis skills and your ability to read the client's instructions in a focused manner, enabling you to work towards the best settlement achievable. Negotiation encourages a sophisticated understanding of the relationship between facts of a dispute, applicable law, and client expectations.

CONCLUSION

■   Ultimately success in oral skills exercises depends on careful preparation, just like any other assessment or developmental exercise.

■   There are six issues that need to be tackled with all oral skills tasks: understanding the nature of the task, managing the task, research, content, delivery and teamwork.

■   Oral skills exercises require you to combine the study skills habits you are developing with your knowledge of legal research in order to construct an argument.

■   A good argument will take you a long way to success, but join it with a strong voice, appropriate pacing, clarity of expression, perfect timing, and keeping a connection with your audience and you will be able to deliver excellent oral skills exercises.

FURTHER READING

C Kee, *The Art of Argument: A Guide to Mooting* (CUP, Cambridge 2007).

D Pope and D Hill, *Mooting and Advocacy Skills* (Sweet and Maxwell, London 2007).

J Snape and G Watt, *How to Moot: A Student Guide to Mooting* (OUP, 2004) This text is extremely user friendly.

R Stott, C Bryan, and T Young, *Speaking Your Mind: Oral Presentation and Seminar Skills* (Longman, 2000).

http://www.firstlight.demon.co.uk/law/mooting/comp.html accessed 22 April 2009 running a mooting competition from Mootnet.

http://www.cedr.com accessed 22 April 2009.

EXAM STRATEGIES

11

" Exams are not unknown events that cannot be planned for; indeed careful pre-planning and execution of focused revision together with wise 'in-exam' strategies are the *only* routes to success in examinations."

S. Hanson

LEARNING OUTCOMES

After reading this chapter you should be able to:

■ competently construct and follow a personal, and achievable, revision timetable;

■ use your lecturers' and tutors' revision sessions to best effect;

■ competently construct useful revision notes and diagrams;

■ work towards the best state of mind for the day of the exam;

■ efficiently plan which questions to answer in the exam;

■ efficiently draw planning diagrams for each question to be answered;

■ describe the best ways of quickly stating information of relevance if you do run out of time in the exam.

CHAPTER SUMMARY

This is one of the most important parts of the journey you have taken this year; it is where you finish the journey and reach your destination. If you have ever been on a long journey and grown tired you will know that often it is the last push that tempts one to give up. Exams require stamina, good knowledge of your own psychology and careful pre-planning of revision and in-exam tactics.

Few students like examinations. While there is a big debate within education concerning whether examinations are a good or a bad method of assessing students, the fact is that this is the main method of assessment that you will encounter on a law degree. Whether you love, hate or do not mind exams, you may not realise that it is possible to prepare strategically for an exam and increase your likelihood of passing and obtaining a good grade.

This chapter aims to demonstrate that it is possible to predict to a certain extent what may or may not appear on the exam paper and to employ the same learnt information economically in different ways for problem and essay questions. It will also give you ideas for ensuring that your revision management and in-exam-timing does not let you down. It looks at planning revision timetables, and tells you what examiners are really looking for. This chapter assists you to reach examinations in a good condition: fit for the task.

FINDING OUT ABOUT THE STRUCTURE OF YOUR EXAM

There will normally be past examination papers available for the module or course that you are undertaking. If you are studying a new module or course then it is highly likely that at some point your lecturer will show you a specimen examination paper so that you know what the structure of your exam is likely to be. If your department uses electronic multiple-choice exam systems your lecturer will give you an opportunity to undergo a mock exam to clarify the approach used. This can be taxing as many students are not used to reading questions and responding electronically within a set timescale.

Whatever advance information you are given, you should note the number of questions on each paper, how many topics are covered and whether there is a tendency for questions to be split into two parts, or a tendency for a topic to be split into two perspectives in the same question with an 'either/or' component. You must be absolutely clear in your mind concerning how much time you are given to answer the exam paper. A misunderstanding about timing can be fatal as it is also an indicator of how well you need to prepare your topics.

Traditional paper-based exams tend to have essays and case studies or legal problems that need to be resolved. You must carefully note the rules (called the rubric) at the top of the exam paper to see if you are free to answer any type of question or whether you need to answer a particular number of each type. It may be that one question is compulsory and then you have a free choice. Or your exam paper may be divided into sections, in which case you need to be clear about what you are required to do in each section.

Find out and make a note of the time, type and number of questions to be answered in each of your exams. A sample chart summarising this information is given in Table 11.1. You can also find a template on the companion website to make your own.

DRAWING UP A LIST OF POTENTIALLY EXAMINABLE TOPICS

It is your job, in reviewing your course, to be sure that you are aware of all potentially examinable topics. Studying past papers can give you an indication of previously featured topics but do not assume that such topics will necessarily come up again. There is no substitute for surveying carefully the topics that are on your course syllabus for your year of study. If you are not sure, seek guidance from your lecturer. However, they are unlikely to answer leading questions such as 'Is the topic of theft coming up on the exam paper?' A better approach would be to ask 'Am I right to assume that theft is an examinable subject that could potentially be on the paper?'

When you are familiar with the topics on your module you need to look carefully at the ways in which each topic can appear on the exam papers. Some topics will always be

TABLE 11.1 A SAMPLE EXAM INVENTORY CHART

Course	Number of questions to answer	Number of questions on exam	Length of exam	Type	
				Closed book	Open book
Criminal law	2	10	2 hours	✓	
Contract	3	8	3 hours		✓ Materials text and statutes text set for exam.
ELS	4	8 in two sections a/b. 4 questions in each. 1 in each section is compulsory and then a free choice.	3 hours	✓	

essays, for example, but other topics may be suitable for essay-style or problem-style questions. Essays and problem questions can be quite wide ranging so be aware of what is normal on your course. It is also important to realise which topics in your course tend to come up in conjunction with each other. Otherwise, even though you have revised a specific topic, you may not be able to answer the relevant question because you did not revise the topic that often accompanies it.

DRAWING TOGETHER INFORMATION ON YOUR TOPICS

The best starting points for revision are your lecture and seminar notes. But of course the existence and condition of your notes over the term or year of the course will vary enormously. You may have missed some lectures or you may have lost relevant handouts.

Some of you will have done the reading requested for tutorials and seminars and made notes in the seminar at the time. Some of you will not. You need to sort out what you have, what is missing, and see if you can take copies from other students. If you know you have lecturer material missing it makes good sense to plan to do this in the last two weeks of term 2, before everyone leaves for the vacation. You can then check with friends about missing materials.

Your law exams are academic exams. Markers of exams expect your answers to exam questions to demonstrate that you have read:

- relevant chapters in your set text and any cases and materials text;

- relevant law cases and statutes, as referred to in your set texts, lectures and seminars or located as a result of your independent study;

- a modest selection of academic journal articles: two or three for each topic if possible.

It is vital that you have academic *and* legal sources to back up your ideas and arguments. In the absence of any sources at all it will be difficult to reach a pass mark, but the addition of academic and legal sources immediately begins to give access to higher results. It is unlikely that you will obtain a pass mark in a legal problem question if you do not refer by name to cases and by name and section (as well as subsection) to statutes. Essay requirements with regard to source material change according to the title of the question asked. However, an essay with only primary law sources (cases and statutes) is lacking as you are expected to use these together with academic materials such as academic journal articles or scholarly monographs.

With regard to statutes you must know:

- the date;

■   the sections, subsections, paragraphs, and subparagraphs of the areas you have studied.

For cases, in addition to content as discussed in other chapters ensure you know:

■   the names of judges;

■   the court;

■   the year.

Draw up a list of relevant references to journals and cases/legislation from your lecture and seminar material. Pay particular attention to any handouts given out in exam/revision sessions. When you have decided what topics you will concentrate on you can then read selectively. Ideally, however, you will have earlier notes from your reading of these for seminars and assessments.

STRESS AND EXAM PERFORMANCE

Whilst few students like exams, they are often the primary method of assessing your understanding of the course. Therefore you need to train yourself to be in the best frame of mind to sit the examinations.

Examiners do realise that examinations place pressure on students and the ability to deal with this pressure is one of the first skills you need to work on. Exams require you to:

■   display your knowledge in a specific area;

■   on a specific day;

■   at a specific time.

This is why students and lecturers often discuss exam 'performance', for exams require you to perform[1]. It does not matter, for the purposes of the exam grade, how good you are before and after the exams. All that counts is what happens *during* the exam. That fact naturally causes pressure. Everything rests on your performance on the day.

While students worry ceaselessly about the idea of the exam they tend to spend less time concerned about their emotional and physical state on the day of the exam. You need therefore to get in training and practise, defuse excessive stress, remain in good health, study consistently and develop a good examination strategy that works for you. It is a good idea to face your fears about failing the exam head on.

---

1   Just as someone performs in other areas such as sport or dance or singing.

What happens if you fail?
Well, life goes on, and you will plan to take the resit!
And you probably won't fail, because if you are reading
this you are doing all in your power to plan to succeed.

ASSUMPTIONS ABOUT WHAT EXAMS ARE TESTING

There are some right and wrong assumptions amongst students concerning what exams are designed to test. Some are more correct than others. Some assumptions are true for some disciplines and not in others. You should take time to consider what your assumptions are. Read through the list of assumptions in Table 11.2 and tick the yes or no box to indicate whether you share each assumption or not.

Once you have considered your assumptions go through the following discussion and see what you got right and where you may have been wrong. Unconsciously your assumptions can determine your attitude to revision and if you only have a range of partially correct assumptions you may cause yourself difficulties in the exam. In reading through the explanations below you should begin to understand far more about what it is that the examiner is looking for.

TABLE 11.2 TESTING YOUR ASSUMPTIONS ABOUT EXAMS

Assumption	Yes	No
1: Exams are a test of how much information I can remember		
2: Exams are a test of the quality of my reasoning powers		
3: Exams are a test of how familiar I have become with the techniques of answering examination questions		
4: Exams are a test of how well I can take apart an examination question		
5: Exams test how quickly I can write in the time allowed		
6: Exams test how well I can argue		
7: Exams test how clever I am		

Assumption 1: Exams are a test of how much information I can remember

To a limited extent examinations are a test of what you can remember. As you can only make links between the question and what you know, your memorised knowledge base is an important aspect of your examination performance. But your rote learning, or memorised work is only the beginning of your answer. The examiner wants to see the proper use of your memorised information to form arguments in answer to the question.

Law exams require, in addition to knowledge of topics in set texts and articles, that you remember the detail of cases and legislation. As you need to know the case name, the court it was decided in, the names of the judges, the date of the case, the facts of the case and the reasoning in the case, memory is important. But the examiner wishes to see you demonstrate that you can use this knowledge of cases to form arguments. You do not get credit for laboriously setting out the details of irrelevant cases. Nor can you get full credit for relevant case details that you do not apply to a problem question. This merely demonstrates a lack of understanding. *Quality* in the use of your knowledge will achieve higher marks than a *quantity* of memorised learning being randomly listed without application to the question in hand. Note, however, that a few leading cases appropriately applied, argued and discussed demonstrates confident understanding and application of knowledge to the issue in hand.

Assumption 2: Exams are a test of the quality of my reasoning powers

This is an absolutely correct assumption. The examiner is testing your reasoning powers and is interested in observing, through your answer, how you think. The examiner is looking to see you demonstrate efficiently and confidently the application of your knowledge in the construction of arguments. You need to choose relevant cases, legal rules and academic texts from your memory and use them to back up your arguments.

Assumption 3: Exams are a test of how familiar I have become with the techniques of answering examination questions

Again this is absolutely correct. The examiner is looking to see if you can sort the relevant from the irrelevant, and identify a good range of the correct issues. The examiner wishes to see you demonstrate that you can think critically, write appropriately in terms of grammar, structure and spelling, and write confident and appropriate arguments in the time limit set by the exam. Being able to do this demonstrates you have good exam technique as well as good examination preparation strategies.

Assumption 4: Exams are a test of how well I can take apart an examination question

Yes they are, and this ability is an essential skill. Without it you may well miss important aspects of the question and will not be able to properly answer it. You could then end up discussing irrelevant matters and setting out your rote learning without customising it to suit the question asked. Examiners dislike this very much and it can lose you marks.

Assumption 5: Exams test how quickly I can write in the time allowed

The answer is both yes and no. You are only given a limited time to answer questions in an exam and part of a successful exam strategy is being able to keep to that time limit and provide an effective answer. This is dependent on your knowledge and skills, but also your ability to write quickly and legibly. You need to know how much you can write in the time allotted for each question. Ultimately you need to know you can construct an answer of relevant points, and refer to key sources and arguments, in the amount of words you know you can write in the time limit. The key element here is to practise writing answers to past or mock exams within the allotted timescale.

- Time management in the examination is an important aspect of examination performance. You may know everything necessary but fail the exam because you just run out of time. Practise timed essay and problem questions, just as you would practise for singing, dancing or sport. In this way you increase your stamina, your speed of thought and recall, and your writing speed.

- Legibility of handwriting is essential so that the marker can read your answer. All of your revision and your writing is useless if it cannot be read by the examiner. So practise fast legible writing.

- Quantity does *not* necessarily mean quality.

Assumption 6: Exams test how well I can argue
Absolutely. The quality of your argument construction can increase your grades at the top end of performance or make the difference between a pass or fail at the bottom. An argument is a series of propositions backed by evidence proving or disproving a given position. All exam essays and problem questions require a well-constructed argument.

The competency of your *relevant* argument measured together with the breadth and legibility of your writing determines your grade.

Assumption 7: Exams test how clever I am
It would be better to state that exams test your learning so far on the course. As such it can be said they test the acquisition of skills, knowledge and intelligence. However, they do much more than just measure intelligence. As we have already seen, exams assess a range of skills from memory and the ability to deconstruct questions correctly, through rule-handling and rule application to final construction of argument using sources to answer the question. Figure 11.1 summarises the full range of skills which examiners are looking for.

1. Correct identification of the issues raised by questions
2. The support of argument by cases, relevant legislation, academic articles and texts of authority
3. A clearly identifiable argument with a CONCLUSION in answer to the QUESTION ASKED BY THE EXAMINER!
4. Evidence of critical thinking and understanding
5. Clear presentation: well structured work in paragraphs, written in sentence rather than note form in legible handwriting. (However if you are running short of time then note form, or use of bullet points is an acceptable way of quickly noting your points)
6. Reference to material that demonstrates you have completed some independent research
7. Evidence of knowledge and understanding and the competent application of that knowledge and understanding to the question asked

Figure 11.1 The range of skills that examiners look for

THE ART OF CAREFUL EXAM PREPARATION

> It is not possible to overestimate the importance of planned, strategic topic picking and then careful, efficient revision of those topics.

Once you know what examiners are looking for, you can use that information to strategically revise your work.

Preparing for examinations requires time, peer support from other students in the same position, and access to your lecturers, seminar leaders or subject tutors (at their allotted revision times) in order to ask any worrying questions you may have. You need to plan revision time carefully, using it efficiently and effectively. It can be easy to do too little at the start and then too much too late. Or you can spend too much time on one area and miss the rest. Or even do too much revision for too long, effectively cancelling out that work by becoming exhausted, stressed and over-stretched. However, if you address revision properly and pace yourself there is no need for this.

To achieve optimum output and pacing it is important to engage in revision time management. Otherwise you may reach the examination with large amounts of material that has not been revised. Or large amounts of rote learning insufficiently understood and 'digested' so that you cannot properly and effectively deploy it.

Preparing a revision timetable

Revision time-management is an important aspect of ensuring peak examination performance. It is essential to draw up a revision timetable to monitor your progress and include in it every topic and subtopic you intend to revise. You should then annotate it with what you actually did. So, by the time of the exam, you know what you have *not* revised as well as what you have.

Planned revision falls into two sections:

- your main revision programme;

- recapping in the day or days before the exam according to your preference.

 A template revision timetable can be found on the companion website. It is really a customised re-edit of the time management charts discussed in Chapter 1. In order to plot the basics on your revision timetable you first of all need to know your exam timetable and the spacing between your exams. This affects the ordering of your exam revision timetable from day 1. It also determines the order of the final look over your revision in the days before an exam. Most importantly, it marks a definite end to exams and some thoughts of celebration and freedom.

You need to decide how many hours a revision session will be, and during what hours. You can always make changes but you should start with a definite plan. The natural rhythm of the day is morning, afternoon, evening and night. To assist you a chart will be set up that mirrors the natural dividers of the day. Each day is divided into three potential revision sessions as shown in Figure 11.2. You will note that there is a one-hour break between each session, and each of the morning and afternoon sessions have a 30-minute break in the middle. Breaks are essential otherwise you will grind to a halt and lose motivation.

Table 11.3 sets out a hypothetical revision timetable based on the template from the companion website. This revision table is for the period 1 May to 15 June and covers nearly 7 weeks. You may need longer and may need use different dates. It allows for 233 revision hours spread over 83 revision sessions.

The givens are put in first, the dates of your exams and the timings of any paid work, or any other occasions when you cannot study, for example family birthdays and special occasions. Relaxation time is also allocated on most days. The third session ends at 9pm so relaxation time is always available after that time. You can customise the sessions and times to suit you. You need to work with your best times, but be aware that there will be times when you have to revise and you are tired. When you are designing your revision

Figure 11.2 Revision session timings

TABLE 11.3 SAMPLE REVISION TIMETABLE

Revision timetable

Session	Week/ Times	Mon	Tues	Weds	Thurs	Fri	Sat	Sun	Comment
	1	MAY 1	2	3	4	5	6	7	
1	9–1			RELAX			PAID WORK	RELAX	34 hours' revision time with half-hour break in all sessions 1 & 2
2	2–6								
3	7–9	PAID WORK	PAID WORK		RELAX	PAID WORK	RELAX		12 Sessions
	2	8	9	10	11	12	13	14	
1	9–1						PAID WORK	RELAX	32 hours' revision time with half-hour break in all sessions 1 & 2
2	2–6								
3	7–9	PAID WORK	PAID WORK		RELAX	PAID WORK	RELAX		13 sessions
	3	15	16	17	18	19	20	21	
1	9–1						PAID WORK	RELAX	40 hours' revision time with half-hour break in all sessions 1 & 2
2	2–6								
3	7–9	PAID WORK	PAID WORK			PAID WORK	RELAX		14 sessions
	4	22	23	24	25	26	27	28	
1	9–1						PAID WORK	RELAX	36 hours' revision time with half-hour break in all sessions 1 & 2

TABLE 11.3—Continued

Revision timetable

Session	Week/Times	Mon	Tues	Weds	Thurs	Fri	Sat	Sun	Comment
2	2–6					RELAX			
3	7–9	PAID WORK	PAID WORK			PAID WORK	RELAX		13 sessions
	5	29	30	31	JUNE 1	2	3	4	
1	9–1						PAID WORK	RELAX	40 hours' revision time with half-hour break in all sessions 1 & 2
2	2–6								
3	7–9	PAID WORK	PAID WORK			PAID WORK	RELAX		14 sessions
	6	5	6	7	8	9	10	11	
1	9–1	EXAM Legal theory 9–11				EXAM Criminology 2 9–11.30		RELAX	30 hours' revision time with half-hour break in all sessions 1 & 2 10 sessions
2	2–6			EXAM Criminology 1 2–3.30					
3	7–9	RELAX	RELAX	RELAX	RELAX	RELAX	RELAX	RELAX	
	7	12	13	14	15	16	17	18	
1	9–1		EXAM Criminal law 9–11	EXAM Contract 11–1			FINISHED		21 hours' revision time with half-hour break in all sessions 1 & 2 7 sessions
2	2–6					EXAM English legal System 4–6			
3	7–9	RELAX	RELAX	RELAX	RELAX	FINISHED			

plan do not leave too much to the last minute. You need to know yourself, act wisely and plan effectively so that you can draw-up a realistic plan and stick to it. It may be a good idea to try and cut back on paid employments during revision and exams, if your pocket and your employer can cope.

It is sensible to allocate a specified revision session to each module. You may allot less time to those with lower exam weightings. Whether you put a large number of same-subject revision together or split it up throughout your timetable is up to you. If you get easily bored by revision you will relate better to change.

A comments column allows for working out the weekly revision hours and study sessions and for any other notes, for instance if you have missed a session.

Note the word revision, means *re*-vision, i.e. re-seeing, looking again at work done. If you neglected to do the work in the first place you will not be engaging in revision, you will be learning for the first time. This generally takes longer than standard revision, so if you have missed material earlier in your course you will need to build extra time into your revision schedule.

How long before the exam should I start revising?

This is your decision and is influenced by a range of factors, including how fast you work, how consistently you have studied all year, how much new understanding you need to acquire and how many topics you struggle with. It is quite possible that when you have done this inventory you have differing amounts of revision to do for each exam.

- DO NOT UNDER-ESTIMATE how much you need to do.

- DO NOT OVER-ESTIMATE what you can do in the time you have.

- PACE YOUR REVISION If you push yourself too much and become too tired your brain will 'switch off' and you will find it extremely difficult to keep going with your revision. If you feel this happening, stop and take time to develop a more efficient plan.

- SLEEP The temptation to revise late into the night is strong for some at exam time, but it is important to ensure you have enough sleep. Your brain is your major asset to be used in passing the exams. It needs sleep to be replenished.

Making an inventory of examinable topics

You should prepare an inventory of examinable topics for each module or course, as shown in Table 11.4 for a hypothetical criminal law course. Your module outlines and syllabus will outline topics and subtopics but be sure to consider all the information given to you by lecturers as well. Place the inventory at the beginning of your revision file for the module or course so you always know what will be required in the exam.

For each module or course you should consider how complete your existing knowledge is. Go through the inventory of examinable topics and consider each in turn, as shown in Table 11.5.

In our example there are several areas that have not yet been covered by the student. They will need to decide whether it is worth spending the time getting up to speed on these topics or whether they should leave them. When making decisions about which topics to cover you should make choices based on your strengths and weaknesses.

For every topic that you do cover, it is best to prepare for both an essay and a problem question scenario, as you cannot always predict how a question will arise on the exam paper. Problem questions require quite extensive primary law sources. Essay questions require both law and academic sources.

Setting up revision filing and developing memory tactics

Once you have collated a full set of notes from:

■   lecture notes;

■   seminar notes;

■   private study notes;

■   case notes;

■   copies of articles

you should condense all the information into key point form. Memorising these key points can be difficult but there are several different approaches you can use. Table 11.6 shows a range of different activities that relate to the learning styles discussed in Chapter 2. You will have your own preference for what works best.

How to keep motivated

Boredom sabotages revision!

TABLE 11.4 A SAMPLE EXAMINABLE TOPICS INVENTORY CHART

Criminal law	Assessment		Is this an examinable topic?	
Topics	Problem question	Essay	YES	NO – Lecturer has told me
The contexts of criminal law • history • media • classifications of criminal acts • official statistics		✓	✓	
Principles and policies • criminalisation • media • women • *actus reus* • *mens rea*		✓	✓	
Murder	✓			
Manslaughter	✓			
Partial defences Provocation Diminished responsibility			✓	
Reform of the law of homicide		✓		
GBH – grievous bodily harm			✓	
Sexual offences			✓	
Theft			✓	
Burglary			✓	
Handling				✓
Robbery			✓	
Criminal damage			✓	
Guest lecture: International Criminal Court				✓
Guest lecture: honour killings				✓ but we have been told that it may be used to inform any essay questions on contexts, reform etc. in the area of murder/manslaughter.

TABLE 11.5 SAMPLE KNOWLEDGE SUMMARY FOR EXAMINABLE TOPICS

Criminal law	Coverage	Type of question I can do	
Examinable topics		Problem question	Essay
The contexts of criminal law • history • media • classifications of criminal acts • official statistics	x	–	–
Principles and policies • criminalisation • media • women • *actus reus* • *mens rea*	✓ Criminalisation only	–	✓
Murder	✓	✓	?
Manslaughter	✓	✓	
Partial defences Provocation Diminished responsibility	✓	✓	✓ Provocation only
Reform of the law of homicide	x	x	x
GBH – grievous bodily harm	x	x	x
Sexual offences	✓	✓	x
Theft	✓	✓	✓ Dishonesty?
Burglary	x	✓	x
Handling	x		✓
Robbery	✓	✓	x
Criminal damage		✓	x

TABLE 11.6 LEARNING STYLES AND MEMORY TACTICS

Activites	Materials
HARNESSING KINAESTHETIC LEARNING STRATEGIES	• Link the information you are learning to doing things. For instance, you could try learning different topics in different places to help recall
HARNESSING VISUAL LEARNING STRATEGIES	• Construct diagrams of interconnections • Construct a mindmap • Draw symbols or even pictures to help you remember cases. All you need in the exam is a trigger to release the door to your memory. Then you only need to learn the trigger • Make some revision flashcards with questions on one side and answers on the other • Make some revision flashcards with a case name on one side and the facts and reasoning in the case and any precedent or interpretation point notes on the other • Make some revision quizzes in the same way • Making these up is of course part of the revision and memorising process
HARNESSING AUDITORY LEARNING	• Speak your notes aloud • Think of rhymes for different things • Record your notes and listen to them • Find a patient friend or relative and explain your topic to them
FORMAL CHECKS	• When you have revised an area write answers to past or specimen exam papers under exam conditions in the time you will have in the exam. Check your answers in your text book • Remember that all of the conventions for good writing apply in an exam • Check your answer for legible handwriting. Ask a friend if they can read it • Check that you have provided evidence for each point in your argument

For many students, revision is not only stressful (because it reminds you that exams are looming), it is boring. This means that however hard you try you may not remember what you revise as your brain has switched itself off.

To avoid getting bored, find the revision activity that best suits you. There are many different revision activities to choose from, as shown in Figure 11.3. All of these make revision active. Consider whether any of these would work for you.

1. Answering practice exam questions
2. Switch topics several times in one revision session
3. Revise using a lot of small sessions (20/30 minutes) rather than a marathon session
4. List key points to each topic
5. Use diagrams to connect knowledge
6. Read, think, and then summarise in writing
7. Summarise notes, and re-summarise
8. Read case notes that you have made
9. Read and make notes on academic journal articles
10. Always aim for a page and no more of revised final notes that contain phrases to prompt your memory

Figure 11.3 Revision activities

Topic-picking

Very few students can learn everything well, and attempting to learn everything can result in mediocre and patchy knowledge that reduces all of your revision to a superficial level. It is, however, possible to learn a few topics very well indeed. Since some exams are designed so that a limited series of topics comes up, many students will select the topics that they are going to revise, leaving some topics to one side. This process is part of the exam 'gameplan' or strategy. Topic-picking in this way is a difficult issue. Attitudes among both students and academics vary.

Topic-picking involves knowing your strengths and weaknesses. It may involve predicting what may, or may not, come up in the examination that you are taking. You need to listen to information given to you from your lecturer and read what is said about the exam in your departmental and subject guides. The next step is to make strategic choices about the number of topics that you can revise in each of the subjects that you are studying. Only you can decide the number of topics to pick. You need to know how the topics splinter into a range of subtopics (for example, theft splits into issues of dishonesty, as well as general problem questions). You also need to know the range of topics that could up in pairs. Here learning just one topic could mean that you cannot answer the question. For example, if you revise murder and not the partial defences, or indeed do not revise manslaughter, you might have difficulty in a problem question designed to test your knowledge of whether the defendant may be liable for murder or manslaughter. Or whether a partial defence applies to murder.

You need to take sensible decisions. If you are convinced a topic will come up but it is a topic that you struggle with and have never understood, think carefully before choosing to revise it. Even if the topic is guaranteed to be in the exam, is there any guarantee that you will be able to understand it before the exam?

THE DAY OF THE EXAMINATION

You have done all the revising you can and now it is the day of the exam. It is worth thinking about what you need to know on the day and what habits you should try to acquire beforehand. Figure 11.4 lists some ways of staying unflustered and relaxed so you are able to perform at your best on the day.

1. Be absolutely clear about the DATE and TIME of your examination.
2. Have a supply of working pens and pencils.
3. Do not overwork the night before, or on the day of the exam.
4. Eat and drink appropriately before the exam.
5. Do not wait near the exam room if you are very nervous. You may pick up on the anxieties of others, or overhear students discussing what may or may not come up. Remember everyone will have different choices of topics.
6. Remember that you have revised to the best of your ability, you have good strategies and you will do your best.
7. Some stress is normal so do not worry about feeling a little stressful.

Figure 11.4 Good habits on exam day

HEALTH WARNING

If you have not properly prepared then there is no point over-stressing, you can only follow through with the exam and hope for some luck

Strategies during the examination

1. **The first ten to fifteen minutes**: Read the *whole* paper through *carefully* and decide which questions you will answer. Check the length of the exam and the number of questions you are told to answer; check for compulsory questions. Make sure you know which questions are 'either/or' questions and which are asking you to do both parts of a question. Think about what the examiner is looking for in each question and whether you can deliver it. Check you have properly explored the language of the question so that you do not miss questions you are able to answer, or miss points in the questions you have decided to answer.

2. **The next ten to fifteen minutes** could be used to plan answers to all of your chosen questions, *or* you could start your first question, planning each question as you go. Whichever process you use, planning time has to be incorporated into the time you have allotted for writing your answer to each question. Do not be tempted into writing

without considered pre-planning of the question on a separate piece of paper. You can plan by making notes or drawing a diagram; think of the strategies used in the discussion of writing in Chapter 9, as well as the deconstruction of arguments in Chapters 7 and 8. Invariably there will be a hierarchy in the questions you have picked to answer, with some topics you know well and some less well. Be rigorous, however, about moving on to the next question at the end of your allotted time for each question. This will open up the next set of marks for you. One brilliant answer rarely makes up for missed questions and other mediocre answers.

3.   **During the planning and writing process** constantly refer back to the question to make absolutely certain you are addressing it. You are being tested on your structured and methodical approach to the questions you answer as well as on your knowledge and its application to the questions.

FOR ESSAYS

Make sure that each of your answers has a brief introduction, a main body and a conclusion.

FOR PROBLEMS

- Give a brief introduction stating ambit of problem.

- Do a flow chart of facts in your rough work.

- Answer each head of liability for each party separately.

- Ensure you make clear the rules that are relevant.

- State legal areas involved.

- Clearly set out issues.

- Apply statutes and cases methodically.

- Conclude for *each* party in relation to *each* head of liability.

4.   Rigidly stick to your timing.

5.   Present your work so that it is easy for the examiner to follow, using the rules preferred in your department for drawing attention to law cases and statutes (for examples using italics, underlining, bold and so on).

6.   Try to leave time in the last ten minutes of the exam to recheck your whole paper for spelling and grammar. If you have been writing too fast you can leave out important

linking words which turn a great point into an incomprehensible point. Check all your sentences make sense. *Neatly* correct any problems. Make sure all rough work has a line drawn through it and you have correctly labelled your questions. This includes labelling parts of questions. If you think of extra materials or points, annotate your question: examiners will follow clear instructions from the exam candidate.

7.   At the end of the exam it may be a good idea to avoid those who are dissecting the paper to see what everyone else did, discussing whether they are wrong or right. This could needlessly upset you and even unnerve you before your next exam.

CONCLUSION

■   Revision skills *and* tactics in the exam are an integral part of your skills. Indeed they are the summation of your year's work.

■   Remember that exams are not unexpected events for which you cannot plan. It is essential to plan for them well in advance.

■   Revise strategically.

■   Answer required number of questions.

■   Use legible handwriting.

■   Plan each answer.

■   Read paper carefully and choose questions strategically.

■   Read and follow all instructions.

■   Stay calm – otherwise your ability to think will be impaired.

■   After the exam draw a line under it and move on to the next one.

FURTHER READING

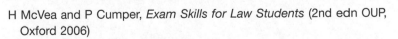

H McVea and P Cumper, *Exam Skills for Law Students* (2nd edn OUP, Oxford 2006)

S Strong, *How to Write Law Essays and Exams* (2nd edn OUP, Oxford 2006).

POSTSCRIPT: CONCLUSIONS AND FURTHER JOURNEYS

" No journey carries one far unless, as it extends into the world around us, it goes an equal distance into the world within."

Lillian Smith

This text has attempted to provide a clear view of the practicalities of studying law, focusing on what are the required skills of general study, reading legal texts, argument construction, writing and oral presentation. We have also discussed ways of developing good independent study habits and approaches to 'breaking into' texts to understand the flexibility and the inherent unreliability of language in a discipline that centres on the power of 'the word' and of language generally.

This brief conclusion finishes by signalling that only a partial understanding is reached if you do not consider the power of the authority of law, attached to the flexibility of words. That is the power of law's context and status, the power of the privilege of law over other institutions, and the power of its interpretation of words over other interpretations. Law is applied, used or created by people acting in roles dealing with the memories of the law. Much time has been spent looking at mechanistic schemes for understanding legal words, legal texts, intertextual and intratextual links and the arguments for the outcome of the case. However, as Goodrich states, 'reading is never innocent'[1].

There are vast dimensions of legal analysis untouched, ready to be tackled by politicians, philosophers, feminists, criminologists or sociologists. And there are a range of ever present, yet buried, motivational issues, such as why did the judge adopt that interpretation? Or which rationale for adopting that interpretation do 'I' believe? We have considered a few raw legal arguments and have noted the reasons given to support outcomes. But valuable issues can also be raised by asking why didn't the judge take another plausible interpretation?

Judgments are the end result after parties and witnesses put their sides, via official and tortuous questioning. They take place in situations where rules of evidence, magistrates and judges control what is and what is not said, by whom, and how it is said. Lawyers, judges and officials control definitions too, as well as choosing interim and ultimate interpretations. Legal texts are never unambiguous representations of the law. They are the words from which interpretations flow. At the level of the obvious, the voice of consensus states: '*we* all know what this means, *don't we?*' Equally, this can be said in a tone of incredulity, or of ridicule: 'we all *know* what this means, don't we?'

In their texts judges build one official story, one official ending. But the story can often be very different, and so could the ending. The bricks for building are words. Despite our focus on study skills, English language skills, legal method skills and their interrelationship with substantive law and solving legal problems, it is the landscape that decides it all. The landscape of the officials, the institutions, politics, the judiciary, the police and policy all have an influence.

The critical thinker has to remain engaged not only in micro-questions within texts, but also in macro-questions at the level of law, politics and culture. This includes considering text as the product of a culture, continuing the search for underlying assumptions.

Much law degree study will revolve around 'fighting' with the language of, and arguments in, cases, reconciling, distinguishing and/or following them and explaining differences of interpretation where some might say there are no differences. Students learn

---

1   P Goodrich, *Reading the Law: Critical Introduction to Legal Method and Techniques* (WileyBlackwell, 1986) 231.

a growing body of rules and, more and more, the overarching context of institutions and culture shrinks into the background. They may be interesting from an academic perspective, but cultural legal content has no place in the everyday life of the law and its mediation of competing interests. It is in the interest of these legal institutional values that the legal 'story' is the one that covers all. But there is a danger that the daily process of *doing* the law blinds the 'doers' (the practitioners) to the motivational influences of some institutional creators of law. The law as language is to be read, interpreted, questioned and seen in its fragmented contexts, to be the object of a healthy scepticism. It should not be invested with qualities it cannot control. Law is not justice, for indeed justice may demand that there be no law.

When deciding what words mean in court, judges make far-reaching decisions and maintain that they do so, not on grounds of morality, religion, justice or ethics, but purely as a true interpretation of the words. They support the orthodox view that law is a neutral instrument to achieve a moral society. Law is objective, rational and logical and one must believe in the ultimate good of the law and the ultimate ability of the law to determine what the law means. A problem can now be seen. As pointed out above, the law is not an autonomous neutral agent; it is used by people in a political and social role. Legal texts can be analysed as social texts created by social actors. Statutes are texts communicated via words created by politicians in compromise and interpreted by judges for a range of reasons, some explicit some not. Can discussions about law, therefore, ever be justifiably separated from discussions about power (especially since access to law-making power is only available to players in the higher levels of politics or professionals in the higher judiciary)?

Law is not logical, nor does it have to be. There is social agreement that, for a range of reasons – political, social and moral – English law should be seen to be fair. But to apply a rule to a problem requires the clarification of the problem and proof that the facts of the problem as presented are the facts that occurred. Rules have developed which state what must be proved by testimonial or forensic evidence and when evidence itself must be backed up.

Due to the history of common law, its oral nature of proceedings, the breaking away of courts from the Royal household, the ultimate ascendancy of statutory law and the complete reorganisation of the courts of England and Wales in 1875 and 1978, we now have a system of law which is based upon the reaction to arguments presented to those officials who decide which argument is legitimate, be they negotiators in offices, tribunals and juries, magistrates' or appellate courts. Major changes will occur shortly with Part 3 of the Constitutional Reform Act 2005 establishing a Supreme Court of the United Kingdom that will replace the House of Lords and assume some responsibilities of the Privy Council in the area of devolution. The legal system, however, continues to be challenged, stretched and changed by the new political and legal order of European Union and European Community law, as well as changes to the law relating to human rights[2].

---

2   Arrangements are on track for the Court to commence in October 2009.

As you finish this journey and look forward to your next, hold some of these issues in mind. As you develop through the stages of your academic legal study you will increasingly be called upon to ponder some of these issues and more; you will be required to spend more time tracing a critical pathway in your work.

BIBLIOGRAPHY

T Anderson, D Schum and W Twining, *Analysis of Evidence* (CUP, Cambridge 2005).

C Burnett, *The Introduction of Arabic Learning into England* (British Library, 1997).

J Bush and A Wijffels, *Learning the Law Teaching and Transmission of Law in England 1150–1900* (London/Rio 1999).

Cardiff Index to Legal Abbreviations http://www.legalabbrevs.cardiff.ac.uk accessed 14 April 2009.

P Clinch, *Using a Law Library: A Student's Guide to Research Skills* (Blackwell, 2001).

S Cotterell, *The Study Skills Handbook* (3rd edn Palgrave Macmillan, 2008).

S Cotterell, *Critical Thinking Skills: Developing Effective Analysis and Argument* (Palgrave Macmillan, 2005).

R Dworkin, *Taking Rights Seriously* (Duckworth 1978).

R Dworkin, *Law's Empire* (Fontana 1986).

C Gatrell, *Managing Part-time Study: A Guide for Undergraduates and Postgraduates* (Open University Press, 2006).

HP Glenn, *The Legal Traditions of the World* (2nd edn Oxford University, 2000).

N Gold, K Mackie and W Twining, *Learning Lawyer's Skills* (Butterworths, London 1989).

P Goodrich, *The Languages of Law from the Logics of Memory to Nomadic Masks* (Weidenfeld & Nicolson, 1990).

S Hargreaves, *Study Skills for Dyslexic Students* (Sage, 2007).

HLA Hart, *The Concept of Law* (2nd edn OUP, 1994).

J Holland and J Webb, *Learning Legal Rules* (6th edn OUP, 2006).

OW Holmes, *The Common Law* (Belknap Press, Cambridge 1963).

E Hoult, *Learning Support for Mature Students* (Sage, 2006).

C Kee, *The Art of Argument: A Guide to Mooting* (CUP, Cambridge 2007).

P Lawrence, *Law on the Internet: A Practical Guide* (Sweet and Maxwell, 2000).

D McGovan, *Reading* (Prentice Hall, New York 1994).

WR McKay and HE Charlton, *Legal English: How to Understand and Master the Language of Law* (Pearson Longman, 2005).

H McVea and P Cumper, *Exam Skills for Law Students* (2nd edn OUP, Oxford 2006).

A Northledge, *The Good Study Guide* (2nd edn Open University Press, 2005).

D Pope and D Hill, *Mooting and Advocacy Skills* (Sweet and Maxwell, London 2007).

G Price and P Maier, *Effective Study Skills* (Pearson Education, 2007).

J Rabinowitz, 'The Influence of Jewish Law on the Development of the Common Law', in L Finkelstein, *The Jews Their History, Culture and Religion* Vol 1 (4th edn Harper and Row, 1970).

DA Schum, 'Alternative Views of Argument Construction from a Mass of Evidence' (2001) 22 Cardozo Law Review 1461–502.

J Snape and G Watt, *How to Moot: A Student Guide to Mooting* (OUP, 2004).

R Stott, C Bryan and T Young, *Speaking Your Mind: Oral Presentation and Seminar Skills* (Longman, 2000).

S Strong, *How to Write Law Essays and Exams* (2nd edn OUP, Oxford 2006).

C Sychin, *Legal Method* (2nd edn Sweet & Maxwell, London 1999).

PA Thomas and J Knowles, *Effective Legal Research* (Sweet and Maxwell, 2006).

PA Thomas and J Knowles, *How to Use a Law Library* (4th edn Sweet and Maxwell, 2001).

W Twining and D Miers, *How To Do Things With Rules* (4th edn CUP, Cambridge 1999).

R Van Caenegem, *The Birth of English Common Law* (2nd edn CUP, Cambridge 1988).

L Webley, *Legal Writing* (2nd edn Routledge-Cavendish, London 2009).

JB White, *The Legal Imagination* (abridged edn Chicago University Press, 1985).

H Wigmore, 'The Problem of Proof' (1913–14) 8 Illinois Law Rev 77.

http://www.cedr.com accessed 22 April 2009.

http://www.firstlight.demon.co.uk/law/mooting/comp.html accessed 22 April 2009.

INDEX